~ Evergreen Ethnographies ~

Hoh, Chehalis, Suquamish, and Snoqualmi

of Western Washington

Jay Miller, editor

1 Overview

12 Hoh Ethnography

92 Chehalis Ethnography

169 Suquamish Ethnography

236 Snoqualmie Ethnozoology 294

295 Index 299

Finding Aids at the back of each article have now become
Table of Contents, as originally intended.

Typo Gnomes are ever present, corrections & improvements welcome

Cover: "We Are Here" 2006 ~ 2013
Russell Beebe, Jack Langford, Agnes Baker Pilgrim, @ Ashland, Oregon

© 2017

~ Evergreen Ethnographies ~

Hoh, Chehalis, Suquamish, and Snoqualmie
of Western Washington

Ethnographies, detailed descriptions of a lifeway – in actions, places, words, and deeds – of the tribes of Washington State have appeared sporadically. Because of their many insights into these cultures, specific studies of rituals, place names, and ethnobiology are also included in this review. The earliest works were by Easterners, published in the East, especially by the federal government in DC. With the rise of universities, printed series in anthropology featured academic studies of specific tribes and languages. Most recently, tribes and reservations have undertaken to self-publish for a general audience, such as Jamestown S'Klallam (Strauss 2002), Makah (Erikson 2002), Coastals (Wray 2002) or, after a lifetime of research, Spokan (Ross 2011).

As preparation for "negotiating" treaties, George Gibbs, of an old New England family, studied local tribes and languages for a decade, publishing his findings in the federal report of the survey for a northern railroad route. His manuscripts are mostly in DC, though some became scattered as family members settled across the country. Half of his more polished ethnohistorical survey, badly edited, was published in DC in 1877. The entire handwritten manuscript resides at the Wisconsin Historical Society in Madison. James Swan (1857, 1971), also out of New England, came to Washington State to stay, actively keeping detailed diaries and journal, an array of sketches, and publishing a pioneer history.

Myron Eells, of a famous missionary family, reported on Twana and others. William Elmendorf (1960) used Eells and his own extensive fieldwork with the Allen brothers to produce the single best ethnography of the region. James Wickersham, a lawyer and Alaska judge, wrote on native legends and technology, as well as providing legal protections for local religious concerns such as the Indian Shaker Church. Later authors included Martin Sampson (1938, 1972), a chief at Swinomish, William Shelton (1932), a Tulalip leader and carver, Cecelia Svinth Carpenter, Nisqually, Vi Hilbert, Skagit, and Nels Bruseth (1926), a pioneer in the Sauk area.

Coming out of journalism and trained in history at Wisconsin, Edmond Meany at the University of Washington wrote a series of newspaper articles on Puget Sound tribes "Native Races of Washington" for *Seattle Post-intelligencer* (1905), which long delayed his reinbursement. Regional fervor awaited the Lewis and Clark Centennial and American Pacific Exposition and Oriental Fair in Portland, 1 June to 14 October 1905.

In the Sunday section, especially the Magazine, there was always at least one article that involved natives somewhere, but as the year went on discussions of local reservations by Edmond Meany were featured, with drawings and photographs to attract reader attention. On 29 January, Famous Indien Relics in Hotel Astor Grill of New York City began the years, while 12 February began the discussion of Chief Joseph, who was about to be reburied and honored. Meany first appears 26 February for Canoe Cedar Has Served Man Since Stone Age. Celebrating Easter on 23 April, color first appears in the newspaper, along with one cartoon. Chief Joseph's reburial is anticipated on 11 June, with there ceremony and Meany's speech on 25 June.

Meany's series begins 9 July with Calispel Ask to Retain Their Land, featuring Indians at School at Fort Spokane, Views on Fort Spokane Indien Reservation, and San Poil Chief Unusual Character ~ Skolaskin. An entire page on 16 July is devoted to Yakimas Present Many Problems, with Views and Portraits Made at Ft Simcoe. On 30 July was Contacts Between Indien Tribes, with Views & Well Known Persons of Tulalip Reservation.

On 6 August was Precious Historical Indian Relics Neglected in Seattle, on 13 August was The Muckleshoots' Queer Reservation, and one 27 August Puyallups and Nisqually Indians, with Views of Puyallup & Nisqually.

On 3 September was Indians on the Edge of the Continent and Their Folklore, with Quinaielt Being Transformed from Hunters of Sea Otters and Whales to Allotted Indiens; and on 10 September was Indians Have Lived At La Push For Countless Centuries, With Ancient Home Of The Quileutes Who Are A Distinct Language Family.

On 1 October was Legends Traditions and Present Conditions of Lummi Indians, with How they Got Fire; 8 October was Swinomish Indians a Composite of Many Tribes and Bands; on 15 October was Washington Redmen Who Helped Palefaces in War for Chehalis; on 22 October was Twana & Clallam Indians Aborigines of Hoods Canal, with Rapid Decline of Once Powerful Tribe, and The Clallams were a Strong People; and on 29 October was Story of Seattles' Nearest Indian Neighbors for Suquamish.

November featured mention of Edward S Curtis & His Indiens, How Humanity Carries Babies, Symbolism of the Swastika, and Chief Peter Brown (How A Thlub) ~ Last Chief of the Makahs, with Thrilling Events of His Life Told by Himself by Lucien M Lewis. December ended the year with Indian Life on Seattle Streets, and, sadly, American Indians Most Misunderstood People of the World.

Though flawed and bigoted, they do include some useful details of contemporary life on various reservations. When the famously precise and eccentric JP Harrington taught a linguistics class at UW during the 1910 summer, Meany was highly critical of his use of a beef tongue to show necessary points of sound articulation and many of the complex technical letters of the Americanist form of the International Phonetic Alphabet. Meany, like many after him, assumed he could make do with the English alphabet, though it has only a third of the letters needed for the discrete sounds of these native languages. Indeed, much of the misguided and flawed information about natives around Seattle and the state can be traced to the early clueless meddling of Meany.

More sustained and scholarly, amateur Arthur Ballard devoted a lifetime to research in south Sound, carefully using IPA letters, only to have his grand work suppressed by his children while it was in being printed in Portland. His court testimony for Muckleshoots and Puyallups, as well as work with other writers, academic and hack, shows the depth of his data.

Following such self financed and self motivated efforts, Franz Boas, establishing academic anthropology at Columbia University, conducted his own fieldwork in the Northwest, and sent his students to specific tribes and locales to fill in the growing record. When money was available, he also funded skilled amateurs, such as James Teit, to do reconnaissance of the region about 1910. Columbia University Press published on Lummi (Stern 1934), and the classic Puyallup Nisqually (Marian Smith 1940).

In Seattle, seeking resident scholarship of serious value, after brief stays by John Peabody Harrington and Thomas Waterman drawn from UC Berkeley, Boas saw UW hire Leslie Spier, Mel Jacobs, Thelma Adamson, and, eventually, Erna Gunther. Spier worked to provide basic information. He published a discussion of tribal distributions in Washington State (1936);

conducted, edited, and published research by a field school among the southern Okanogan (1938); and cowrote a work on the Wishram (1930), Chinookans of the Columbia River. Companion books on other Chinooks were done by Verne Ray (1938) and Mel Jacobs (1959).

Since nepotism rules limited employment only to Spier, his wife Erna Gunther, with her own Columbia PhD, devoted her time to raising their two sons and researching among Klallams (1925, 1927) and Makahs. After her legal marriage contract (not license) with Leslie Spier ended, and he left for fieldwork in the Pacific, she replaced him at UW. Johnson Williams, Philip Hugh Howell (pen name ~ Jorg Totsgi), and Mary Ann Lambert ~ Vincent, all Klallams, also published selective information.

Publication outlets began in DC, then New York, before moving west to Berkeley and Seattle. If the Smithsonian published the earliest works, the UW Publications in Anthropology published the majority:

1920 I (1): 1-67 Makah Whaling ~ Waterman, 1925 I (4): 113-170 Klallam Tales ~ Gunther, 1927 I (5): 171-314 Klallam ~ Gunther, 1927 II (3): 57-81 Puget Sound Tales ~ Ballard, 1929 III (2): 57-81 South Puget Sound Tales ~ Ballard, 1928 II (4): 83-128 Middle Columbia Salish ~ Teit, 1930 III (3): 151-300 Wishram ~ Spier & Sapir, 1930 IV (1): 1-84 Puget Sound Indiens ~ Haeberlin & Gunther, V: 1-237 Sanpoil Nespelem ~ Ray, VI: 1-190 Quinault ~ Olson.

Linguistically unique, Quileute on the coast attracted a range of linguists from major universities, with Jay Powell and Vickie Jensen (1976) providing a brief ethnography and George Pettitt (1950) a study of culture change researched while he served at the Coast Guard station at La Push. Their current role as "werewolves" in the *Twilight* books and movies has encouraged their own push back and self expression in museum displays and media events.

Of some note is the comparative study of Olympic Peninsula tribes by Singh (1966), an Indian studying Indiens who eventually entered politics at home in India. Its look at traditional economics compares well with the more contemporary discussion by members of coastal tribes themselves in Wray (2002).

Now regarded as outdated and old fashioned, unless undertaken by a tribe itself, these comprehensive descriptions nonetheless provide a basic data-rich foundation for all future studies: personal, applied, and for legal defenses.

Ethnographies

Adamson, Thelma   1934   Folktales of the Coast Salish.   Memoirs of the American Folklore Society 27. [Reprinted 2004]

Amoss, Pamela

1978   Coast Salish Spirit Dancing ~ The Survival of an Ancestral Religion. Seattle: University of Washington Press.

1981   Coast Salish Elders. pp. 227-261 in Other Ways of Growing Old. Pamela Amoss and Steven Harrell, eds. Stanford University Press.

1982   Resurrection, Healing, and "the Shake": The Story of John and Mary Slocum. Charisma and Sacred Biography. Michael Williams, ed. Journal of the American Academy of Religion, Thematic Studies XLVIII (3/4): 87-109.

1987   The Fish God Gave Us: The First Salmon Ceremony Revived. Arctic Anthropology 24 (1): 56-66.

1990   The Indian Shaker Church. Northwest Coast. Wayne Suttles, ed. Handbook of North American Indians, Volume 7: 633-39. Smithsonian Institution Press.

Ballard, Arthur

1927   Some Tales of the Southern Puget Sound Salish. University of Washington Publications in Anthropology 2 (3): 57-81.

1929   Mythology of Southern Puget Sound. University of Washington Publications in Anthropology 3 (2): 31-150.

1935   Southern Puget Sound Salish Kinship Terms. American Anthropologist 37 (1): 111-116.

1950   Calendric Terms of the Southern Puget Sound Salish. Southwestern Journal of Anthropology 6 (1): 79-99.

1951   Deposition on Oral Examination of Arthur Condict Ballard. November 26, 27, 28. Testimony before the Indian Claims Commission of the United States, Docket 98. Carolyn Taylor, court reporter. 2 volumes.

1957   The Salmon-Weir on Green River in Western Washington. Davidson Journal of Anthropology 3, 37-53.

1999   Mythology of Southern Puget Sound. Kenneth (Greg) Watson, ed. North Bend, WA: Snoqualmie Valley Historical Museum.

Barnett, Homer   1957   Indian Shakers, A Messianic Cult of the Pacific Northwest. Carbondale: Southern Illinois University Press.

Barsh, Russell, Joan Megan Jones, and Wayne Suttles   2006   History, Ethnography, and Archaeology of the Coast Salish Woolly-Dog. In Dogs and People in Social, Working, Economic or Symbolic Interaction. Proceedings of the 9th Conference of the International Council of Archaeozoology, Durham, August 2002. Lynn M. Snyder and Elizabeth A. Moore, eds. Pp. 1-11. Oxford: Oxbow Books.

Boyd, Robert   1996   People of the Dalles   The Indians of Wascopam Mission.   Lincoln: University of Nebraska Press.

Boyd, Roert, Kenneth Ames, and Tony Johnson   2013   Chinookan Peoples of the Lower Columbia. Seattle: University of Washington Press.

Bruseth, Nels   1926   Indian Stories and Legends of the Stillaguamish, Sauks and Allied Tribes. Arlington (WA) Times Press. [1950]

Carpenter, Cecelia Svinth   2002   The Nisqually, My People. Tahoma Research.

Carpenter, Cecelia Svinth, Maria Victoria Pascualy, and Trisha Hunter 2008 <u>Nisqually Indian Tribe</u>. Images of America. Charleston: Arcadia Publishing.

Castile, George, ed. 1985 <u>The Indians of Puget Sound</u>. The Notebooks of Myron Eells. Walla Walla: University of Washington Press for Whitman College.

Collins, June
  1949 John Fornsby: The Personal Document of a Coast Salish Indian. Smith 1949: 287-341.
  1950b The Indian Shaker Church. <u>Southwestern Journal of Anthropology</u> 6: 399-411.
  1974 Valley of the Spirits: The upper Skagit Indians of Western Washington. Seattle: University of Washington Press.

Curtis, Edward 1913 <u>The North American Indian</u>, being a series of volumes picturing and describing the Indians of the United States, the Dominion of Canada, and Alaska. Written, Illustrated, and Published By Edward S. Curtis. Frederick Webb Hodge, ed. Volume 9 of 20.

Eells, Myron
  1886 <u>Ten Years of Missionary Work among the Indians at Skokomish, Washington Territory</u>. Boston: Congregational Sunday-School and Publishing Society. [Shorey reprint 1972].
  1887 The Indians Of Puget Sound (nine parts). <u>American Antiquarian</u> 9.
  1889 The Twana, Chemakum, and Klallam Indians of Washington Territory. Smithsonian Annual Report For 1887: 605-681.
  1985 <u>The Indians of Puget Sound. The Notebooks of Myron Eells</u>. George Pierre Castille, ed. Seattle: University of Washington Press.

Elmendorf, William
  1935 The Soul-Recovery Ceremony Among The Indians of the Northwest Coast. Master of Arts Thesis. University of Washington.
  1946 Twana Kinship Terminology. <u>Southwestern Journal of Anthropology</u> 2: 420-432.
  1948 The Cultural Setting of The Twana Secret Society. <u>American Anthropologist</u> 50, 625-633.
  1960 The Structure of Twana Culture. Pullman: Washington State Research Studies, Monographic Supplement 2. (with Comparative Notes on the Structure of Yurok by Alfred Kroeber).
  1961a Skokomish and Other Coast Salish Tales. Washington State University Research Studies 29 (1): 1-37; (2): 84-117; (3): 119-150.
  1961b System Change in Salish Kinship Terminologies. <u>Southwestern Journal of Anthropology</u> 17 (4): 365-382.
  1970 Skokomish Sorcery, Ethics, and Society. Chapter VI: 147-182, <u>Systems of North American Witchcraft And Sorcery</u>. Deward Walker, ed. Anthropological Monographs of the University of Idaho 1.
  1971 Coast Salish Status Ranking and Intergroup Ties. <u>Southwestern Journal of Anthropology</u> 27, 353-381.
  1993 <u>Twana Narratives</u>. Native Historical Accounts of a Coast Salish People. Seattle: University of Washington Press.

Erikson, Patricia, with Helma Ward & Kirk Wachendorf 2002 Voices of a Thousand People~ Makah Cultural & Research Center. Lincoln: University of Nebraska Press.

Frachtenberg, Leo
  1920 Eschatology of the Quileute Indians. American Anthropology 22: 330-340.

1921 The Ceremonial Societies of the Quileute Indians. American Anthropologist 23: 320-352.

Gibbs, George
1855 Report on the Indian Tribes of Washington Territory. Pacific Railroad Report 1, 402-36.
1877 Tribes of Western Washington and Northwestern Oregon. Washington: Department of the Interior, United States Geographical and Geological Survey of the Rocky Mountain Region, Part II: 157-241.
1970 Dictionary of the Niskwalli (Nisqually) Indian Language - Western Washington. Extract from 1877 Contributions to North American Ethnology 1: 285-361. Seattle: The Shorey Book Store Facsimile Reproduction.

Gunther, Erna
1925 Klallam Folk Tales. University of Washington Publications in Anthropology 1 (4): 113-170.
1927 Klallam Ethnography. University of Washington Publications in Anthropology 1 (5): 171-310.
1928 A Further Analysis of the First Salmon Ceremony. University of Washington Publications in Anthropology 2 (5): 129-173.
ms. Culture Element Distributions: Puget Sound (Duwamish, Skokomish, Klallam, Makah). Berkeley: Bancroft Library.
1949 The Shaker Religion of the Northwest. Indians of the Urban Northwest: 37-76. Marian Smith, ed. NY: Columbia university.
1945 Ethnobotany of Western Washington. The Knowledge and Use of Indigenous Plants by Native Americans. Seattle: University of Washington Press. [1973]

Haeberlin, Herman
1916-17 Puget Salish, 42 Notebooks. DC: National Anthropological Archives # 2965.
1918 SbEtEtda'q, A Shamanic Performance of the Coast Salish. American Anthropologist 20 (3): 249-257.
1924 Mythology of Puget Sound. Journal of American Folklore 37 (143-144): 371-438.

Haeberlin, Herman, and Erna Gunther 1930 The Indians of Puget Sound. University of Washington Publications in Anthropology 4 (1): 1-84.

Hilbert, Vi, Jay Miller, and Zalmai Zahir 2001 Puget Sound Geography. sdaʔdaʔ gʷəɫ dibəɫ ləšucid ʔacaciɬtalbixʷ. A Draft Study of the Thomas Talbot Waterman Place Name Manuscript and Other Sources, Edited with Additional Material. Seattle: Lushootseed Press.

Hulse, Frederick
1955 Blood-types and Mating Patterns among Northwest Coast Indians. Southwestern Journal of Anthropology 11 (2): 93-104.
1957 Linguistic Barriers To Gene-Flow; The Blood-Groups of the Yakima, Okanagon, and Swinomish Indians. American Journal of Physical Anthropology 15 (2): 235-246.

Lambert [~ Vincent], Mary Ann
1961 Dungeness Massacre and Other Regional Tales. Port Angeles: Privately Printed.
1960 The House of the Seven Brothers + Trees, Roots and Branches of the House of Ste-tee-thlum. A Genealogical Story of the Olympic Peninsula Clallam Indians. Port Angeles: Privately Printed.

Miller, Jay
  1988 <u>Shamanic Odyssey</u>. The Lushootseed Salish Journey to the Land of the Dead, in terms of Death, Potency, and Cooperating Shamans in North America. Menlo Park, CA: Ballena Press Anthropological Papers 32.
  1999a <u>Lushootseed Culture and the Shamanic Odyssey</u>: An Anchored Radiance. Lincoln: University of Nebraska Press.
  1999b Chehalis Area Traditions, a Summary of Thelma Adamson's 1927 Ethnographic Notes. Northwest Anthropological Research Notes 33 (1): 1-72.
  1999c Suquamish Traditions. With Warren Snyder. Northwest Anthropological Research Notes 33 (1): 105-175.

Olson, Ronald 1936 The Quinault Indians. University of Washington Publications in Anthropology 6 (1): 1-190.

Powell, Jay, and Vickie Jensen 1976 The Quileute ~ An Introduction to the Indians of La Push. University of Washington Press.

Ray, Verne
  1933 <u>The Sanpoil and Nespelem</u>, Salishan Peoples of Northeastern Washington. University of Washington Publications in Anthropology 5.
  1938 Lower Chinook Ethnographic Notes. University of Washington Publications in Anthropology 7 (2): 29-165.
  1939 <u>Cultural Relations In The Plateau of Northwestern America</u>. Los Angeles: The Southwest Museum, Publications of the Frederick Webb Hodge Anniversary Publication Fund III.

Richardson, Allan, and Brent Galloway 2011 Nooksack Place Names. Geography, Culture, and Language. Vancouver: UBC Press.

Richen, Marilyn 1974 Legitimacy and the Resolution of Conflict in an Indian Church. University of Oregon: Anthropology PhD Dissertation.

Ross, John Alan 2011 The Spokan Indians. Spokane. 871pp.

Ruby, Robert, and John Brown
  1992 <u>A Guide to the Indian Tribes of the Pacific Northwest</u>. Norman: University of Oklahoma Press.
  1996 <u>John Slocum and the Indian Shaker Church</u>. Norman: University of Oklahoma Press.

Sampson, Chief Martin
  1938 The Swinomish Totem Pole, Tribal Legends. Told to Rosalie Whitney. Bellingham, Washington: Union Printing Company.
  1972 Indians of Skagit County. La Conner: Skagit County Historical Society Historical Series 2.

Seattle Post Intelligencer 1905
  29 January Magazine p1 Famous Indien Relics in Hotel Astor Grill.
  12 February Magazine p9 When We Fought Chief Joseph by JW Redington.
  26 February Magazine p1 Canoe Cedar Has Served Man Since Stone Age.
  26 February Magazine p9 Magic Rites & Incantions among Malays; Magazine p10 Tardy Honor for a Neglected Heroine ~ Sacajawea.
  2 April Magazine p1 Hong Kong.
  9 April p5 Panama Canal Zone; Magazine p1 Lewis & Clark.
  16 April Magazine p1 The Real American Girl and her Characteristics.
  23 April Easter color first appears, a cartoon.

30 April Magazine p18 Koriaks.
14 May p3 Harmony as Understood by Primitive People Igorrotes Albert Gale.
28 May p6 Future of Our Indians as Forecast by Commissioner Leupp Outlook not bright
4 June Magazine p3 An American's Adventures among the most Exclusive Savages in the World ~ Eskimos
11 June p14 Elaborate Ceremonies Will Attend Erection of Monument to Chief Joseph.
18 June p5 Where Kissing is Unknown.
25 June p12 The Reburial of Chief Joseph ~ Meany Gives Address.
4 July Magazine p2 They Plan Petticoat Government; p8 With Light Fantastic Toes ~ Moulin Rouge Girls Dress as Indiens.
9 July Magazine p11 Calispel Ask to Retain Their Land; p12 Indians at School at Fort Spokane; Views on Fort Spokane Indien Reservation; San Poil Chief Unusual Character ~ Skolaskin.
16 July p16 entire page Yakimas Present Many Problems; Views and Portraits Made at Ft Simcoe.
23 July Magazine p4 Girls Who Must Do All The Lovemaking.
30 July p13 Contacts Between Indien Tribes;Views & Well Known Persons of Tulalip Reservation.
6 August p3 Precious Historical Indian Relics Neglected in Seattle.
13 August p11 The Muckleshoots' Queer Reservation [p10 Iron Chink].
27 August p6 Puyallups and Nisqually Indians; Views of Puyallup & Nisqually.
3 September p6 Indians on the Edge of the Continent & Their Folklore; Quinaielt Being Transformed from Hunters of Sea Otters & Whales to Allotted Indiens.
10 September p6 Indians have lived at La Push for Countless Centuries; Ancient Home of the Quileutes Who Are A Distinct Language Family.
24 September p13 Appeal for Natives by Rev EJ Knapp Protestant Episcopal missionary against Eskimo abuse in Alaska.
1 October p6 Legends Traditions and Present Conditions of Lummi Indians; How they Got Fire.
8 October p6 Swinomish Indians a Composite of Many Tribes and Bands.
15 October p6 Washington Redmen Who Helped Palefaces in War; Legends of the Wishkah & Hoquiam Rivers.
22 October p6 Twana & Clallam Indians Aborigines of Hoods Canal; Rapid Decline of Once Powerful Tribe; The Clallams were a Strong People.
29 October p6 Story of Seattles' Nearest Indian Neighbors ~ Suquamish.
12 November p11 Edward S Curtis & His Indiens.
19 November magazine p8 How Humanity Carries Babies.
26 November p2 Symbolism of the swastika; p6 Chief Peter Brown (How A Thlub) ~ Last Chief of the Makahs; Thrilling Events of His Life Told by Himself by Lucien M Lewis; Magazine p4 Blondes Highest Type of Human Race.
10 December p7 Indian Life on Seattle Streets.
17 December Magazine p4 American Indians Most Misunderstood People of the World.
24 December p2 Neptune's Christmas Present to Old Hucksee by Zoe Kinead.
Shelton, William 1932 The Story of the Everett Story Pole. Everett: Kane and Harcus.

Sicade, Henry 1940 The Indians' Side of the Story. <u>Building A State, Washington, 1889-1939</u>, XIX: 490-503. Charles Mills and OB Sperlin, eds. Tacoma: Washington State Historical Society.

Singh, Ram Raj Prasad 1966 Aboriginal Economic System of the Olympic Peninsula Indians. Sacramento Anthropological Society Papers 4.

Smith, Marian
  1940a <u>The Puyallup-Nisqually</u>. Columbia University Contributions to Anthropology 32.
  1940b The Puyallup of Washington. Acculturation in Seven American Indian Tribes, Chapter 1, 3-36. Ralph Linton, ed. NY: D. Appleton-Century Co.
  1941 The Coast Salish of Puget Sound. <u>American Anthropologist</u> 43: 197-211.

Smith, Marian, editor
  1949 <u>Indians of the Urban Northwest</u>. New York: Columbia University Contributions to Anthropology 36: 1-370.

Snyder, Sally
  mss. Sally Snyder Collection, Melville Jacobs Collection, Special Collection, University of Washington Libraries.
  ms. Folktales of the Skagit. Copies at Lushootseed Research and University of Washington Archives.
  1964 Skagit Society and Its Existential Basis: An Ethnofolkloristic Reconstruction. University of Washington: Anthropology Ph.D. Dissertation.
  1975 Quest For the Sacred in Northern Puget Sound: An Interpretation of Potlatch. <u>Ethnology</u> 14 (2): 149-161.

Snyder, Warren
  1956 "Old Man House" on Puget Sound. Washington State University Studies 24, 17-37.
  1968 Southern Puget Sound Salish: Texts, Place Names, and Dictionary. Sacramento Anthropological Society, Paper 9.

Spier, Leslie
  1935 <u>The Prophet Dance of the Northwest and its Derivatives</u>: The Source of the Ghost Dance. Menasha: General Series in Anthropology 1.
  1936 Tribal Distributions in Washington. Menasha: General Series in Anthropology 3.

Spier, Leslie, editor.
  1938 The Sinkaietk or Southern Okanagon of Washington. Contributions from the Laboratory of Anthropology 2. Menasha: General Series in Anthropology 6.

Stern, Bernhard 1934 The Lummi Indians of Northwest Washington. New York: Columbia University Contributions to Anthropology 17: 1-127.

Strauss, Joseph H. 2002 <u>The Jamestown S'Klallam Story</u>. Rebuilding a Northwest Coast Indian Tribe. Sequim, Washington.

Suttles, Wayne 1987 <u>Coast Salish Essays</u>. Vancouver, BC: Talonbooks.

Suttles, Wayne, editor. 1990 <u>Northwest Coast</u>. Handbook of North American Indians. Volume 7. Smithsonian Institution Press.

Suttles, Wayne, and William Elmendorf 1963 Linguistic Evidence for Salish Prehistory. <u>Symposium on Language and Culture</u>: 41-52. Viola E. Garfield and Wallace Chafe, eds. Proceedings of the 1962 Annual Spring Meeting of the American Ethnological Society. Seattle: University of Washington Press.

Swan, James
- 1857 The Northwest Coast, or, Three Years in Washington Territory. NY: Harper and Brothers. [University of Washington Press, 1972]
- 1870 The Indians of Cape Flattery, at the Entrance to the Starit of Juan de Fuca, Western Washington Territory. DC: Smithsonian Contributions to Knowledge 16: 1-105.
- 1971 Almost Out of the World. Scenes in Washington Territory. The Strait of Juan de Fuca 1859-61. Tacoma: Washington State Historical Society.

Taylor, Herbert, and Garland Grabert, editors. 1984 Western Washington Indian Socio-Economics: Papers in Honor of Angelo Anastasio. Bellingham: Western Washington University.

Tollefson, Kenneth
- 1987 The Snoqualmie: A Puget Sound Chiefdom. Ethnology 26: 121-136.
- 1989 Religious Transformation among the Snoqualmie Shakers. Northwest Anthropological Research Notes 23 (1): 97-102.
- 1989 Political Organization of the Duwamish. Ethnology 28: 135-149.
- 1992 The Political Survival of Landless Puget Sound Tribes. American Indian Quarterly (Spring): 213-235.
- 1995b Duwamish Tribal Identity and Cultural Survival. Northwest Anthropological Research Notes 29 (1): 103-116.
- 1996 In Defense of a Snoqualmie Political Chiefdom Model. Ethnohistory 43 (1): 145-171.

Tweddell, Colin 1953 A Historical and Ethnological Study of the Snohomish Indian People. Docket 125, Indian Claims Commission. [1974 Coast Salish and Western Washington Indians V. David Agee Horr, ed. Indian Claims Commission, Findings 120: 475-694. New York: Garland Publishing, Inc.]

Waterman, Thomas
- 1920 The Whaling Equipment of the Makah Indians. University of Washington Publications in Anthropology 1 (2).
- 1922 The Geographical Names Used by the Indians of the Pacific Coast. The Geographical Review 12 (2): 175-194.
- 1924 The Shake Religion of Puget Sound. Smithsonian Report for 1922: 499-507.
- 1930 The Paraphernalia of the Duwamish 'Spirit-Canoe' Ceremony. New York: Museum of the American Indian, Heye Foundation, Indian Notes 7 (2): 129-148, 295-312, 535-561.
- 1973 Notes on the Ethnology of the Indians of Puget Sound. New York: Museum of the American Indian, Heye Foundation, Indian Notes and Monographs, Miscellaneous Series 59.

Wickersham, James
- 1896 Pueblos on the Northwest Coast. American Antiquarian 18: 21-24.
- 1898 Nisqually Mythology, Studies of the Washington Indians. Overland Monthly 32: 345-51.
- 1899 Notes on the Indians of Washington. American Antiquarian 21: 269-375.

Wike, Joyce
- 1941 Modern Spirit Dancing of Northern Puget Sound. University of Washington: Anthropology M.A. Thesis.
- 1952 The Role of the Dead in Northwest Coast Culture. Indian Tribes of Aboriginal America: 97-103. Sol Tax, ed. Proceedings of the 29th International Congress of Americanists.

Williams, Johnson 1916 Black Tamanous, the Secret Society of the Clallam Indians. Washington Historical Quarterly 7: 296-300.

Willoughby, Charles 1889 Indians of the Quinaielt Agency, Washington Territory. Smithsonian Institution Annual Report.

Wray, Jacilee 2002 <u>Native Peoples of the Olympic Peninsula. Who We Are</u>. Norman: University of Oklahoma Press.

Wright, Robin, ed. 1991 <u>A Time of Gathering</u>, Native Heritage of Washington State. Seattle: University of Washington Press.

Hoh Contents

13 Introduction   14 Forward ~ JV Powell   16 Richard Daugherty and Hoh Ethnography ~ Miller and Kirk   17 Home Drainages   17 Lodges Clubs Orders   18 Hoh and Quileute Chronology   19 map   21 The Notebook Transcriptions ~ Miller

22 ARTIFACTS
   Baskets   Canoes   Houses   Fish Traps   Adornment   Fire   Snares ~ Traps   Dogs   Bow ~ Arrows ~ Spears   Tools

34 FOODS
   Sealing   Whaling   Salmon   Smelt   Elk   Halibut   Herring   Sea Lion   Ducks   Porpoise   Plants   Storage

46 SOCIETY
   Birth   Twins   Puberty   Quest   Songs   Cures   Raids   Ranks   Slaves   Doctors   Names   Murder   Travel   Pranks   Burial   Languages

58 GATHERINGS
   Parties   Klokwaly~Wolves   Tsayuq~Fishers   Clubs = Elks   Whalers   Weather Forecasters~Tcalalayu   Invitees   Shakers

73 APPENDICES

   Checklists 73 Questions 73
   Kin Terms 75
   Linguistic Domains 77 Meanings   Trees   Animals   Sea Life   Birds   Shore Life   Seasons
      Times   Directions   Measurements   Spans   Weights   Distances   Numbers 1-20
      Forecasting
   Places 82   Hoh Household Census 85   Acknowledgements 86

87 Bibliography 91

JOURNAL OF NORTHWEST ANTHROPOLOGY

VOLUME 44	Fall 2010	NUMBER 2

THE HOH TRIBE IN 1949: RICHARD "DOC" DAUGHERTY'S ETHNOGRAPHIC NOTEBOOKS

Jay Miller, Editor

ABSTRACT

The 1949 field notebooks of Richard Daugherty's ethnographic work with the Hoh Tribe of western Washington State were compiled, organized, and occasionally extracted and re-arranged to facilitate publication. Additional material was prepared by Jay Powell and Ruth Kirk and included to set the context of the material in light of current knowledge of the Chemakuan Linguistic Isolate.

Introduction

The Hoh and Quileute represent the most distinctive living communities on the Northwest Coast because their language is unaffiliated and unique to the Olympic Peninsula. It may have ancient ties to Wakashan languages of southern British Columbia, but it has long stood apart. With dormant Chimakum, Hoh and Quileute speakers composed the entirety of the Chimakuan (formerly Chemakuan) language isolate.

In 1949, Richard D. Daugherty, an anthropology graduate student at the University of Washington, spent months collecting ethnographic information on the Hoh. The information was documented in four notebooks, and more or less forgotten after Daugherty moved on to a career in archaeology. In 2009, he lent me the four field notebooks from his 1949 work to transcribe and publish.

To facilitate publication, the transcription is presented as follows. First is a Foreword by fellow ethnographer and linguist, Jay Powell, who worked with the notebooks in the 1990s. This is followed by an historical and cultural overview by me and Ruth Kirk. I came to the Northwest fascinated by language isolates, having finished a dissertation on the Keresan Pueblos of the Southwest and visited the Yuchi of the Southeast; both are isolates. Kirk is a writer and photographer on National Parks, Nature, and Northwest history and archaeology; she and Doc were married in 2007. The transcribed material from the four notebooks is then presented essentially as it appears in the notebooks. Five short sections are then provided that focus on specific topics found scattered in different places within the notebooks: checklists, kin terms, linguistic domains, places, and a census of Hoh village houses. Finally, a bibliography of references relevant to the Hoh Tribe is provided.

Foreword
by Jay Powell

I think now of the first time I opened "Doc's" field notebooks almost 20 years ago. Some memories do not fade. At Verne Ray's suggestion, I had called Richard and asked if it would be possible to have a look at his Hoh River fieldnotes. And he said, "How about tomorrow…and I'll even buy you lunch." Over dessert, he handed over a paper bag containing the four faded composition books. I opened the one on top and just started to laugh. On the inside of the cover was written:

If found -
Please return to R. D. Daugherty, Dept. of Anthropology, University of Washington, Seattle 5, Wash. or 5127 46th N.E. Seattle 5 Wash.

Reward

In fact, despite that notice, until recently these books had been lost for almost five decades. And more is the irony, by the time they were "unearthed" we were all shocked that Daugherty, The Great One of northwest coast archeology, had started out as a graduate student doing pure ethnography.

Readers should know immediately that those notebooks, edited into this publication, represent an important contribution. Over the years, Farrand, Reagan, Frachtenberg, Andrade, Swindell, Pettitt, Ram Singh and the other "first voices" (see bibliographic overview) all mentioned the Hohs as if they were a band of Quileute speakers, largely culturally indistinguishable from the Quileutes of La Push. Daugherty was the first observer to set out to document the Hoh's lore and identity as a distinct community. And that he did. We and the Hohs themselves are all richer for it.

Like most fieldwork, Daugherty's success in eliciting a satisfyingly complete picture of Hoh traditional life derives from his relationships with Billy Hudson and Stanley Grey, his informants (an old term now replaced by "consultant"). Born about 1883, Hudson was an elder and head of a respected and noble family, and he was able to describe life on the lower Hoh River with clarity and delicious detail. Hudson's narrative flows page by page, describing community life, status, the annual cycle of hunting, fishing and gathering, inheritance, the potlatch and a complex spirit world. Grey taught him about spiritual and artistic traditions. We have no sense of the extent to which Daugherty directed the narrative with questions, but my experience with the Quileute and Hoh *talhaykila potsokw* ('old time people') was that they required and put up with very little prompting. There is input from others as well, but we are very aware that the picture we are savoring is the artistry of Billy Hudson and Stanley Grey.

With few exceptions, Daugherty records information without commentary. It is the raw data of cultural description. The margins were not decorated with hypotheses or comments. The notes are the broad transcription of information, of a young fieldworker focused on getting down the gist and details of an articulate and loquacious expert. Hoh elders were used to being listened to. Once when I interrupted Quileute elder Hal George with a request to repeat something, he looked at me and said, "Jay, when an old man is speaking, shut up and listen." It is clear that the young Daugherty was a good listener. Maybe Mel Jacobs, a founding anthropologist at UW and one of Daugherty's teachers, told him as he told me, "Your job as a fieldworker is to be an amanuensis, not to hold a conversation. Take lots of pencils and write like hell." When I look at the pages of data in those notebooks, I think about writer's cramp and the fieldworker's natural urge to get down every fact in a consultant's voluble account. Daugherty got down an amazing amount of detail—all of it important to us now.

Daugherty had a good ear! As we progress through the notebooks, he starts to include more Quileute words, as if he were getting comfortable with the recognition and recording of Quileute sounds. His phonetic transcriptions are good from the beginning, a product of the "four-square" approach to anthropology teaching: cultural, linguistic, physical and archeological. Those of us who are interested in Hoh personal names, place names and the recondite cultural vocabulary of the Hoh natural and physical world are grateful for that phonetic accuracy.

I personally appreciate the charts and maps that are plentiful throughout and, as the saying goes, are worth a lot of words. They are evocative of generalizations, the building blocks of understandings. I recall looking at the map/chart of the assignment of net sites along the Hoh River and realizing that all but one of the site-assignees had either a Hoh father and a Quileute mother or a Hoh mother and a Quileute father. This realization, based on the ultra-rich data of the chart, led me to seek out other evidence of village exogamy within the tribe and to write "The Ethnic Unity of the Hoh and Quileute." Such is the value of ethnographic notes half a century later; and such is the value of Daugherty's contribution, which previously has been largely unavailable.

This edited version of Daugherty's notebooks assures that this rich description of Hoh beliefs and lifeways will not again be lost and will be easily available. That is the gratifying payback for us ethnographic fieldworkers as we record the words and stories of the last of the old timers who remembered the way things used to be. Our notebooks turn oral history into written records that would otherwise have died with those old people. It is like catching a dodo bird by the toenail as it flies off to extinction. And the *Journal of Northwest Anthropology*, as usual, is playing a role in this documentation, preservation and dissemination effort.

Richard Daugherty and Hoh Ethnography
by Jay Miller and Ruth Kirk

Richard D. Daugherty, or "Doc" as he is respectfully and affectionately known, was born in 1922 and raised in Aberdeen, Washington, at the inner tip of Grays Harbor. His father owned a car dealership and his grandfather ran a sawmill in nearby Junction City. As a boy, Doc avidly hiked, skied, and rock climbed, as well as hunted and fished for the family's table. After a year at college in Ellensburg, where he was introduced to anthropology, he transferred to the University of Washington (UW). There, World War II interrupted his studies; and he joined the U.S. Navy Air Corps as a blimp pilot based in New Jersey, flying out over the Atlantic on convoy escort duty and submarine patrol. After Germany surrendered and submarine surveillance was no longer needed, Doc taught meteorology and navigation at the Navy Air Navigation School in Oklahoma.

When the war ended, Doc returned to UW, where he graduated in 1946, and immediately started on his PhD, initially in ethnography. His courses included a class by Verne Ray and a summer introduction to archaeology in the form of a field school directed by Arden King at Cattle Point on San Juan Island (one of Washington's earliest field schools). In 1947, he undertook an archaeological survey of the Washington coast on foot, locating 50 archaeological sites that would later became important sites of excavations (Miller 2010), such as Minard and Ozette (Daugherty 1947).

In 1949, after a rigorous class in fieldwork methods from Verne Ray, Doc temporarily moved his wife Phyllis and baby daughter to a shack at the mouth of the Hoh River, south of the Quileute village of La Push. Every day he rowed across to the Indian village where he eventually filled four notebooks with ethnographic information, working particularly with Stanley Grey and Bill Hudson. After several months Doc returned to the UW and found his interest shifting from ethnography to archaeology (Fig. 1).

Consequently, the Hoh notebooks languished, never written up or published. But they had their own exciting life since they remained in the safe of the UW Burke Museum for decades until George Quimby found them and returned them to Doc in the 1990s. Doc loaned them to Jay Powell for seven years, who used them in his Quileute research and for the Hoh web site. Powell then sent the field notebooks to Barbara Lane as she assembled data for a fishing rights case around 2003. She returned them to Doc, who then loaned them to Jay Miller to transcribe and organize into this ethnographic overview, sixty years on.

For Doc and his students, archaeology promised vigorous, outdoor activity. At that time there were few trained archaeologists available to make river basin archaeological surveys, before major dam construction got underway in Washington and elsewhere in the West. These projects also provided ready funding for career and department building.

Doc had a thirty-five-year career at Washington State University (1950–1985), building a program recognized internationally for its interdisciplinary approach to archaeology. His excavations at Lind Coulee, Marmes, Ozette, Fort Nisqually, and elsewhere are legendary; dam construction projects from the Columbia and Snake rivers to the Peace River in British Columbia and the Nile in southern Egypt and northern Sudan continued on his agenda. Appointed by President Johnson to a national committee, his advocacy of federal protection legislation and historic preservation policy helped to establish current standards and funding.

Widowed in retirement, Doc married writer/photographer Ruth Kirk in 2007 and they continue archaeological consulting from their home near Olympia, Washington.

Fig. 1. Richard D. "Doc" Daugherty
at the University of Washington, 1949
(Daugherty personal files).

Home Drainages

The Hoh River has its headwaters off Mt. Olympus, flowing as the main stem of a regular dendritic pattern (Fig. 2). Smaller tributaries include its South Fork and creeks now named Braden, Nolan, Anderson, Pins, Lost, Winfield, Alder, Willoughby, Clear, Linder, Tower, Pole, Dismal, Spruce, Twin, Snyder, Taft, Jackson, Mount Tom, Mineral, Slide, Falls, Martin, Ice, Cream, and Elkhorn. These names have hidden from the public any of their ancient Hoh cosmic and spirit associations.

The drainage of the Quileutes is more complicated. Near La Push, the Dickey River (which includes an East Fork and a West Fork flowing from Dickey Lake) joins the Quillayute River, which has the three main branches of the Soleduck River (fed from Lake Pleasant, Beaver Creek, Bear Creek, and the river's North Fork); and the Calawah River (with North and South Forks fed by Elk Creek, Sitkum Creek, and the Bogachiel River.

Goodman Creek, fed by Minter Creek, flows into the Pacific half way between the Hoh and Quillayute river systems. Mosquito Creek is to its south.

Hoh Lodges—Clubs—Orders

Although much of Hoh ethnography is shared along the Northwest Coast, a distinctive feature, condensed in Doc's notes is the six lodges, clubs, sodalities, or orders which drew membership from prosperous Hohs (Powell 1990, 433; Powell and Woodruff 1976: 81, 91, 198, 211, 249, 441):

Hoh

1. λokʷa•li — wolf, black paint, warriors
2. ċa•yiq — fishers, sealers, Salmon
3. kiƛaʔk̓ʷaɬ — hunters, Elks, "uprivering"
4. sibaxʷola•yoʔ — whalers, "oily-voiced"
5. čala•layoʔ — seers, forecasters, Weathermen, "southern voiced"
6. ʔixʷaolaʔa•ʔlayoʔ — doctors, shamans.

Often called secret societies, they represent special privilege and guarded rank, based on knowledge that is protected and only in that sense "secret." Only #3, #6, and maybe #5 have Chimakuan origins. The others have obvious regional links, especially in their songs, which feature words from neighboring tribes, including Wakashan Kwakiutlans (1, 2), Makah (4), and Quinault (5). This last may have come from Hoh at a time when Quinault was the dominant language there. Hoh is called "South River" in Quileute.

In Kwakwaka'wakw the word tʔsetʔsayeka means "secrets," being shortened to Tsaykik as the club spread to other communities. A distinct category of family privileges involves tsasa'a = love songs.

Hoh and Quileute Chronology

The name "Quileute" derives from the native name for the village at La Push, whereas "Hoh" derives from their Quinault name. Over time, the Quileute and Quinault languages seem to have alternated in prominence along the lower Hoh River, which may have been the actual source for the Weather Forecaster order. Hoh ancestors are ṗiṗisodaċiɬi "upside-down people," with smelt as their special gift. They call themselves čala•t̓ which is sometimes also used for Quinaults.

As the world was changed before humans arrived, *Kwati* (The Changer) found timber wolves (as animal spirit people) living at Quileute and he transformed them into ancestors of today's human people. At Hoh, he found beings walking upside-down trying to use smelt nets with their feet. Kwati turned them right-side-up and taught them to harvest their promised smelt with hand-held nets. To the south among Tsamosan Salish, the Changer was known as Mispʰ, who later became Old Squawk Duck. Hoh, Quileute, and Chimakum form the Chimakuan language isolate, unique to the Olympic Peninsula.

Chemakum, who called themselves *axoqulo*, occupied a palisaded village on Hadlock Bay, fed by Chimacum Creek, on the western side of the Quimper Peninsula above the mouth of Hood Canal. Situated in the rain shadow of the Olympic Mountains, their territory was more arid than surrounding areas, and this helps to accounts for their persistence there. Known as belligerent and likely slavers, they were attacked by Snoqualmies and later by Suquamish, led by Chief Seattle, who lost a son in the battle. Survivors took refuge with Skokomish. Later, in 1854, about 70 members had 15 small houses on Port Townsend Bay. Party to the 1855 Treaty of Point No Point, they settled, in 1860, 18 houses on Point Hudson, and intermarried with Klallams. They became fluent in both Chimakum and Klallam, and used nasals (M, N), which are characteristic of Straits Salish.

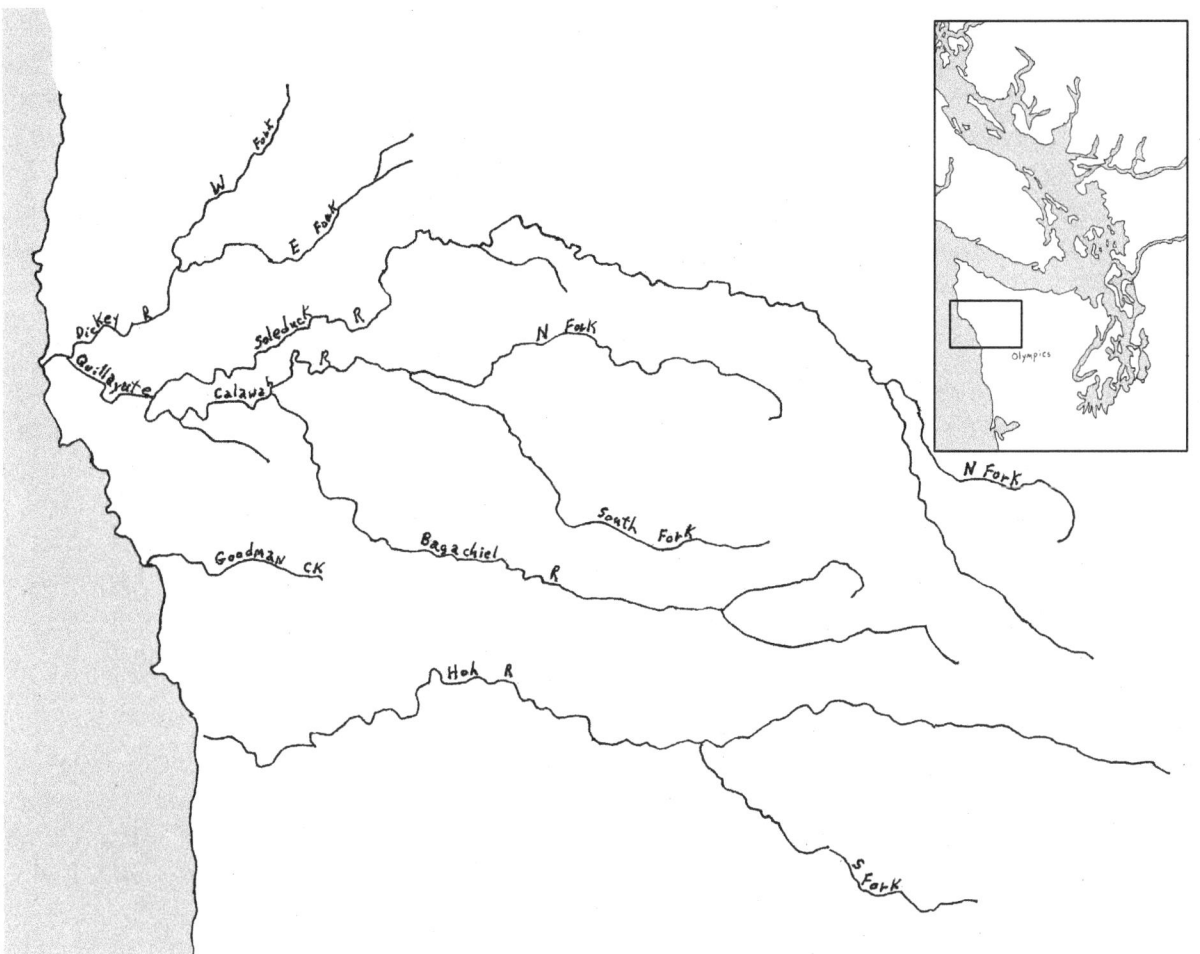

Fig. 2. Map showing location of rivers mentioned in text (drawn by Jay Miller 2010).

Hoh and Quileute married among leading families of the coast, and shifted to orals (B, D), like the Makahs. They incorporated memberships in the special or privileged lodges, and strongly defended their territories. Europeans learned to be wary. For example, Spanish crews on the *Sonora* in 1775 and British on the *Imperial Eagle*, captained by Charles Barkley, lost members of landing parties. Russian and Aleut survivors of the *Sviatoi Nikolai*, wrecked off Quilleute in 1808. Survivors, including three women and a lone Englishman, fortified themselves on the Hoh only to become enslaved. Some were traded elsewhere, some died, and others were rescued by an American ship in May 1811. A report by Timofei Tarakanov of their suffering begins the historical record [Ownes and Donnelly 1984].

Present at the first 1855 treaty council at Cosmopolis, George Gibbs, ethnographer for the commission, had yet to learn of Chimakuan distinctiveness. By the second council at the Quinault River (negotiated 1 July 1855, signed at Olympia 26 January 1856, ratified 8 March 1859), Chimakuans were included (though the Chehalis were not). Chimakuans refused to relocate to the Quinault Reservation, however, and eventually Grover Cleveland signed executive orders for reservations in their homelands at La Push (19 February 1889) and Hoh (11 September 1893). As lead signers for Chimakuans, the chiefly names of Howeattle and Kilip became confirmed as the most prominent of the hereditary name-titles.

Bureau of Indian Affairs agencies were located at Neah Bay and at Quinault in 1863. A subagency has been located at Hoquiam since 1933. In 1889, while Quileutes were away picking hops, a local settler intent on homesteading at La Push burned all 26 houses in the village. The BIA supplied lumber for the community to rebuild, but irreplaceable heirlooms were lost. In 1895, many residents joined the Shaker Church, founded by John and Mary Slocum near Olympia in 1882. Indian Agents tried repeatedly to suppress services of this faith, but their persecutions encouraged more converts.

After the Civil War, when federal officials assigned reservations to Protestant denominations, the reservations along the coast of Washington, because of close ties with missions in the Columbia and Willamette Rivers, were placed under the Methodists, who started schools and churches. When James Swan held school in 1864 at Neah Bay, a few Quileute students attended. A day school began at La Push in 1882, when Alanson Wesley Smith and his wife gave names to residents that they drew from notables in U.S. history and the Bible. Smith (whose sister Harriet married Dan Pullen, local trader and arsonist) retired in 1905. Albert Reagan took over the school 1905–1908, collecting stories and other ethnography, as well as a charming set of children's drawing now with his papers at Brigham Young University.

Individual allotments began 4 March 1911 but the limited size of the Hoh and Quileute reservations led assignment of parcels on the larger Quinault Reservation (originally approved 4 March 1904, reversed 1906, and reapproved 4 March 1911 until 1913). Far from accepting allotment as the end of the matter, Hoh and Quileute (Indian Claims Commission, Docket 155) pursued compensation for undervalued land, rejecting the court's first determination of $25,000 in favor of receiving $112,152.60 on 17 April 1963 for division among both tribes.

In 1920, tragedy struck when a storm at sea drowned 42 sealers, sparing only six men and two canoes that were rescued by the passing steamer *Multnomah*, and were taken to San Francisco, where they were put ashore to return home. One of six rescued, Dr. Lester credited his power for the men's deliverance. The others were Frank Harlow, Eli Ward, Burt Jones, Charles Sailto, and Frank Fisher (as reported in Doc's notes).

Academic research began with Leo Frachtenberg in 1916–1917, followed by Manuel Andrade in 1928 working with Jack Ward and monolingual Sixtis [Ward ?]. George Pettitt, while stationed at the La Push Coast Guard base (a lifeboat station since 1930) during World War II, studied Quileute acculturation. He later supplemented his notes with research in Washington DC archives while stationed there, and published in 1950. Jay Powell and his wife Vicki Jensen began Chimakuan studies and publications in the 1970s and their work continues today. Today, Quileutes figure in the internationally best-selling *Twilight* books, erroneously assuming their first ancestors were genetic werewolves, rather than transformed pre-Quileute Wolf Spirits.

Treaty-rights issues continue. In 1981, in *Hoh vs. Baldrige*, Hoh, Quileute, and Quinault sued and won against U.S. Secretary of Commerce Malcolm Baldrige, forcing the federal government to manage the ocean fishery in accord with treaty rights. Today, the Pacific Fisheries Management Council oversees this compliance.

Most recently, Hohs have gained higher ground for their reservation by purchasing property and by land transfer from the National Park Service, enabling them to move their community above storm tides and tsunami hazards.

The Notebook Transcriptions
prepared by Jay Miller

At the end of 2009, Richard D. Daugherty lent me four field notebooks from his 1949 work with the Hoh Tribe in Washington State to transcribe and publish (Fig. 3). The field notebooks have been transcribed as found (Fig. 4). In general, entries are sequential by notebook 1 to 4, and placed within parentheses (notebook: page) set at its beginning to avoid confusion. Transcriptions were as accurate as possible, with all strikeouts included. Doubtful passages were reviewed with Doc, who read them for corrections. Since Doc was working through the subject outline taught by Verne Ray in class, much on one topic is placed together. In cases where related information was found on a different page, the material was extracted and moved. Citations for Hoh Notebooks are between parentheses, with the number of the notebook and page, such as (4:97) for page 97 of notebook 4. Additional punctuation includes wider spacing, equal signs = to indicate translations or equivalences, and curved brackets { } around inserted information, usually from marginal notes with arrows pointing to the allied topic on that page but sometimes as recent clarifications by Doc and Ruth. Whenever a name, time, and date appears in the record, they are included in square brackets [ ]. Several illustrations have been reproduced and placed near the appropriate text.

In consultation with Jay Powell, it was decided not to update Doc's transcriptions since they, for the time, were "pretty good." The standard reference, however, remains Powell and Woodruff (1976). A subject matter finding aid is provided (Table 1).

Fig. 3. 2010 photograph of Richard Daugherty and his Hoh field notebooks
(Jay Miller photograph, September 2010).

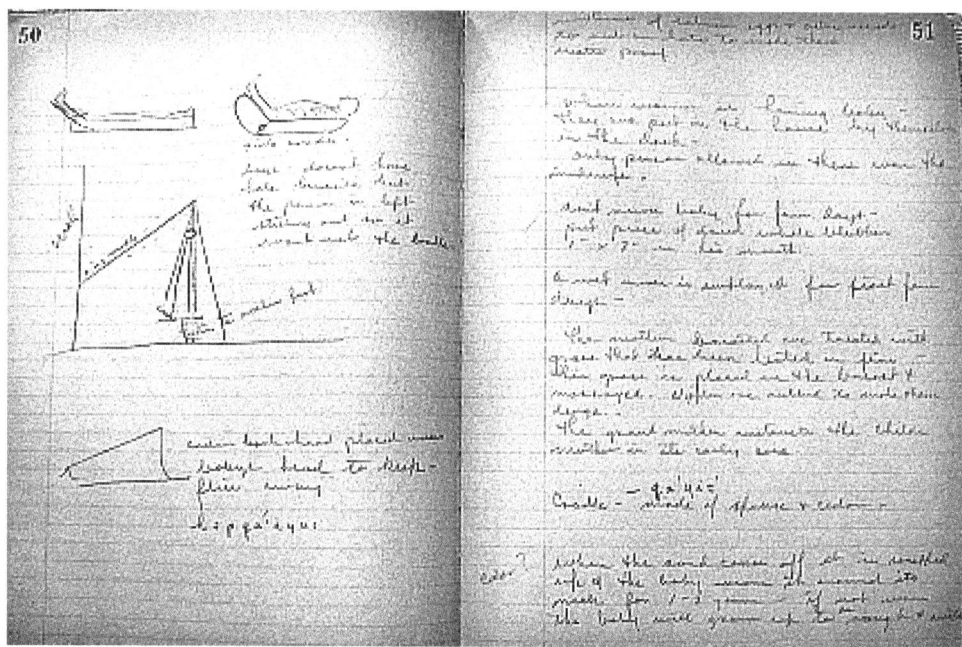

Fig. 4. Photograph of example notebook page
(Jay Miller photograph, September 2010).

Artifacts and Possessions

Baskets

cedar

Baskets (1:7) Mrs. Stanley Grey at La Push—baskets. Get string from hop fields for twine for baskets. Gathering basketry – spruce root & cedar – Swamp grass or mountain [bear] grass May–June good for gathering cedar bark – Sun dry cedar bark—Young limbs split to form base of basket—Split vine maple used for baskets—3 in.or less in diameter. Split easily.

(1:33) cedar bark pockets = qla•ac qla'c (1:40) leaves = qʷa•yuxteix basket = po•o'q

Egg gathering – seagull eggs – Ate them fresh - boiled - hard boiled. (1:119) Eggs lowered in basket by small line.

Canoe

Canoe (1:6) canoe blank is now greased to facilitate removing from the woods.
Canoe making (1:7) Cut log to length desired—split it in half, level it for working. Shape ends first—all eye work. Use axe—formerly burned out inside. After shaping outside, the inside is dug out. Now use wedge & sledge or only axe. This is done in woods—then turn canoe over, drill holes from inside along bottom before turning over. Then flatten bottom around hole—measure for desired thickness—use stick with hook after working bottom, then work sides, then turn over. 3 in. for bottom 2½ in. on sides. Nail on this or cross pieces (cedar limbs) (about 6), this is temporary until canoe is taken out of woods.

(1:8) drawing of upside down canoe with 3 guide holes, draw knife on pole "to get into V of ends." (1:9) After canoe is home you save cross piece. Cross piece used for pulling canoe out of woods, these fit inside canoe, measure back end of canoe—go back in woods & get piece to fit it. Rough out shape with axe. Use medicine in fitting end pieces—mix charcoal & oil.

[drawing (1:10) of Nootkan canoe with sail, labels]   same names on middle sail
  (first sail) = t'awaxpotsxuł middle sail = xalɛ•ywałpotsx^{w}ł mast = tcuyaq^{w}ł
  bowman = t'a•sax^w mid = kslɛ•yex^w captain = h'a• yil

Large sail tended by bow man, small sail usually tended by captain, but may be tended by middle man (Fig. 5).

Work (1:11) on sides & then bottom—cedar plugs for knot holes. From outside towards inside. Galvanized tin on inside over plug.

  sealing canoe = alo•tx   yacabałkat (1:53)
  whaling canoe = abe•yut
  head piece = t'awa hotct < t'awa bow
  stern piece = ha'yilitct
  cross piece = a'ayahuxt (? first letter)
  nailing = pi'pi'łxix̣
  bottom = otcodəq^{w}at
  sides = otciuq^{w}at (? stress)

  R = piłatcuq̓^{w}iyut
  L = yat'oq^{w}iut ~ yat'oq^{w}iot

  bow piece fitted on canoe = tłtłatct (1:52)

[drawing of paddle] (1:54)

Some people used mats for sail made of cedar (1:55).

  Captain = h'ay'il
  Bowman = t'awax^w
  Mid man = qale•ywax^w
  Paddles of yew wood, maple = xaliyət

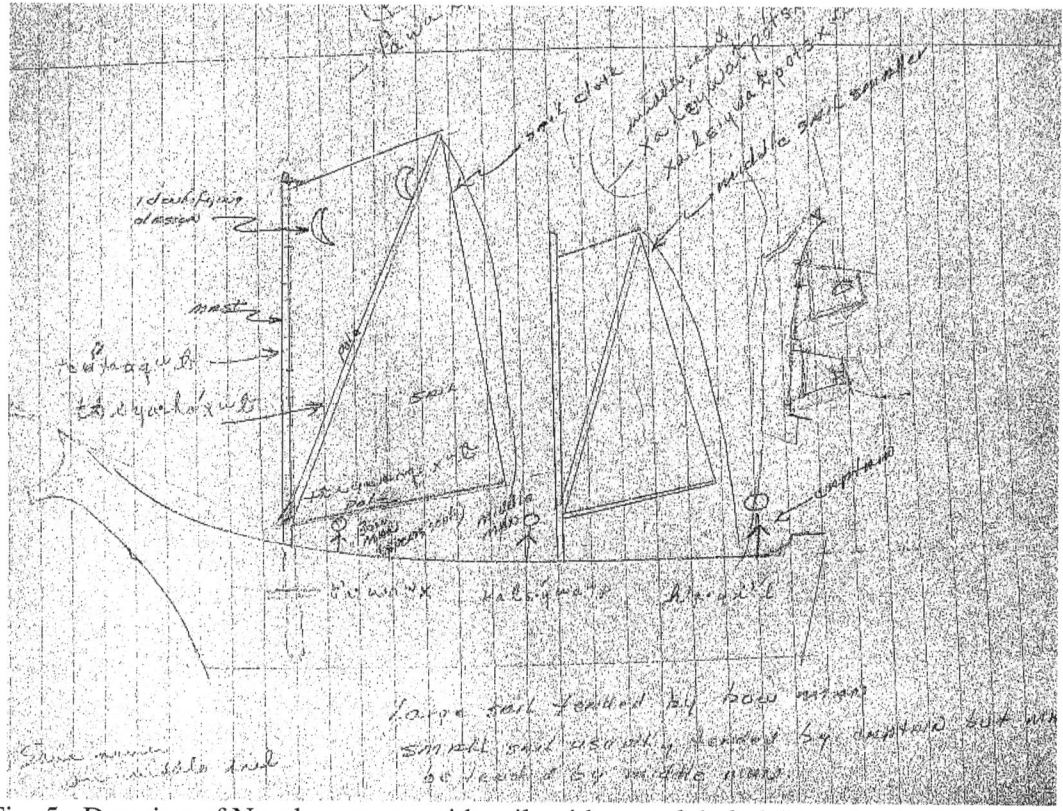

Fig. 5. Drawing of Nootkan canoe with sail, with parts labeled (Daugherty 1949, 1:10).

House

House (1:48) drawing of shed roof house from side. (1:49) W. Hudson Houses—Living houses had shed type roof—long axis of dwelling along beach. "Smokehouse" had gabled roof. Walls—planks run horizontally—two posts sunk in ground side by side with narrow gap between. Planks laid between & secured with cedar limbs.

    Cedar planks = supi•iya
    Uprights = tca'tca• 4–6"
    Rafter = sit'q^{w}ət
    Door in middle on side facing back = t'ati•gat some had 2 doors on front and one on back
    Pole leaning against door = tɬiya•x^{w}əɬ
    Pole across door = tɬiya•te•pex^{w}əɬ ɬixots•pex^{w}aɬ
    Side posts 10–12' apart—buried 3–4'
    Poles holding planks of door = q̇əda'ṗlk^w

Smoke hole (1:51) opening in roof—hole located between fires 3 x 2 ft.—sliding plank to cover in bad weather. Smokehole called = xəxso• , open the smokehole = x̣ə•xsib , smoke hole cover = xəx^{w}səx^{w}əɬ , "cover up that smokehole" = xix^{w}sib , pole to open smoke hole = tɬia•xsix^{w}əɬ

Hoh

Roof planks (3:16) of houses are sometimes laid on lengthwise—sometimes vertically [drawings of gable roof with perpendicular planks, shed roof with both plank styles]. Roofs all of shed type—prior to whites—later on, occasional smokehouse was made with gable roof.

Nets

Net (1:4) diagram of squarish dip net and small Nootkan canoe

hand   Made line from nettle fiber—cut and sun dried—when real dry they soften them up—twisted on thigh also used for fishing net
        Nettles = pəda•k'k̓ʷł
        Fish net = [blank]
        Drift net = blank

(1:82) [drawings of dip net drift net with canoe & stone V]
(1:96) [drawing of dip net from top]

Nets (1:83)
    dip net = k̓ʷtse•yq̓ʷtił yew wood hoop = hitc'a•k̓ʷt spruce or fir for handle
    pole net = xla•yətsalk̓ʷłwa weir = [blank] □

Net on end of two poles held between two canoes—twelve ft. wide—2 ft. opening held about 8 in. from bottom called = b'q'o•d o'łqʷłwa b'q'o•d.
For drifting—net 8 ft. or 10 ft. in length—line to top of net on each side to hold it open.

net (3:116)
called = boq'o•d pole net, wrapped with deer hide so it makes no noise. Strings tied to fingers, 12 ft. across mouth, 15 ft. long {land ?? }, 1.5 ft. high.
Devil's club used to make tail of mesh & keep it open so it won't tangle.

Nettle fiber (3:117) used for twine in netting—long pole 16 ft. long—reach bottom in deep hole in river. Two canoes (4 persons)—people in stern hold poles—persons in front paddle & scare fish into net—if too heavy with fish it is dragged ashore & emptied.

Fish Traps

cone trap = s'qʷɛ•ləb (1:83)

Open end for unloading—yew wood hoop—strips of vine maple tied with spruce or cedar, limbs (twisted), drive stake on each side to hold trap in place—used only in fast water.
rocks = tłe•ł
rapids = a•qsət

(1:84) drawing of cone trap
(1:98) [drawing of weir trap] (Figs. 6, 7, 8).

Hoh

When fish trap (1:85) is loaded a man puts canoe under end & opens trap end to empty fish. Chase fish into trap with canoe—caught silver & blacks [salmon] only used in fall of year.

(1:97) [Sunday, 27 Feburary 1949, Wm Hudson]

Fish trap = t'o•pa^h Find shallow place—maple & hemlock poles—dive [down to set] them in river—5–6ft. apart—clear across the river—have braces on downstream side—brace every pole {tied with cedar limbs} small maple or hemlock or willow 20–25 in. long across—2 poles. Wattle work—small vine maple or hemlock woven 1½–2 in. gap, 1 ft. wide and 5–6 ft. long, turned over to clean off leaves—twice a day—extends 3–4 ft. above water.

> Net = p'o•yəałid
> Wattle wove = itsi•xła
> Upright poles = kato'pa^h
> Braces hemlock, vine maple, or willow = tl'ia•yha•it . Tied together with spruce & cedar limbs. Repair it each year after high water—reused trap again.

All year round (1:99) open trap once in a while & give people upstream a chance to catch fish. Scaffolding built on both sides—called = ?? made of split cedar planks, 4 ft. wide—8 ft. long, 3 places on weir—scaffolding owned by individual persons—rented out. Caught fish going up river as well as coming down. Trap owned by one 2 or 3 men—8 traps known to informants. No trap lower down than 5 or 6 miles from mouth. Fish put in canoe—fish divided up, given away. People lived at site of fish trap.

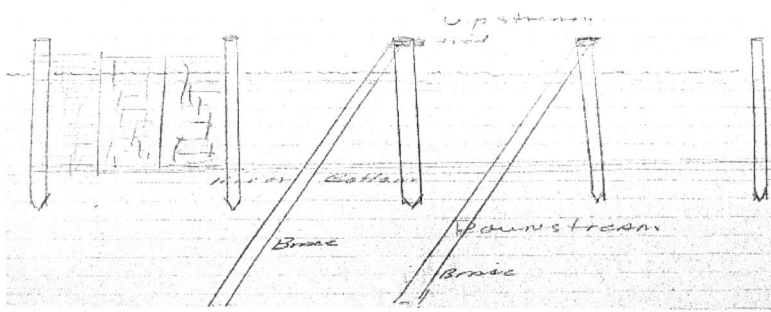

Fig. 6. Drawing of fish weir (Daugherty 1949, 1:98).

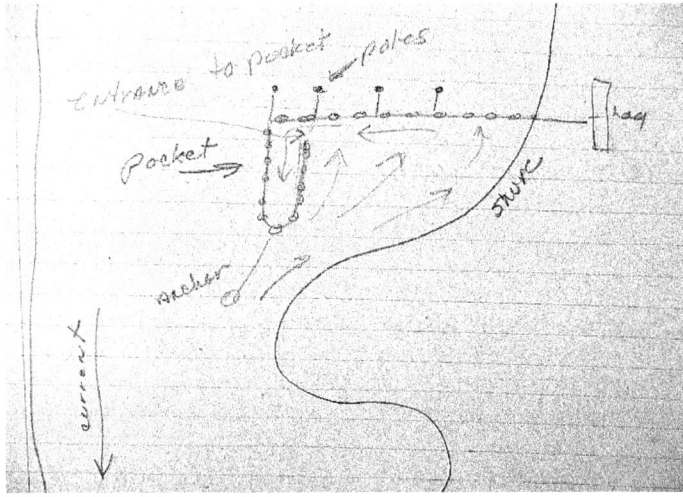
Fig. 8. Drawing of full weir (Daugherty 1949, 2:26).

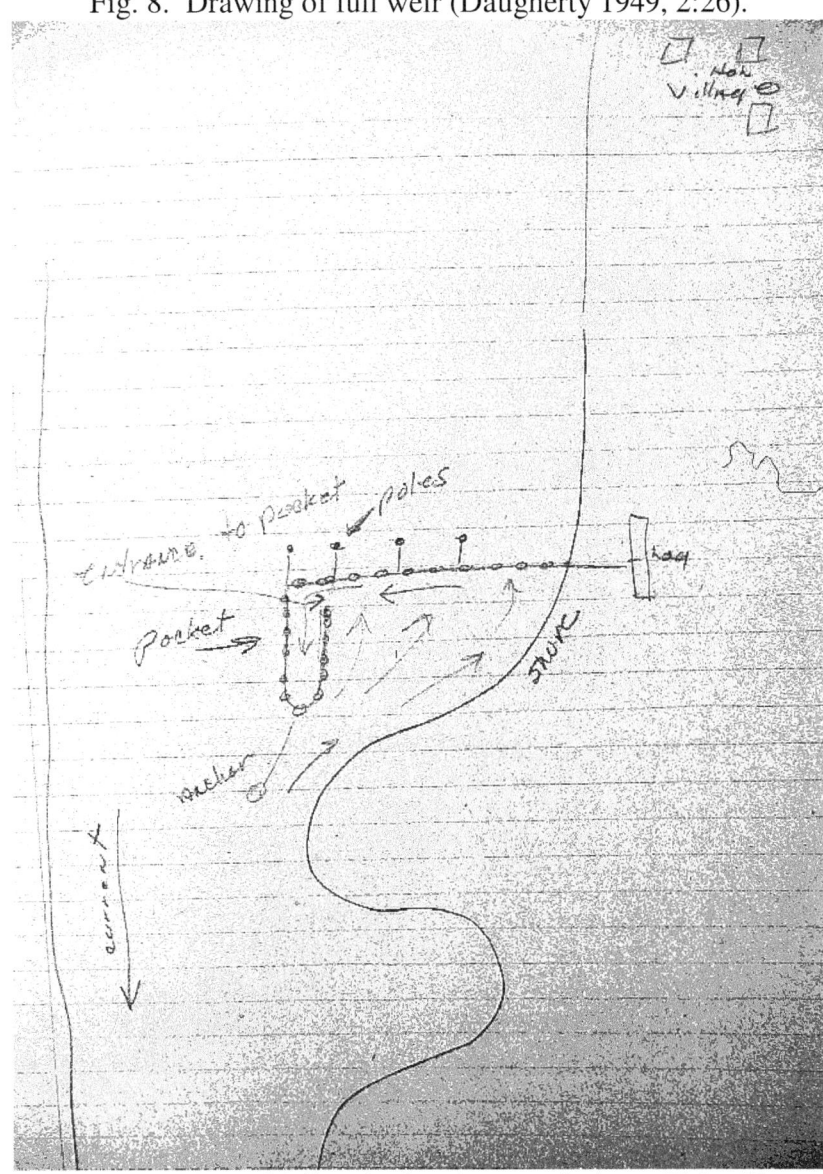
Fig. 7. Drawing of full weir showing proximity to Hoh village

Hoh

(Daugherty 1949, 2:26).

Adornment

Red sand (1:103) from beach—cooked near fire & powdered. When going to use it, it is mixed with oil—bright red—also used for rouge.

    red paint = po•tcitłok̯ʷłə

    black paint = ci•pa powdered charcoal mixed with oil.

    yellow paint = po•doqʷałwa roots of holly-like bush used (has grey berries) boiled.

    boiled hemlock bark—dark brown = cipawi [dark] pici•su [brown] now used for dying nets.

Amulet belonging = qʷdu•də•d'k̯ʷł. Informant stressed ability of good eyes – in being a successful seal hunter (1:109) [4 March, 10 am, Bill Hudson]

Mixture of salmon eggs & ochre used to rub on hats to make them water proof (3:51).

    dentalium - = tl'błasłix (1:95)
    blue beads = xas•diłx̣ Makah = tciti•dək

Cedar bark—skirts covered front only, ♀ = tałala•dəx̣ .

Fire

Fire making (1:117) informant never saw it done—use fine dry cedar bark, gather dried cottonwood roots in summer time drill + base of dry cottonwood roots keep fire going all the time. Spruce limbs hold fire well. They carried it with them—Bill doesn't know how [clam shells ?].

Fire making (3:31) Dry cottonwood roots—gather it in summer—firedrill & platform made of dry cottonwood roots. Fire is never allowed to go out, or borrow fire from other houses driftwood knots—spruce usually—used to keep fire during night. Braided cedar bark wick placed in dish of oil—sea lion, whale, seal—for lamp at night, a wooden bowl of maple or alder.

Big smokehouse had four fire places—2 at each end [drawing of long house with X in each corner] At big gatherings they had fires down the center of house. Green wood—alder, maple, vine maple—use when drying fish—causes some degree of discomfort in the house.

Dogs

Dogs trained to hunt coon, wildcat, bear—tree these animals—hunters built fires under tree with lots of smoke, 4 or 5 hunters ready with bows & arrows when animals came down—aim for eyes of animal (4:61).

Snares—Traps

drawing of elk snare (1:50) elk trap = sit'ixi•d (1:51)

elk whistle = soo•spilaət (1:101) made of bamboo—claims it is new.

Elk snare = sitexid (4:61) 6 in. diameter vine maple bent over—rope made of sinew from along back bone of elk (1:51) 3/8 in. diameter [Drawing of bent over tree branch with loop pegged on ground]. Then shot with bow & arrows, mussel shell points for arrow.

Bear hunting (4:63) bear trap = a•atiya't , trap , bear trap = aq̇i•ligət , pile lot of rocks on ground—trap obscured by moss hung in trail – salmon for bait [drawing of top piled with rocks, side view of log bottom and top with bear between 2 trees].

Bear trap—find creek where bear gets fish—fish for bait. bear trap = a'atiyaət (1:50). bear trap (1:52) bear trap two poles laid on each side of creek 12 ft. parallel with creek.

Curved poles & dirt. Built along stream bank to catch bear when he's fishing (Fig. 9).

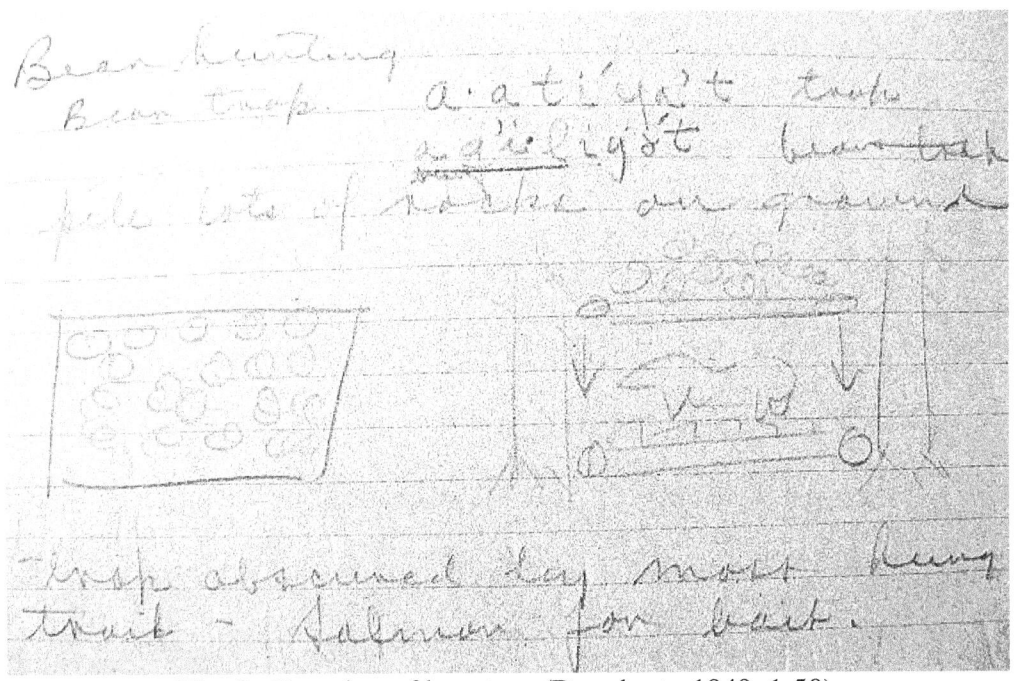

Fig. 9. Drawing of bear trap (Daugherty 1949, 1:50).

Bow—Arrows—Spears

bow = t'ax̱ʷło yew wood, white cedar (1:51)
bows sharp shell on end of bow

Hoh

gut – sea lion bow string = ťahox^{w}ł

arrow = hai•tut
[wing feather of shag {cormorant} = hi•skid]
arrow feather from wings of shags = water proof = tłoo•ł
shell & = si•ig
bone points ground = x̣a•x̣

Salmon spear ~ harpoon (1:99) made the same as seal spear—also called = [blank]

Prongs even—made of wild cherry—formerly used bone point—for elk—put spruce gum over it. Little longer than seal spear called = [blank]. Looked for salmon spawning & speared them.

Tools

Hand axe (1:9) one for rough work—(wide blade), for fine work (narrow blade), handle of maple. Large adze used in fitting ends also. Ends fastened on with fir or cedar pegs. Long handled, broad blade chisel for working inside ends. Draw knife & box plane for hard to get to places where jack plane can't be used. Final adzing after smoothing is for decorative effect & also keeps from checking. Railings go along sides —fir cedar or spruce. Goes about 8" over the end fingers (1:101).

Hand adze called = tlaxo•sks , means "chipping off."

Spoke shave used diagonally (1:9).

Whet stone – Smooth black rock for sharpening stone (1:9).

Hard rock from which pestle is made—called—ła•tłit (1:42).

[drawing of sharpened end, hand-held egg-shaped tool (1:78).]

Knives—Used to use mussel shells for knife—ground it on stone = siq'tił—sharp on end.

Knife = siq'xalix Mussel shell also used for blade on whale harpoon (1:79). q'tc'tad = made of large mussel shell—used to butcher fish, drawing (1:102).

Sledge or maul for driving poles (1:83). Maul (1:85) large rock held between hands used for maul.

Octopus hook (1:80) blue stone—commercial product, drawing of stick with bone hook.

Octopus were boiled and eaten (1:81). Long pole 10' long with nail on end—get "blue stone" and tie it on end of pole with rag—push pole in against octopus and leave it—the action of the blue stone in the water makes the octopus come out of hole. Made octopus vomit. Formerly made hook of bone. Attached to pole.

Sea bass fishing (1:81) Devil club—wood is white with bone hook attached—baited hook—wood weight to keep from turning—trolled with it. Held line in right hand when paddling on right side causes line to jerk. Sea bass = q'li•tu Devil Club = tcitcapuł

Canoe bailers = ka•w^{h}ł—of alder or maple—dug out—drawings of 3 types = tcałka•w^{h}ł (1:101).

Wooden boxes = tl'tlya•du (1:101).

(1:102) [drawing of bark shredder] (1:103) bark shredder—made of flat piece of bone—whale bone—bark lapped over board—beat on edges, rounded edge.

Spoons mussel shells used, wooden spoon made – alder & maple, maple especially good—handle about 2 in. long—some big spoons might hold a pint (3:13).

Bathing (1:117) people used to jump in river every morning—men, women, children makes them tough to make them clean. Informant knows of no sweat houses. Stone thrower—not known to Bill Hudson. Hygiene was an important aspect of life discipline, career success, and effective tool use.

Masks = q̇^{w}alabaq^{w}ł long—fore & aft iyiłq^{w}ł [Tylor Hobucket has = iyiłq^{w}ł] (1:97) [Sunday, 27 February 1949, Wm Hudson] (Fig. 10).

Rattles (1:42) [drawing of scallop shell for rattle, loop pectin rattle] name of rattle = tłale•iləx^{w}əł Made by hanging large pectin shells on two pieces of wire—handle made by tying several large feathers to wire with wrapping of cedar barks. x̣i•a^h = act of singing a song, sung with rattle. Shells—on wire loops—feathers – cedar handle. A rattle was brought to Neah Bay from BC and sold. Elks club = tsɛ•w^{h}ałayux .

Fig. 10. Drawing of mask (Daugherty 1949, 1:97).

Drum = kle•lk̇^{w}ł built wooden box of spruce or cedar, 3 ft. height, 8 ft. long, 1 ½–2 ft. wide—3 men sit in row on top of box & kick side with heels at big gathering. Thunderbird design painted on front—box placed against wall when in use (1:101).

Hoh

Foods

Farmed on top of James Rock—river outlet on N side of river (1:5). When SG was young man gardened variety of cabbage, carrots, apples (4:57).

Sealing

Sealing (1:11) Sealing grounds from 5–30 mi.—22 canoes went out over morning—2 sails on a canoe—bow and middle. Large sail on bow—small in middle. Go out in morning—1–2 o'clock in morning. Captain & bowman stay up all night to judge weather—surf heavy on N side—good weather—south side bad weather {weather forecasting} sometimes alternate positions on way to sealing grounds. Harpoon, seals, lunch box.
Sails used in breeze—2 sails—one in bow {identifying marks on designs on sails — crescent, whale, eagle} One man takes care of canoe when sailing in—light breeze—others sleep—3 men to a canoe.

Used oars and oar locks in bow & middle. Captain steers with paddle.
Begin in March—3 tries till June—keeping going till you spot a seal. {Middle man usually has not learned to be captain or bow man.}
Seals sleep on back—flippers crossed—seal looking towards tail. Approach seal from head end 50–70 ft. away—just captain paddles

[Drawings of seal spear [harpoon]
prongs called = xabo•dət , point = bi•yuq' , elk bone point, line = k̓ʷa•ditsiya (1:12).
Spear called = tsɛ•y'q' (1:13) pole 16 ft. long

At about 30 ft. away canoe is turned diagonally by captain—bowman raises up and spears seal when head is under water.
Spear shaft—straight grain fir 2 short pieces of crab apple. Foreshaft—2 pieces of elk bone riveted to blade made from metal of animal trap or steel saw.
Elk bone riveted to blade and then wrapped with net twine and this was covered with spruce pitch or gum. The pitch was put on warm {with knife}, then allowed to cool. The knife was heated and then the pitch was spread smooth.
(Frank Fisher one of sealers who was taken to San Francisco [rescued in 1920 in storm]).
Canoe bailers [drawing "loop around wrist"]

To hunt seal (1:37).

Permit needed for seal hunting now (1:89).

Seal (2:15) [9 March 1949] were close long ago—5 min[utes] out—used 2-man river canoes & paddlers. Seals used only for meat & rendered oil & took stomach out, cleaned it and then blew it up & hung it to dry for several days, then put seal oil in it. Informant didn't know of any use for skins. It didn't make any difference whether fur seal or hair seal were caught. Both used in same way. Hair seal caught all year round speared on rocks – waited until seal reached water before spearing so that the seal wouldn't break the spear.

Bags called = pi•xʷə seal oils = tsia•xʷa (generic term = oil) , q'xados = (fur seal)
Hair seal = ha'ta•l
Five (2:17) miles south of La Push at Strawberry Point is good place for hair seal
tadəx = means "tail end," at end of point, 40 or 50 in a bunch rest there.
tsixolaa•tal = 5–6 mi. N of La Push
After pulling in seal, they club it, called = [blank], made out of a kind of wood. Last time BH went sealing was 1940, because during war sealing curtailed. When at sea, they cut seal open & remove entrails to lighten load. Pups not saved as meat too soft to eat. Sometimes went as far as Destruction Island in one day & spent the night there & then went out early in the morning.

People (2:19) who used to live on Destruction Island—2 families were Hoh people
iaidə' = one man who used to live there lots of hair seal on Destruction Island.

Seal hunters not allowed to sleep with woman for hunting season, but can sleep together during bad weather—only applies for spearman. Had to go outside every half hour to look at weather—couldn't sleep all night before sealing. Uncertain if child birth taboos pertain. Leave for sealing just before day break. When out about 5 or 6 mi. – they look back at land & if they see a little valley fog—low—means good weather. If the fog is high (clouds) (2:21) it will spread out & indicates a blow—if spreads to S means NW wind—good if spread to N means SW blow—E wind best weather.

See Cape Flattery—if fog coming out of or from Strait of de Fuca—and spreads out over water means heavy easterly wind—makes it hard to return home. Spearman who has been judging weather all night, sets sails & then sleeps all the way going out. Navigate by sun & waves.

Formerly 27–30 canoes—go out at once. Land at Rickson Point in rough weather—small bay—good landing place = botsaya'wa (means "short beach"). When sealing, they carried seal bladder bags full of water and dried fish to eat.

rehash [in ink in corner] of Quileute sea mammal hunting (3:1) [T Hudson]
The sealing grounds are from 5–30 mi. off the coast—22 canoes went out one morning — 2 sails on a canoe

      bow = t'awaxpo'tsxʷł
      middle = xalɛ•ywapotsxʷł
      parts of sail = identifying marks on designs or sail—crescent, whale, eagle, etc.
      mast = tcutcuqʷł
      diagonal strut = tɬiya•hoxʷł
      bottom pole = tɬiyasiqxʷł
      bowman = t'a•waxʷ

Hoh

mid. man = kalɛ•waxʷ
captain = h'a•yil

Large sail tended by bow man, small sail usually tended by captain but may be tended by middle man. Sometimes alternate positions on way to sealing grounds. Middle man usually has not learned to be captain or bowman. Would leave about 1 or 2 o'clock in the morning – the captain and bowman stay up all night to judge the weather.

At La Push (3:3), if the surf is heavy on the North side of the river it means good weather. If the surf is heavy on the south side, it means bad weather. Take a lunch box. One man takes care of canoe when sailing in a light breeze—the others sleep—3 men to a canoe. In recent times, oars and oar locks in the bow & middle. Captain steers with paddle. Began sealing in March or when weather gets good enough to risk going out. In June, keep going until you spot a seal—you then know you have reached sealing grounds.

Seals sleep on back with flippers crossed or paddling with just one, head bobs up and down. When head is under water, they are looking towards the tail.
Approach seal from head end—when 50–70 ft. away, just captain paddles, at about 30 ft. away canoe is turned diagonally by captain—bowman raises up and spears seal when head is under water.

drawings of seal spear [harpoon > shaft prong finger piece blade] (3:4)

Seal harpoon (3:5) pole 16 ft. long of straight-grain fir with prongs of crab apple. Wrappings of wild cherry, peeled in February. Wrapped first with sinews & covered with bark, toggles of elk bone riveted to blade and then wrapped with net twine, and this was covered with spruce gum. The pitch was put on with a knife while warm, then allowed to cool. The knife was heated and then the pitch was spread smooth.
Finger grooved piece at end flange [with 3 notches] = hi•tsxaɫət , line holder on shaft = tcibi•tsiuqʷɫ , composite point = bi•yuq , line = a•ditsiya

Billy Mason sealing crew (4:14).
Tommy Payne—qixəbəɫp
Harry Pullen tsəxəla
Howard Johnson taxweɫ-
Howard Wheeler (Hoh) tcio
Hoh Williams (Hoh) a•yɛc
taxa'wiɫ

Whaling

Thomas Paine—whale hunter. Eight men in a canoe—went out 1 or 2 mi., when they spear the whale they were carried 8–10 mi. out.
One time I remember there were 4 canoes hunting—the 1st day of April—Jerry Jones— he speared whale—put up pole with flag as signal that whale is speared all others come to help. Whale turned and went under canoe (other) and smashed it.

Hoh

Harpoon—point—made of saw blade—connected to elk bone (antler) foreshaft spruce gum glue it to foreshaft—¼ mi. of ¾ in. rope made of cords of whale—dry it—hit it on rocks every day to soften it. Whale sinew – line called = tłix̣dE .
Pole has 3 pieces—front piece 5 ft., mid piece 4 ft., last piece 3 ft.—pole of yew wood (only) 3 piece takes spring out of pole.

[drawings of canoe bows with details on 3 lines] (1:38)
    1) main line (leader—bladders tied to it) 14 ft. long tłi•xdi
    2) 1 ½ line 20–22 ft. long ts'ido•xʷa
    3) 3/8 in. line—¼ mi. long (cedar limbs) x̣ʷatsida•sx̣ʷał

Whaling canoes—8 man (1:39) 5 ft. beam—28–30 ft. long—high on the bow. 4 or 5 big bladders—all different in size—longest 1st & so on to smallest. Floats made of [entire] hair seal skin called—pɛi•xʷa . Each hunter had identifying design on bladders

Lines—
    1) main line tłi•xdi {bladder tied to this} = 14 ft. long [cord ? x ?]
    2) 1 ½ in. line = ts'ido•xʷa 20–22 ft. long [cedar limbs twisted]
    3) 3/8 in. line =   x̣ʷatsida•sx̣ʷał ¼ mi. long [cedar]

Other harpoons thrown by other canoes. Each person gets particular part – according to position in canoe. The first man to harpoon whale is the owner and divides the whale.

Bowman (1:41) made & owns whole outfit, such as Tommy Paine. Eight whale hunters here (La Push) around 1900. Bowman went someplace where cave is & takes clothes off & dives in water & goes down & gets mouth full of water & comes up & spits it like a whale—toughen body by rubbing with twigs.
Whale hunting—only in summer or spring. Got 3 in one season. Whale used for oil—smoked blubber, whale meat dried. Soak in water to prepare for eating. Kept oil in hair seal bags & bags from whale.

On the hillside (2:27) above the village, it was noted that there was ca. 4 ft. of midden exposed where the bank sloughed off. A large amount of whale bone was noted—also fragments of human burial.

Preparation (2:31) of whale meat, especially summer whale—heat rocks—cover with hemlock bark—splash water on rocks for steam, put on meat, bark, cover with flat leaves.
    leaves called = qʷa•yux
    leaf = tlo•tc'ił
Blubber—cut in slices—4 in. thick & hung by strings in smokehouse—for winter use. Before eating is soaked in water over night – cooked on rocks. [Wm Hudson, 25 June 1949, 2 hours, 8:00 pm].

Hoh

In rendering (2:89) whale oil—Cut blubber in pieces about size of loaf of bread, slice like bacon, boil oil out, take out of pot & tie two pieces together with cedar bark, hang to dry for winter—to eat, it is soaked & boiled, & eaten with dry fish.
hide of whale = ba•xwagit

Whaling—8 men in canoe (3:19). Sometimes 7 men—one in the middle
La Push old whale hunters –> Tommy Payne = qixəbaɬəp , Henry Pullen = s'qəli , Mason = yahətəp , qaqalado , waxəb , Tom Sox = q'glicg'a . New at La Push –> Harold Johnson = t'xedəb .
Hoh –> Hoh Williams = t'xedəb , Howard Wheeler = sixoɬbiq , ? Jones = xixi•əglabiq' , John Jackson = tc'qetuq .
Whale hunters have to make up all the equipment = spear of yew wood—heavy—in 3 parts, harpoon end—5 ft. long, middle 6 ft. long, top 2 ft. long. Spliced pole is better—a whole pole is too springy.

Spear pieces (3:21) topped with hook & bound with braided whale sinew. A lady braids this. Can't braid it while menstruating—if she does it while menstruating, it is believed the cord will break & spear break—over this is wrapped wild cherry bark—dog fish belly skin is used for sandpaper to put final finish.
Use yew wood paddles for whaling—good spring to it.
Harpoon also wrapped with whole sinew braided—ends fastened to short sticks—one of which is held between feet & other in hands—in this way a real tight job is done. Modern harpoon blade made from [metal] hand saw, old ones made of mussel shells.
Bone attachment of elk horn. Soak elk bone in urine before working, makes bone softer. Urine kept in wooden chamber pots, only man's pot used—women's may have menstrual blood in it. Soak for 2–3 days, women's menstrual blood would make it brittle & it would break.

Before (3:23) going out whaling, the whalers would stay out all night looking at weather—4 or 5 canoes go out at once. When they see whale spouting, they follow it. The whaler that hits whale first owns the whale—others who hit it, get share. Small bladder at end of cord, stored as coil in canoe either in small bladders or in a basket—large line coiled near bow. Bladders of hair seals turned inside out tied ends & arms. Inflating hole is stuffed with pith of elderberry stem except for small hole for wooden peg. Blew up 4 bladders to be ready. Three different sections of line. Lines all tied together before whale hit, floats already tied on, lines fastened along shaft. 2nd man throws first bladder at same time harpoon is thrown. (3:25) Bladders finally grab end of line & pull canoe closer & closer to whale—hit with second harpoon.

Whaler stands in bow—right foot placed behind him on first cross piece—good brace & gives added impetus to through [throw], left foot placed in bow, harpoon resting in bow V. 2nd man holding on line tells whaler when whale is coming up. Two canoes – one on each side of whale—put line under jaw & closes mouth [jaws tied together]. Man climbs on head & cuts hole in lower jaw & fastens piece of elk hide (1½ x 3 in. wide)—this is tied to tow line—

Hoh

3 bladders on top of head & two over middle for towing. Two canoes tow whale—paddling. (3:27) First bladder right next to whaler. Varied lengths of bladders 2nd 60–80 ft., 3rd 200 ft., 4th on end of small line. 1st bladder tied at knot with 3 wraps in front of knot & then several wraps behind—so won't slip back then.

    summer whale—big black = t'axa•tsi
    winter whale = tita•qwal
    whale = qwatl'a

Large rope – made of twisted cedar limbs, 50 ft. of middle rope. No women allowed around when making rope – menstruating [danger] – whale will break it. If one menstruating watched whaling, the whale would swim far out to sea. Women ask each other if menstruating. Women must stay home by order of wife of whaler.

Whaling canoe (3:29) is 40 ft. long. Take waterproof lunch baskets of dried fish, fried bread (in lard), dry meat, water – in kegs or bladders. Headman furnished this food. Owner of whale gets hump – dried tła•lit = hump of whale is only top half, has more oil there – considered best part, dry whole thing until it softens, then cut it & make lots of oil.

Form sections of whale line (3:32).
Dixon Paine's brother used to go out to James Island—swim from point to rock under water—dove down & held rock for a while—came up like a whale spouting with arms outstretched—go down again & hold on to weeds on bottom rock – come up again – swam into cave & did same thing – then dressed, went home, talk to "<u>help</u>" to get whale.

He was also a medicine man—had good canoe he got in payment for his services. Wore only blankets & long shirt when whaling—no shoes—pants, etc., use real black blanket warm—arms free—wooden pin fastened blanket—wrapped tight. All wore blankets.

[drawing of torso with blanket wrapped around it and corner strap over right shoulder pin at side, belt around]
Used (3:33) to sing while towing in the whales (whale hunters song ?).
When beaching whale—the whalers bring long line into beach & the people pull the whale in – pull when breakers lift it up.
whale hump = tła•lit (3:34).
Interior (3:69) people would visit the coast during the whale season to get on one of the canoes to get a share of the whale.

Whaler-Mason = yaxətəp (4:15) he kept his own crew & captain of canoe = gitxis—as soon he gets close to the whale. There is herring where the whale is. He opened his mouth—full of herring. Whaler harpoons him as he lay on surface. Harpoon & hair seal bladders [floats], seven bladders tied to line. Four harpoons hit whale & whale gets weak. Man behind spearman holds line & tells spearman when the whale is coming up.

Hoh

Red blanket on top of pole is signal for other canoes to come to aid of one who has harpooned whale. Have long spear with 18 ft. iron point to jab whale behind [its] front flipper to kill him—hit heart. Help each other to kill & tow the whale.

Hoh whalers (4:17) used to go out with Quileute whalers.

Had a little trouble—Hoh & Quileute. A man from Quileute ran away with a Quileute woman to Hoh River. Man from Queets was after that lady. One night they are watching each other. They don't go to sleep. They watch. Quileute man ran away with gun that belonged to Hedot'a, Hoh man. The man from Queets told people that the man from Quileute stole the gun. The man from Quileute hid gun in the brush. Hedot'a gets mad—doesn't want to lose gun (musket). Hedot'a asks Quileute man to confess. Quileute man blames Queets man. Finally Hedot'a shot Quileute man. Quileute man sent man to get gun he had hid, so Hedot'a got his gun back. Sent word to Quileute to come & get dying man. SG's father went with crowd in canoe to get man. Man walked up James Island to home, by himself [to show his power, then died]. He had big family & they decided to go & ask for some stuff (from Hoh Rivers). They can sue to pay for funeral. Ask Hedot'a to pay for that man. Hedot'a tried not to pay any attention to Quileute. (4:19) Finally he gave up—was afraid of them. They were going to start big fight if he didn't pay. Paid blankets, etc. Used to make soft elk hide for blanket—also bear skin—old times—rabbit hide—duck hide (mallard & surf), grouse.

Sinew of whale near flippers & tail (4:44).
Brew from a boiled devilfish used to give strength to neck & hair—for wrestling—rubbed on arms.

Salmon

net locations at Hoh (2:13) [8 March 1949]
   Bryant Cole
   Frank Fisher – best place to fish
   Reginald Ward
   Chris Morgenroth
   T Hudson
   Lilly Williams
   Scot Fisher - 2nd best
   Herb Fisher
   Wm Hudson

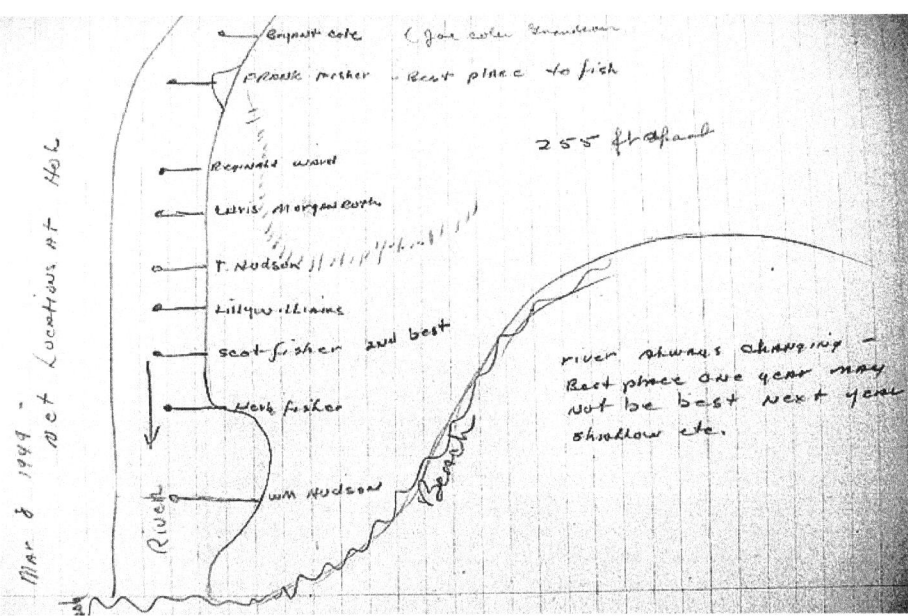

Fig. 11. Drawing of Hoh salmon net locations set 155 ft. apart, 8 March 1949 (Daugherty 1949, 3:13).

River always changing—best place one year may not be best next year, shallow, etc (Fig.11). Gill Netting Salmon (2:27)

Net is circa 25 mesh wide x ? long factory-made linen, commercial wooden floats and [heavy] leads used, also lines. Several poles are driven in the river bottom to which lines are secured to which the net is fastened. One end of net is tied to log (etc.) on shore. A pocket is made on offshore end of net on the theory that fish seeing the net will attempt to swim around the end of the net & become caught in the pocket. Most of the salmon enter the river at high water. When the nets are checked, the owner works the net over the bow of the canoe to check for tears, and to free the net of moss, leaves, and sticks. Fish that are caught are removed from the net, clubbed, and tossed into the canoe. [with arrow line to p26] (2:26) map of gill net stations

Theodore Hudson (2:35) dries about 100 salmon (years supply) = coho, dogs, steelhead, kings (fall silvers). Dries lots of smelt – freeze them. Kept in cool dry place – cardboard carton.

(2:37) Fish smoked over night & then canned. Elk meat smoked for preservation now – canned in tin cans, some smoked.

Made falls (3:69) in streams of hemlock logs & in high water they would go below the falls with special falls nets & catch the salmon. These nets were about 3 ft. in diameter and a bag 3–4 ft. deep. Same knot as in dip net. Hoops holding out net of yew wood, bent by using kelp. Insert wood inside kelp stem, heat it to soften.

Fish trap (3:73) made of 7 or 8 hemlock poles tied together with spruce line rope. The main poles driven in over vine maple [bands]. These sections are held in place by water current – can be put in rapidly when river rises.

This net (3:75) can be used in deep holes by having long poles (16 ft.)—tie bag to pole at right height above bottom of river.

Fish heads are roasted by fire in halves – backbone roasted. Fish only until they have enough for the year—had ideas of conservation to preserve fish supply.

When flowers (3:85) bloom on the elderberries, they know the first run of spring king salmon will begin – this is signal to set fish traps.

First salmon (3:83) cut with mussel shell knife—roast it by fire—don't cut it up, not boiled—everyone eats first salmon.

Smelt

Hoh (1:5) good spot for smelting—April – September [First try at drawing of dip net, shifted & enlarged to p4] Purse seine in surf for smelt.

Salmon eggs (1:85) put in spring salmon fish bladder or seal bladder—and dry them for winter use.

> Fish eggs fresh = tdi•qəs
> dried = s'bisuwa "stink eggs"
> Smelt = t'o•pix̱ large =   small =   night smelt = o'o•pac
> dip net = a'a•yił

Lay eggs on gravel beach of smooth gravel, no sand Feb – August

Large silver smelt (1:87) April – September. Dip net—today used drag seine at half tide & incoming tide. Smelt were dried over fire—smoked, tied smelt to lines to lines at head. Hang on long pole near fire & dry for 3 or 4 days, then placed in basket (of split vine maple).

Smelt (2:24) are now sold to commercial buyers—the price ranges from 4–20¢ ? per pound. (2:25) Smelt fishing (dipping 20 June 1949 6/20/49)—a watch is kept from hillside above village since one can see the whole beach, south to Ruby Beach. They watch for flocks of seagulls which sit on the beach or dive into surf after incoming smelt. Sometimes the smelt can be seen "flashing" as they are cast on the beach.

When the smelt are located the men get their dipnets and go down to the beach. The best times for smelt are at the half tides (going out ?). When the run is heavy, the men dip the smelt in, carry them up to the gravel area on beach, and dump them. The women put them in tubs, buckets, boxes, baskets, etc.

Hoh

When dipping, the dipper places the lower cross bar (the one away from him) on the bottom in time to have the wave break and dump the fish in the dipnet. If only a few are caught, he constricts the net [drawing in at side], just above the fish in the bottom of it, with his hand & thus preventing these already caught from escaping while making subsequent dips. Thus it is not necessary to empty the net after each dip. As much as 100 lbs can be taken in a single dip during a heavy run. When the surf is rough, one often gets more rocks and bits of wood or kelp than smelt.

Hoh River (2:31) best place for smelt along coast. Sun-dried smelt – spread on smooth gravel beach—spread any way just so they <u>don't touch</u>.

When smelt (2:33) first start running, they are unsuitable for drying because they are too fat. Smelt are tied on cedar bark string about 1 inch apart on 12' strings, turned once a day, hung on racks inside the house [drawing of smelt on loop rotated hanging from pole]

Sun-dried (2:65) smelt = qa•li'tso—laid on rocks of beach, turned several times—too much rain will spoil them [about 5 days to dry].

Eat boiled smelt by dipping them in melted shortening (= pi'ts) (2:72).

First (3:83) smelt—not boiled—roast on stick against fire.

If (3:89) a person wants to stop the smelt from running—u•qul to•piks "no more" + "smelt"– he will take a male & female smelt & bury them deep in the sand along the beach where the smelt run.

In order to get smelt to run again, these smelt must be dug up and dragged down the beach in front of the incoming tide. After this, lots of smelt will run because they are angry at what happened to smelt that were buried & come up on the beach to fight.
Bill Hudson said (3:89) One time at Hoh River some Indians from Queets (Quileute) were camped on beach at south side of river. There were lots of smelt running but some of these people (4) wanted to see the canoe races at Coupeville & didn't want the smelt to run while they were gone. Two ladies got a tub of smelt & buried them behind a drift log on the beach. They left for Coupeville, suddenly the smelt stopped running & didn't "hit" again for several days. Some children playing on the beach with sticks were digging around & found the pan of smelt. They took these (3:91) smelt down to the beach and through [threw] them in the water. The smelt began to run again on the next tide.

<u>Elk</u>

Bill (2:31) went with Joe Cole up mountain for elk hunting—got bull—dug hole—built fire—put rocks on—got hemlock bark 4 ft. long—cut brisket & laid on bark (fattest part

Hoh

from brisket to testicles) – put leaves on top—then little sand—cook ½ –1 hr. Broth stays on bark – considered excellent.

When (2:33) it is misting—good for stalking—animal hears dropping [dripping] from trees & can't hear hunter. itixliu = crazy (time ?)

> fattest part of Bull Elk (belly) = qʷsa•dəxʷł rump fat = t'a•lux
> elk = qi•qił
> fat surrounding insides = łixat
> kidneys = ts'qʷiuk̇ʷ

Friday 24th one spike deer shot (2:39) [27 June 1949] Saturday 25th—one doe shot—only hind quarters saved (Wm Hudson). One bull elk shot (T Hudson)—meat canned—could have shot a second bull but didn't—meat divided—T Hudson & ? Wilson. 2 ducks shot previous week.

Cooking (2:49) fresh meat—method called = tsixpa•təs—impale meat on stick—and lean over fire [drawing of meat, stick, fire] Cook until there is no more blood dripping out, then it is done—
> meat = assa•yət all kinds, all parts

At present deer & elk meat are mainly roasted (pot roast) and fried by Wm Hudson & many others. Hooves, nostrils & tongue were formerly eaten – dried for winter use. Elk & deer were hunted in summer when meat is fat.

To store (2:51) the elk fat or tallow, the bladder of the elk was dried and then the fat was put in it. When it was to be served, it was put by the fire to heat and soften. Formerly took intestines and cleaned them & stuffed them with pieces of meat & fat. Tied & cut in sections about 10 in. long. These were cooked on rack over the fire ^ stored for winter. (2:50) What kind of intestines?

> Elk bladder called = pei•xʷə
> Took whole bladder dried it and stored whale oil in it.
> Elk belly called = utcqe•dit
> Urine bladder = du•x̣ʷal

Dried meat, fish, whale kept in cedar bark containers, stored in rafters—containers called = q'wayitc'i•sə , had square shape, made of strips of cedar bark 1½ in. wide.
cuwʰa – village on this side (4:46) of Tyee on Sol Duc River.... Elk hunters—live there year around—occasionally came to La Push & bring elk meat.

Halibut

Halibut (2:59) fishing in summer time, mostly low tide—flounder, devilfish, bass (cut meat up) troll for bass—white meat. (2:61) These halibut were not very large.

Hoh

Herring

Herring (2:65) rake them—used to rake (comb) smelt long ago – they split bone —later wire or nails ca. 3/8 in. apart on one side of rake, used fire (split) 10 ft. long (approx), use rake like paddle & dump smelt in canoe (on back swing) – get them in river, also in surf. Herring dried for winter use. Stored in cedar bark basket. No longer fish for herring, too fat – hard to dry.

Perch – Bill doesn't know.

Sea Lion

If you (2:69) kill a sea lion it will rain—Sea Lion Rock on Fogged rocks. Joe Pullen is the only one now who hunts sea lions—uses gun—month of April. Sea lion skin is eaten—laid on fire until charcoal forms—scrap it off & wash it & cook it again by boiling for a long time. Just the neck part of skin is eaten—it is the thickest—fat & meat eaten.

  hapi•s pat = cooking fish over the fire on salmon berry stem.
  q̓ʷɬspat = leaning against fire. (2:91) .

Ducks

Like (3:73) to eat young fish ducks, used boq'o•d set between two canoes—on riffle—water fast young ducks can't swim upstream. Would drive ducks down to net from 5–6 mi. upriver. Used same thing for salmon.

Porpoise

Porpoise (3:83) were hunted late in evening because the phosphorescence of the water made it easy to follow them. Beecher Wheeler hunted them at Hoh using sealing gear – good eating. Hunted whenever they could be found. Porpoise found close in – but outside on rocks, can hear them spout.

Sea lion meat bad in spring & summer – they smell bad.

Plants

Elderberries (1:41) favorite—cook them buried in sand—build large fire—put rocks in fire—heat them—put fire out—lay out large pieces of hemlock bark—put berries in—cover with leaves—cover good so sand won't get in & then bury in sand, remove sand = make square or rect. Basket (po•o'q) – fill basket & cover with leaves. Bury this in marsh (1:42) Salal berries – dry them. Wash them, smack them with [stone] pestle in wood bowl.

  Pestle hard rock = ɬa•tɬit

Hoh

Vine maple best for drying meat, alder also used (2:9).
    salal berries = xoo•d (2:19).

(Hoh) (2:29) [21 June 1949] salmonberries are now eaten fresh with sugar & cream, frozen & canned.
    Called = tc'a•łwa

Blackcaps (2:67) gathered in foothills of Olympics at headwaters of rivers—ripe from last of July to middle of August—good sweet berries.

[written on a diagonal] 38 quarts of strawberries canned, 30 qts. of strawberries in locker by Pansy Hudson (2:72)

Theodore Hudson, Pansy & Howard went to logged off area around Lake Quinault to hunt & gather wild blackberries. 9 July 1949—Theodore & Pansy, Bill H & Mary went to upper Hoh for blackcaps (2:77) [8 July 1949].

Salalberry paste & loaf—crush them and flatten in cakes, dry cakes for winter use
Get pail elderberries (2:80).
Fruit & vegetable truck stops at cable bridge—Wed morning 9–10:00 AM Wolf fish ?

Seal club (2:81) made of yew wood—Bill doesn't know of any particular shape or design.
Many families canned 11 qrts & 1 pt of black caps yesterday.

Elderberry ripe now (10 July 1949)—pick clump of berries & shake off berries, also cook them & they come off – bury then in sand & cook them.

Wild (2:89) rhubarb = tło•pit—boy type—peels better from outside. Girl type split and peel from inside. Gathered in spring & peeled, eaten now with oil.

    also = ba'ax^w
    to dip in oil = p'itsia•x^{w}a   to dip = p'it

Yesterday (2:93) Bill & Mary, Theodore & Pansy, Howard & Blackie went up to S fork of Hoh to pick blackcaps & wild blackberries. Theodore's family picked only blackberries. Howard & Blackie are good berry pickers. Alva doesn't go because of her heart trouble.

Indian barley Neah Bay = kitci•d other kind = ho•x^{w}ap (3:42).

When flowers bloom on the elderberries, they know the first run of spring king salmon will begin—this is signal to set fish traps (3:85).

Hoh

Braken fern = qa•q̇wə' Dug the roots – roots are coiled up & placed in fire in smokehouse – frequently turned to keep from burning, came from Quileute Prairie, gathered in early fall, gathered one large basket full. Some stored raw but [most] dried on poles over fire.
Prior to eating, the root is pounded with stick until soft enough to peel. Eat only the outside – not center. Dug with digging stick made of crabapple—dug along edge of bank because it grows so deep.

Lady fern = ts'ikwe'—grows in rotten log in woods – sometimes in ground, pineapple shaped. Baked in pits of hot rocks—covered with skunk cabbage leaves—cooks over night. Lots grow at Queets, way up Bogachiel River. Gather basket full. Men & women both gathered them (4:41) [Thursday, Stanley & Connie].

Bulbs were peeled & eaten after dug with digging stick (4:42).
pila'pila' = – [fern] tops used for lining baking pits. Grow all over = had-poqɬ-pət – used for medicine—chew & swallow it—good for chest congestion—some boil it in can in Fall – use upper part (leaves).
qaq^{w}a'apət = roots used for food.

keksto la'pət = (deer fern) (4:43) when chasing elk & tired—chew leaves & swallow juice.
ba'awx = (horsetail) peeled, gathered in spring, tips or heads are sometimes broken off & roasted on hot rocks.
tu tu'tsi' = same as ba'awx
xi'ya' = yew wood, whale spear—boil wood, needles, & rub potions on oneself when they bathed to make them strong.

Pine bark (4:45) secured from Sound Indians, chewed when spitting blood—stops right away.
In wintertime, wore rabbit skin blankets & wildcat skin around neck.
yaktsə = Sitka spruce
Clover used for medicine in stomach diseases.
Boil spruce cones & drink infusion. Limbs used for ropes.
ti•ɬa = hemlock – bark peeled & used for roofing material for summer house—used for medicine—bark pounded & powdered & boiled for good drink—good for TB & bad colds—hemlock bark used to make kettle for boiling water with hot rocks.

bark of old trees used for fire wood
qle'xits' = fir
cattail = tsi'tsay' (male) t'ola•x (female)
Pondweed – surf grass ? x̣a•pu' = hook game, shoot arrows at it,
basketry = piditc tud
Rye grass = k'ak'epət   masts = k'ake'tsa•boɬ   roots are rough & rub body to give strength when bathing – cause bleeding. Used to be lots growing in front of Quileute village.
tule = tcida•ax – Lake Pleasant village, used for making mats.

Hoh

The (4:48) whole family including children shared in the activities of gathering wild plants. Places are known where all plants are found.
Strawberries not saved for winter.
Salal berries dried by fire & stored in baskets.

Elderberries are cooked in fire pit—layer of hemlock bark—skunk cabbage leaves—then cover —wet cover with leaves of skunk cabbage, then cover with ca. 6 in. of sand & build fire over it—burns all night.

t'oqwa' = skunk cabbage (4:49) During hard times, this is eaten, eat roots, rub "tits" with root to bring milk.

camas = k'wala
snake berry = tsə'a'tsixłpət ripen in fall, eat now
trillium = kokots'tudaktc'ił

Storage

Boards (3:33) placed across rafters to support stored food, keeps it dry & free from vermin. Watch stored food—brush & clean it to keep from molding & keep bugs off. Occasionally take it out in bright sunshine to check it & wipe off mold & redry it.

Canoes are usually started to be built in spring & summer—before fall run of fish. Get all equipment ready for fall runs of fish in the spring & summer—cut & trim poles for trap, make wattle work, and make drying racks for fish.

Food at Wm Hudson's (2:120) [24 June 1949] is Liptons tea, Hills Bros coff[ee], Seedless raisins, Fishers flour, Pilot bread, Sliced peaches, Centennial waffle flour, 2 dozen clams (razor), 25th June hind quarters of deer, 25th & 26th June Elk meat.

Food (3:119) in Stanley Grey's House—bananas, mother's oats, instant cake mix, cherrioats, C&H sugar, lard, Hills bros coffee, brown beans, dried eggs, Lipton tea, graham crackers, potatoes, home canned apricots, dried salmon, dried smelt, com[mercial] jam, canned jam, butter.

Society

Birth

Newborn baby (3:49) is put on mat with legs flexed & cedar bark placed underneath them so cord won't be rubbed off. Baby bathed before breakfast—hold baby under arm & when it comes out of water—hold it up & shake it—and blow on its back. After dried, lay on stomach & rub shoulder, back, & hips to broaden shoulders, flatten back—lay on back & rub chest—also rub forearm from wrist to elbow or they will have small wrists—legs the same. The nose is squeezed together, so it won't be flat, push corners of mouth towards center—so mouth will be small—cheeks pushed up, so they won't hang down—

eyes rubbed toward outside, so they won't cross—bridge of nose pushed up, ears pushed out—so they won't fold—then always put back in cradle until 2–3 years old.

[drawing of cradles, legs bent up, hammock with string to mother's toe] Girl's cradle had hole drilled in back for urine outflow. (3:50) Boys—doesn't have hole beneath, but the penis is left sticking out, so it won't wet the cradle. Cedar bark hood placed over baby's head to keep flies away = həpqa'ayus (Fig. 12).

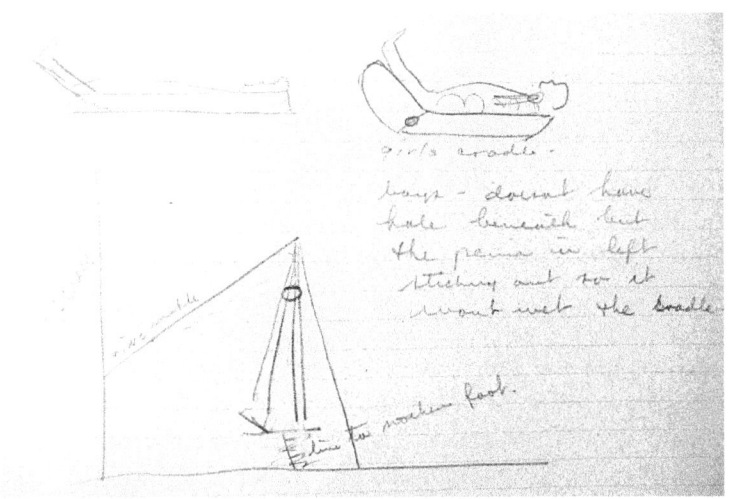

Fig. 12. Drawing of baby cradle (Daugherty 1949, 3:50).

When (3:51) woman is having a baby—they are put in house by themselves in the dark—only person allowed in there was the midwife. Don't nurse baby for four days — put piece of dried whale blubber 1 x 3 in. in its mouth. A wet nurse is employed for first four days. The mother's breasts are treated with grass that has been heated in fire—this grass is placed on the breast & massaged. Nipples are rubbed to make them large. The grandmother instructed the child's mother in its early care. When the cord comes off, it is wrapped up & the baby wears it around its neck for 1–2 yrs—if not worn the baby will grow up to be rough & wild.

    cradle = qa'yit'—made of spruce & cedar
    x^{w}ətsa' = soft shredded cedar bark (3:52)

When a child is born its age is recorded by tying a knot in sea lion gut (4:2).

Indian doctors (S Grey's father) would be called when baby was to be born. Would drink from bowl of water & blow this on expectant mother's head. This would insure an early delivery—would "make the baby loose" (4:77).

Twins

Women (2:9) were not kept away from river when fish are running, but a man or woman with newborn child were not permitted near river, most especially with twins. Joe Pullen had twins when he was young. He was kept in the house for ten days with all windows covered—had someone care for them. No fresh fish could be eaten—last year's fish could be eaten—but dry fish only.

If twins (3:87) or triplets are born to a family, the family must move out into the woods, away from the rivers, for five months. They mustn't eat fish (fresh ?) or the fish will stop running. {Throughout the Northwest, twins and salmon have a special relationship and they have to be kept distinct for a run to continue. During famine, however, twins will approach a stream to draw salmon to them. Twins evoke the duality involved in the rhythmic death and return of salmon.}

Puberty

Girl's puberty (3:53) made to sit for four days without food or sleep—sometimes fed dried fish, but she is not allowed to hold the dried fish—mother prepares it—can't eat anything hot, if you do while you are menstruating, it will harm the teeth—drink only a little water.

Softened cedar bark used to wipe face—rub up, not down—deer bone marrow cooked to use for face cream. If you go to sleep, your eyes will wear out soon. If you laugh, your face will wrinkle soon. Someone takes daughter down to creek early every morning—she holds rock on lap & sits in creek with water to chin until numb—done every morning for four mornings—sometimes sits under falls, such as (3:55) tcibtsaya = falls at Goodman Creek.

Jonah Cole's mother sat under falls at Goodman creek until numb—looking for power—finally she got help—got a song – got doctor power. One time on upper Hoh, she tried her power. She sat submerged in water until numb—she saw fish duck—fly up river—she through [threw] her power at it & it fell on the water dead.

When girl reaches puberty, she can't eat fresh fish for one year & can't drink hot things (3:83).

Dentalium shells = x̣asdix̣ (4:71) 2 in. length real expensive (valuable), worn at girl's puberty ceremonies in headband across forehead.

Cosmetics (3:77) [toilet articles, 17 August 1949] Sap of hemlock—used to rub on face—smells good—especially women—paint cheeks—eye brows—brown color—used in hair for de-lousing, because slightly sticky. Seeds (ground ?) used with elk tallow to give it good smell & brown color. Elk tallow pounded & boiled with a little water—white color—put in salmon bladder or elk intestine (cleaned out), 12–14 in. long—cut in short pieces.
Shredded cedar bark towel = xʷat'sa• – also used for napkins [pads] of women.
Combs—made of bone—worn in hair at back. Elk shoulder blade—often carved at back—hair was worn long by men—shoulder length.

Hoh

Urine used for washing hair (3:79) Small boys taken to river by fathers & their hair washed in urine & skin rubbed with nettle fibers, cedar limbs, or spruce limbs. Different families used different things. Lectured about becoming a strong man – great hunter, etc.

Red ochre (3:79) placed on face when going berry picking to keep from getting sunburned. Red ochre used as rouge—some placed it just on the cheeks & some placed it all over. After eating, the people would get a mouth full of water & rinse out mouth.

Men (3:81) coiled hair in bun at back & held it in place with an 8in.long bone pin with hook at end (like a crochet hook).

Marg's mask is a Tlokwaly mask.

When (3:85) it thundered, they thought it was a big bird. They burned old clothes & they believed that the bird will smell this strong smell & go away.

Used (3:85) to have nose plugs through hole in nasal septum, made of bone. Dentalia used for earrings, each ear pierced—with bone point. Ears pierced when baby is born, put small piece of pitch wood in hole to keep it open—flush with surface of skin.

Etiquette (3:85) girls must not gorge themselves, mustn't make any noise, must eat slowly. Girls mustn't laugh or talk too much—be silly.

Quest

Powers (3:9) Whale hunters go in caves—swim like a whale to seek "help." Seal hunters go out on rocks—roll around on sharp rocks—body all cut up. In Elk society—help is always Elk. Hair seal hunters—have songs & help. Trapping is new—no society or power—no power on fishing. Tlokwaly power—powerful—painted face all black. You have to look for the power you want. In Tlokwaly ceremony, when they pull out [from skin] the bone pins – they rub the spot & blow on it—it doesn't bleed or anything.

Both men & women get power (3:57). Some people look for power—were told by parents—some receive without looking for it. This power inherited – get some songs & dances—more of an invitation. My grandfather, according to Morton Penn, was a tahmanawis man—he would get me in the evening—put on his headdress, would make me get hold of rattle (see description) (3:59) made of cedar bark—with two handles on lower sides, deer hoof rattles. [Morton Penn himself in 1945 worked with George Pettitt, an anthropologist from UC Berkley serving in the Coast Guard and stationed at La Push. Penn's grandfather had light brown hair and was 80 when he died in 1906].

When old man died, he had 7 or 8 sticks 5 ft. high – different designs [made in 1902] winter—I hid them in the woods—were stolen. One had little bird on top with outstretched wings—have to go through Tsayuq & other "little stuff" before he can become doctor.

Hoh

To give power—line up the people—each with one stick—he gives them the power & the sticks shake—the bird on top revolves. Old man could put his hands in hot coals of fire to get the power in there—also in boiling water to receive doctor power—must be clean—free from disease—eat only a little. He would touch no food until he had taken a bath. Must be clean to get tahmanawis. Esau Penn is tahmanawis man [but] getting discouraged with tahmanawis power because he lost 4 sons & his wife & his power wouldn't work to save his family.

Nephew (3:60) of chief = qilip [Kilip] part ~~Quinault Indians~~ Lower Chehalis Sooez (3:61) named = qʷətutiɬ (Makah ?) when he first got power, called = qʷayəbi until his
death, other name = yɬixbəx—lived four miles up the Quileute river—live with another
couple who owned other half of trap—his wife went out—full moon—little clouds obscuring moon—saw big boat with lots of lights—seemed to hang in air but close to water—she thought about it & went back & told the old man. He went closer—he prepared himself to receive a power if that was what it was. He got close enough to see it was a tahmanawis. The river rose & he found himself, when he came to, way back in the brush. When he came to, he was afraid to come home, stayed out long enough to be sure his tahmanawis wouldn't leave him. After 3 months he was ready to sing—sing for 5 days & 5 nights & then they have power for good. Don't eat during these 5 days & nights – he got the doctor power, 5 different times, the last time in 1898 – additional power comes each time. (3:63) [3:62 doodle 3:63 doodles] He could take a person with (TB)—looked like worm—maggot with long fuzzy nose—and take it out if caught before too long. He knew when he couldn't cure some things. Would get blankets—canoe, etc. Monk Williams doesn't get anything, had doctor & Shaker power too.

geɬakʷ aɬ = means "up stream"—comes from the Interior, although people on coast did belong – must belong to see it. If non-members are there, they are seized & moved around the fire & forced to join. People see them & put up wealth for them to join. Leaders of groups have inherited right to initiate new members, to son or grandson. Leader has to sing & announce so & so is joining & tells how many days before this person becomes an active member—the initiate is carried in or led in by two people & they dance with him—imitates the dance of the leader.

Stanley Grey (4:7) was fishing at nighttime—wintertime—had canoe on land—waiting for steelhead salmon. Saw a fish duck head [from] bow of canoe on small log—he was sitting in canoe – snow on the ground. He said, "After midnight, I heard something coming up the river – it was a man fish duck – he lands in water & splashes it in front of me. I see 'it' coming up – real white – the head is black. It is moonlight. I received the Tsayuq from this bird. It was real white & had a little dog – he was laying down in the canoe. He stood up & started barking. I believe he chased my help away. I got a song & dance. It can help person who has lost his soul. It searches for person's soul through singing, people help him by drumming." If a person walks around at night & hears something strange, he may lose his soul & become sick. (4:56) S Grey can tell several days before that person has trouble & will get sick. He feels it, comes to him in a dream.

Hoh

At a small lake north of Quileute river named diłdotci'l (= means ?) "A man went hunting up there–hunting elk–he didn't get any, he was returning home empty handed & feeling very ashamed since the thought he had a great help (4:53) for hunting elk. He came to this deep place & dived down in there–they later found his body on the ocean beach near La Push. The devil is in this deep hole with no bottom (in lake) (4:51) [S Grey, Monday, 18 August 1949].

Songs

No seal hunting songs or power—whaler has power—gets song from inside song sometimes sung at gatherings. Elk hunting song received when in the woods, song comes with power. Bill Hudson tried to get Shaker power—but could never "feel of anything" (1:109).

>Whale hunters society = tsibax^{w}layu
>Elk Club = tsilig^{w}əliyu , songs = tluq^{w}ali [Tlokwaly]

Run skewers through skin, had meal after ceremonies, ate dried fish smoked eggs & potatoes [powdered face black with charcoal]. Had big bonfire = wllaisəb - one man grabbed hot coals & threw them around in the house (1:109).

Indians have lullaby song—Nona knows quite a few songs—Mary will put up 2 dollars to know who has lullaby song (2:118).

Singing (3:43) Man sings love song in group—to girl—she may rise after words & return the favor by singing her love song = tsatsa'a—have long sticks with which they beat on long poles hung around smokehouse—Love songs usually sung during girl's puberty ceremony—4 day ceremony—girls don't eat or sleep. Grandfather tells people they can tsatsa'a all they want, so he gives a big party. The girl is secluded behind some mat curtains, so she can hear but can't see. The people sing songs for the things they want & [that] the girl's family must give [to] them.

(5) k̓ ig^{w}ał a new dance—brought from Alaska by Sitka George (42 years ago) & others they learned it when they went sealing on the schooners [George = q^{w}əwsə] (3:45)

Williams tahmanawis—<u>Tlingit</u> . k̓ ig^{w}ał = only slightly at La Push. Some songs brought from Alaska, others were received (new). gi•a qi•yił = big shots own private songs, but not many had them—belong to family. Stanley Grey, Bill Hudson, North fork of Calawah, [always did] closing song at parties.

Esau Penn claims he received Stanley Grey's father's songs. SG doesn't believe it because he doesn't use it right. Stanley Grey's father was a great doctor (4:8).

Hoh

Cures

One year in November (1920 ?) (1:19), we went with a kid (who was around 25). We went out hunting from La Push to Sol Duc Hot Springs. Standing timber was still along road—road curving by Hot Spring, road all crooked. We went up the mountain, 3 of us, went up the mountain we was hunting. Made camp on Bogachiel peak. A nice sunny day—stars at night. Towards morning it stated raining. Rain, rain, rain, poured-down rain. Woke up at 4 in morning, soaking wet, we got our water from [off] tent—cooked with it. Still raining, we was going to Lost Lake. On Bogachiel side. We was going hunting in flat by lake. Lost Trails. In afternoon gave up. We didn't see anything – no game at all. I suggested we go down below spring but up the hill—saw one deer but didn't shoot it—we were hunting elk & afraid we might scare them away. Getting dark. It was dark when we got to the camp. We went home. Stormy night, SW Wind. Drove to Forks. Car was going fine. A couple miles from main highway (on road to La Push), the driver spoke up, (that was my dad, Wm Hudson). He said, "Did you see that two lights?" We said, "No." He says, "I'm going to speed up & catch up with (1:21) that car." We drove 3 miles & got to Quileute Prairie Hill. He said, "You can drive now," so I tried to catch the car. I drive six miles & you can see everywhere. No light.

Finally we got to Mora at mouth of Dickie, Old Mora Post Office & store. We put car in garage & went down to canoe & paddled down to upper dock. Left canoe there & walked along puncheon road to village. When we go to the house, we came around through the alley, through the back door. As soon as we came in the house, my dad sat down & told mother he had seen two lights (at saxwiɛsli = name of place "thin spot in trees"). That is the place I saw the two lights & told my boy to drive. The next day he got sick. That's the first time he ever got sick. He got his throat sore & then was spittin blood. We brought white doctor down. Goverment doctor. One or two trips. He got a little better. He said, "My head is heavy it is bothering me all the time. The back of head is always heavy." He took sick for several years. In fall and continued through winter. (1:23)

Took him to his sister's at Calawah bridge (1/4 mi. below bridge). This was in 1925. I didn't know he took sick again. It was December month. I brought Indian goverment doctor. The doctor just looked in the door and said, "You'll be alright in a few days." The doctor was afraid to come in—he was afraid of him—he was spittin blood, blood – one basin after another. I and Roy Black [line to note on 22] & other boys.

He was sick again—one big piece of blood as big as a strawberry—shaped like strawberry—when that was gone, he felt better. It was March & he was feeling better. My brother thought it was his tonsils. We took him to St. Joseph Hospital in Aberdeen, took them off. Stayed several days. He was getting better – improving. Summertime he got well.

Suddenly in fall he got sick again. Well, he got laid up again pretty bad. We called Indian doctors, medicine men, Doctor Lester—old fellow—best, the best we had down there. Cost a fortune. Gave away one big canoe [for sealing, new] & money, big stove, blankets—but it didn't help at all. Kept on laying in {but he didn't take it. I guess he got ashamed}. (1:25)

In bed for three or four months—till March. His sister was religious woman—belong to Shaker Church. Used to come & help him – helped him pay the doctor. The oldest sister suggest calling Indian doctor (Shaker) from Oakville. He got medicine too. She came over to Dad one morning. Asked permission to bring him over. He said, "It's up to you"—she wrote letter right away. They sent a telegram to Bill's sister (that they were coming), came on stage. Called from Mora to La Push for someone to go after them. I went after them. I didn't know them at all, old fellow. Paddled down to village. Quite a crowd at beach. They just looked. Aunt was there. Bill's sister asked them to dinner before seeing Bill—this they didn't do. They wouldn't eat. They had their minds on my dad. We'll go see him first.

This man went through the alley & followed our trail—came in through back door {(1:24) just as dad had come in the night he saw the light} into sitting room. The old man, his head was heavy. This man saw him & started singing with his own power. He said "You saw something strange (1:27) when you came home from hunting trip, which you shouldn't have told—you would have got a great power & been a doctor man." He wouldn't be ashamed—he'd have all kinds of songs to sing.

That is where his mistake was, in telling everybody. This guy sing & then he got through & went to Bill's house for dinner—but were coming back. But now they were going to Shake. They kept it up whole week, a couple hours in day and again at night. It helped him a little bit. They went home. Bill's sister drove them to Port Angeles.

He was still bad—still having body heavy—hurt most at back of neck. We invited a dozen old people over that, had Elk songs, Tlukwaly wanted to find right song. They knew he wanted a song. He wanted a song to sing, wanted to sing Elk song—that is beginning of his songs. We got interpreter & split up stove wood for sticks to pound on floor—didn't want to use drum. We found (1:29) he wanted to sing an Elk song. We do that for a month, every evening—3 or 4 old people in house, every evening until he learns song well. When he learns that song well the older people were through.

Have interpreter—she sings loud. If interpreter sings different he (Dad) beats floor with stick & wants to start over. Sings right along with him. He was a hunter—the song cured him. When he goes in woods, he hears song and cannot sing it—gets sick until he learns to sing them.

Happen again a year later. An Elk song with different words & song—he finally sang song—we done same thing again—he's well again. He never had songs before this. When he's sick in bed for a week he gets song. After he gets song anyone can sing it & don't have to be a <u>tahmanawis</u> man. Anyone can borrow it to have a song to sing in house (meeting house). (1:31)

Hoh

Name of W Hudson's song = t'si•xʷałayux . William Penn has songs – but he was a trapper, has trapper songs, Whaling songs. All Elk songs are called = t'sixʷałayux. When sing Elk songs or Black song, they sing these first, and then announce floor is clear and other songs can be sung.

When (3:81) people sing for something they will keep singing & singing. His friends will help him. A big man will not refuse to part with anything, otherwise people will think he's cheap. Jimmy Howe was a big man at La Push long ago. After he died, Harry Hobucket wants his place (was Harry's mother's cousin) but he can't make it. A person must return a good amount for articles danced for, or you will not be considered a big man.

Raids

Near (3:117) James Island = axa•lat , village on top called = hoq•tot, one man was drift fishing—big canoe left on other side so they were not surprised. A big war canoe came—Indians with muskets. The lady saw it. The man didn't believe her. They were Makah—they tried to catch him—grabbed him by belt but it broke—he dove in water & swam away. Lady jumped out on beach & ran to James Island. She said, "Wake up every body"—some believed her—others didn't. Some go to trail to watch, (3:118) Canoe goes & hides behind point at 2nd beach. Seagulls make lots of noise flying around. They know people are around. Daylight come. The Makah didn't bother man [= k'ɛ•ypilatsi ?] hunting hair seal—they said, "Let us catch the man we are after." Four or five canoes waiting. The people said, "Hurry & catch seal meat. Let's go trolling for salmon." Finish feast.
Little bay for canoes on outside of James Island—a secret place. Makah come in close to beach & cut off canoes trolling—people on top make smoke—put this fire out & make another on north side—means go home by north route. The lead canoe holds up big mirror—move it to look at them—not to paddle home.

Man on top killed lots of Makah as they were trying to head off the returning Quileute. Caught man & cut off his head—captured boy. Makah sold the boy to Nisqually—called Quileute John—chief's son—later wanted his sister to visit him—she went with others – saw his race horses. He later came to Quileute with Nisqually. Middle aged, one eye gone, had lots of property.

Ranks

The "chief" was the head of the extended family, such as Howeattle = gləkick'a , Tommy
Payne = gilip , who lived above Forks (3:69).

Ranks (4:69) chief = a•atcit , subchief = tcitc'a•atcit arbitrates trouble—a chief is supposed to act the part—carry himself with importance. [ʔa•čit = chief, rich man]

    xawicats' = Howeattle was head man

Hoh

sub chief = bistase•blis.

The chief before him was his father—also named Howeattle. Howeattle family comes from kwaladisq^w up the river

Stanley Grey (4:73) says that the Hoh had no "chief"—only whale hunters are leading people—Hoh Williams tla•uts, also a sea otter hunter.

Slaves

Slaves (3:34) Mr. Wolf at Neah Bay—slave from BC. Lady who married Andy Johnson was a slave. She later married Philip, had daughter who married white man — lived in Ballard.

Beads (3:35) used dentalium shells blue beads = ga•sdix , blue beads—one fathom—used for trade, also gave as presents, used to buy slaves.
A rich man (3:35) had 5 or 6 slaves captured in war ~~slaves could only marry slaves~~ [with arrow line to p34—slaves lived with masters]

If a man escapes & returns home—he is referred to as a slave. If slave tried to escape he may be killed, beaten, or sold. Slave is a bad name—no way of returning to former status. Bill doesn't know of anyone at La Push, Hoh, or Queets who are descendants of slaves. Slaves work for masters—cutting wood—fishing—make canoes—do everything – get seafood.

Slave (3:37) may have had a power before capture & may attend parties, but is always referred to as slave. Slave could go whale hunting but never as head whaler. Children of slave & non-slave—called half slaves. Women & children captured as slaves — children raised for slaves.

Doctors

Doctor (3:11) power is different—look for doctor power—come home & sing what he received – he show what he received. {This section could as easily have been placed in the Gatherings chapter.}

Monk Williams received doctor power – he showed people a stick about 8 ft. long – painted around. 5 or 6 people hold it—Monk puts his power in it & people start to shake – Monk gets shorter stick (5 ft. long) & stands in front—stick stands on end by itself while Monk dances around it. The stick never fell over. Monk now has Shaker faith & has dropped the doctor power.

A man's son often gets same power as he has but it is not mandatory. A man's power helps him when sick (3:13). The doctors (shamans) fished & did other work as well as other people, but doctors were rich.

Hoh

When (3:13) there was a big gathering, doctors get together & perform. One doctor would get hold of his tahmanawis and through [throw] it to another—they would throw it from doctor to doctor.

Queets (3:15) had good medicine man = bəs•p'. One lady = tsibo'su (same) was sick—long ago—lady had no clothes on – he got her soul & put it on over her head – his organs were hanging in her face – she bit at them – he dodged away and smiled—finally he's through—next morning he jumped in river & bathed —sick woman in house—he came back & sat in front of fire—the sick woman put her fingers in her mouth & points at his organs & says "good food"—bəs•p' jumped over fire & raped her right there.

Tłqicq'a = man who received Indian doctor help (4:1). People had a big smokehouse in middle of village—on the hill. He had 3 long poles—moving face on end, white spiral line around it. He asks who wants to shake the pole in the crowd. Three poles tied together—he unties them—stands them about 3ft. apart, person holding each, lots of people sitting around walls of smokehouse. Da'xos floats around (like balloon is simile), with this he recaptures souls—people select which stick they want to shake. They ask who is going to drum for them. They have six drummers. Six men went to place where they are going to drum.

Then doctor selects two ladies to stand up—wearing rabbit hide blankets = ho'qsɛt. They gave each of the ladies one blanket. He says "When I start my song, you two ladies sing right away that song which you have been practice[ing] before." The doctor starts his song & the ladies sing their song to the people. The song belongs to the stick. (4:1) [Stanley Grey 10:15–Monday 2 August 1949].

    all the people are singing = ałitlicxaba po•ox
    Pole = łostowo•tsoq^{w}ł pole shaking
    deer hoof rattle = sək̓ł These rattles are tied on the long poles, tall enough to reach roof of the smokehouse.

    łəgo•ya = (Stanley Grey's) [(4:2) drawing of human effigy red & white] (Fig. 13).

    yəw^{h}e•los = light colored body "gives light" & searches for soul in the night
    pitiqisili = means light in the body

Doctor man asks for four men to hold statues. These four small statues nearly life size but with no legs on them – deer hoof rattles on elbows. Each had a song, had (mink) fur clothes on, had eagle feather – white & shag (black) feathers. Chinese pheasant (?) [for] some of the feathers were split, called = watcqwał – make lots of noise when shaken with deer hoof rattles.

Finally (4:5) the doctor starts his singing & starts his "help," then this brings the soul back [= oby q'lə'c]. Doctor help received in wild places—especially by streams. Makes place to lay down up in tree on limbs—makes a bed. Builds fire below & puts whale blubber on fire – brings lots of wild birds – owl, etc., at night time, stay there until he receives his help.

He heard something – then lightening flashes – then he tries to pay attention to what kind—he becomes not like anybody [else]—he jumps down & hugs what he sees & he faints—receives help—seems to be that a man has face painted—arms & legs painted —black (called xa•wa') & white—only a hazy vision is seen—man has feathers on head —face is human-like yet different.

Stanley Grey's father was a great doctor. (4:9) <u>Causes of sickness</u> – Soul loss. Dr hires someone (another doctor) to go with him & help him. Doctor lays down on floor. Face down on floor — singing (soul goes down ?), hold soul in their hands & place hands on top of head & run hands down over body. Sick person is lying in bed — not close to doctor.
(4:13) Some doctors get start on assisting other doctors by shaking = ł'koya.

Names

didiba•łx (1:90) If a man wants to change his name from his ~~father's~~ mother's side – he can get a name from his father's side. Names are those which were formerly used but are not used at this time.

Name from paternal grandfather—with line to Floyd Hudson

Wm Hudson on Hudson genealogy (1:91) [26 February 26 1949 Saturday]
Party given — get elks (1:93) to feed people.

Dema Cole (1:93) turned her first name over to her granddaughter. Names for children are taken from names of older generations. Grandparents or great grandparents give names—names given by maternal grandparents.

Sometimes party given by grandchild. (1:93) Bill Hudson gave party at Hoh River and gave Theodore a name from his (Theodore's) mother's side. Party also given by Floyd — dishes given away to visitors—big dinner.

Murder

Bill Hudson (3:13) [15 July 1949] If a man kills someone — his family makes payment to family of dead man. If payment is not made — the dead man's family will seek to kill the killer [check ?].

Travel

People (3:13) never went to Puget Sound long [ago].

Hoh

When (3:13) people went to hop fields, they took lots of dried fish, smelt, whale, got flour and coffee at Port Angeles & Port Townsend.

Hoh against Quileute in bone game (4:73). Winter whale considered best, found during April.

Pranks

Young fellows t'q'e•dəb

These 3 boys (3:14) were picking wild cherries – they came to good bunch. 1 & 3 started eating them, 2 had an old white blanket. 1 told 2 to spread his blanket under tree to catch berries but he was torn. 3 laughed, so 2 said Alright, & they spread it. 1 went up tree (no clothes on) — he shake a little — said, Watch out, I'm going to shake harder, moves his bowels at same time. 2 gets mad & curses at the others — said his folks will be mad at them. 1 wrapped up everything in blanket & told 2 to take it home. 2 began to cry. 2 throws the blanket away. His folks asked him what he did with the blanket — 2 told them what happened.

tɬkicqa—had Elk power & doctor power & Tlokwaly power (3:15) Taholah & Queets — had tlokwaly, Elk, Tsayuq, Whaling powers
For 2 years (3:16) Scott Fisher hired fellows to fish for him because he got money from officee — got $4000 — only has $600 left. He has a daughter — in training ? school in Seattle.

Burial

Burial customs (4:71) body removed through hole in side of house—unfastened boards—placed body in canoe [drawing of tub like canoe] flat rocks placed across open ends of canoe – then body & canoe placed in branches of tree. Usually the nephews of a man would make the arrangements. They were paid for helping by being given 2 or 3 strings of beads = x'xatɬiyaxi' (beads) (one string) = length from outstretched finger to nose.

Languages

Stanley Grey (3:103) noted "the Hoh use own language...." SG says he used to know Chemakum—a different language (4:15). Clallam & Chemakum spoke same language according to Stanley Grey (4:68). [because most were bilingual in these distinct languages]

Gatherings

Parties, Clubs, Give-Aways, Funerals

First Salmon ceremony, give party, also First Elk meat (2:9). Whale party (2:112).

Parties ~ Give away (1:17) money, clothes, blanket, glassware, most valuable gifts go to chief of visiting group—invite La Push, Queets, Taholah, Neah Bay. Elk Dance Club. Black (Devil) Dance, Tlokwaly [28 January 1949, T Hudson, 7:30].

A long time ago, people ate only dried fish & pudding of flour & water (for birthday party they now have a large cake made & fruit). Stanley Grey has song of how Steelhead travel that is sung before eating, then eat – called = Tsayuq. Jonas Cole, Stanley Grey & Frank Fisher danced at Tulalip, took oranges and elk meat. Used to have regular winter dances within smoke house. Only sing now around La push, Hoh, Quileute, no dancing. <1-19> William Hudson has several songs.
Neah Bay have same dance & songs as at Hoh & La Push – Tlokwaly. Have Elk dance. Makah have masks & head gear that Hoh, Queets, Quileute didn't have.

(1:31) When inviting people to "party" at Hoh—group goes to Queets & goes from house to house & sings song they are going to sing at party—Elk etc. [Queets people] call them to stay before they go back home. Do particular order of inviting people. Then go to La Push & do same thing (all song are Elk songs, for example)—may be invited to dinner by several families. People who are invited, give presents to people who sponsor party—money, blankets, dishes, etc. Come back home & wait for time of party. Before they eat—those people thanked who received money at invitation.

Rattle & special song for big gathering = tɬəleylǝx^{w}uɬ (1:43). Song used is with tɬi•iɬ – q^{w}uɬəw . Singing song = i•a^h . Each wealthy man sings his song—all sing & clap. Called = i•a^h , each family had a song. Any one in family can use song. Gatherings held in winter time.

Small baby joined Elk club = tsɛw^{h}aɬayux . Each member person has on Elk song.

Mrs. George Winton gave party & gave what is left of her food – peanuts, fish, bread, coffee. He gave party himself after getting these. Whoever wanted to join put up a party (1:45) & give presents away—dishes, bowls, baskets, towels—small gifts person who joins uses family song. Annie Hopkins—knows all the Elk songs.

Morton has Tlokwaly, Elk, Tsayuq, Doctor (3:64).

Tlokwaly = Wolves

<λok̓^{w}ali> Tlokwaly (2:5) 3 or 4 leading men—bad guys—have small dish of charcoal at door—as soon as you get in there – they paint your face if you belong—if you don't belong, you stay over on one side. Everyone had his own song, all join in & sing his song, go clear around—everyone had short stick & pounded on board—then the 4 leading men start it again—getting rougher (2:7).

One fellow go & grab fire & threw [through] it all around. One fellow grab big piece & put it on his back—everyone then dances, one foot & then the other. Fireman (a certain man) starts fire again—only one man starts fire.

Women folks get dry fish & cook it & eat it with whale blubber. Whoever want to join they must notify 4 or 5 leading men—paint novice face—if a person wants son or daughter to join – must notify leading men & give a present to each person at gathering—wooden spoons, harpoon point, old belt?? made of dry spruce limb—twisted spruce limb around neck to keep from splitting, canoes. (2:9) Tlokwaly song—Joe Cole—would sing the song before giving presents away.

Elk Club—winter & early spring (2:114)

Tlokwaly—winter time—Molly Caplanaho—has scars on her arm where she was cut during Tłokwaly dance when she was young.

Bill's father (2:115) used to lead in Tlokwaly. Bill knows all his songs, especially 2 good songs. Bill's father had elk bone pin & would run it through his body.

Club colors (3:6) Tlokwaly black paint—a woman usually paints faces. Tsayuq = red & white stripes vertically on both cheeks. Each Shaker has own song.

Mrs. Frank Fisher brought Mary a box of weaving grass & an old coat because of Ross Tsailto's death<3-6> [13 July 1949].

Rules of Tlokwaly (3:67) can't sleep with wife for 5 days—will take you before crowd & bawl you out. People act as individuals. Last one (Tlokwaly) was given by Tylor Hobucket for oldest daughter to join. People (3:66) from BC made special trip to give Tylor Hobucket the mask & song & dance (Tylor poor singer—out of tune).

Tlokwaly—mainly for rich people—to join one must give away a great deal. Rank depended upon – membership in different societies – wealth – family – individual – what he has done for his people. Old man Hobucket was chief – he had no sons – so his nephew was chief.

Tłokwaly—Family had children—they select oldest & 2nd oldest – to give party among the tribe. Younger ones are left until later. Beads &c collected to give to people who have had parties before & now belong. Invite some young men (2 or 3 recent) to get small rocks—they pack those rocks, as much as they can carry (in baskets) around to every house in the village and throw the rocks on the roofs of the houses – make a big noise & the people in the house wonder who is leading—(secret at this time – find out at party). In afternoon of next day, these boys go around to the houses with rattle & Tlokwaly song. Rattle is owned by man whose business it is to go around village & make invitations (3:95) [Stanley Grey, Wed 14 (?) August 14 1949].

Hoh

The leader & boys go out in brush & pick branches off salal bush to be used by young people. Party held at Captain Mason's house. Young people carrying in all the salal branches. People are gathered at old plank house ready for party. People going in are covered with (3:97) salal brush—obscuring their entire body. Dirt floor in house. Two men with Elk [insignia] tail feather fans – are leaders = younger (1st tso•wɛ•yuqʷəp) (and ya•wəqɬəp). Others come to help leading men called (older) = (tɬa•xʷa•xəd) & (tsuqʷa•tsit) (yaq'la•do) (wiba•xəd).

When the brush dancers come in—each dancer has wooden whistle in mouth—made of bark. Leader sings out a short chant & swings the door open. The (two) wolves come in wearing wolf clothes—ears—long tail—act crazy like—growling. [(3:100) wolves called du•ɬəb, [have] eagle feathers on the mask.] Then came in the brush dancers also acting crazy & line up around the smokehouse, (25–30 young men).

Had 4 big wooden box drums which 6 men sit on each & kick with heels—3 men on each side of drum – sounds like thunder. Two boxes on each side of door. Four men are boss for the fires in the house (2 fires)—one man called = wəqaiyso , second = o•biq' [bosses for fires]. (3:94) In giving the invitations those people who are invited are named. Stanley Grey was among young people carrying in the salal brush.

2 water man (3:99) = 1st = ya•wəx 2nd = tsəltcayiɬ . During the dance, if anyone drinks or warms themselves by the fire without asking the bosses, they are fined. Watchmen will take knives & cut their clothes off & then these people must pay food, berries [as fine]. Ladies pay berries & lacamas—men pay dry fish or meat, whale. After the dancers are finished with the brush dances, they go out & throw the brush in the river.

Old man (named = wila•isəb) starts his song with a rattle around big fire—song means dead face—"These clothes which I wear belong to dead face." Starts to act like he's getting crazy around & around the fire—he pulls start at one end of village (after midnight) – 1st bunch goes into the houses first & are followed by second bunch – four men dressed as wolves from the first bunch.

Four other men wearing wooden masks (like human face & dressed in rabbit skin clothes) [try to make people smile]. These are called = gwaləbəqʷəɬ—come dancing into house
throwing invisible things to one another. People in house can't smile or laugh, leader has black bear hide blanket, had bone pins made of bones of dead people – had hair on one end (dead people's hair), called = tɬqe•ləqʷəɬ —3 sizes—small for young people, middle size, & large size. Used for punishment—if a person makes some kind of mistake—large pin used. Same men have knives through sides [of body]. Big logs & coals from fire & throws them into the crowd—he kills the fire. His help lets him kill the fire without being burned—that is what his song means.

After the people (3:101) had gone home, yawəpɬəp & tɬa•xʷa•xəd , each has a gang of people—all wear masks, deer hoof rattles on legs, & in hands – carry pitchwood torches,

Hoh

Party (3:103) is all done—usually lasts for 5 days & nights—for rattles are passed around from different people to sing their songs. After the party, the presents are passed out. During party, each large family is ready to fight other family of tribe. Last lunch – if non member eats with member —he is punished with bone point through upper arm. After lunch, they give away presents of beads—if a person has put up two parties, he gets two strings of beads—some have 5. Also give wooden spoons away, called = tła•sə'. These spoons used for drinking broth left in kettle after meat is cooked – knives, poles, paddles, bailers, harpoons for salmon. People who do lots of singing, get larger present—for helping people in the crowd. (3:105) Some receive bow & arrow, some get wedges & mauls—the hide of elk from its shoulder is wound around head of wedge.

People want their children to join because of added prestige & also because Tlokwaly is for people who are not afraid of any pain or danger—perhaps connected in old days with warriors. Song—means shaking in head—a bird—their help in killing. The older people who were warriors had Tlokwaly power—mean men—their songs were to typify their feeling & tell of their strength. Songs are obtained through dreams—dreams that they kill a person & receive a song. Members get song around middle age & use it themselves.

Stanley Grey (3:103) noted "the Hoh use own language," occasionally conflict of minor nature between Hoh & Quileute. (3:106) Stanley has Butterfly dance, Eagle dance, Tsayuq. Bernice Jones is head of Tlokwaly. Sintos Ward—willed to Bernice to take care of food—Joe Pullen's wife.

Stanley Grey (3:107) has four Tlokwaly songs, also can inherit songs from father. Stanley Grey Tlokwaly songs sung at Makah Day or other parties. When he is asked by leader to open table to let people eat – he sings his Tlokwaly song. Stanley Grey put up party for his daughter—300 loaves of bread – cases of peaches cases of pears etc. Ideal is of giving a bigger party than others—some jealous of the party that Stanley Grey [gave]. Bernice Jones receives 1st present at La Push, Emily Cleveland 2nd, Tylor Hobucket's daughter 3rd, Lillian Fisher 4th, Jack Ward 5th, Joe Pullen 6th – [Just] one name mentioned for whole family.

Tsayuq = Fishers

Tsayuq = All of Bill's brothers and sisters were Tsayuq, Bill wasn't. When they want child to join they gave party – they announce it will be a Tsayuq party (2:113) [14 July 1949].
Each person has own song—when one person stops, the person next sings, left to right. Person stands up and both hands are waved from side to side in front of the person (Neah Bays hold hands up and move them around sides & front of head) person can be young (5 or 6 months) or old. Family gives presents to others. Young people use family song – later on may get song of their own get power by dream or hear it—hear song

Hoh

Neah Bay (2:113) led by Young Doctor—kwikwał have fans & dance, canoe songs. Young Doctor got songs in sleep when he was sick. Dreamed they were bringing them in canoe around the world & will get well when he gets home.

Tsayuq' dances (2:115) in winter time because power comes in winter time—early—dances at Johnsons Party at Neah Bay—have Tsayuq power—have power with them all the time. Some people have 3 or 4 songs. Many have parent's song.

Mary got very sick & they thought she would die—couldn't move hands, didn't eat—could hardly talk. They covered her face with good silk handkerchief because they didn't want to look at her—she could hear them talk as if in a dream. Lighthouse Jim said he felt bad because he thought Mary would die. "When night comes, I told myself," my mother said, "I wonder if it would help if we got people together to sing—somebody comes & asks if it would help—I'm too weak to answer. They gather 8 or 10 people & they start in singing. There were two persons I wished would sing again—I liked their song—it made me feel better—the other songs didn't come to me. The last person sang—I went to sleep—first time for a long time." The next night they called the (2:117) people again—first time people sang & then I went to sleep & the 4th night I could look around, I felt lots better, I could eat a little bit & got stronger. My mother called people & they sang again. She gave lots of payment. I always like Tsayuq after that. Joe Pullen is Mary's cousin.

Mary never got her own song but a song comes to her occasionally in the last two years. She's not sure whether it's really her song or one she has heard. She is going to sing it to Molly to find out.

Hudsons: Theodore—Elk , Jane—Tsayuk , Floyd—Elk (2:116).

Adelle Martin (2:116) gave party last winter for her daughter to join Tsayuq & also for her birthday (10th). They gave away lots of things. They live at Queets—they wanted Elk party but couldn't find a leader, so they made it Tsayuq party. During party, Adelle brought out 4 steelhead, 3 gallons fruit, 2 lbs coffee, 6 loaves of bread, & 10 lbs peanuts—had men bring them out & carry them around room & back to door where they came out. She announced she (2:118) was going to give it to waxəb (Floyd Hudson) who had given her some presents at a big party he had years before. Lots of presents were given away—[went] 3 times around room. Bill, Floyd, Theodore were not at party. Food given to person at end of party—extra food called = ła•kwa•tsl [??].

Tsayuq (3:57) [in ink] people receive power [with] distinctive dance, distinctive rattle design, distinctive songs [from Morton Penn, 10 August 1949]. Face painting—3 vertical stripes on each cheek—red costume—long headdress of cedar—hangs down, long, colored brownish red. Back is plain cedar color, covered all over with down of seagull or male fish duck. Color—baked clay, Can get Tsayuq power at any age. Ceremony lasts 5 days & 5 nights, usually in early fall or late winter.

Tsayuq (3:66) a fish song, people must bring in a steelhead or salmon. One man about 25 years ago sang a Tsayuq song in which he told about [how] floats on his nets were dancing in the waves. People didn't like this because they thought it was too modern. But what he really meant was the floats he saw through his Tsayuq help that helped him to catch fish.

(3:68) Tsayuq headdress—Mrs. Gold—Elk headdress, Elk rattle, Tsayuq rattles, & tokwaly rattle—made like raven, [also] had wooden masks.

Tsayuq (3:113) "Lots of [eggs] on the coast, I climb up every rock—biggest rocks. Hunting for sea gull eggs. I pick up enough to use, come to dream I was flying around the rocks—shirt full of eggs, tied at waist with snake. I can not break [it]. The snake told me song will come. I land over at Cape Rock with my dream. I saw snake & flew in my dream, two eagles each side, see nest [one eggs in nest. Offered egg in dream & saw creature inside]. Snake becomes dragon – see hole in rocks, look down & see lots of white rocks, get song. The song belongs to the sea coast. High rock with hole—sea goes through from S to NE, lake below. I look (3:115) SE & there is green grass—big field—there's a man [man named = yawəx] in the field—he raises lots of boys—makes lots of money—butchering boys. Dragon's home in rocks—that's why I'm not short of money when giving party because the man makes lots of money killing the boys and selling them. I was proud and happy.

Dragon home called = xɛxɛxtuya' (3:114) Dragon makes the lightning, which, when it bites a tree, makes the bark peel off in a spiral fashion around the tree from top to bottom – 8 in. strip Winter salmon – steelhead = titałiłq^w .

Tsayuq (3:115) people have different types of rattles—double row of sets around smokehouse—had two rattles for singing, sounds like roar of surf, sing about steelhead salmon for winter.

Clubs = Elks, Whalers

Elk Society (3:7) [14 July 1949] each person had his own Elk song—today none of the young people know songs painted face with dark red—reddish brown color—horizontal strip 4 in. wide across face—above tip of nose covers eyes. Only Elks have face painted, one woman does this at all the parties. When person dances & sings—the others sing with him.

One time I invited Neah Bay, Queets, Hoh, Quileute—for Floyd when he was 12 years old—had 2 elks. Some used parents' songs. Bill had one or two songs – Got his song on elk hunt when rolled in fire. [Bill also has Tlokwaly pin from N fork of Calawah (3:8).] Man receives power in woods after he does the killing—Comes home & invites friends & sings song. Elk parties in wintertime. Bill's children & grandchildren in Elks society—June also Tsayuq—now they have meetings in houses & there is no room to dance—just sing. Ceremonies in winter because during summer people are too scattered — also

Hoh

(3:9) lots of food to feed people – also lots of elk tallow = pi'ts & jerked meat. Much work to do in summer.

Whalers (3:38) may have warm black blankets because whale is black. Taft Williams = g'lo•tciyił = leaf, an old Hoh whale hunter [?? Q or G at start of name ??] (3:39) [drawing of leaf]

Hoh was recognized as the same group as La Push (3:39). Hoh & La Push people never had any trouble between themselves—good relations. They attended the winter parties of each other. Invitation sent by one or two (3 or 4) men, who walk down the beach in the winter—too rough for canoe—highest ranking people asked first, given gift, such as

Hoh – Floyd – takes father & mother	$5
Elva	$4
Scotty	$3 or 4
Herb	$3 or 4

Old folks mentioned last

Bernie Jones, Stanley Grey's granddaughter > youngest daughter's youngest daughter = suqsa•yił child. Lillian Fisher as grandmother gives things for her. Peale Penn, Helen Hobucket, Arleen Sailto, Lovetto {Eastman} Black, Lawrence Jackson

Elk club (1) = tsex^{w}əłayu' <3-43> [35 hours to date, 29 April 1949]
Whale club (2) = tsiba łayu'
(3) tsatsaa – singing group [love]
(4) Tsayuq –

Elks (3:45) club members have head gear with elk horns on it   Hold on to stick. Person has to put up party to join Elks Club—announced that person wants to join—give presents away. Face of new joiner is painted – across eyes. New joiner dances with old members until dance is learned. People must follow the directions of the leaders or they are fined—ex[ample]—if drummers miss beat. Fines—peanuts—things to eat, small calf. (3:47) At subsequent party—the amount of the fine is determined—formerly fines were dry fish & other food stuffs—rest of members eat [it]. At Floyd's party, Bill had it announced that he wouldn't bother their present of $780—he returned this money himself $50, $55 returned. Party cost Bill over $1000.

Only one dance used "double tail dance" (3:65) If first comes Elk dance, then maybe comes the Tsayuq. It must be announced that it will be a double tail dance—formerly couldn't laugh, smile, look at one another. At Tlokwaly – if a person was seen laughing—the person who saw him would take a burning stick from fire & throw it at you, or lips would be pinned together with bone pin.
Parents have to pay for child membership in these societies—then when the person is invited he is paid – whether he dances, sings or not. If person wants to join—he

announces that he is going to give party this winter—before then, people go around & throw pebbles on roof of house of people to be invited.

Elk songs (3:66) sung when hunter gets into a herd — it will mix them up — so hunter can get one—also aid in tracking.

Stanley Grey
    Whale society = tsibax^{w}łayu   ts'ayuq
    Doctors songs =   tc'la•layu   t'łoqwali
    Elk society =   tsi•x^{w}əłayu
    Love songs for girls at puberty = tsas'a•
    Love songs to sweetheart = a•ałits'sis   "I am very glad to see my sweetheart."

One time (3:91), one of the party at La Push (Harry Hobucket) started dancing for a new 14 ft. canoe that Bill Hudson had built. Bill had built the canoe for a white man & had a check for the canoe ($30.00) in his pocket, but he hadn't delivered the canoe yet. Bill didn't want to give up canoe since it was promised, but Harry Hobucket kept dancing & singing for the canoe & wouldn't stop. His friends were helping him. Finally Bill said alright he could have the canoe. Bill sent the check back to the man who ordered it. H. Hobucket's father came over & asked Bill when he would deliver the canoe so they could have food ready to receive them. Bill said next Saturday they would deliver the canoe.

When the time came six dancers danced into the big house carrying the canoe. Bill was in front (3:93) to sing his Elk song & do his dance. Then everyone began to do their dances & finally someone made the announcement that they were delivering the canoe that Harry Hobucket had danced for & that Bill had returned the ($30.00) check. (This made him a big man.) In return, Harry Hobucket gave Bill $1.50 & a thin sheet blanket (black), the total worth being about $1.75. Bill was angry at so small a payment but being a big man could say nothing. People regarded the small payment by Harry Hobucket as being not the mark of a "big man" & although he received the canoe for a small amount – his position in the group was lowered. People say he could never be a "Big Man." He did not have the money to pay for things.

When Bernice Jones (3:115) got married to Casey Jones, she got $449 dollars. Billy Hudson gave several boxes of silver salmon, danced in with them but wouldn't stay mad.

SG's granddaughters (4:9) Bernice & Emily have dance costumes made by Mrs. Grey after design dictated by S Grey. They are used when they put up a party—Eagle style. Arms extended with feathers on them. Tlokwaly dance.

SG has Butterfly Dance, Eagle Dance, Steelhead Dance, Tlokwaly Dance (4:11). Stanley Grey was going to put up a flagpole in his yard with an eagle on top – his help – received flag for dancing for cannery owner at Queets—didn't raise pole because his grandson died. Might do for great grandson. Butterfly Dance—SG has 18 costumes—sang for it. SG got song through dream. His help for leading dancing. Steelhead Dance, Tsayuq, SG father's ghost—doesn't go to sleep at night—bothers at night time.

Hoh

Weather Forecasters

Tc'ala•layu (2:116) a dance & song—they have a good time with it. Some real old people have power for this—a doctor power—they jump around. This is different from Elk & Tsayuk. Always use peanuts at Elk party. Bill Hudson is leader of Elks

tc'ala'layu (4:13) for well off men {such as Dr Obi, Doctor Lester, Esau Penn, Frank Fisher (4:12)}, using songs which they believe are better for getting greater wealth. Dancing by jumping up. Songs say they have lots of property. If man finds five white pups on rock on beach & the pups lick his legs—he receives wealth power. Don't catch the pups—just see them. Dream it first & then go look for it.
People in tc'ala'layu'—after they join they receive help to become doctors. Idea is power resident in the sky—SG father—had ship in sky—Tlokwaly—tc'la•'layu.

Details

Bill Hudson (4:21) White paint made of burned bone which is then ground up & mixed with oil. Mary's mask is Tlokwaly—made by Jerry Jones, Mary's uncle. Masks are shown by people at meeting & give presents away—presents are returned later [at other hosted events]. At Neah Bay last Friday, money was given the family of Jesse LaChester by many people. People sing & dance & then gave money. In old times when a person died, they destroyed a lot of property.

Long time ago, Tommy Payne (4:23) lost a song, 12 years ago – he ~~gave~~ threw away all his whaling equipment—gave his canoe away to Sally Black (he's her brother-in-law). She gave $75 for the canoe & blankets. She invited lots of people (long after death)—she is going to pay canoe off to TP & have eats. Jim Black gets upon floor & talks good to Tommy Paine. Two or three years later, ? Pullen made a speech & asked Tommy Payne to come back to whaling. Dixon Paine his brother made more equipment for him. He went out that summer.

Before person goes to a party, they fast so they will have a good appetite – fast for 1 or 2 meals (4:27). g'iya' = to fast—tied up. The visitors want to eat all the food if possible. qi•yił = closing song at parties, sang by big shots—use large clam shell rattles. During a Give-Away—when one of the boxes or baskets has been emptied of the gifts, one who intends to give a party at a later time, will walk out & take basket. At Elk Dance when they give-away things – they spread a blanket or sheet on the floor—pile stuff on it. After everything has been given away—they say, Here is a blanket for "our father" (the leader of the Elk club), such as Floyd Hudson, Bernice James.

After Jonas Cole's ~~wife~~ sister died—Bill's wife & Bill got sick—they haven't used the smokehouse at Hoh River. Healer's wife is religious (4:29). Hoh was looked up to in past years – had lots of money. Theodore was going to put up party for Junior after he got out from training school. You invite only the head men of family, rest follow [after], ex[amples] are Floyd Hudson, Elva Hudson, Bernice Jones, Herb Fisher.

Hoh

Old lady Ward (Jack Ward's mother) (4:31) carried invitations [to Elk Party 10 August] Bernice Jones is head of Elk Club & Tlokwaly. Mrs. Fred Penn gave Elk party for her granddaughter (married to Taholah man)—party for their daughter (Mrs. Penn's granddaughter) Mrs. Fred Penn is sick & wanted to give the party before she dies. Mrs. F Penn gave the baby (1 year old?) an Indian name = tsa'osastəb) [Agnes Penn's aunt is Mrs. Frank Fisher]. Food—brought by relatives, such as Fishers—deer & salmon, salmon was roasted around fire. Other food—salmon berries, red huckleberries, strawberries, peaches. Mrs. Penn's relatives did the cooking for second meal had salmon stew. (4:33) Mrs. Charlie [Lela] Tsailto brought berries & fruit. Invitations to Harvey James & his wife.

Invitations (4:35) are handed out in order of location by~for house in the village. Start from far end of village & go from house to house. Go to door & sing 2 songs—march right in & invite head of house by name.

La Push invites:

Fred Woodruff & his wife Sarah (helped cook)
Tylor Hobucket & family
Jack Ward & his mother
Walter Paine & his wife
Hazel Bright
Rex Ward
Bobby Ward
Floyd Hudson & wife B
Monk Williams
Venny Black & wife
Joe Pullen & wife
Ray Black & wife
Dewy Cleveland & daughter & wife
Annie Hopkins
Grace Jackson & 2 sons
Stanley Grey & wife
Bernice Ames & son

Hoh invites:

2nd Frank Fisher & wife
3rd Scott Fisher
5th Theodore Hudson & wife & 2 older children
1st Billy Hudson & wife
4th Herb Fisher & wife

Hoh

tsexax (4:34) Stanley Grey brought 2 bags of peanuts for his great grandson—hired Pansy & Elva to spread them around hall. The significance being that the peanuts represent the dropping of the herd of elk.

Party held at Annie Hopkin's (4:35) house started at 2:00 PM & last until about 10:00 PM. Party begins with individual songs & dances—2 drummers—Stanley Grey sang Elk dance songs at supper, sang tcalalayu. Robert Lee from Queets started this, [with] Esau Penn & Frank Fisher. One person gets up to sing & dance—everyone helps him sing. Joe Pullen & Stanley Grey were drumming, dancers use rattles. Rattles pass from person to person—counterclockwise around house. (4:37) Had supper after dancing. Appoint man to open meal—Robert Lee opened meal with tscalayu.' Queets [invited Esaw Penn, Julia Lee ([his] mother), Robert Lee, Col Martin & wife. Bennie served food (Mrs. Woodruff took his place). Floyd Hudson also served food—inherited right—get presents for this. After dancing, presents are given away—dishpans, dishes, shirts, blankets. Presents distributed according to location of houses. Big men get better presents (4:38) food—berries canned for forthcoming party. (4:39) Eva & Junior Hudson each gave the little girl $5.00—a few others gave her money—Col Martin gave a little money. Elk parties don't allow Tlokwaly or vice versa.

Quileute & Neah Bay & BCs had big fight at Queets ? = tl'dixbit (2:97). Dick Payne related story to Bill (2:98). Big party—invited by tl'bix'bit people (2:99). Quileute & Neah Bay & BC go in canoe—fully armed. Neah Bay and BC line up in canoes on beach to keep Quileute from landing. Quileute accidentally shot a BC, started fight. One Quileute armed with sharp knife killed lots of enemy, finally killed with spear. They cut him open & found his heart covered with fur showing he had wolf power (= xa'wiłbałux. That night the wolves came howling around & proof that he had wolf power.) He got caught & name of this brave man now belongs to Walter Payne = i•sitciul. Most of Quileute fled.

At Carl Black's funeral—his family didn't give any presents away or gas money to people attending the funeral. This was received by people with astonishment since Carl Black was well known all over—it was felt that this was an insult to Carl Black. At Tlokwaly, Carl Black (3:64) painted person's face—look after fires & build them—passes water around—give pounding sticks—kept tied in bundles—owns building. These specialists are paid for this work by person who gives party—Had to give away things to become one of these specialists.

Asked Morton Penn to go to Shaker meeting and put his tahmanawis on the floor – in this way through God's power they could tell if he really had a tahmanawis power. They were curious if he had the power. If you get a power, you will be sick for a year unless you sing. Person can become members of Tsayuq but not sing songs – no power.

Modern Shaker Funeral 24 February 1949 (1:65)

A small child, age 3 years 1 day, died 22 February 1949. The funeral was held on 24 February 1949. Invitations were extended to people from Oakville, Queets, Hoh, La

Push, & perhaps other people (perhaps Elwah also since an expression of sentiment was received from a woman there.)

At 12:00 noon the bell on the Shaker Church was rung several times to inform the people to come to eat. A meal was given to all who attended the funeral in the dining hall adjoining the church. Approx. 80 people attended. This number includes mostly adults, but children & small babies were also brought. I did not attend this dinner and can only report the last portion of the affair which was witnessed from the outside. At apparently the termination of the eating, the people who were seated along either side of a long table, which ran the length of the building, arose. At a signal, each made a ¾ turn to the left, and in single file made several (3?) circuits of the table in a counterclockwise direction, to the accompaniment of bells, chanting & the rhythmical stomping. The tempo was rather fast, ca. two beats per second. I believe at this time only one person was ringing bells. The bells were rather large bronze bells (circa 5 in. in diameter.) with straight wooden handles. [(1:66) drawing of inside of Shaker church] (1:67) Candles were burning on the altar. A cross & bells also there. Nothing further was observed until the people emerged from the dining hall to enter the church. [Fig. 14 (1:70) drawing of the dining hall]

The men were seated along the left side of the church & the women along the right (Fig. 15). The Indian preacher was Charley Howeattle. Also there was bishop (Shaker) from Queets (William Bennett). A short sermon was given in Indian but whenever the words "my friends", "my brothers & sisters" were spoken, they were spoken in English. At intervals there was genuflection by the preacher & the congregation, as well as final "amen." The bishop rose and gave a short sermon in English, and the prayer in Indian. He then read a brief obituary of the dead child.

Six candles were lit by C. Howeattle & handed (1 each) to 3 men, who stood on left of casket & 3 women who stood at right of casket, in a line, one behind the other, facing the altar. The front woman (Lila Fisher) chanted a long prayer. Then she led congregation in a chant. At frequent intervals, individuals in the congregation spoke out, while she was giving the prayer, to make brief statements in Indian languages.
During the chant the congregation stood, (1:68) several of the people in the congregation were crying, but there was no emotional outbreaks of wailing or screaming. (1:69) most people facing the altar. During the service, a number of the younger people payed [paid] little attention to what was going on, talking and moving about in the rear of the church. The older people paid no attention to this commotion.

At the termination of the services the casket, which had been closed, was opened. At a signal from the preacher, the people arose and, men first, filed past the coffin & then went outside. The child was dressed and was lying feet toward the altar, on its back. The coffin was a modestly priced one of the common type found in all funeral homes. It was gray with silver handles. The coffin was resting on the undertakers wheeled, collapsible dolly. The Forks mortuary handled the body and brought it to the church in their hearse.

The casket was removed from the church & placed in the hearse. The funeral procession to the graveyard was led by the hearse. No apparent position in the procession was noted. However, the family might have been in the car following the hearse.

When I arrived at the graveyard, the casket was in position to be lowered into the grave. It was placed in a wooden (1:71) shipping case & was resting on two 2 x 4s lain lengthwise across the grave. Webbing straps were used for lowering the box & casket into the grave. At the graveside service, the top of the shipping case was not nailed on until just before lowering the casket into the grave.

The bishop gave a short sermon ending with the familiar "ashes to ashes, etc." The coffin was lowered into the grave & the grave was closed by the three men who had been asked to dig it by the family.

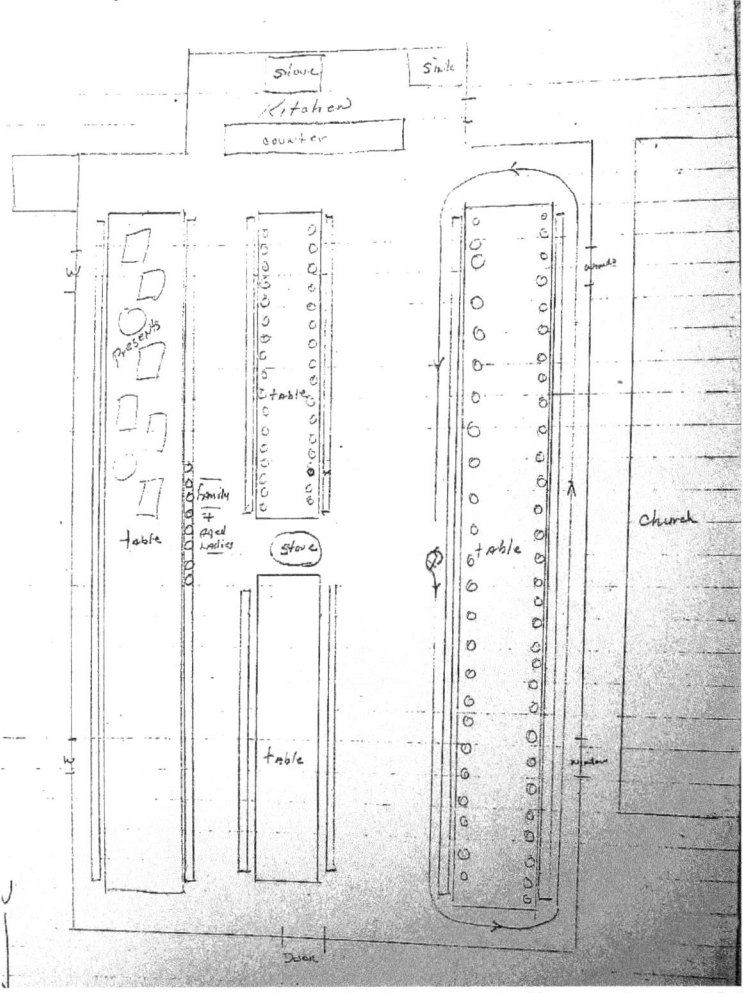

Fig. 14. Drawing of inside of Hoh Shaker mess hall (Daugherty 1949, 1:70).

After the service, most of the people took the occasion to wander around and visit the graves of friends and relatives.

At the graveyard, as well as before, there were no emotional outbreaks & very little crying. In fact a good deal of joviality was observed – kidding one another about getting cars stuck, etc.

Numerically, only about half of the people who were at the church service attended the graveside service. Rain & lack of transportation probably accounted for many not going. Also many remained at the dining hall to prepare for the dinner that followed the return from the graveyard. (1:73)

Upon entering the dining hall, I noticed some people already seated at the tables and others standing around talking. My informant and I took seats at the center table. Some food was already on the table and more was being brought in. The menu consisted of baked steelhead, mashed potatoes, canned corn, lima beans, home canned elderberries, peaches, canned pears, canned strawberries, canned cherries, & coffee.

No one began eating until all the food was on the table and everyone was seated. The seating was haphazard. No one appeared to have an assigned place. There was more food than was eaten. Young and old alike were seated at the table. Four aged women sat opposite the five at the left hand table. They didn't eat & spent most of the time caring for the small children.

After the meal was finished number of men arose, one after the others, and in longer or shorter speeches thanked (in Indian) the people for attending, especially those who had travelled far. The relationship of these men to the family of the deceased could not be determined. Mrs. Lila Fisher (California) arose and gave a long extemporaneous prayer in (1:75) English. Following this, everyone led by Mrs. Fisher sang a repetitive chant—"Jesus is good, Jesus is very very good." This was repeated at least a dozen times. The bishop then arose and gave a short prayer. C. Howeattle brought in three pairs of bells and gave then to three different men, including the Bishop.

On a signal from Mrs. Fisher, all at the left table only, arose and, making a ¾ turn to the left, made those counterclockwise circuits of the table chanting "Ho-ya^h." The rhythm of the bells and stamping of feet was fast, ca 2 beats per second. This completed, they sat down at their places again and attention was turned to the giving away of gifts to all adults and adolescents. [(1:74) The men who had dug the grave first received three dollars apiece, lesser amounts were handed to others who had helped in other capacities.] Small children were excluded.

A typical gift consisted of a plate, small plate, saucer, cup, and a dollar bill. Bowls & cut glass dishes were also included. The more prominent men (perhaps ½ dozen) received their gifts first but the ranking seemed to end there. About midway along I received a gift of a soup bowl and sugar bowl

Every 4th of July there's a Shaker meeting at Mud Bay (2:67). People from all over come. This year a bishop died (Frank Bennett, Quileute). His wife is an Elwah. She wanted to take him to Elwah. Their sons—Walton 2nd, Herbert 4th, Raymond 3rd, Lawrence 1st, girl died of pneumonia. Mary Johnson, Nora James Barker, Harvey James, all ½ brothers and sisters.

Hoh

They came to Mud Bay from California on 4th of July & also from Oregon. Bishop Bennett was well liked—his aunt was Rebecca Cole, his cousin Horace Bright, Obi family his relative, Joe Pullen, Stanley Grey's uncle? (2:69) Herb's wife from Johnson, California, on Witchpec, a Klamath.

[Funeral held on 9th Saturday July at Elwah] Bennett's mother dreamed that he was going to die & he would return home covered with blood. Dreamed this twice. She always took care of him & talked to him before he left on a trip.

Shakers (3:10) Mrs. Black was Bill's sister. Bill's brother David brought Shaker faith to La Push. 3 yards of calico used to be a common present.

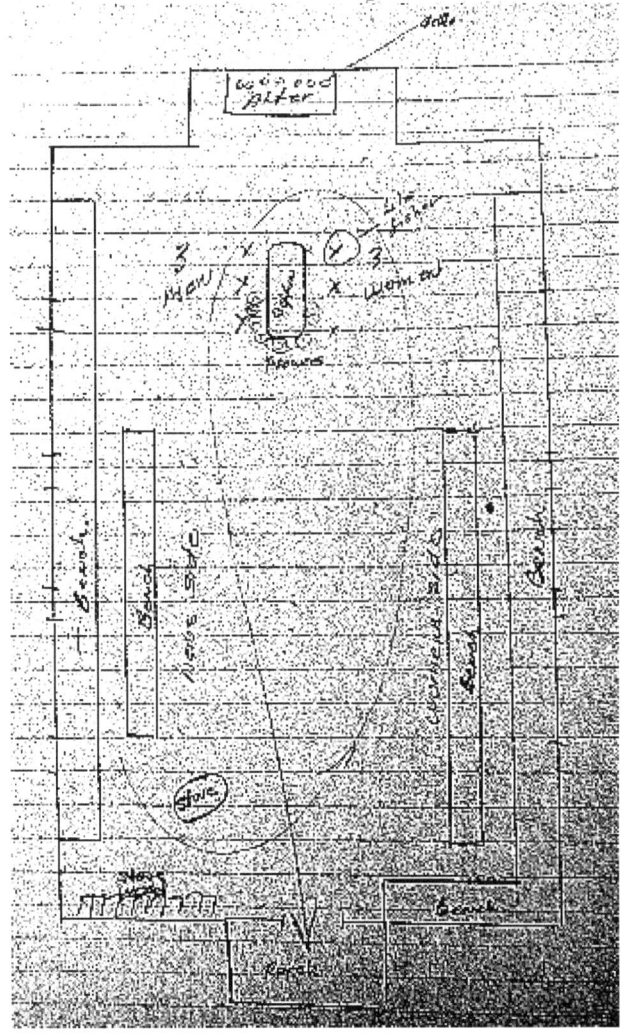

Fig. 15. Drawing of inside of Hoh Shaker church (Daugherty 1949, 1:66).

Checklists

Note: Doc was taught to constantly review collected material to check for gaps or irregularities. These are his running lists from each notebook, with checks beside those he went over again.

Quest[ions] ? – (1:15)
    1. how are masts attached in canoe - ?

Hoh

    2. how are lines rigged ?
    3. how are line on spear rigged ?
    4. are floats used in sealing?

Questions (1:47)
    names of canoe parts—whaling, sealing
    Indian's names of people
    See page 43
    Photography—rattle, drum, spear (seal), harpoon (whale)

Topics (1:120)

- weirs √
- dip nets—names √
- drift nets—names √
- salmon harpoon √
- elk calls √
- bailer — names √
- adze—name √
- wooden box √
- cedar bark shredder √
- cats cradle—yes √
- warfare
- games
- knowledge
  - nature √
  - calendar √
  - constellations √
  - directions √
  - measure √
  - numerations finish
  - medicines & cures
- village & locations
- bird hunting—equipment
- traps & snares

- slavery
- birth customs
- childhood
- adolescence
- marriage
- death & mourning
- property & inheritance
- best places for various game etc.
- quivers
- plant food
- sweat houses √
- fire making
- stone thrower
- skin dressing
- boxes & dishes
- dyes & paints ??
- household group

Inside front cover <# 2>

- Sea otter
- Clam beaches
- Sea anemones
- Secret society
- People at Jackson Creek
- First salmon ceremony
- First salmon ceremony taboos

- color
- murder
- adultery
- marriage
- herbs & medicine
- ear piercing
- kinship tenure

Hoh

equipment for trout, halibut, sole cod, rock cod, sea bass

marmot   beaver   land otter   coon   wildcat   rabbit   mink   wolves   squirrels   hats   tattooing   hairdressing   face painting   weaving   joker or buffoon   shamans   months   seasons   salmon spear

Questions & subjects (3:120)

    function of shamans
    shaman's organization
    trade
    slaves—Bill doesn't know
    murder
    spoons
    first salmon ceremony—other animals
    fire making
    intertribal relatives
    money & money values no [know] little
    personal care
    birth customs
    burial & mourning customs
    dreams
    ghosts & souls
    ritual before whale hunts — prayers — to whom directed ?
        — whalers sing when bringing in whale ? cover whale with feathers
    taboos in whaling
    clothing or dress of whalers
    mortars & pestles
    ceremonial treatment of animals
    animals not eaten
    famine foods
    rock baskets & straps [rocks to throw on roofs prior to party ??]
    sign language
    medicine & cures

Inside front cover # 4
    SG—8.00–15–19.00
    4 headresses 20.00
    beaded olivella neckless & dress 20.00
    Tluqwali rattle 25.00

Hoh

Kin Terms

Note: Kinship terms, especially in this unique language were of great importance for understanding social organization, with Doc working from a genetic list of possible biological relationships.

(2:72)	GM	GF	grand parents	
younger = tco's	M	F	mother	father
old = łipo'qo (older) (pref) [prefix ??]	Z	B	sister	brother
my = ta•d (pref)	D	S	daughter	son
your = tcid (pref)	A	U	aunt	uncle
her = la'ya'ki• nephew	Nc	Nw	niece	

(2:73) 10 hours to date kinship terms
mother = ka'
father = o•lo'
son = tsi'tsqʷaaťot (your son)
daughter = ťxet (ťxe•təx̣qʷatc my daughter)
maternal grandmother = kətciya•ks
 " grandfather = hida'yaəks o•loya•ks (woman = o•layas)
paternal grandmother = same as GM ?
 " grandfather = hida'yas (wisətsobətabatc)
grandmother = aba•
grandfather = tiiəłaba•
my mother = ta'dka
my father = ta'do•lo
your mother = tcika'
your father = tcido•lo
mother's brother = pa•lo'yaks
 " sister = a•loyaks
 " older brother = [blank]
 " younger brother = [blank]
 " older sister = [blank]
 " younger sister = [blank]
♀ sibling = [blank]
♂ sibling = [blank]
father's brother = q'di'so•lo
 " sister = tłopətiyas
 " older brother = [blank]
 " younger brother = [blank]

" older sister = [blank]
" younger sister = [blank]
aunt = käistot' aunts
uncle = tc'i•la uncles
cousin = [blank]

(2:75)
mother's sisters son = a•lohiłqʷaks
" daughter = same
mother's brother's son = hiłqʷa'kspuletot (brother = puletot)
" daughter = [blank]
(my) father's sister's son = təło•pahułqʷks
(my) father's sister's daughter = təło•patsitspa'yaks
(my) father's brother's son = hidatotwałoyastit   titsk̫ʷayas
My father's brother's daughter = [blank]
Mat[ernal] great grand father = [blank]
" Mother = [blank]
Pat[ernal] Great grand father = [blank]
" Mother = [blank]
Great grand mother = [blank]
" father = [blank]
great grand parent (s) = [blank]
parents = [blank]
parent = [blank]
2nd cousin = [blank]
3rd cousin = [blank]
mat[ernal] Great aunt = [blank]
" "uncle = [blank]
pat[ernal] great aunt = [blank]
" " uncle = [blank]

Linguistic Domains

Note: Vocabulary was collected by sematic domains according to category, theme, or topic to assure some consistency.

(1:121) Vowels
a — f<u>a</u>ther
I — s<u>oa</u>p {??}
ɛ — s<u>e</u>t
O — c<u>o</u>ld
U — sm<u>oo</u>th
ə — g<u>oo</u>d
e — <u>a</u>te

Hoh

Meanings (1:58)

-yut = at end of word means complete, ex. — ya•xsayut = complete spruce tree, branches and all
itsa = diminutive end for word i.e. fawn, calf, kitten, etc.
q̇xo•didapət
ti•iyał = ♂ of a species ?
yuxuqʷət = ♀ of a species ?

Trees (1:59)

cedar tree = tsa•pis
hemlock = t'i•ła
spruce = ya•xsə ya•xsayut = whole tree
fir = tłiłxi'ts
alder = q'a•qali'a
cottonwood = q'odoqʷ
vine maple = l'a•xał
willow = ł'a•qał
yew = xi•yax
cascara = q'xo•didapət powerful stuff

Animals

elk = x̣ix̣ił bull = ti•iyał cow = yuxu•qʷət calf = q'q'itsa
deer = h'yayicqa buck = ti'iyał doe = yuhuqʷəthwayic•qa fawn = q'dihwayucqa'tsa
black bear = aqi•l female = yuhuqʷətaqi•l cub = agi•litsa
cougar = wi•daxʷts'a
bobcat = da•idat'
skunk = tsɛ•ix̣
muskrat = tc'xʷi•qʷayuł same name as large rat
mink = q'əda•yis "fish eater"
raccoon = q'q'a•wit
beaver = d'a•d'i
land otter = li•ya•at
wolf = lawa•ts'a•xil
coyote = [blank] □ (1:60) rewritten words in ink from p 61

Sea Life (1:61)

summer whale – black = t'xatsi•qwl
winter and spring – black, smaller = tita•qwal
hair seal = h'ata•l

fur seal = tlado•s
sea otter = xakudi•swa
sea lion = ɬəxwsa'lat same name for Sea Lion Rock, breeding ground on S side of Carol Island

silver = iluq'si
steelhead = k̓ʷawiya or titatiɬ "winter fish"
black = sa'ts
dog salmon = xadi•da'oalitaɬ or yado•qʷ
humpy = xotu•ca (few only)
blueback = ya•las (few only)

rainbow trout = [blank]
jack salmon black mouth = cicp'ila
dolly varden = tl'dadatɬutsa
sucker = tcuqʷtsid
bull head = xawadi

Birds

ducks = di•dos
mallard = diq'diq'
widgeon = [blank]
canvas back = [blank]
teal = [blank]
spring – pintail = [blank]
butterball = k̓ʷiyuyuxwal
sawbill = qʷi•d
coot surf duck = balal   (1:63)
geese = ho•hoqʷal
seagull = kwaləl
crow = ka'yo
raven = ba•yuk'
jay = kwackwac

Shore Life (1:79)

Butter clams = [blank]
Little necks = soto•kwəd
Mussels = six
Octopus = ya•
Razor clams = yalikələ

Hoh

Seasons

    winter = totq^{w}t iłq^w steelhead = winter fish
    summer = t'xats t'axats (A.)
    autumn = spring = qwa'yət'
    spring = ya•lowəł
    month =wi•łpititcu < wił   one day = [blank]   today = x'e•ltia   names of months ?

Times

    sun = pitotcu
    afternoon = ləxwal
    morning = tci'i
    tomorrow = ta•włx also {used} for yesterday
    night = awi
    moon = awi•pititcu
    noon = t'tcuxłił
    yesterday = wiłxtiya'
    day before yesterday = qitoktiya'

Directions

    N = łalo•lik
    S = sixla•wat
    W = yəxo•ł
    E = ləwi•ł
    Up = ts'xi•ł
    Down = qupi•ł
    Right = piłtca•wił
    Left = yata•wił

Measurement (1:113) 5 Mar 1949 B Hudson

    Span [blank]
    River canoe = 4 spans + ¾   [blank]
    Fingertip to fingertip extended = 1 span   [blank]
    Fingertip to sternum – ½ span   [blank]
    Fingertip to opposite – ¾ span   [blank]

Spans

    ta•sil = 5 fathoms
    ba'yasil = 4 fathoms
    ławul = 2 fathoms
    wi•łwə = 1 fathoms

qʷali•l = 3 fathoms
ts'qo•til = 1/2 fathoms
tsadiwiłwə = ¾ fathoms
h'etətqaqsli = 1/4 fathoms
witsoq̓ʷa = index finger – thumb
witc'e•utsuq' = 2nd finger – thumb
tas•k̓ʷədit = 5 finger width
ba'yas = 4 finger width
k̓ʷa' = 3 finger width
ła' = 2 finger width
wi•ł = 1 finger width
təłk̓ʷadit = ½ finger width

Weights

heavy = ti•la
light = huw'ə

Distances (1:115)

long distance = sa•wil
short distance = hak̓ʷil
high = ts'xi•lx
low = ku•pił

Numbers

1 = wi•ł
2 = ławi
3 = qʷali
4 = ba'yas
5 = ta•si
6 = tc'xla•si
7 = ława'tsitsi
8 = ławe•tałi
9 = wi•łtałi
10 = tci•łt'o•pa
11 = to•pawiłtsiu
12 = ła'wi'tsiu
13 = qʷalitsiu
14 = ba'yasitsiu
15 = ta•sitsiu
16 = tc'xla•sitsiu
17 = ławatsitsitsiu

18 = ławe•tałi'tsiu
19 = wi•łtałistiu
20 = ła'tciława•sta

Forecasting (1:104)

    When waves hit rocks hard, it is rough outside
    If game is fat—rough weather
    Early run of fish—steelhead—means rough winter

Weather (1:105)
    judge weather before sunrise & before sun sets. Red sunrise in morning = p'tcisxal , sign for rain & S wind blow
    if sunrise is clear—good weather
    red sunrise—ring around sun—also means rain tomorrow—called = xle•yal (means sun wading in water)

Constellations (stars all) (1:79)
    Morning [blank] evening [blank]
    Big dipper = means dipper, also name for canoe bailer.

Places

Note: Place names were collected because they reveal cultural, seasonal, and historical use of the landscape.

W. C. Lehman (1/18/48~9) said (1:1) Two burial grounds on N. side of Hoh River on either side of camp (cabins). He believes the camp is on the site of a former village. Fisher & Hudson are good informants.

Mrs. Fletcher (daughter of early white settler) speaks Chinook jargon. She "told about myth in which members of Hoh village were chased inland by raiding group. They camped beside a lake and nearly all died. This was because they saw a whale in the lake: the[y] knew it was a whale because bubbles could be seen rising." Mrs. F. thinks they might have camped by one of the numerous natural gas seepages in the area, (accounting for bubbles in the lake) and were asphyxiated. The lake is undefined.

Mrs. F. also mentioned that the Hoh are noted for frequently having red or blondish hair. This is supposed to be due to the inbreeding of the Russians who were captured by the Hoh. Russians being wrecked at Quileute & captured by Hoh.

Good clam beach (1:15) at Goodman (or Jackson) creeks & also at Steamboat Creek.

Abbey Rock at Ruby Beach was once used by Hoh Indians as a defensive position in time of war. Lived on top of island. [Chris Mogenroth, 4:30–6: pm]

Hoh

Reef at mouth of Hoh is good spot for rock clams at low tide. Night smelt once caught in surf on incoming tide in evening.

Village at La Push was below hill. Dan Pullen wanted most of site for claim – lost case in court. Formerly river mouth on N Side—house built on spit—S of rock. Beach formerly was wider (extended out further). Beach at La Push was good for landing canoes—best place to go out from for seal hunting. Clallam Bay Indians came to hunt seal. Few from Tahola (4–5) (1:35) [William Hudson, 9:30–11:00].

Mora = ho•qsuq^w—a fishing place—some live there all year round. Others live here only during fishing season. 1 or 2 big smoke houses. Might be four families living in smoke houses—4 families (1:49).

Place name – rock SW of Abbey Island = qa•tayaxat "pull hands" (1:53).

    Abbey Island = tc'ała^x tc'idał
    Hoh head = yi'tciłx^w
    Rock off Hoh head = tatci•tsa•h (young Destruction Island,
        breeding ground of shags [cormorants])
    N side Hoh head (nook) = łixła•xtal Alexander Island
    Hoh River = tcalalqq^w
    Frank Fisher = xiya•wəd
    Hoh Village = tcala•d
    South Rock = dixiti'
    Little rock S of mouth of Hoh = yak̓^{w}'əp
    N Rock = wil•uyəxi (mens 'tall')
    Needles = siluxtayiłal (clam bed & needles)
    Beach N of Needles = qiqtal (landing place)
    Destruction Island = tatcusx^w
    James Island = aqa•lat (1:57) [W Hudson, Feb 24 [49]]
    La Push = q'te•yut
    Rock next to James Island = tatiəti•xtcu (graveyard rock) Name of grave
        Old people would favor James Island, buried there.
    Quileute River = q'le•yut q'wa•ya
    Bogachiel = boq̓^{w}atc'i•l means "muddy"
    Calawah = q'lowa means "half way" (half way between Bogachiel & Sol Duc)
    Sol Duc = su•łtuq^w Long ago Indians used to stay on Sol Duc = aq̓^{w}asuq'
        means "above the bend" for summer camp [Soleduck]
    N fork of Calawah = dəq'aq'aiq^w
    S fork of Calawah = ha'tca•lit' old camp near headwaters
    Needles off La Push 1st dulatsatał 2nd qiqsustal
    Small rock next to James Island = xaxɛ•i
    Small island next to graveyard = k̓^{w}alala•tal little birds dig hole in rock
    Island where mussels are found = tsidułiwas•utal

Hoh

Punishment for children—Bill doesn't know (3:17).
> One or two houses were at various sites up river—but often move home to La Push in December, January, February during high water—have big times at La Push, where they also had houses.
> cuwʰa—between Beaver and Forks—on the Sol Duc River.
> səlelit = on Bogachiel River – close to Forks prairie, but Charlie Grader took it away from local Indians.
> duqʼaqyu = village at N fork of Calowah

> drawing (3:40) of Hoh village vicinity with rocks, beach, point, river.
> village = tcʼla•qʼ people = tcʼla•t

Tatoosh (3:41) is a woman married to Destruction Island [her husband], but she got jealous & left him, dropping her son off at Hoh Head. Someone told her to stay there, but she wanted to return & look for her child but they wouldn't let her return.
This son of Destruction = tatcistsa [map of places in story]
Brown's Point—Steamboat Creek = Klalock = qʼle•ləxʷ

Dickey River (4:51) villages—tabəli—the real children there were Sextis mother, SG mother, Annie Hopkins mother, Lewis Bennett's mother [S Grey, Monday, 18th August] Located below tlitciyaqʼ (between Quileute Prairie & Forks) creek—6 mile above mouth [6 miles]
> doxodatctidaʼt—village name, one house owner—xaxawiyəd, large family had a fish trap across the river.

Above this, another trap (q̇i•yət = trap) belonged to gi•dicq̇i•yət / gi•dic = his name, an Indian doctor at big bend in river – a good place for beaver (4:52). Had platforms on trap to hold fish. Indian would beat on trap with club to call someone to haul fish to shore. Cedar limb basket trap—holds one canoe load of fish—open end upstream —Open bottom end of bag & let fish slide into canoe = soqwe•ləb.

3 of them, side by side, ¾ mile below trap across river [drawing of triple traps] of Calkins Eastman, ?? Wash Howeattle, David Hudson.
Sol Duc River kwaaladisq̇ʷ (Coon's Place) Connie Grey's father, Old chief Howeattle = xawicaʼɬa . xastutcbəlt = lowest aɬəbik = last tətcto•a = ??

3 miles up from forks of river on N side had fish trap across.
In the operation of basket traps—the owners help each other. People would come to La Push to hunt seal & whale & women.

diɬdotciʼl (means ?) A man went hunting up there for elk, left empty handed and felt very ashamed. Came to this deep place & dived down in there. They later found his body on the ocean beach near La Push (4:51, 53).

Hoh

Sol Duc continued (4:55)
cux^{w}a^h 4 or 5 miles above U.S. 101 bridge across Sol Duc (N side)

Had fish traps [by houses]:
   1. old man cilabab' (David Hudson's wife's father)
   2. xik̃^{w} wayəb
   3. tawlano^h
   4. others yawəx̣ (Will Essa, married Clallam Indian girl, her father head man of Clallam. When interior people hear of whale being killed by coastal people, they would bring elk meat down & trade for the whale).

Bogachiel = totco•leybiq^w ~ totco•łe•biq^w just above wooden bridge on S side of river [two houses] kitx̣is owned trap across there   yicɛlituq^w – da•wəx – (lived in yicɛlituq^w ('s) home).

p'itci•tayit' = 3 miles above former—S side of river—fish trap (4:57)
tso•tso•wałat = 2 miles above former trap 2 houses > father = ayu•łalis (S Grey's name now) son ho•yəwiłił (S Grey's father) = four families at each house – left this place because water was not swift enough for trap. Tore down houses & moved them up stream in canoes in summer time to
tsidi•t = – N side river—built another trap across.

When SG was young man gardened varied cabbage, carrots, apples (4:57).

Calawah River – S side—near Forks - tsix̣o•x = (upper name) one big house = tsib'lis (owner) = tl'^{iq}icka'a tł'qicq'a – ha•qił Had lots of dogs for hunting elk (4:58)
Bill Hudson's mother – his sister [arrow line to Charlie Williams]

tco'lolasili' (tall trees) = S side of B[ogachiel] River – 3 miles above former, 1 long house—large family—had trap (4:59)
Calawah runs into Bogachiel
     Tsile•lit – 3 mi above mouth of Calawah – S side one big house—Charlie Williams = hoho•'tl – one small house – tłix̣abəx = (old man Penn), great hunters (with dogs in summer), had fish trap.
Charlie Williams had 3 wives at one time—1 from Hoh, 2 from La Push [line to p58 BH's M]

(4:64) [drawing of Hoh village, each house numbered 1–23]

Village House Census

Note: A census of households is a vital component of basic fieldwork because it indicates who lives where, with whom at a moment in time (Fig. 16).

[Hoh village] Houses were named for owner (4:65) [S Grey, Friday, 23 August]

Hoh

SW end of village i.e.
1. kitxis house his cousin yaxətəp (whale hunter)
2. oBay [Obi] & his family
3. saweyuk̓ʷəp & hayi'ł (his father-in-law)
4. wilo•yawə (long house ca 200′) chief Howeattle's house, talakas = (talacus Eastman), abe•ti = (wałwayəqut)
5. d'beyił - q'leywəd (s) house (2 names xelədux (his cousin (paternal) axławitw' (son-in-law)
6. wilay'sub łixatuwis (no relation)
7. ho•yəwitił (below hill on East)
8. hobucket – cilaba^h (also man at shuwhah) ??
9. yustcä•is <4-67>
10. ql'kic'q'a
11. q'dɛ•kc
12. ya'aiłəp
13. ts'qlɛ'
14. d'do•pił

This was all of the big smokehouses – there were smaller dwellings belonging to upriver people who lived in them when they visited.

15. California Hobucket
16. kixəbəłəp
17. xix^{w}ayəb
18. yi•cäle•tux
19. x'xawiyəd
20. yä•du'
21. sa'ks (wa'xəb)
22. həstatcił (Mr Hudson)
23 wiba•xəd

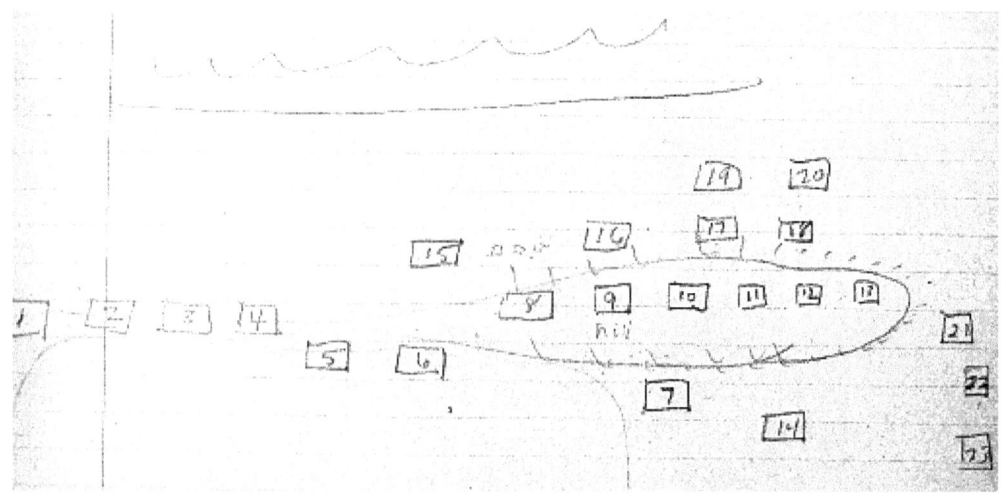

Fig. 16. Hoh village census (Daugherty 1949, 4:64).

ACKNOWLEDGEMENTS

Thanks to Richard (and Phyllis) Daugherty and Ruth Kirk for letting me fulfill a promise of forty years. To be in Washington State is to be indebted to Chimakuans. Aid and abetting during the final days came from William Seaburg, Barbara Brotherton, Laurel Sercombe, Vi Anderson Hilbert. Amelia Susman, and those who came before: Erna Gunther, Herman Haeberlin, Viola Garfield, Wayne Suttles, Bill Elmendorf, Leo Frachtenberg, Ronald Olson, and Manuel Andrade, as well as all the elders.

BIBLIOGRAPHY

Almy, Tina
  1977 *The Quileute.* University of Washington, Anthropology 299, Summer Quarter. 56pp.

Andrade, Manuel
  1931 Quileute Texts. *Columbia University Contributions to Anthropology,* 12. New York.
  1933 Quileute. *Handbook of American Indian Languages,* 3. Columbia University, New York.

Beckham, Stephen Dow
  1969 *George Gibbs, 1815–1873: Historian and Anthropologist.* Doctoral dissertation, University of California at Los Angeles. Ann Arbor: University Microfilm International.

Boas, Franz
  1894 Chinook Texts. *Bureau of American Ethnology, Bulletin* 20. Washington.
  1901 Kathlamet Texts. *Bureau of American Ethnology, Bulletin* 26. Washington.

Boyd, Robert
  1996 *People of the Dalles: The Indians of Wascopam Mission.* University of Nebraska Press, Lincoln.
  1999a *The Coming of the Spirit of Pestilence: Introduced Infectious Diseases and Population Decline among Northwest Coast Indians, 1774–1874.* University of Washington Press, Seattle.

Boyd, Robert, editor
  1999b *Indians, Fire, and the Land in the Pacific Northwest.* Oregon State University Press, Corvallis.

Collins, June
  1949 The Chemakum Language. In Indians of the Urban Northwest, Marian Smith, editor. *Columbia University Contributions to Anthropology,* 36. New York.

Curtis, Edward
  1913 Salishan Tribes of the Coast. *The North American Indian,* 9. Plimpton Press, Norwood.

Daugherty, Richard
  1947 Survey of the West Coast of Washington from Cape Flattery to the Columbia. Manuscript in possession of the author.
  1949 Hoh fieldnotes, four volumes. Manuscript in possession of the author.

Densmore, Frances
  1939 Nootka and Quileute Music. *Bureau of American Ethnology, Bulletin* 124. Washington.

Donald, Leland
  1997 *Aboriginal Slavery on the Northwest Coast of North America.* University of California Press, Berkeley.

Eells, Myron
  1886 *Ten Years of Missionary Work among the Indians at Skokomish, Washington Territory.* Congregational Sunday-School and Publishing Society, Boston. [Shorey reprint 1972].

Ernest, Alice
  1952 *The Wolf Ritual of the Northwest Coast.* University of Oregon Press, Eugene.

Farrand, Livingston
  1902 Traditions of the Quinault Indians. *Memoirs of the American Museum of Natural History* 4, Publications of the Jesup North Pacific. Expedition III: 77–132.

Frachtenberg, Leo
  1917 Ethnological Researches in Oregon and Washington. *Smithsonian Institution, Miscellaneous Collections*, 66, No. 17. Washington, DC.
  1920a Eschatology of the Quileute Indians. *American Anthropologist,* 22(4): 333–340.
  1920b Abnormal Speech Types in Quileute. *International Journal of American Linguistics,* 1(4):295–99.
  1921 The Ceremonial Societies of the Quileute Indians. *American Anthropologist,* 23(3):320–352.

Gibbs, George
  1877 Tribes of Western Washington and Northwestern Oregon. In *Contributions to North American Ethnology* 1(2). John Wesley Powell, editor. Department of the Interior, United States Geographical and Geological Survey of the Rocky Mountain Region, Part II: 157–241, Washington.

Hobucket, Harry
  1934 Quillayute Traditions. *Washington Historical Quarterly,* 25(1): 49–59.

James, Karen, and Victor Martino
  1986 Grays Harbor and Native Americans. Report for the U.S. Army Corps of Engineers, Seattle District. October.

James, Karen
  2007 The Hoquiam Indians. In *Cultural Resource Study Report of the Port of Grays Harbor Industrial Development District Parcel Number 1, Hoquiam Washington.* Astrida Blukis Onat James Phipps, Karen James, Kathryn Bernick, Timothy Cowan, and Lacosta Browning Lykowski by authors. Report No. 200511.03. BOAS, Inc., Seattle. August.

Jones, Joan Megan
  1977 *Basketry of the Quinault.* Quinault Indian Nation, Taholah.

Kirk, Ruth
  1967 *David, Young Chief of the Quileutes: An American Indian Today.* Harcourt, Brace, and World, Inc., New York.

Meany, Edmund
  1920 Indian of the Olympic Peninsula. *The Mountaineer,* 13(1): 34–39.

Miller, Jay
  2010 Start-up: Richard "Doc" Daugherty's 1947 Archaeological Survey of the Washington Coast. *Journal of Northwest Anthropology,* 44(2): 257–265.

Morganroth III, Chris

2002 Quileute. *Native Peoples of the Olympic Peninsula ~ Who We Are:* 134-149. Jacilee Wray, ed. Norman: University of Oklahoma Press,.

1991 *Footprints in the Olympics: An Autobiography.* Katherine Flaherty, editor. Ye Galleon Press, Fairfield, WA.

Norton, Helen

1979 The Association between Anthropogenic Prairies and Important Food Plans in Western Washington. *Northwest Anthropological Research Notes,* 13(20): 434–449.

1980 Evidence for Bracken Fern as a food for Aboriginal Peoples of Western Washington. *Economic Botany,* 33(4): 384–396.

1985 *Women and Resources of the Northwest Coast: Documentation from the 18th and Early 19th Century.* Doctoral dissertation, University of Washington, Seattle. Ann Arbor: University Microfilm International.

Olson, Ronald

1925–1927 Field Notebooks 1–12. University of Washington, Special Collections, Seattle. Accession 2506.

1936 The Quinault Indians. *University of Washington Publications in Anthropology,* 6(1): 1–190.

Owens, Kenneth, and Alton Donnelly

1984 *The Wreck of the "Sv. Nikolai."* Western Imprints for Oregon Historical Society, Portland.

Pettitt, George

1946 Primitive Education in North America. *Publications in American Archaeology and Ethnology,* 43(1): 1–182.

1950 The Quileute of La Push, 1775–1945. *Anthropological Records,* 14(1): 1–120.

1970 *Prisoners of Culture.* Charles Scribner's Sons, New York.

Powell, Jay

1990 Quileute. In *Handbook of North American Indians,* Vol. 7: 431–437, *Northwest Coast.* Wayne Suttles, ed.

Powell, Jay and Vickie Jensen

1976 Quileute. *An Introduction to the Indians of La Push.* University of Washington Press, Seattle.

1980 *Quileute For Kids,* Book 6. Quileute Tribe, La Push.

Powell, Jay, and Fred Woodruff

1976 Quileute Dictionary. *Northwest Anthropological Research Notes,* Memoir 3.

Ray, Verne

1937 The Historical Position of the Lower Chinook in the Native Culture of the Northwest. *Pacific Northwest Quarterly,* 28 (4): 363–372.

1938 Lower Chinook Ethnographic Notes. *University of Washington Publications in Anthropology,* 7(2): 29–165.

Reagan, Albert

1908a Some Notes on the Olympic Peninsula, Washington. *Kansas Academy of Science, Transactions* 22.

1908b The Shake Dance of The Quileute Indians. *Proceedings of the Indiana Academy of Science.*

1911 Sketches of Indian Life and Character. *Kansas Academy of Science, Transactions* 23

1917 Archaeological Notes on Western Washington and Adjacent British Columbia. *Proceedings of the California Academy of Science*, 4th Series, 7 (1).

1921 Hunting And Fishing of Various Tribes of Indians. *Kansas Academy of Science, Transactions* 30, pp. 443–448.

1925 Whaling of the Olympic Peninsula Indians of Washington. *Natural History* 25 (1): 25–32.

1928 Ancient Sites and Burial Grounds in the Vicinity of Queets, Washington. *El Palacio*, 25 (19): 296–299.

1934a Plants Used by The Hohs and Quileutes. *Kansas Academy of Science, Transactions* 37: 55–70.

1934b Some Traditions of The West Coast Indians. *Utah Academy of Science* 11: 73–93.

1934c Various Use of Plants by West Coast Indians. *Washington Historical Quarterly*, 25 (2): 133-137.

1935 Some Myths of the Hoh and Quillayute Indians. *Kansas Academy of Science, Transactions* 38: 43-85. Lawrence.

nd Quileute Notes, unpublished manuscript. Bureau of American Ethnology archives, Washington DC.

Reagan, Albert, and L. V. W. Walters

1933 Tales from the Hoh and Quileute. *Journal of American Folklore* 46 (182): 297–346.

Riebe, Viola, and Helen Lee

2002 Hoh. In *Native Peoples of the Olympic Peninsula: Who We Are*: 116–133.. Jacilee Wray, ed. Norman: University of Oklahoma Press.

Singh, Ram Raj Prasad

1966 Aboriginal Economic System of the Olympic Peninsula Indians, Western Washington. *Sacramento Anthropological Society*, 4.

Ruby, Robert, and John Brown

1992 *A Guide to the Indian Tribes of the Pacific Northwest*. University of Oklahoma Press, Norman.

Shaffer, Anne, and Jacilee Wray

2004 *Native American Traditional and Contemporary Knowledge of the Northern Olympic Peninsula Nearshore*. With Beatrice Charles, Vince Cooke, Elaine Grinnell, Chris Morganroth III, Lela Mae Morganroth, Melissa Peterson, Viola Riebe, and Adeline Smith. Olympic Peninsula Intertribal Cultural Advisory Committee, Coastal Watershed Institute, Kingston.

Suttles, Wayne, ed.

1990 Northwest Coast. *Handbook of North American Indians*, Vol. 7. Smithsonian Institution Press, Washington DC.

Swan, James

1870 The Indians of Cape Flattery, at the Entrance to the Straight of Fuca, Washington Territory. *Smithsonian Contributions to Knowledge*, 16 (8): 1-106.

1880 *The Surf-Smelt of the Northwest Coast and the Method of Taking Them by the Quillehute Indians, West Coast of Was Territory*. U.S. National Museum, Proceedings for 1880. 3: 43–46.

Swindell, Edward, Jr.

1942 *Report on Source, Nature, and Extent of the Fishing, Hunting, and Miscellaneous Related Rights of Certain Indian Tribes in Washington and Oregon, Together with Affidavits*

Showing Location of a Number of Usual and Accustomed Fishing Grounds and Stations. U.S. Department of the Interior, office of Indian Affairs, Division of Forestry and Grazing, Los Angeles.

Turner, Nancy J.
 1975 Food Plants of British Columbia Indians. Part 1 Coastal Peoples. *British Columbia Provincial Museum, Handbook* 34. Victoria.
 1979 Plants in of British Columbia Indian Technology. *British Columbia Provincial Museum, Handbook* 38. Victoria.

Willoughby, Charles
 1969 *Indians of the Quinaielt Agency, Washington Territory.* Facsimile Reproduction of 1886 Smithsonian Institution Annual Report, 1889. Shorey Book Store, Seattle.

Workman, Larry
 1997 Land of Trees. *Scannings from Quinault Country, the Grays Harbor Region, and Beyond, 1774–1997.* The Quinault Indian Nation, Taholah.

Wray, Jacilee, editor
 2002 *Native Peoples of the Olympic Peninsula: Who We Are.* University of Oklahoma Press, Norman.

Chehalis Contents

95 **INTRODUCTION**
    Introduction
    Editing Adamson
    Sources
        Upper Chehalis
        Cowlitz
        Other Tribes

105 **ENVIRONMENT**
    Housing
    Woodworking
    Clothing
    Tools
    Fishing Gear
    Baskets
    Pets
    Sky
    Earth

111 **FOODS**
    Salmon
    Fish
    Shellfish
    Hides
    Meat
    Birds
    Plants
    Seasonal Work Parties

                      SOCIETY

116 **RANKINGS**
    Royal Chiefs
    Slaves
    Generosity
    Class Examples

119 **LIFE CYCLE**
    Birth
    Twins
    Training
    Teachings
    Stamina
    Questing
    Mask
    M1   [M1 = First Menstruation]
    Mary Iley's M1
    Names
    Marriage
    Marriage Examples

Chehalis

    Adult Duties
    Hair Care
    Painting
    Tattooing
    Death
    Burial Examples
    Reburial

131 INTERACTIONS
    Smoking
    Sweating
    Crimes
    Hospitality
    Trading
    Warfare
    Gaming
    Medicines
    Dicta

RELIGION

137 Origins
    Quest Stages
    Dreaming
    Visions
    Inheriting Spirits
    Insignia
    Personal Encounters
    Specific Powers
    Spirit Examples

143 NATIVE DOCTORS
    Odyssey to the Land of the Dead
    Growlers Cult
    Shakers
    Luck

148 POTLATCH

TALES

150 Background
  Short Stories
      Wild Men
      Flood
      River Clams
      Boil and Dung
      Robin
      Thrush
      Grizzly
      Bear
      White Ghosts

Chehalis

        Stockade

153   Bluejay
        Bluejay Bungling Host
        Bluejay
        Bluejay
        Bluejay and Girl
        Bluejay 3
        Bluejay 4

155   Xwane
        Xwane
        Xwane and Crane
        Xwane
        Xwane and the Girl

156   Animals
        Steelhead
        Steelhead
        Steelhead
        Skunk
        Spear
        Raven
        Urine
        Chipmunk and Psa
        Lake Psa Danger
        Beaver Psa Danger
        Mink and Whale
            Noah
        Mink
        Mink and Cougar
        Crow's Son

160   "French Stories"
        Obstacles
        Gifts
        Marriage
        Handless Girl
        Boy Wins King's Daughter
        Bull
        Seven Heads
        Little Jean
        King and Two Queens
        Little Jack 1
        Little Jack 2

Appendix: Other Sources   163
        Sahaptin Upper Cowlitz (Melvlle Jacobs)
        Twana of Hood Canal (William Elmendorf)

167   Bibliography 168

CHEHALIS AREA TRADITIONS

JAY MILLER

Abstract

Ethnographic materials on the aboriginal inhabitants of the Chehalis River and environs are assembled herein from the 1927 notes by Thelma Adamson to include the topics of Environment, Foods, Rankings, Life Cycle, Interactions, Religion, Native Doctors, Potlatch, and Tales, both native and French derived. An appendix adds materials from other sources, and a finding aid lists subtopics.

INTRODUCTION

As preparation for my book-length overview of Puget Sound ethnography, following up a prior study of its major ritual -- the shamanic odyssey to the land of the dead (Miller 1988, 1999), the 1927 notes on Chehalis, Cowlitz, and neighbors by Thelma Adamson were typed into a computer and boiled down into the present work. Similar efforts also produced Suquamish notes based on those of Warren Snyder that will appear separately. Strongly motivating these contributions has been increasing despair that anthropologists, expecially in the Northwest, have been actively denying their own founders, even as local native peoples constantly remind each other not to forget their elders. This growing contrast only adds to the larger sense of loss.

This article, therefore, mostly brings together materials on the traditions of the Chehalis, who once lived at Mud Bay before moving to the river that shares their name at the south end of the Olympic Peninsula, a haven for the greatest cultural and linguistic differences in Washington state.

While the northern peninsula was more recently occupied from Vancouver Island by Makahs (Wakashan Nootkans) at the tip and Klallam (S'Klallam, Straits Salish), more ancient inhabitants were Chimakuan speakers such as the now extinct Chimakums near Port Townsend and the Quileute living at La Push. Lushootseed (Puget Salish) speaking Suquamish were on the Kitsap Peninsula and the Twana Salish were and are along Hood Canal.

Coastal Washington, south of the Makah and Quileute, was occupied by Salishan Quinault and Chehalis, with Lower Cowlitz nearby along that tributary of the Columbia River, dominated by Chinookans, master traders of the region.

Small bands of Athapaskan-speaking hunters occupied upland regions on both sides of the Columbia. In Washington these were the Kwalhioqua, also known as Willapas, with a Suwal subgroup on the east. According to one tradition, those Athapaskans who had lived along the Skookumchuck River moved across the Columbia into modern Oregon to become the Klatskanai, and their lands presumably reoccupied by Southern Lushootseed from Squaxin Island.

Chehalis

Great diversity occurred in this southeastern corner where Salishans, Athapaskans, and Chinookans met and mixed increasingly after all were decimated by European diseases in recent centuries. Reoccupying these lands, Sahaptians intermarried with Salishans and were settling downriver toward the coast, enjoying new pastures for their horses.

The Upper Chehalis River, in particular, was the interface between four language stocks. There Sahaptians known as Taitnapams or Upper Cowlitz neighbored Salishan-speaking Upper Chehalis and Lower Cowlitz, along with those Athapaskan Willapas sometimes known as Mountain Cowlitz. Indeed, despite speaking languages of three very different stocks, all of these Cowlitz, according to Dr Verne Ray, their expert witness, engaged in behaviors which identified them as a single tribe to themselves and to others. The Willapas lived in the hills drained by the river of the same name. The Cowlitz River headwaters were on the slopes of Mt Rainier, near others flowing into eastern Washington. Ancestors of Sahaptians now on the Yakama Reservation walked along these waterways, upriver and across to trade and intermarry among Salishans, establishing bilingual Taitnapam - Cowlitz Salishan villages on the Lewis and Upper Cowlitz Rivers.

The Chehalis River drains into Grays Harbor, with its entrance marked by Point Brown on the north and Damon Point on the south, where Westport now occupies the site of a major Lower Chehalis town. Located upriver from the mouth, tributaries are the Hoquiam at Hoquiam, Wishkah at Aberdeen, Wynoochee near Montesano, and Satsop near Elma. The native Satsops spoke Upper Chehalis but interacted more with the Lower Chehalis.

Along the main river are modern towns such as Cosmopolis (where Governor Isaac Stevens held an aborted treaty council in 1855), Montesano, Elma, Malone, Porter, Cedarville, Oakville, Rochester (near the present Chehalis reservation), Chehalis, Doty, and Pe Ell. Gate, herein called Gate City, is on the Black River tributary leading to Mima Mounds Prairie and on to Olympia. This is the route followed by John Work (1912) of the Hudson's Bay Company in his 1824 journal.

The Chehalis River bends and twists along its curved route. First flowing north, it loops eastward toward Centralia at Claquato, the place where Moon was stolen in this important saga of chiefly origins, then shifts west by north from Oakville to enter Grays Harbor at Aberdeen. Tributaries enter along the way. Scatter Creek borders Grand Mound Prairie, where a Star came to earth. The Skookumchuck River, homeland of John Slocum, founder of the Indian Shaker Religion, enters the main river near Centralia, as does Hanaford Creek. Klaber and Boisfort are on the South Fork, while the main course includes Ceres, Rainbow Falls, Dryad, and Pe Ell.

The headwaters of the Chehalis River approach those of the Willapa River, which drains into Willapa Bay after passing through Raymond and South Bend. On the north side of Willapa Bay at Toke Point, the Shoalwater Reservation was established for the Lower Chehalis, Chinook, and Willapas who refused to move upriver to the reservation near Oakville or upcoast to the Quinault Reservation at Taholah. On the south shore is Bay Center, where Franz Boas collected texts from Charles Cultee, a speaker of two Chinook dialects married to a Chehalis woman.

Editing Adamson

The bulk of this description was collected by Thelma Adamson (see Seaburg, this issue) as a graduate student at Columbia University under the famed Franz Boas. After collecting folklore texts in 1926, she turned more to ethnography in 1927. After almost sixty years, all that

Chehalis

remains of her Chehalis ethnography is a carbon copy of roughly typed notes divided up according to materials given by named individuals. The original notes are lost, but the carbon was saved, like so much else, by Melville Jacobs of the University of Washington.

In an attempt to make these notes more useful and available, Jay Miller typed them into a computer during December 1994 and January 1995. The original order of source (elder, informant), sometimes date, and unarranged subjects under a centered heading was revised by creating new computer files according to topic, combining materials from several sources on the same topic unless they were substantially different. As a result, any slight repetition that may appear involves variations of basic data.

Segments of information are identified by page number and initials of source inside curved brackets, such as {000 jm}. When topics were only coded by some form of a Chehalis word, such as that for first menstruation, a substitute such as M1 replaced it. The time frame was clarified whenever possible, and references to "now" were changed to "1927." Native phrasings "directly" copied are indicated by quotation marks. Obvious typographic errors were silently corrected, others presented along with a suggested interpretation between square brackets [], and a few were left for later explanation, if possible. Amplifications or explanations are also set within brackets [ ]. After twenty five years of research in Washington State, Miller was also able to qualify and better present whatever comparative information was supplied to Adamson when she was very new to this region.

Under each topic heading, data are arranged by page number, smallest to largest, to facilitate rechecking against the carbon. Since these materials were collected during longer interviews, whole segments of data were sometimes moved as a group to better convey a sense of the flow of the discussion about that subject or topic.

In many cases, idiomatic Indian or Red English expressions indicate that Adamson [marked ThA in the text] was recording verbatim statements. This flavor is conveyed by confused pronouns ("the man she"), use of terms such as smashed for shredded, and expressions such as kinda, holda, nowdays, and chaw. The subtle reduplications, as in "to stick the stick," suggest that speakers were thinking in or influenced by Salish. In a few cases, where the best relocation for something was uncertain, a section was copied to another topic in addition to being included within a longer segment of material at full context. All of the underlined words are as they appear in the original notes.

Since the surviving carbon is irreplaceable and indispensable for scholarship, these topics are arranged by page number of the carbon followed by the initials of the elder. Their initials were taken from the Upper Chehalis Dictionary by M Dale Kinkade (1991), which reproduces all of the linguistic forms attempted by Adamson in these notes and in her 1934 published collection of texts, Folk-Tales of the Coast Salish, a memoir of the American Folk-lore Society, Volume XXVII. Indeed, through the kindness of Kinkade, these notes were typed from the very same photocopy of the carbon which he used to extract the words that appear in the dictionary. The continuous page numbers, penciled in by Dr Kinkade, provide the citations used here for the entries.

The most visible differences between the carbon and this rearranged work are the removal of dashes, replaced by commas, and of most parentheses. Gaps left for native words marked by double question marks [??] or distinct listings of supposed variants of native terms have been combined and moved into connected paragraphs.

Chehalis

In October of 1995, Miller boiled down the rearranged topics into understandable English summaries which are presented here in a fifth of the original space. The intent was a close paraphrase of the information, with "exact phrasings" always marked by quotation marks to indicate they are in a native voice.

All of the Chehalis words (but not the Cowlitz, Taitnapam, or Lushootseed [Puget Salish]) in these notes appear in the Kinkade 1991 dictionary as correct forms, but the most significant ones are included herein, along with its corresponding number in the dictionary. Where the technical spelling of a word is reliable it appears in **bold**, while those that remain uncertain are in *italics*.

The names of individuals and places, listed in separate appendices to the dictionary, are treated with other kinds of notations. Place names, which occur in its Appendix A, are listed by their own number preceded by the letter A. Personal names, Appendix B, are listed by page number [p 336 or p 337] followed by a letter for each of the four columns [A and B on p 336 or C and D on p 337] and the number counted from the top of each list to that name.

In all cases, the Kinkade dictionary is the most reliable source for the native terms. While Adamson's grasp of Salishan grammatical and phonological complexities was not firm, gaps in her typed forms include not only spaces for handwritten diacritics, to be added later, but also are the fault of sticky keys, particular the "a" in that day of manual typewriters. After working with the carbon for some time, it is also obvious that she was, at times, a poor typist.

Several consistent substitutes have been used for native words and designations, or, like the term "potlatch," have been adopted as accepted conventions of use. Since the term she often used for the stage of the female life concerned with first menstruation also meant a range of associated phenomena, the abbreviation **M1** replaces the native term. Spirit ghost ally was briefly **sghal**. The notes are peppered with the abbreviation ta. for tahmanawas, the Chinook Jargon designation for anything dealing with the supernatural, deriving from **tah**, a word for spirit or spiritual ally. No other term had the right sense so **tahmanawas** has been spelled out at every occurrence in these notes. Similarly, the native term **pəsa** or **psa** has been retained to refer to supernatural monsters and other dangers. Because the Animal People of the mythic age were supernatural, their names are spelled with capitol letters, such as Cougar, Bluejay, and Boil.

To help the computer keep things straight, however, internal commentary by Adamson, designated therein as TA has here been replaced by ThA. Place and tribal designations appear in the dictionary, but for convenience, following native usage, ethnic groups, settlements, and place names have been rendered as English plurals, thus, **ts!ehalis** = Westports.

Adamson's material represents an impressive early ethnography and is particularly useful for religious and theological topics. The work was done as an aspect of the research for her doctoral dissertation on Tricksters and Transformers under the direction of Franz Boas, who also arranged for Thelma Adamson, along with Melville Jacobs, to become founding members of the Anthropology Department at the University of Washington in Seattle. In 1927, both Boas and Adamson were conducting fieldwork with the Chehalis.

Notes in the manuscript indicate that Adamson had copies of <u>Klallam Folk Tales</u> (1925) and the freshly published <u>Klallam Ethnography</u> by Erna Gunther (1927), who, before and after Adamson, chaired the Anthropology Department at the University of Washington. These notes have been traced to the appropriate pages in Gunther. It seems likely that the published version of this Chehalis work would have followed the same order as the section headings of Gunther.

Chehalis

Adamson's focus on Chehalis apparently grew out of Boas's earlier interest in Chinook, the aboriginal traders of the lower Columbia River who were devastated by epidemic diseases by 1830. Charles Cultee, speaker of two Chinookan languages, was married to a Chehalis woman and using her language when Boas (1901) met him. Other survivors also settled among the Chehalis, although American officials intended the Chinook to relocate to the Quinault Reservation, whose headquarters remain at Taholah on the Washington coast.

Personal Initials (modified from Kinkade 1991, xiii-xiv):

    bd = Bertha Davis
    ds = Dan Secena
    gs = George Sanders
    mh = Mary Heck
    ph = Peter Heck
    jp = Joe Pete
    js = Jonas Secena
    jw = Jack Williams
    ly = Lucy Youckton
    md = Marion Davis
    mmd = Mrs Marion (Bertha Heck) Davis
    mi = Mary Iley
    pb = Pike Ben
    mpw = Mrs Pete Williams
    msc = Mrs Simon Charley
    sh = Silas Heck

Sources

All biographical and tribal comments scattered throughout the carbon are assembled here, along with any published by ThA in her 1934 <u>Folk-Tales of the Coast Salish</u> and by M Dale Kinkade (1991) in <u>Upper Chehalis Dictionary</u>, including place names from his appendix A [marked as A + number].

Upper Chehalis

Random comments about these people have been assembled here, though some are unclear or confusing.

Upper Chehalis [q̓ʷay̓ayiɬq] lived along the Chehalis River from around modern Chehalis to a little west of Oakville, including Oakville and Rochester prairies, large parts of Mima and Grand Mound prairies, and many smaller ones (ThA 1934: ix).

Upper Chehalis was once spoken from Elma upstream almost to Rainbow Falls. Silas Heck identified 5 bands: Mud Bay and Black River (called here the Bays), Teninos, Chehalis town (called here Ilawiqs), Pe Ell - Boistfort (Boisforts), and Oakvilles (Kinkade 1991: v).

Among these 5 bands were 3 Chehalis dialects: Satsop, Oakville (ch series, Bays and Oakvilles), and Tenino (k series, Teninos, Boisforts, Ilawiqs). Satsop, while speaking Upper Chehalis, interacted more with the Lower Chehalis. In this rearranged collection, Tenino Chehalis was spoken by Marion Davis, Mary and Peter Heck, Robbie Choke; Oakville Chehalis

Chehalis

by Dan and Jonas Secena, Pike Ben, Joe and Maggie Pete. For unknown reasons, Silas Heck spoke the Oakville dialect while the rest of his family used Tenino (1991: vii).

ThA mentioned that the land from Rochester to Tenino, where Scatter Creek flows, had a distinct designation as Q!waxtn [1689].

Among the Lower Chehalis, Westport was literally called "sand" [329 čaxə?s, *cf* 1657] and was an aggregate of Lower Chehalis more than a distinct tribe.

Wynoochee lived across from Porter Creek, where they hunted elk. They dug wild carrots at Malone [downriver from Oakville].

The Satsop language has replaced the older form of Upper Chehalis among the younger generation {58 md}.

Chehalis rarely married east of the Cascades. Spencer, a Yakama chief, married the daughter of Yawnish but had no children before they separated. She then married Chehalis Jack. [See also in Appendix about Mrs Dan Secena, a shaman from Ellensburg, who told her life's story to Melville Jacobs.]

Chehalis went to Cowlitz to borrow canoes to go to Vancouver and Portland to trade. They dried eels at Willamette Falls in Oregon City. French and other traders wanted beaver hides from them. Later they went on horseback.

Chehalis later went to Monticello, called mansəla [mansla] to work for the French during harvest.

An Upper Chehalis town was located at Cedarville (a fish trap, 4 large houses, smaller ones), where Santos was the last person to live. Satsop would come and spend the winter there {240 ph}. In turn, Upper Chehalis stayed with Satsop at their town at that river mouth.

Upper Chehalis lived between Rochester and Ceres. The Willapa were below [west, beyond] Ceres {69 ph}. An important town was located on the open prairie near [modern] Centralia.

Only the Teninos [906] had an account of their own origins, traced to the marriage of a royal daughter and a Wolf. Mary Heck's husband, Sam Smith, Mrs Marion Davis and the Sanders "belong" there. [Sanders ~ Sandersons were southern Lushootseeds] Teninos were like soldiers, mean fighters and good hunters. Each of them could eat a quarter of a deer. To insult them, people called them "dogs," meaning less than wolves.

Trails to Olympia went from Tenino to Tumwater, or along the Black River through Waddle Creek {241 ph}. Suckers were dried at a lake on the Tenino trail. Women gathered moss and sank it into the lake on Black River to catch small fish, but people could only canoe as far as Little Rock, where they portaged upriver.

Grand Mound, where part of a Star came to earth, had a spring half way up the side. The Star was too big to live on the earth so it only left a small bit behind. Just to the east are many small mounds that once were porpoises [1612] before the Flood.

Brush Creek divided Grand Mound Prairie and was known for its winter abundance of red salmon. It was dry in the summer.

At Lequito [Claquato], Moon was born, according to the epic.

Before the Flood separated everyone into animals and humans, birds were the boss of all the people. Moon changed all that.

At Black Creek, across from Lequito, a man killed his wife and ran off with his five daughters into the mountains. Later, Taitnapam hunters saw smoke, found them, and thought

Chehalis

they had gone wild. But someone convinced this family to settle among the Taitnapams [941], where the girls married {69 ph}.

At nearby Lincoln Creek, Chehalis and others dug camas. Hunters followed it up into the Blue Mountains [Doty Hills ?] for elk.

Upper Chehalis and Black River ["made lake" A17] languages were close, but the people were different. Black River town was at Gate City, where Maggie Pete's father came from. Many of these people were fair, with black eyes and brown hair.

A monster bird lived near the Black River bridge, perhaps a condor, but people were afraid of it because it was able to bite off heads {151 sh, 164 md}.

Upper Chehalis and Newaukum spoke the exact same language, and most Upper Chehalis summered there for hunting and berrying. Newaukum was named for the crayfish there [literal meaning is "big prairie" A78].

Two first cousins ran away and married. They had three children, one of whom was Mary Heck's father, when Mary Iley's great grandfather found them among the Upper Chehalis and welcomed them back to Newaukum {1 mi}. Thereafter, the Iley's and this family called each other cousins.

Some Upper Chehalis summered at Dryad and Ceres, but hunted at Willapa. Good camas prairies were located near Robbie Choke's and Pierson's.

The people at Klaber spoke another language, more like Cowlitz. Boisfort people were Cowlitz, marrying among Upper Chehalis and Lower Cowlitz. Fred Wesley and Julia Pete belonged there.

By way of further clarification of these extracted notes, in her published introduction, ThA (1934: ix) noted that the largest group of tales came from Upper Chehalis, living on reservation at Oakville, Washington. Prime sources were Peter Heck {ph} Marion Davis {md}, Jonas Secena {js}, and Pike Ben {pb}. Peter, then about 60, sometimes served as interpreter for his mother Mary Heck {mh}, over 90 years old.

Living at Oakville, Mary Heck (**kwil'inut**, p336 B1) had six children: Peter, George, Emma, Silas, Lizzie, and Adam. Emma was the mother of Bertha, who married Marion Davis (Kinkade 1991: viii). Peter Heck said that his mother's ancestry included Tenino and White River (Muckleshoot Lushootseed). His father's included the Westports and a group just above Elma {24 ph}.

Silas Heck, Peter's brother, was married to Lucy, who was mostly from the Wynoochee, who had lived both near Montesano and at Damon's Point. Oyhut [modern Copalis] was related to many of those tribes {149 sh}. ThA (1934: xi), however, traced her to the Humptulips, as paraphrased here.

Lucy Heck, about 70, lived at Oakville but her ancestry was Gray's Harbor and Humptulips River. She was raised along Chinoose (Chenois) Creek. Her tales were learned from Pete Simmons, her step father, who died when about 100. He only told her stories prior to her marriage. She told the tales in the Harbor dialect, with Silas Heck, her husband interpreting. She died in the winter of 1927 before ThA returned.

Similarly, Jonas Secena, about 40 and blind, interpreted for his father Dan Secena {ds}.

Chehalis

Joe and Maggie Pete also supplied ThA with information. Joe had spend his youth among the Nisqually. His mother was a sister to Dan Secena's father (Kinkade 1991: viii). Maggie Smith Pete was sister to Ed Pete and mother to Blanche Pete Dawson, who had aided Boas's fieldwork while she was a school girl.

Marion Davis was born at Centralia. His grandfather and father were Cowlitz {50, 229 md}. His mother, Liza, related among the Cowlitz, Puyallup, and Nisqually (1991: viii), moved to the Upper Chehalis from the White River when she was five and she taught him some Lushootseed Puget Sound tales also recorded by ThA.).

Marion Davis and Pike Ben were older than Peter Heck. Mr Ben told a group of Mink tales that ThA did not regard as properly Upper Chehalis. Mrs Ben was a Puyallup and several sources insisted that "Mink belongs to the Sound."

Bertha Heck (Mrs Marion) Davis was the daughter of Mrs Emma Heck, her mother's mother was Upper Chehalis, and her father and father's father were both Nisqually {222 mmd}.

Jack Williams was from Gray's Harbor, his mother from the coast across from Astoria on the Columbia River, and his father was from the Wynoochee Valley, Montesano, Columbia River, Willapa, and Gray's Harbor {91 jw}. At Montesano in 1927, ThA (1934: xii) collected tales from elderly speakers, Jack Williams for Wynoochee and Mrs Simon Charley for Satsop.

Mrs Simon Charley was 60 years old. Her mother was Satsop, her father was Gray's Harbor (from Montesano down), her mother's mother from Squaxin, her father's father was Humptulips, and her grandfather's father was Satsop through his own mother and mother's father. Her father's father belongs to *Wapu:ttci*, who lived near the bridge to Aberdeen {87 msc}.

While the ThA notes refer to George Saunderson, the family is known as Sanders (Kinkade 1991: viii). George Sanders [ThA's Saunderson] was born at Cleber [Klaber], but left there when he was 5 years old. He spent most of his life at Rochester. His mother and both her parents were Lower Cowlitz, his father and father's mother were from the Scatter Creek people [A34], his father's father was Nisqually {112, 113 gs}. George was also the source for a remarkable collection of interlinked texts about the Changer, drawn from the Nisqually and Chehalis, called Honne, Spirit of the Chehalis (1925) by Katherine Van Winkle Palmer. Its publication made Adamson's 1926 fieldwork more difficult.

Queen Susan [p 336 A20] was mentioned several times. She was an outstanding example of advantages of a high ranking woman. She belonged to the "best family" as the sister of Chief Yawnish, but relied on her own capabilities. She was one of the very few women to be doctors with a spirit ghost ally [*sghal*] that allowed her and her powers to retrive "souls" of people, especially children, from the land of the dead. She also had luck [1441] power, and because she was too powerful, was suspected of poisoning people who disagreed with her {141 sh, 153 md}. She also had a third unnamed power, and was middle-aged when Marion Davis was still a young man.

Cowlitz

Taitnapam were Sahaptian speakers, the Upper Cowlitz including those at Mossy Rock (the *Wanukwt*), at Nesika, and at Silver and Tilton Creeks (ThA 1934: x).

The [Salishan] Lower Cowlitz lived along that river from Toledo to Castle Rock, roaming as far south as Kelso. Subgroups included the Toutle River Cowlitz (si:'q'w), those at Newaukum River, and those near Pe Ell and Boisfort.

Chehalis

Lower Cowlitz lived on the prairie half a mile above present Toledo, where they had a trail through Mossy Rock (Wanukwt, Upper Cowlitz, Taitnapam) to Klicktat across the Cascade Mountains {32 md}. They had a big village [A153], down the hill from the Catholic mission, that had plank house 30 feet long. Other Upper Cowlitz were on the Lewis River near Mt Rainier.

Cowlitz were also at Jackson Prairie. Marion Davis's father was raised on the Jackson farm and took their family name. Peter Tom, half Wanukwt and half Newaukum [Nwakame ?], brother to Mrs Jack and Frank Tom, lived there above the main store road. Frank Tom lived in the Willapa Hills. The population at Jackson died during an epidemic when many sweated and then swam in the cold river.

When Taitnapams saw a boy who was a good hunter, they wanted to marry their daughters to him. People who were lively in work and life were preferred as spouses. Taitnapam Upper Cowlitz included Mary Iley, Sophie Smith, and Mrs George Jack. They spoke it among themselves and the Wanukwt, but used Chehalis with others. [See appendix with information about Mary Eyley from Melville Jacobs (1934: 231), who identified Kelso as mansa'la [Montecello], where some French [Canadians} settled. To Jacobs, Mrs Eyley described a myth as a canoe, tied up at halts and drifting during digressions.]

Cowlitz were rich, with many horses and packed storehouses. Each kind of food had a separate house, such as for dry camas, dried berries, dried fish, dried venison, or for hide blankets {120 ly}. They had five good salmon creeks with prized trap locations. They owned many shells, horns, beaver pelts, deer hides, baskets, songs, and names {121 ly}.

Lower Cowlitz went to Castle Rock for the fishing, and to Kelso. A big town was at the mouth of the Cowlitz River with many four-fire winter houses, each 40 feet long. Where they camped for camas or berries, they used cattail mat tents.

Upper Cowlitz went to Bay Center by getting to Boisfort, canoeing down the Chehalis river to Westport and then going on {129 ly}. Canoes, later horses, took them to Nisqually, Mud Bay, Puyallup, and, rarely, Skokomish [Hood Canal]. Cowlitz got clams at Olympia and Mud Bay, or traded for them from those at Tumwater. The trail was in woods from Chehalis to Centralia, then prairie to Tenino and beyond.

Upper Cowlitz materials were supplied by Mary Iley, her sister Sophie Smith, James Cheholts, Lucy Youckton, Mrs. Northover [only in 1926], and Minnie Case. Lucy Youckton lived at Oakville and suggested the names of others, who were scattered because the Cowlitz had neither a reservation nor a land base (ThA 1934: x).

Mary Iley, about 70, lived at Nesika on the Upper Cowlitz River, but visited widely {250 ph}. ThA finally met her in 1926 at Wapato on the Yakama Reservation staying with her sister, Sophie. Minnie also lived at Wapato. Mrs Johnnie Johnson, a sister of James Cheholts, lived among the Yakama but refused to give any tales. In 1927, Mary was with her son at Morton, where Melville Jacobs worked with the entire family collecting Sahaptin texts. Their brother James was then at Rochester.

The sisters Mary, Sophie, and Lucy belonged to the bilingual Newaukum Cowlitz who intermarried with Taitnapam. The father of Mary and Lucy was Lower Cowlitz, their mother was Taitnapam and Yakama. Mary was married to a Taitnapam. James was born on the Toutle River, as were his mother and father. Mrs. Northover was born near Toledo. Minnie Case belonged to the Boisfort group (ThA 1924: xi).

Chehalis

Lucy Youckton's father, a great hunter, was Lower Cowlitz, her father's mother was from Tenino, her father's father was Cowlitz, and her mother's mother was Taitnapam. She was born on lakamasili [Lacamas ~ Illahee, camas land in Chinook jargon] Creek, a little more than half a mile from Cowlitz Prairie, where many camas and cattails grew. She had a Lower Cowlitz uncle, named *wvk'm-nos Kal*, who was a great old man "to tell her everything. When get to be a woman, be kind to people." He had about 4 wives at the same time and 2 or 3 houses, with round, hanging doors. Each house was located near a food source like a salmon stream or berry patch {117, 122 ly}.

Joe Peter and his wife Agnes were mentioned because he was Mrs Youckton's sister's boy {118 ly}.

Other Tribes

In 1926, ThA collected tales from Mrs Mary Adams on the Skokomish Reservation at the heel of Hood Canal, also obtaining Puyallup Lushootseed tales from Jerry Meeker, who was there visiting. Both speakers were over 50 (ThA 1934: xii).

No living sources were found for the upland Athapaskans, here called Willapas.

The Willapa [Kwalhioqwa] lived as far as Dryad, intermarrying with the Pe Ells [A86]. They used a trail between the Willapa and Chehalis rivers to go and dig clams at Tokeland. [It is now paved as State Route 6 between Chehalis and South Bend.] Old Youckton belonged at Willapa, where people went to hunt elk. Perry Youckton (about 70 in 1927, half Willapa and half Tokeland) was married to Mary Heck's aunt, who was Black River and Chehalis.

These Athapaskans were called upstreamers or inlanders in Chehalis [A 473]. They spoke Salish with Chehalis and Athapaskan with the Pe Ells {35 ph}.

Tokeland was home to Lizzie Johnson's mother's father. Her husband was part French and named Pe Ell. The town was named for him.

Chehalis

ENVIRONMENT

Housing

Houses, with sides of standing cedar planks tied on (without pegs or nails), were built so their length ran parallel to a river or stream with doors at both ends. [Early travelers noted this up and down placement of native house boards, and Fort Chehalis (1860) was built the same way (Van Syckle 1982: 36, 152, hereafter EVS).] (At Grand Mound, because the Chehalis River ran east and west there, the houses happened to be oriented to the sun, but this was a secondary consequence of their following the waterway {365 ds}.)

Firewood was stored just inside the doors. During a freezing spell in winter, a mat tent might be made inside these doors to keep out the cold. Sometimes, there was a double door. An outside one hung like a pendulum so it could be moved back and forth to allow passage. The inside door was fitted, longish and squarish, so it could be locked with a cross bar.

Planks were wedged from cedar logs, and could take two months to finish. Those with knots were used for the sides, while those without knots to let in the wet were used for the roof. Gaps were left along the peak of the gabled roof line to serve as smokeholes.

Most houses had two fires, used by four families, but a house could be as much as 80 feet long and 40 feet wide for a six-fire house for 12 families (two families share a fire), about as large as houses got {150 sh}. Their doorways could be fastened closed using a string that hung down {267 ph}. In colder spots, houses were dug deeper {205 mh?} and had a thick layer of dirt piled along the outside of the walls as insulation. The area outside the house was bare, no platforms like those of the Kwakwaka'wakw [formerly Kwakiutl] of British Columbia {39 ph}.

Inside each house was a packed dirt floor, fires, and beds. Built as platforms along the sides, these bunks were four-feet high, surfaced with cedar planks, and covered with (2-6) layers of mats about six feet long and 3 or 4 feet wide {154 md}. They were used as seats during the day and as beds at night.

The man who built the house, or managed and paid for the construction, was regarded as the owner. After his death, it was inherited by his close relatives, beginning with his wife, then his sons, but it was the family home so all shared it {364 ds}. If a family died off, the house was moved to another location that was regarded as safer or more lucky. Once the house was moved, the owner had no claim to the prior site {295 ph}. Anyone could move there. Ownership consisted of occupancy.

Houses were swept daily using a broom of bundled buck brush {286 ph}. Blankets were hides, but wealthy families had bed spreads woven of dog or mountain sheep wool {81 ph?}. The woolly dogs were raised locally, but the sheep hides were traded from the Klickitat [Yakamas]. Large mats were used as inside walls. Dried salmon and other food hung from the rafters above the fires.

The house of a chief was larger and dug deeper {184 md}. Slaves slept inside, without assigned locations, ready to work. Contrary to the Skunk story [below], there were no little outbuildings where slaves lived. That was a literary device of Marion Davis, who told the story. A chief might also build a large house just for a potlatch and leave it standing as a monument. A potlatch was like Christmas, with someone standing in the center of the house and telling the helpers to whom to give presents {39 ph}. Chief John Heyden built the last one in back of where Secena lived in 1927. It was only torn down when it began to collapse.

Chehalis

Villages were clusters of these houses along a shore associated with a particular band of people. Remains of a village at Gate City are now gone {108 ph}. For example, Upper Chehalis were from Cedarville to Lequito {296 ph}. Teninos had Scatter Creek, Skookumchuk, and a section of the river {99 ph}.

During the summer, people moved upriver to camps where they used flat-roofed cattail mat tents. Smaller sweat houses were also used all year long {256, 269 ph}. Unlike the Klallam, fish were never dried in these summer homes because they would instead spoil first. Rather, they were hung from the rafters of the winter plank houses.

Woodworking

Every family needed the firewood of two or three trees every winter {186 md}. Both women and men packed wood. People would find a dead or dying tree and set a slow fire to burn it down. Several days later, they would go back and chop up the wood, load it into a canoe, and bring it home. Backpacks and, more recently, horses were also used to carry wood.

Firewood was stored inside the doors, while bark and twigs was kept under the bunks. People did not like to have to get wood in the rain.

Fires were mostly small, except when a chilled hunter or fisher came home. Then bark, wood, and limbs were added to the fire. To increase the flames, pitch or seal oil was added.

A firedrill was used to make a fire. A glowing punk was made of braided willow root {101 ph}, carried inside a large clamshell only by women.

Cedar bark was pried off trees in June and July when it was loose. Strips should be wide, up to six inches or the width of two hands for use as soft baskets, women's aprons, and shredded towels {286 ph}. Women mostly did the work, but men helped if needed.

Every woman was busy making mats, which were used for walls, padding, plates {84 ph}, and covers. Small round mats were used for playing the disk game {154 md}. Shredded cedarbark served as towels, skirts, pads. Shredded cedar was sometimes dyed red using alder bark. Spoons were selected clamshells or carved from yew or alder wood. Dishes were made of hard wood, often maple.

Everyone preferred to travel by canoe, although there were trails {102 ph}. When whites were taken downriver to the harbor by native guides, they came by wagon to Little Rock, where they loaded into river canoes. The harbor canoes, for saltwater, were too "wild" [erratic], too sharp pointed to keep straight in a riffle. Sometimes they hitched a horse to a canoe to drag it overland to the Cowlitz River.

Many canoes at Kelso bought from the Chinook had a front painted black or red, same as their paddles.

Clothing

The woven cedarbark skirt overlapped at the back and was made more sturdy in front {7 mi}. They came below the knees and were longer in back {78 ph?}. Other skirts were also made from strips of muskrat, badger, wild cat, mountain beaver or raccoon hide, twisted while they were wet. A cape made of cattails kept off the rain.

Blankets were made by sewing together 6 or 8 such pelts. These animals were so easy to catch that a woman could make two or three blankets in a week. For these blankets and warm clothing, the fur was left on the hide. Deer and bear pelts were used full size {191 md}. Chehalis traded with Puget Sound tribes for a blanket woven of duck feathers {333 ph}.

To make leather, fresh hides were soaked overnight to loosen the hair, scraped, and rubbed with mashed brains as a tanning agent {26 ph}. The next day, the hide was rinsed, wrung out, and rubbed with an abrader to soften the fibers. Mrs Youckton and Mrs Secena were very skilled tanners. Some men knew how to tan, but mostly women did it. In 1927, soap and lard were used for tanning, along with deer or cow brains.

To color the leather, a slow fire of rotten logs was built in a pit and two deer hides, loosely sewn together, were tented over it to smudge into a yellow tint. After many hours, such smoked hides shed water and always remained soft.

Both men and women wore buckskin leggings when they went into brush, for example, to pick berries. The word used for leggings in chinook jargon derived from Ojibwa, Great Lakes Algonkian, via the fur traders.

Dentalia (tusk) shells, dangling in strings, were used for earrings and other objects of wealth {78 ph?}. As elsewhere along the Pacific coast, natives did not know that their source was Nootkan traders from the west coast of Vancouver Island, where the shells were ingeniously dredged up from the ocean floor several hundred feet deep. Instead, a race of dwarfs with tiny mouths, used to suck out the insides, was believed to supply the shells to the trade.

Women made beads of clamshells and wore them in necklaces {78 ph?}. Young men gave strings of such beads to their lovers.

Men sometimes wore a shell through a hole in the nasal septum, as did a few women. Winter was the time for head coverings, which were not worn in summer. Men could use the head of a deer or other animal as a hat. An otter hide, beaded and decorated, made a hat that was "too high toned" and likely to cause jealousy {122 ly}.

Some used a basket hat. Taitnapam women wore nice basket hats that were all white, all yellow, or white and black, made by Cowlitz matrons {122 ly}.

As undergarments men wore something like a diaper [bikini, briefs] made from leather. Some women also wore them under the skirt {119 ly}. The leather for these was particularly nice and soft.

Girls at Grays Harbor liked to wear beaded strings just below the knees, along with another three bands above the ankles.

People wore moccasins, stuffed with fur in the winter. Deer hide was used for moccasins because elk hide did not last. A toe [ThA "tow"] strip was sewed to the moccasin and wrapped over the arch and around the ankle {292 ph}. In deep snow, snowshoes and snowboots were used {380 js}.

Tools

A woman owned everything she earned or made {281 ph}, and took it with her when she divorced. The same applied to a man.

Stone tools included a hammer, about a foot long, with a rounded bottom and a tapered top to use as a handle {102 ph}. Made of grey stone, such hammers were used to pound stakes or wedge off planks by men, and to make flour of dried fish or meat by women {284 ph}.

Each woman had a dibble (digging stick) made from yew with a handle of elk horn. Women twisted string and chord on their hips and do not seem to have used spindle whorls.

Chehalis

Copper was found near Toledo and used for paint.

Cowlitz got large spoons from some kind of ocean being {8 mi}. Oblong basins were carved from curly maple. Stirrups were made from oak, boiled half an hour and bent to shape. Mary Iley's father knew how to make all of these. Round wooden water buckets were traded from Canadian Indians who made them.

Spoons were made from boiled and shaped mountain goat horns {61 md}. Suitable clamshells were also used as spoons.

Bow strings were made from sinew taken from along the backbone of deer. Bows were made from carved yew, arrows from fir or from arrowwood. The use of armor was uncertain, but ironwood slats might have been worn over the chest and back.

The only musical instrument was a long pole used to keep time by pounding on the roof during a dance {102 ph}. Only the Puget Sound tribes had musical instruments such as [square] drums, rattles, and whistles.

Deer, elk, bear, and other animal bone was used for beads, needles, and awls.

Fishing Gear

Before salmon came up the river, fish traps were put up. Certain people always had a trap in place in time for the spring [324] salmon, using it through the fall salmon run in October {27 ph}. As many as five people could be involved with making such a fish trap [272], helping one another cut lots of little sticks that were needed and lengths of vine maple [1362], maybe 5 feet long and about an inch or more in diameter {28 ph}. These poles were sharpened at the bottom, stuck in a line into the stream bed, and tied together with willow bark every yard or so. This fence was braced with slanting poles set against the water flow. Basketry cylinder traps, made of interlaced hoops, were set in the water to hold salmon until they could be gathered.

A whole tribe might build a trap together, but the chief had the most of the say about it {367 ds}. A trap could be built in a day, ready to catch fish that night. The first-caught fish was roasted on sticks and everybody was invited to eat so that the trap would be lucky. Even lazy people were welcome. Similarly, when fish were distributed, everyone got a share, regardless of what, if any, work they had done. There were never quarrels or disputes for that would offend the salmon.

Spring runs were from February until the last of June. The water was high, so a net was not used. All of the salmon was dried. To roast any, it had to be soaked overnight.

Black salmon [1662] was the first one in the fall, maybe in September; then came red [428, pink] or dog [1212] salmon. They were speared [cf 1340] and cooked by being boiled or roasted on sticks. These fish always dug into a riffle and so could be speared in the backbone sticking out of the water. Steelhead [1473] came up both the Black and Chehalis Rivers.

Suckers [2419] were in the rivers all year around. They were speared, using a small net to make a drive for them since they always went in a bunch. Men in canoes floated on both sides of the river and hit the water with paddles to drive the fish toward another canoe with a set net.

Chub, another fish, were also in sloughs or slow, still water [833]. In the spring, fat ones were caught on bone fish-hooks or with a little set net [2515]. They are caught at night when there is no light.

Chehalis

Red mouth, plentiful all year around, were caught in the spring when they were good and fat. Trout [1235] were taken with a fish-hook any time of the year, while steelhead or salmon trout [493] only come after the salmon in the fall. People looked for salmon eggs to use as bait, particularly from a white salmon with a small mouth caught below a riffle, where they stay waiting for the eggs [?].

While local nettles, carefully gathered because they sting, were used for fish line {28 ph}, nets [1557] were made from nettles [1592] traded by the Yakamas {369 ds}. The dried nettles were soaked in water, then women used a finger cap [thimble] of coarse white material to scrape the bark off, remove the fibers, and twist them into double strands on the hip. This cord was spun fine or coarse, depending on what kind of net was intended {28 ph}.

Night fishing was done from a canoe with a fire burning on a bed of dirt in the middle. The spear was made of split fir, tapered nice and smooth, with 3 hardwood prongs attached with cherry bark {107 ph}.

Baskets

Upper Chehalis made soft and hard baskets {7 mi}, along with mats. Soft ones, with a bottom woven of roots and grass sides, were used to pick berries in the mountains. Cowlitz women's hats were woven of grass and willow bark twine.

Hard baskets were used for cooking [1576]. The Upper Chehalis only began to make hard baskets with imbrication after they saw that whites wanted to buy them. They copied Wynoochee and Lower Cowlitz baskets {36 ph, 125 ly}. Mrs Heck learned to make them from Minnie Case's mother. Hard spruce [hemlock] twined baskets [728] may have once come from the Gray's Harbor or Satsop region, but spruce does not grow in the Chehalis neighborhood {37 ph}.

A quick pack basket for firewood was made of little cedar limbs, split and twisted into an open weave. Other hasty baskets, assembled as needed for berries and such, were made with any flexible bark {191 md}. Either men or women could make such an emergency basket, according to Mrs Youckton.

Women made small mats [735] of cedarbark or cattails to use for drying food, such as berries, or for a table cloth on the floor when serving food {190 md}, also baskets filled with shredded cedar bark to sell to gamblers {286 ph}.

Sweet grass itself [1427 **qaqcxʷ**]came from the Harbor, where it grew in the mud {49 mmd} and was gathered in during the months from July to September. Women would pull it out, wash it, clean it, and hang it in a shed to dry slowly. If left in the sun, the grass would break up too quickly. Sweet grass was used as attractive trimming. At a marriage exchange between the inlaws, the half that was the bride's mother's gifts were trimmed baskets, some with beads inside.

Mountain grass [115] was gathered at Skokomish in the old days, but, if they had the chance, it was best gathered in August on Mt Rainier, when mountain berries were also {50 mmd} ripe. People traded a dress, cloth, or skirt for it.

Cedar bark was dyed red with alder, or black by burying it in mud. Rusty cans, stove lids, and old rusty kettles were also used to dye cedar bark {50 mmd}. Mountain grass was dyed yellow by soaking it overnight in boiled Oregon grape bark {79 ph?}. Special dyes were gotten from Taholah (Quinault).

Chehalis

By 1927, people used a store bought coloring (Diamond brand name), but such commercial dye did not fix as well with sweet grass as it did with raffia. In 1927, baskets were made and traded for cloth, household goods, curtains, or maybe a chair. Chehalis made a modern basket of mountain grass, woven over ribs of cattails and covered with designs all over.

A twined market basket was made of white sweet grass by Mrs Williams, who used cedar bark with mountain grass over a bottom of raffia on back {95 mpw}.

Basketry designs were passed down in families. Women did not dream or envision new ones {189 md}.

Pets

Dogs and horses were native pets before whites came with cats {48 ph}. Other people said that the first horse came from the French and was seen at Tenino, brought by the Nisqually from the Yakamas {368 ds, 129 ly}.

The Hecks had a pet raccoon, which begged for food and was treated like a person {192 md}. Young beavers were also kept, but not bear cubs because they were too mean. Children used to catch a mud puppy (water dog, salamander), dress it, and put it on a tiny cradleboard like a baby.

Every single bone of the first fish caught each Spring was carefully placed in the fire so animals could not eat them {119 ly}. In the fall, some families mashed Chinook salmon bones and mixed them with berries to eat like hash.

A dog howling at night meant that someone was going to die. People did not like the sound {287 ph}.

Dogs and babies talked to each other. Dogs were like people and so could eat the bones of hunted elk and deer {380 js}.

Youcktons made pets of young deer, beaver, wild cat, and owl {119 ly}.

Sky

Movements of the stars and sun were used to tell the time and seasons.

A piece of star broke off and plunged into the earth to make Grand Mound {59 md}. Some stars were people before the earth capsized. The dipper was an elk with three or four people and a little dog hunting after it.

A falling star is off to meet a lover. A comet meant the world was close to ending.

Morning [Moon] was a baby stolen by two women at Lequito and taken west before being rescued by Bluejay to become the Moon {58 md}. His brother became the Sun. Everything bad was burned {386 js}. This is the story of the founding of the chiefly lines {345 js}.

Rainbow was never pointed at {275 ph}.

Earth

Shooting an arrow at night was dangerous because a boy might hit the eye of the earth, who would pinch and kill him by winking {153 md}. When the earth winked its eye, a life was shortened [crushed].

Chehalis

FOODS

The best food providers remained celibate or chaste during a fish run or hunt {166 md}.

Salmon

First Spring or Chinook salmon was cooked and eaten by all the men on the Cowlitz {11 mi}. All the bones are returned to the middle of the river and told to say "I got hurt" so all the other salmon would come to show concern, just like adults do when a child said this. To feed everyone, to stretch the first salmon, beef, sausages, cakes, and doughnuts were also served. Cowlitz now gather together for first wild strawberries, blackberries, huckleberries, and spring greens.

Upper Chehalis cooked the first salmon as soup in a large kettle {28 ph}. It was always cooked by a man, never a woman.

For Lucy Youckton {117 ly}, first salmon was cooked with dried camas and served in a small wooden dish on a cedarbark mat. Everyone invited brought a spoon to eat some of this soup. Old women came, but not girls.

Along certain sections of the river, the salmon had to be cut in specific ways. They always cut along the backbone and spread the flesh to the side. Sometimes, the flanks were cut up to the tail and hung on either side of a pole to dry. Once dry, the fins had to be cut off or the flesh would sour.

Women dried the fish over a slow fire, then packed it in cedarbark or cattail open-work baskets. Sometimes, the fish was packed carefully, layer by layer, at an end of the house. Dried salmon was soaked overnight before it was cooked. The tail piece was fed to children in hopes they would marry a chief and become well off. It was the poorest part of the fish and so acted as a reverse prayer. Peter Heck thought that it was also an excuse for the elders to be greedy and eat the best parts.

Backbones were dried separately, often for soup or mashed flavoring. Salmon heads were cooked on sticks propped around a fire. In 1927, heads were dried on strings. Salmon eggs were dried loose over fine mesh rack or inside a fish bladder, sewn fish skin, or deer stomach {51 md}. Dried eggs were mostly eaten in the spring with mouthfuls of peeled salmonberry shoots. Only the blood, gills, and intestines were not used.

Fresh salmon was propped open like a butterfly and roasted between split sticks like tongs.

People at Grand Mound never fished in the Chehalis River, instead taking good, fat silversides from Scatter Creek in December. Boys were sent up toward Tenino to watch for the high water that marked the run. These salmon stayed there until spring. This arrival was so sudden that a man who lived with his grandmother accidentally cut open his stomach and died while in a hurry whittling a spear to get the first of the run {31 ph}. Since then people have prepared well in advance, taking care that the salmon leader got up safely, so all the others would follow {148 sh}.

A crooked nose salmon had to be well treated because it was dangerous. In the towns of the salmon beyond the horizon, the smoke from this fish's house comes out crooked {250 ph}.

Black and red salmon runs can be forced downriver by putting smashed blood and eggs into the water {186 md}.

Chehalis

Fish

Smelt [1568] had to eaten whole, but it was taboo to eat the tail. The fish got mad if you were local and cleaned it {5 mi}. If you took off the head, guts, and bones, smelt would kill you. If you were a stranger, the fish were tolerant.

Smelt were caught in a net {119 ly}. If someone ate just smelts, they would die with something like puke coming out of their nose, ears, and mouth unless a doctor came to cure them. Smelt had to be mixed with berries or camas, maybe some Chinook salmon oil {120 ly}.

Flounders were also taken from Mud Bay by searching the bottom with the feet. In the old days, a sharp stick was kept between the toes to hook [impale] the fish. They were good in June {107 ph}.

Eels go upriver at night. Any who travel by day were no good. They were caught below Dryad at the dark of the moon using a pitch torch, mostly in April when the new leaves came {102 ph}. They were caught by hand, with 5 fern roots on each palm for traction, and bitten below the eyes to snap the backbone. The use of knives was forbidden. Eels were dried on sticks, up to 10 on each. In August, eels were big and spotted. Eels were sometime caught from a platform built across the river.

Eels wanted to be cooked with the head off [for Taitnapam ?]. The cut off heads were roasted on sticks. If you throw a head far off, it will live for a long time. If you throw it close, it dies quickly {5 mi}. Mary Iley's father never ate eels because they were like his power. From Oakville up the Chehalis River, the stick was put through the eel's mouth; maybe from Oakville downriver, the stick was put through the neck {38 ph}.

Eel oil was used to soften and water proof moccasins.

Sturgeon were bad luck to see {11 mi}, but its flesh was eaten near the mouth of the Cowlitz. They come up as far as Kelso naturally, where they used a bait of smelt and salmon, but they can be seen as a bad omen anywhere.

Dried sturgeon was traded from Bay Center or Grays Harbor. [Famous sturgeon hunters were Putsenay, a Hoquiam shaman, and Cosmopolis Pete.]

Shellfish

Chehalis got clams from Mud Bay, dug by both men and women, dried over a fire on a stick, then strung on cedarbark for transport and storage. Oysters and mussels were eaten fresh, not dried {107 ph}.

Hides

Cougar, badger, and mountain beaver fur was buried so the grease would soak in and then knitted into blankets, each worth one slave or much of a bride price {8 mi}. Elk skins were traded for bison hides. Blankets were made of squares of bear or beaver fur {5 mi}.

Whole elk skins were used to wrap a body for burial or reburial. A tough elk hide was used to test the strength of a boy's hunting power. If his arrow went through, he would succeed {114 gs}.

Deer hides were smoked [smudged] through in half an hour, but most were left for half a day {167 md}. Saved brains were mashed and mixed with hot water to soak into the hide.

Chehalis

Meat

A hunter had to have proper power and respect it by taking sweat baths and rubbing his body with cedar or fir boughs {114 gs}. He could not eat fresh meat before hunting. In August, all the hunters in a place might agree to go on an elk hunt for several days. A boy went along as messenger. They got enough for a whole winter supply on one trip, killing up to 20 elk.

Seal meat and oil-filled stomachs were traded from the Harbor, and eaten with dried sturgeon {284 ph}. Seal oil was drunk only by Taholah Quinault, Lower Chehalis, and Bay Center Chinook {130 ly}.

Pits were dug into trails to catch [trap] deer or elk. Fences were built for deer drives {78 ph}.

A hunter sang his spirit song before starting out.

Elks were hunted in the fall along the North River. Many small hunting canoes were left there for men to use {79 ph?}. They were also hunted along the Satsop, the Skookumchuck, and in the mountains near Boisfort {335 ph}

Deer were butchered by removing the skin, cutting off the legs, taking out the insides, saving the blood, and slicing up the flesh to eat then or to dry. Liver, heart, lungs were saved {51, 166 md}. A piece of the deer was burned in a fire for his spirit before the rest was eaten. Mary Heck's husband would burn the ears {151 sh}. Bones were cracked with stone maul for their marrow. Blood and fat was used for soup, along with backbone segments. Meat from the head was only eaten by men or old ladies. Brains were saved and used for tanning.

Bears were butchered in the same way. Their blood was made into a soup. Hides and grease were used, but the meat was rarely eaten because it was strictly a personal preference.

Before a woman recited dicta [power words], she rubbed bear oil on her hands and touched the afflicted body part she wanted to relieve {183 md}.

Bear skulls could be placed as a path by someone with power so a stream or river would then make a shortcut {183 md}.

If a wounded bear attacked a hunter and he squealed like a woman, high and shrill, the bear would not harm him. If he screamed like a man, he would be maimed ("chawed") or killed. It was best to shoot a bear through the heart {190 md}.

Tanned bearskins were traded from the Mossyrocks and Yakamas.

Skunk grease was used to treat a boil or headache. This meat was sometimes roasted and eaten.

Mountain rat intestines were cooked and eaten in the fall when they ate grass.

Chipmunks were eaten by Taitnapam, but Chehalis children only used them for hunting practice {252 ph}.

Beaver meat was a favorite boiled {23 ph}.

Elk tallow from the foreleg was like candy {335 ph}, but Silas Heck preferred that from the thigh. It was also used to keep the face from chapping and for greasing guns.

Not eaten in the old days were dog, rabbit, muskrat, fox, wolf, mole, nor mice {254 ph}.

Chehalis

Birds

Eggs of duck, pheasant, and grouse were eaten {107 ph}.

Mallards were hunted at Chehalis with bow and arrow, later guns, and then roasted or boiled. Black ducks only came to Mud Bay.

A net, over 10 feet high, was hung across a riffle for ducks and geese. People ate the meat and saved the feathers for pillows and blankets. The five duck feathers worn by women with a certain spirit were selected at that time. Duck-wing feathers were good for arrows {191 md}.

Pheasants [actually native grouse] were snared while drumming on a log (mating), lured by a decoy made of moss. The bird became jealous of a rival and choked in the noose {108 ph}.

Crows, bluejay, or smaller birds were never eaten.

Thrush brought the rain so if one was killed and thrown in the river, it would storm.

Hummingbird nests brought luck. If a hummingbird hovered around a girl, the old people said it was measuring her for a dowry. The buzzing meant "one string, two strings, and so on."

Yellowhammer (a flicker woodpecker) feathers were used on boys' arrows {292 ph}.

Cranes or storks [a local term though these are introduced species] used to nest at Grand Mound and the Nisqually Delta {189 md}. They flew in a V led by a captain. Children ran underneath them praying, "Leave me a big salmon backbone," so their families would not starve that winter.

Larks were avoided because if a child struck one, he or she would never stop quarreling. A quarrelsome woman was called a lark {251 ph}.

Pigeon, called "crying bird," was eaten but not preferred. The very first one was a person who lost all his children and cried and cried until he became a bird.

Eagles were killed for feathers. A big doctor always had on a fine wing feather from an eagle. Eagle spirit was good for hunting, gambling, curing, and war.

Hawk was the leader of all the birds so people left it alone.

Plants

Berry patches were burned over every two or three years to get a continuing good crop {73, 79 ph, 124 ly}.

Berries were picked into baskets lined with leaves {96 mpw}. Each fall, everyone went to pick in the mountains. Old women picked the first ones and held a feast. After everyone brought their dried berries back home, more feasts were held, served out of wooden troughs {132 js}.

Red elderberries were "canned" in soft baskets shingled with layers of maple leaves {270 ph} and kept fresh by being submerged in a slough, where thieves sometimes poked for them.

Raspberries and blackberries were made into a dried cake that was sliced during the winter.

A girl about to become M1 held a "bridle" stick, loosely tied behind her neck, in her mouth, while picking berries so she could not eat any. Old women later inspected the stick for stains, just to be sure {140 sh}.

Chehalis

Strawberries were so abundant at Grand Mound that you could smell them drying on a hot day.

Only women dug and prepared roots, while the men gambled or raced on foot or horses {69 ph}.

Sword [probably bracken] fern roots were used for medicine, and ground up for flour. Fronds were used to spread out berries to dry or for wrapping camas to roast. The roots were charred, scraped, pounded up, and sometimes mixed with salmon eggs, or baked overnight in a pit {127 ly}.

Wild rhubarb, carrots, camas, and sunflower roots were baked for storage. Wild sunflowers, growing at Rochester and Grand Mound, were sometimes used to make a sort of root beer. Tiger lily roots were gathered from prairies in the fall and boiled {56 md}.

Acorns were gathered, baked in a pit, and eaten with salmon eggs. Some were buried in the mud over the winter. They were bitter if the tannin was not leached out.

Nuts were collected in the fall, but people had to be careful to say "There is just one nut" in front of a treeful or the crop would disappear.

Camas or lackamas were dug from marshes, steam baked in a pit, and dried or ground up for storage {72 ph}. Often camas was baked overnight, mashed into a loaf, and dried to be sliced up during the winter. Blackberry cakes were used the same way {69 ph}. A M1 gave her next dug camas to an old woman for luck, otherwise she would be eating up [shortening] her own life.

Spruce roots were dug up for making baskets.

Willow roots were ground up fine to make tinder for starting fires {124 ly}, and the inner bark began to be used for basket trim, dyed black, instead of using rope or a quick, convenient twine.

Wild cherry bark was used for a tough binding, especially on salmon spears {190 md}.

Alder bark was chewed to make an orange-red dye. In 1927, though, people did not want to chew it, so they pounded it with a hammer and soaked it in water {183 md}.

Moss was gathered and cleaned to use as diaper stuffing {125 ly}. Catnip leaves were put on a baby's head to make it sleepy.

Blossoms and flowers were to be avoided by children because they were said to belong to the ghosts {132 js} because they bloomed in the spring when ghosts were leaving and so could take a soul away {140 sh}. [In other words, spring flowers came as ghosts were leaving and so could "hand off" a soul, particularly that of a vulnerable child.] New cedar saplings were the same way. If berries had a second crop or lasted into the winter, these too belonged to the ghosts.

Lilies and wild cherry blossoms were people long ago who transformed in a graveyard {325 mi}. Early white lilies were the worst [most dangerous] {325 mi}.

Seasonal Work Parties

In the spring, everyone fished the runs and dried salmon for the winter. They used weirs, traps, nets, gaffs, spears, and arrows. The nets were made from nettle fiber and were dyed to match the water color of a stream. During the summer, they harvested roots, berries, and nuts. Men went hunting in the fall, particularly for elk, then for deer and bear. During the winter, families holed up in plank house towns.

Chehalis

Families owned weir sites. The Sanders built theirs at Klaber below Ceres {115 gs}. One man could put it up alone after they had axes and saws. In the old days, they needed a work party, treated to a big feast, and all could thereafter share in the catch. The weir was built with many small poles of maple or fir tied with cedar or hazel. A 25-foot cottonwood braced the back. A shaman blessed the finished construction. Builders used it beneficially in turn, but others had to return some of their catch to the group.

Houses were also built by work parties. The ground was dug out and leveled before the bunks and walls were built inside the depression. Racks were constructed along the sides to hold mats, foods, and goods. Planks were made from cedar using elk-horn wedges, yew wood mauls, and stone hammers, preferably by someone with carpenter power. Then the planks were adzed and planed, before floating down the river to the construction site. Sometimes, the wood was gathered in the spring, seasoned all summer, and used in the fall.

The chief looked over the building to make sure it did not impose on others. The house should reflect the status, position, and class of the owner. At Grand Mound, the town went across the prairie to the present state [reform] school. Sanders had a "living room" house there, and another for cures "like a church." White homesteaders later destroyed these house remains.

In February, everyone had to be very still, all loud activities were forbidden and taboo {206 mh?}.

SOCIETY

RANKINGS (Social Classes)

Like other nations of the Northwest, Upper Chehalis recognized the three social classes of royal chiefs, commoners, and slaves. The first two were freeborn, but not the third. High chiefs, low chiefs, commoners, and slaves might be further distinguished {360 js}.

Royal Chiefs [20 'als]

Chiefs were royal in the old days. Their line was founded by Moon while he was on earth. Sometimes they were called **taiyiman** from the Chinook jargon word for chief or leader, **tyee**. No matter how much money a person had, they could not be a chief, "not in their hearts." A chief was born not made. A chief, first and foremost, kept things going smoothly within the tribe and dealt with outsiders whenever they came. He had to be smart, know about all the families in the region, and speak many languages {372 ds}.

People gave things, food and presents, to a good chief so he never had to work hard. He was always fed and given the most at gatherings like feasts and marriages. Fur blankets, dentalia shells, and canoes were important gifts, then later horses and trade blankets {364 ds}. A chief also owned and managed a fish weir or trap to feed his people.

The chief told people to be friendly and not go against one another. If someone building a house needed help, the chief would ask people to assist {50 md}. After a murder, the chief was the judge deciding on the compensation that would make it even with the victim's family. If the chief could not decide or the families agree, then the murderer or someone in his family was killed to resolve this family feud, provided both victims were of the same class and rank.

Chehalis

A murderer had to fast and swim to purify himself or he would die. He would only hold a bite of food in his mouth briefly before spitting it out {274 ph} during 10 days. He would drink only a tiny amount of water. While he was fasting, his own family negotiated compensation and settlement with the family of the victim. The best go-betweens were royals.

Chief also punished thieves. After whites came, a chief could order someone lashed. A jury of wise men helped the chief decide. Of course, if a family did not like the decision, they might hire a doctor to work sorcery to get revenge {274 ph}.

When a chief died, everyone mourned as he was buried in a big canoe. The chief would inherit from a father, an uncle, or a brother. A younger brother might also inherit the wives of the dead chief. Sometimes, the brother was just a regent for his nephew, the chief's son.

A chief lived in a big house with his many wives and owned slaves, who lived "like dogs" without regular sleeping places. Slaves were taken in raids or sold far from home, unless they could be ransomed back by their family {85 ph}. Peter Heck's mother's aunt was ransomed from Skokomish (Snohomish ?) warriors at Port Madison [Suquamish] and cleansed with a potlatch. The children of slaves remained slaves, unless someone royal took pity and freed them. Slaves who married royals had the "taint" washed off with a potlatch, but, behind their backs, people still insulted them, saying they gave their family "bad blood" {256 ph}.

Slaves

Slaves could get spirit power or be doctors, but their owners could take their pay. A fine fur blanket was worth one slave in the old days. A famous chief, *YuliltitsL*, at Grand Mound, had 40 slaves because he was so kind, and they asked him to buy them. He also saved two early white men from frostbite.

A chief wanted his slaves to work so he sold the lazy ones. Slave women wore their hair in a bob. They dried salmon like other women. Slaves were treated well as long as they worked. When they died, their bodies were put out of the way but not otherwise buried or mourned {392 js}.

A slave was known by the name of his or her own tribe. An enslaved Snohomish was called "snohomish" {243 ph}. They never had a personal name or a separate identity.

Peter Heck's grandfather had five slaves, three men and two women. He sold four of them before he died, but kept a young woman to take came of Heck's father while he grew up. She did this faithfully until she died of smallpox {268 ph}.

Generosity

A chief had to marry a daughter from another royal family, often of another tribe. One of Yawnish's daughters even married east of the mountains among the Yakama. She was one of the very few to marry so far away. Mostly royals married along the coast. A chief gave presents to "buy" a foreign wife, but a commoner did not {362 ds}. They just "lived together" and probably even belonged to the same tribe.

A chief hosted potlatches, and a big chief had a special house built for his own lavish potlatches. John Heyden had the last one built, about 1875, for a potlatch celebrating the piercing of his daughter's ears {70 ph, 130 ly}. A chief from another tribe made the holes for this royal daughter when she was about 10. Many people came from all over Puget Sound.

Chehalis

About $1500 was given away. This potlatch lasted five days. Jim and Charlie Walker helped Heyden with the expense.

A name was usually given to that person when their ears were pierced. For royals, these were famous inherited names. Sometimes, a power gave spirit names to a father before the children were even born [cf Lushootseed Press volume on Susie Sampson Peter].

Children of chiefs were royal and carefully treated. As infants their foreheads were flattened with pressure to mark them for life {85 ph}. One woman kept her daughter secluded in a box [cubicle] until her marriage so she would be much honored. Slave women watched and guarded her all the time. Royal children were raised to have a good character and to speak well.

Other potlatches were for a reburial or to renew a grave. The body was removed so new clothes, new gifts, or a new casket could be supplied.

A royal woman could not be chief, but she took charge of the other women and knew about picking berries and digging camas. Only men were chiefs. Royal women managed female activities, while their women slaves did the hard work for the chief's household.

Class Examples

The Upper Chehalis chief was *Yawnish*, who was born and buried at Grand Mound. He held a class to teach stories to boys and told people what was right to do. Yawnish did not have much money because he had many children to feed from the young woman he married after his first wife died {268 ph}. He was a "Boston man" who only had one wife at a time. His house was behind the old school at Oakville.

John Heyden had the bones of Yawnish, Queen Susan, and Lizzie Johnson's sister reburied in a single coffin at Grand Mound {130 ly}. Yawnish and Queen Susan were brother and sister. Heyden was their nephew.

Tsinitiya was an important chief before Yawnish {268 ph}. He had many wives from all over, including Cowlitz, Nisqually, and Astoria. He had many slaves. He subsidized young men when he went gambling. His son was *Ananit'x*, a drinker who was murdered at the Harbor by a jealous husband. [State court records say he was killed for siding with the Indian agent.] After Tsinitiya died, a son became chief before Yawnish succeeded him.

Teninos and Cowlitz had their own chiefs. Black Rivers had a little chief of their own, but were under Yawnish for overall advice. Same applied for little chiefs at Oakville and Skookumchuck {112 gs}.

Syk'amen ("light") was a common man who lived between Chehalis and Satsop, moving by canoe. He had three wives who had separate beds in the same house. When he died about 1900, only one wife was alive after the government took the others away from him.

Chehalis

LIFE CYCLE
Birth

Unborn babies came from the sunrise in the east {98 ph}, traveling through the air along the path of sunlight {141 sh}. [Tillamook of the Oregon coast also had a belief in a land of unborn babies, where they lived and even married waiting to be born.] While the dead lived in the west, the unborn lived in the east. Anyone could see the fire of the dead, but only a spirit could see the dead themselves or help a doctor to see them. People also felt when ghosts were nearby. Peter Heck's father once rushed home from winter hunting near Independence when he sensed the dead.

Pregnant parents should not look at anything deformed or suffering because their baby might come out that way {132 js}. A mother ate slowly and carefully to keep the baby safely small. These parents could not be lazy, working all the time to stay fit and strong {113 gs}. The woman never ate anything that stuck to the sides of a pot or paused in doorways for that would delay the impending birth. A few months before delivery, the mother began drinking a wild rose infusion (of boiled bark) to speed the birth.

The baby was born in a separate hut, assisted by a midwife or kinswoman. The mother squatted with hands on the ground. To make a baby turn before delivery, the mother held her breath and shifted her stomach. Two rocks were struck beside the baby's ears just after birth to make sure it will always hear. The newborn was washed in cold water, sprinkled with ashes, and wrapped in rabbit fur or a soft blanket {3 mi}. For the next year, the baby was carried in a cradleboard, made by the father, to make it grow straight. If freeborn, the baby's forehead was weighted and flattened as a mark of class.

Mother and baby were secluded. Taitnapams waited five days {2 mi}, Chehalis waited ten days with a girl and nine with a boy. Anyone could go near a baby boy, but only women went near a girl baby. The place of seclusion was heated by hot rocks in a deep hole, covered with ferns to steam and smell nice. New hot rocks were added twice a day. The mother's breasts were held over this steam, and rubbed with white moss or shells to improve the milk. The baby nursed on demand, but the new mother still did not eat anything fresh, raw, or bloody.

Bands of wildcat skin, put around the woman's abdomen two months into the pregnancy to hold it tight and keep the baby small, were cut and retied to help her belly to heal. The umbilical cord was cut but not tied. When the stump fell off, it was put into a beaded buckskin bag, sometimes hung from its cradleboard. Taitnapams gave it to the child at about the age of ten to take into the woods and tie to a little fir tree. [This made the child close to nature and "fresh air".] Chehalis burned it completely to ashes.

The afterbirth was put into a tree with an offering of beads or buttons. That of a boy was placed higher than that of a girl {224 mmd}, but if it was too high the child would want to climb all the time. The offerings "paid" the afterbirth to keep the child from getting "silly" or hurt. Some families buried the afterbirth. [Though unstated, Chehalis, like other tribes, probably placed the afterbirth and cord in a place that would benefit the character of that child, such as, a tree for a hunter.]

According to Chehalis, the mongoloid spot at the base of a newborn was caused by the afterbirth hitting the fetus because it was lazy being born {246 ph}. An old woman might use dicta to speed a birth, but men did not know such formulae. If a baby did not arrive after two or four days, a native doctor was summoned.

A Greyback Louse went to "heaven" to report each birth {276 ph} and decide if its arrival would be marked with good or bad weather.

While a first birth was supervised, at later births the mother was alone. Mary Iley was splitting wood when she went into labor, gave birth, fixed the fire, dressed the baby, rested near the stove, and got fresh milk for the baby's older brother. The baby was enticed ("primed," like a pump) to suck with warmed bear grease rubbed on the mouth. Children could be nursed until they were three or four years old. While they were nursing, women did not menstruate or conceive {126 ly}.

An unmarried royal girl killed her baby because she could never raise a bastard. She should have aborted it to avoid scandal.

A baby who was someone reborn would have marks, usually on the earlobes or at the locations of grandparent's scars {141 sh}. A chief was always reborn since they were trained never to die, always returning among their own descendants {340 js}. Mrs Davis noted that her own eldest daughter seems to have been reborn in her son's daughter, and they intend to give her aunt's name to the grand daughter {226 mmd}. If the person had come back into another but related family, they would give another name.

The new father used the sweat house for two or three days. The new mother went to the sweat house for two days after her 10 day seclusion with a daughter or for one day after her 9 days with a son. If a father wanted his baby son to be a hunter, he hung a tiny bow and arrows from the rim of the cradleboard {138 sh}.

The baby was massaged to shape it. For boys, shoulders and legs were stretched. For girls, the nose was squeezed, cheeks pressed downward, foot arch indented, and buttocks lifted. Some families prayed to Thrush while doing this {246 ph}. Babies were bathed morning and night. A slow growing baby had very cold water poured over its buttocks to cause a growth spurt.

A cranky baby was bathed in cold water and wrapped up warmly to sleep. A neglected baby became sickly and a special doctor had to go to the land of the unborn in the east and coax its soul back [cf Chehalis]. It wandered away along the earth, leaving tracks to be followed, and then flew at tree height (or as high as its afterbirth was located in a tree?). The doctor sang a song that slowed or halted the baby along the way. If the baby stopped to listen, it would be cured; if not, it died.

Twins

Instead of calling twins [527] two babies, Chehalis used the term for "wolf" [1469] since these canines had double litters {3 mi, 60 md, 104 ph}. Twins were fragile and rarely lived to become adults, unless they were boy and girl. Cowlitz had a word for twins, but also called them "wolf" or "cougar" [2129].

Training

Children of a household were made to get up early and swim, diving away from the bank so they will have plenty in life {105 ph}. An old man was their trainer. If their legs were not red when they stood beside the fire after bathing in cold water, he hit them with a paddle or stick and covered them with cold ashes to make them go and plunge again. They were told "not to lie to their own life." They swam for a long life, good luck, and a good home.

Children played together when small, but after they got to be ten and started questing, boys and girls stayed apart. A boy, rarely a girl, was given a stick to take to some remote place and leave in hopes of encountering a spirit. The trainer went there to make sure the stick had been left and the boy did not cheat. Sometimes the quester was expected to pile stones at a spot to prove he or she had been there. Important spirits lived where there were no other people. While spirits visited humans in the mundane world, they did not give power then.

Teachings

Every evening in good families, children heard "teachings," mostly about being helpful and energetic, particularly with the elderly {4 mi}. "Help out, wherever and whenever you can! When you visit, do housework, split firewood, or get water. Eat whatever is put in front of you. If a woman is making a basket and leaves the room, work on the basket to help her. Also, when you are host, give people good food and a nice time."

People will know the character of children and say, "Here comes that bad one or that good one. Coaxing made a child good. Never make fun of anything or anyone. Never laugh at what you do not understand." A child who listened and obeyed all the teachings led a long and rewarding life.

Children could not eat food stored for over a year or they would become deaf {132 js}. They should be good to all elders in the hope that a grandparent or other oldster would promise them "Since you have been good to me, I will leave my soul to you when I die so that you can live a long time." This made the child proud {262 ph}.

Children were sent to visit relatives when they were old enough to have sense and learn about their relations. They might stay a long time, sometimes years. Even strangers were welcome as long as they helped out with food and chores.

Teachings were like the Ten Commandments, but involved all the world of living things. The Earth listened and punished those who did not live right. After hearing a story, children had to swim {54 md}.

Stamina

Some boys were sent out to run naked in hail, rain, and thunder storms to get a strong power and make them hearty, tough, and healthy. They swam where it was cold, but not icy because "ice" also meant "very poor" and was an ill omen. Whenever a boy got home from a cold quest, he could sleep beside the fire.

When snow accumulated on trees, boys and girls charged through them to get cold, wet, and tough. The boldest did this 5 times, although it was very grueling.

Boys and men practiced weight lifting with boulders. Some, as at Lequito, were specially prepared. Towns or tribes would challenge each other at weight lifting, foot racing, or wrestling. Later, people learned boxing and horse racing.

Chehalis

Questing

A questing boy bathed at least every morning and evening, if not more frequently {56 md}. A boy who did not sweat, bathe, or swim was considered dirty and "full of sin." A clean body attracted a spirit because it could see the heart of someone pure and clear. To get a powerful one, boys dove into deep water holding heavy rocks. Diving was an act of courage and daring. To be successful, diving had to be done 5 times. In the salt water, a boy rubbed his arms, legs, neck, and back against the edge of the canoe to chafe the skin before diving {192 md, 260 ph}. Older women also chafed the boy's skin to increase their ordeal.

One old man insisted that his grandson dive near Olympia, but sharks ate him {259 ph}. Desire was not enough, a family had to know about using supernatural protection to safeguard its novice questers.

Over a decade after a power was acquired, the man or woman sang in public during the winter. People then were sure that they had a spirit power. In some cases, a young man would prove this by telling hunters where they could find a deer or other game to kill and serve to that gathering. The spirit provided this meat to the people who helped the man to sing and announce his power. Finally, goods and gifts (like beads, clothes, and cloth) hung along the inside walls were given out to the guests {161 md}.

Later in life, a family member might inherit the spirit of a close relative. Silas Heck felt his father's Wolf hunting power following him after his father died in 1915 {138 sh}, but he rejected it because he was a Shaker. Similarly, at Little Rock, Peter Heck saw their own father's hunting spirit as an ugly woman wearing five duck feathers in her hair. A spirit can best be inherited when someone already has another spirit to help welcome and control the new one.

A family might take revenge by imposing one of its spirits as a "chronic" inheritance in another family, where it was unknown, unexpected, and potentially very lethal.

When he was 18, Mary Heck's grandfather died in an epidemic and was buried inside a bark house near Grand Mound. His Bluejay spirit brought him back and gave him the ability to go to the Land of the Dead, recovering souls. After 10 days, his mother went out to weep at his grave and found him. He told her he had gone to a big gathering of the dead, but he was naked, so his own father sent him back.

Mask

Taitnapams had a mask like a **psa** danger. If a child was mean, nasty, or always crying, someone would put on this bark mask of an old woman (Basket Ogress ?) and scare the child into behaving properly. Once the child saw her, men tried to catch her to drive her out of the house. The person who wore the mask was paid with dried camas, berries, or fruit.

M1

Menstruation first started when some girls made fun of an old man bleeding from the eyes. They laughed at him. He wiped off the blood, threw it at them, and, everafter, women have had their monthlies.

When a girl became M1, she was taken to a hut near the house for five months. She wore a hood "blinder," with dangling noise makers like deer dew claws, shells, or bells, to warn others away {122 ly}. She could not look at small children because they were weak and vulnerable to her power {31 ph}, which might detach their souls {54 md}. The M1 could only look down because paralysis was usually a sign that an M1 had looked, deliberately or inadvertently, at that future invalid {169 md}. While the girl was isolated, often for the first time in her life, she was never entirely alone since older women watched out for her, using protective dicta. If she needed help and no one was near, she pounded on a board. She must never shout or cause any disturbance.

A man at Satsop had a magical bow and arrow that made the elk drop dead by merely holding it up {95 mpw}. When his daughter became an M1 and went into seclusion, a Lower [?] Chehalis shaman decided to steal this girl and punish her father for either lying or bragging. But when the shaman got to that man's house, he found elk lying all over and everyone drying meat.

A girl could only eat dried salmon, fresh camas, or anything else from the ground because that came from the work of woman. She could not eat anything fresh or bloody without risking a hunter's luck or her own welfare. She must never drink from flowing water or she would die of consumption when her heart flooded with blood {325 mi}.

A girl who was prepared for the onset of M1 found a white tree out on a prairie and painted it red to highlight her readiness. She also put red paint along the part of her own hair. Her father had a bed of cedar boughs inside a bark-covered hut all ready for her {117 ly}, with a new fire made inside. This fire could never be brought from a house, it had to be started fresh for the M1 {203 mh?}.

At M1, a girl's face and lower arm, especially fingers, were painted bright red. She wiped this paint off with shredded cedarbark each time before she bathed, which often meant wading into water shoulder deep. She rubbed hard to scour her skin and toughen it. If she bathed at a place that was dangerous with **psa**, women used dicta to calm them. Once, a woman painted and named three rocks for the water dog **psa** who lived at a place in the Chehalis River.

To keep track of five day intervals, M1 wore five cedar bands around her right wrist, removing one each day before swimming {126 ly}. A new mother did the same thing, using 5 knots in a deerskin cord and untying a knot each day. Some girls wore tight garters at wrists, ankles, and below the knees {203 mh?}. Some wore a tight belt to lessen hunger pains.

To scratch her hair and tend it, each M1 used a tip of horn, a sharp stick, or a comb either of lashed together twigs or carved of alderwood. Unlike other tribes, she had no drinking tube, which was only used by the very sick.

The M1 worked hard, often preparing fibers and making both soft and hard baskets. She gave these baskets to old women so they would pray that she have a long life.

Often, an M1 stayed secluded for five months, but some took a whole year {117 ly}. M1 never ate fresh fish nor meat, only dry camas, dry berries, dry seeds, or dry roots according to the Taitnapam. A Cowlitz M1 also ate fern-root mush.

If M1 came during berry picking season, the girl wore a bridle, a white peeled stick kept between her teeth, so she could stay busy by helping to pick but did not eat any berries. The stick bridle was inspected each evening to make sure there were no berry stains. If she ate any fresh berries, her reckless use of power endangered the harvest for the next year.

Salal berries were a **psa** to an M1 because they belonged to ghosts, who used the longest stems for canoes {204 mh?}. It was χaχaaʔ [sacred and forbidden] to eat them while an M1.

Seclusions should last 10 days for the first and second times, then five days thereafter. For monthlies that lasted two days, women stayed in a hut three nights {7 mi}. Younger women secluded for each monthly, but older women usually just stayed quiet at home.

Chehalis

Change of life [menopause, *siatsnaw/,* **syaćnaw**] came at about the age of 50.

Mary Iley's M1

When Mary Iley began to menstruate {3 mi}, she was scared and hid until her sister found her, saying "Do not touch your hair. Bend it up and out of the way. Put something over your head like a hood. Stay small. Do not lie down. Do not stretch. Stay compact."

Mary continued, "I made a tiny fire with lots of pitch. Like other Cowlitz and Taitnapam, I made ?? *saletcvn* [seclusion ?]. My hair was braided, looped, and wrapped with buckskin. Beads were tied on the ends. I could not touch my hair or head or I would get headaches. My mother or aunts combed my hair. My father made me two sharp scratching sticks, and I wore them suspended on a long necklace of beads. My face and arms to the elbows were painted red. Someone painted me this way every day.

"I stayed warm and fasting for five days, then bathed. Every morning, I bathed and rubbed myself with five little bundles (half a palm in size) of hemlock sprouts until only sticks remained. This scouring kept hair from growing over my body. I was not supposed to drink, but I got thirsty on the third day. My mother said I had to eat before I could drink.

"I finally slept on the third night and ate on the fourth day. I ate dried rice, a bit of sugar, and two dried pancakes. I ate the same on the fifth day. If I had lasted the full five days, I would have been strong.

"I stayed out of the house for two months. I never saw my little brother or any other small child. The last five days, mother made me pack firewood and pile it beside the house. I kept busy so I would never be lazy.

"For five months, I wore a hood so I could not see the stars or the Moon. I stayed shy. I only looked at girls, never any males. Men were afraid of M1. I never ate fresh salmon or bloody meat. My food had to be roasted on a stick and then dried. I could eat fresh berries because they were women's work.

"If I had to wade across a stream (even though I was forbidden to go near running water) I threw dirt or dried leaves upstream so it would float down and hide my passing, otherwise the salmon would never return to that stream.

"After five months, I could eat fresh salmon. During every later monthly sickness, I went outside for five days, but after I married, my husband would not let me go out, so only one of my babies was born outside.

Names

Family names were inherited {6 mi}. Royal families owned important names and gave a feast and presents when each was bestowed in public, singing family songs to everyone.

Sometimes spirits gave names to someone before they were married or had children. Such a name would "warm up" the baby so it would get a good spirit and song later, like its parent {15 mi}. Tahmanawas names might not be potlatched since they were personal, unique, and specially given.

A doctor who could go to the Land of the Dead might be given a name for his or her child by a spirit ghost, perhaps to have its own former name continued {163 md}. Jack Knoodle was given such a name for his son George.

Chehalis

Mary Heck's father's spirit singled her out from her sisters to help him cure. Her spirit name was *misal&mx*, her name when she was young. She got another one when she married {395 ph}. If she wanted to "condemn" this name, so no one else could use it, she could take another final name for the end of her life {285 ph}. Mary Heck's husband, the father of Peter and Silas, was named *xekwim/* and then **kʷuqʷɬa** [336 B4], after his father's father.

At his wedding, Peter Heck was named **yanm** after his father's father, with the announcement that "the dead man has now returned" {82 ph}.

Some names were nicknames. George Jack was called "raven" to tease him. His father had three or four wives in a row like his Raven power {132 js}. Lena Heck was called "lake."

When someone died, the family might remove [retire] a word that was like that person's name. The dead were sacred so it was an insult to continue to use such words. For example, when a man died whose name was "ax," they made up a new word for this implement. When a woman died whose name sounded like "iron," they used the chinook jargon word *chickamin* for "metal, money, and iron" instead {37 ph}. The Lower Chehalis changed their name for "deer" to "jumper" or "grey face," because a man died whose name sounded like the old word {140 sh}.

After a few years have passed, they will bring back a name by giving it to someone in a younger generation of the family – a grandchild, nephew, or niece. Names were changed throughout life.

If a Chehalis woman was married at Quinault and wanted to give her grandfather's name to her new baby, "naturally" [of course] she came back to have that name called out among the Chehalis, who would hear it at a potlatch. Those who accepted gifts would be acknowledging as witnesses the bestowal of that name or giving up their own claims to it {140 sh}.

White names could also be inherited. Mucy Bill Simmons was the third one in his family with that name {140 sh}.

Some families even had names for their dogs or other pets {72 ph}.

Anyone could be insulted by calling them a "slave" in public {132 js}.

Marriage

Families exchanged goods at a wedding. The parents provided half of the gifts for their side, the other half coming from their relations {2 mi}. The exchange was not equal; the groom's side gave more then the bride's since she went home with them. Gifts were mats, blankets, baskets, elk skins, beads, and foods. The boy's family gave more household goods, and the girl's more foods. Important families gave slaves to help the new couple. Cowlitz gave horses {120 ly}.

The boy's parents began the negotiations for a marriage, and continued giving gifts for the duration of the marriage. When the husband's mother came to visit her inlaws, she wore a fine dress and hat, which she removed and gave to the other mother-in-law. The mothers-in-law should be like sisters, and the fathers-in-law like brothers.

Boys married after 15, girls after 10. A chief gave permission to marry into another tribe, but people had to be careful. Satsop and Skokomish women had "easy minds" and did not stay faithful {82 ph}.

When Taitnapam saw a boy who was a good hunter, they wanted to marry their daughters to him. People who were lively in work and life were preferred as spouses.

Chehalis

Important families would betroth their children while they were small to become inlaws. Personal likings were not important, only the family rankings. If a boy or girl were opposed to the match, he or she could only run away and hide. If a boy and girl were devoted to each other, they ran away and hoped for forgiveness after they had a child. When the couple returned decent and well-behaved, the parents gave gifts to each other and became inlaws. If one of the couple was a slave or low class, the parents never reconciled to the mating. People who married relatives, of whatever degree, were called "dogs" because they could not recognize their own relations {272 ph}. Brothers and sisters would sometimes swap or take spouses from each other {270 ph}.

Royals always married among themselves. By strict rule, they married until death. Chief Taholah at Quinault married the mother of Chief Masin from Scatter Creek {113 gs}. A royal wedding was expensive in order to show who the children were. Gifts from her family covered the path the bride walked between the two sides. After these were given away, the groom's family laid down more gifts along the same path for distribution. Then the families displayed their inherited dances and songs before giving new names to the bride and groom and hosting a big feast {120 ly}. Sometimes, hostilities were settled by having the offspring of the feuding chiefs marry, forging an alliance.

A common marriage signified only common children "born to the dust," while royal babies are "born on top of the heap" piled with treasures {272 ph}. Children of poor or slave families were called "bastards" because their "fathers were unknown" in that they had no pedigree or ancestry.

Before a marriage, the inlaws gathered to get to know each other. At the ceremony, the bride's side and the groom's side sat about 200 yards apart {364 ds}. Women of the bride's side tossed beads, blankets, and gifts for all to take. The bride, wearing a cap covered with beads and earrings down to her shoulders {3 mi}, was led across by two old women and seated on the groom's left side {82 ph}. Old women from his side removed the blanket hiding the bride, finalizing the marriage when the wife and husband actually saw each other.

The groom's side always gave more than the bride's because they took the woman home. If the families were royal, their chiefs spoke about the consideration needed for a good marriage. Inlaws exchanged food and gifts as long as the marriage lasted. After children were born, the families were linked and an aunt or uncle was expected to replace [re-wed] a spouse who died. A sister married a widower or a brother the widow so the children would be cared for by a relative who became a step-parent.

After a husband died, the wife was supposed to stay with his family and marry his brother or cousin. If she married a stranger, the prior children would always have trouble because they had no "real relatives." If the wife died, her sister, niece, or another girl in the family was expected to marry the widower. She felt it was a duty to her family {150 sh}. A special kin term applied to these re-wedders [1042.10a **smakʷtuɬn**]. The parents and family of the deceased could decide if they would allow the widow or widower to marry someone else. If a widow did, the former inlaws gave back some of the dowry. The widow mourned for a year, wailing loudly each morning if she truly grieved. Her hair was cut off above her ears and she re-wed when it grew back.

Women were not to tap their feet or seem distracted. If a jealous husband saw his wife wiggling her toes with her legs crossed, he suspected she was thinking of a lover and might stab her in the heel with a knife.

Chehalis

A man without character ("bad in his heart") might marry his step-daughter, but most men would not do so. A woman never married her step-son. An unlucky man who married a dutiful wife, who bathed and prayed, would become lucky.

Shamans often could demand a wife. A girl might be given to a doctor in payment for a cure {15 mi}. She either was married to the shaman himself or to his son or nephew. She had no choice in the matter, but she could desert the marriage after an honest attempt over a year or so. A doctor envious or jealous of a pretty girl about to be married might kill her for revenge {16 mi}.

Marriage Examples

Lucy Youckton's father had three wives who lived with him, but he was left with one after the oldest one died, and the youngest one got mad and left {120 ly}.

John Smith was a young man "not thinking of women" when his father or uncle died, leaving a wife named Maggie, whom they had "paid" a lot for so the families forced them to marry. John refused, so they put them in bed together, but he ran off. Maggie waited for days until John came back, and they became congenial {272 ph}.

Syk'amen ("light," sickman) had three wives, an old one from Scatter Creek Prairie and two young ones with many children. He favored the middle one, a Satsop woman, and always took her in his canoe. The other two wives had their own canoe, but always quarreled. After Syk'amen died, the youngest wife (Satsop and Puyallup) married a sailor from Chile and learned Spanish. They lived and died in Oakville {271 ph}.

Two first cousins ran away and married. They had three children, one of whom was Mary Heck's father, when Mary Iley's great grandfather found them among the Upper Chehalis and welcomed them back to Newaukum {1 mi}. Thereafter, the Iley's and this family called each other cousins.

Chief Tsinitiya, half Cowlitz and half Upper Chehalis, married the daughter of a Lower Cowlitz chief, giving 10 slaves, 10 horses, and beads. Her family kept her well hidden all the time because she did not have a flat head marking nobility so someone might make fun of her. She could not cook or work, but she was royal. Since she never went out, she did not know how to ride horseback. At the wedding, she fell off the horse. Immediately, her mother scattered beads all over the place where she fell for everyone to pick up. Tsinitiya already had 7 wives, but this girl was the only one to have children {4 mi}.

Mary Iley's mother's father (a Taitnapam named *watatanx*) had four wives, only two of whom had children {11 mi}. The oldest wife had two daughters and the other one was her own grandmother, whose daughter was Mary's mother. The oldest drove one wife away and fought with the others, who were cousins. She beat them, and cut up baskets they were working on.

Once, her grandmother had worked on a coiled hard basket that she kept hidden, but the oldest wife found it and cut it up. The grandmother shouted, "You treat me like a dog. You slashed my hard work. Now I will beat you for good." The women fought while the husband had Mary's mother in her cradleboard. Her grandmother struck the oldest in the face, getting the best of her. The husband tried to separate them but her grandmother knocked him down. He took his knife and slashed her arm to the bone in three places.

The youngest wife, who was childless, took Mary's mother in the cradleboard and medicated the grandmother. Then they left, walking across the top of the fish trap. They

Chehalis

wandered all day long for five days in a row, only coming home late at night. Finally, the grandmother decided to move to Mossy Rock, joining her sister, Lewey's mother. [cf Melville Jacobs (1934, 239) worked with Lewy Costima, an Indian Shaker in his sixties at his farm at Bremer near Morton in August of 1927.].

Soon, the husband began to seek his wife. He was out of gun powder and wanted to hunt along the way. He got to Mossy Rock, but his wife hid for 10 days waiting for him to leave. He knew that if the cuts healed before he got her back, she would always get her way for her spirit was very strong.

At Mossy Rock, the husband was refused powder by his nephew (actually a second cousin), who was a brother to the cousin wives. For this insult, two days later, this man died, speaking like the husband at the end, which confirmed the uncle as a sorcerer.

The youngest wife heard that they were coming to kill her husband and she tried to protect him. She slept with him every night. One morning, the hired killer named *mo'o/* ?? found him and shot him with four loads of shot, like they use for grizzly bears. Blood and flesh covered the youngest wife, but she was not harmed. She washed and prepared the body for burial, wrapping it in an elkhide. No one else would help, so she had to bury him in a hole left by a huge fallen-over cedar. She placed two guns, three brass kettles, and other goods in the grave. Then she filled in the hole and disguised its location.

The other wives divided up his goods, but would give her nothing. She threatened to tell what they had done and so was bribed with a buckskin and a blanket. They burned down his house and pretended that the husband was lost and they were looking for him.

The youngest wife moved to Mossy Rock and married a series of her murdered husband's brothers, but none of these unions lasted. Several of them beat her and left scars, others died. She had several children, but died while still young.

A Cowlitz married a beautiful slave girl, who worked very hard. In time, however, a slave man named *qa'os* took after the girl and she yielded. The Cowlitz let them marry because *qa'os* also worked hard, taking care of the horses, getting water and firewood.

Sometimes a man traded away a slave girl before his son entered puberty to avoid temptation {14 mi}. To be polite, young slaves were sometimes called brothers or sisters.

Adult Duties

A carpenter had a special craft, assured by his spirit power. His tools were elk horn wedges, stone hammer, scrapers, and knives {73 pb, 290 ph}.

Hunters left without eating and were gone all day long. They sweated or bathed for about 5 days before to purify their bodies and remove human smells. They never hunted at night, except when trapping eels {106 ph, 150 sh}.

Women mostly managed their households, but some females got spirit powers to doctor or to excel at basketry, berrying, or tanning {121, 128 ly}. Women's work was to get plant foods, tan deer or elk hides, make mats or baskets, shred cedar bark, and sew clothes.

A husband or wife could own separate things, but they shared and helped each other. A wealthy family would own the land where their house stood, canoes, later, horses, and maybe a fishing site {99 ph}. Berry, camas, and hunting grounds were common property, even used by Nisqually and Cowlitz.

Chehalis

Hair Care

Hair was parted in the middle along the crown of the head. Women put theirs into two braids, men into a ponytail. Using tweezers or fingers rubbed with ashes, men plucked out their facial hair; women their eyebrows, covering the location with dark red paint.

Sometimes bear grease was rubbed into the hair to keep it soft and glossy. A special plant medicine was used to thicken thinning hair {277 ph}. Combs were carved of yew or oak; one per family. Thin sticks were also interwoven to form comb teeth. Hair combings were hidden or burned so they could not be used for sorcery against that person.

Mourner's hair was cut after a death. For a son, everyone in the family had their hair cut. For a husband, the widow had her hair cut to the ears {275 ph}.

Paint

Some paint was traded from the Yakama. Another, like a reddish bread dough, was dug from the riverbank, baked in a pit over night, and mixed with elk tallow. Faces were painted all over to prevent chapping from exposure to wind or sun. The part of the hair was painted to appear attractive, particularly to a spouse.

An M1 painted herself with red paint and washed it off, cleansing her of sin. Paint was also applied to make dicta more effective. It also improved love medicine, which had to be purchased from other tribes.

An old man once painted his face to court a young girl (Marion Davis's sister) at the agency school, but he was sent away by the teacher, Mr Bell, and threatened with jail {55 md}.

White paint was made from cottonwood ashes {254 js}.

Black paint was only used by Growler cult initiates.

Tattooing [1722]

A few people had a tattoo applied as dictated by their spirit, such as a Skokomish and Upper Chehalis woman who had a small circle tattooed on each cheek. Mary Heck's mother had tattoos all over her legs, which showed below her skirt, and an elk and deer on each breast. Her cousin Kate had hearts on each cheek {282 ph}. Some women had tattoos on the legs and lower arms, done with a gooseberry thorn and the ashes of burned raspberry canes.

Men did not tattoo in the old days. Now, sometimes, a sweetheart "will put it on" out of devotion. Marion Davis had a tattoo saying "Tillie" on his arm {55 md}.

Death

When someone's soul left forever, he or she died. Sometimes an owl, lizard, snake, beetle, comet, or omen warned the family in advance. The body was washed, dressed, and wrapped in cattail mats and an elkskin. A wake was held for 2 or 3 days to allow friends and kin to gather. Children were sent away for their protection. The body was never taken out the door, but instead through a hole in the wall made by removing boards {97 ph}.

In the old days, corpses were put into canoes placed in trees, such as one at Gate City when Marion Davis was young {53 md}. Sometimes the canoe was cut in half to make a bottom and a top {76 ph?}. Once secured among tree limbs, other family members who died might be added to the canoe, which had holes bored in the bottom for drainage. Any grave goods put with the deceased were broken or damaged, sometimes by nailing them to the tree, so their connection with the family would be broken and they would be whole in the afterworld {244 ph}. A woman's favorite basket was put on a pole to wave in the wind {370 ds}.

Once people became Christians, they buried the dead and hired a grave digger, who chewed white fir while working {245 ph}. Then he had to sweat and fast for a time. In the old days, grave diggers had special power, as from Wolf, to allow them to do reburials.

After the deposition (or burial) early in the day, a feast was held and everything movable the deceased owned was given away. If a woman died after picking fresh berries, these were given away or, if no one wanted them, burned up. The family gave all these things away so they would not have reminders of the loved one, who might lure them to the land of the dead. In the old days, non-related people took everything as soon as someone died.

The house stayed in the family, unless its owner died, then it was torn down and the pieces moved {149 sh}. Houses were expensive since it took two weeks just to make a plank, but it was fumigated and cleansed after each death.

A doctor might look over the close family survivors to make sure no ghosts or spirits were clinging to their grief. If any were present, he or she removed them {370 ds}.

If a royal person died, the chief spoke at the wake and funeral to remind everyone of his or her deeds and family connections.

Before the funeral, people gave money and gifts to the chief mourner to spend on new clothes for the deceased, a coffin, or food to feed those who attended the funeral {193 md}. At the dinner after the burial, the mourner announced the donations and paid back a token amount (a few dollars) to those who prepared the body, dug the grave, acted as pall bearers, cooked the food, or gave money. If there was money left, some was given to all who attended. In 1927, Joe Pete usually did the talking as "em-cee" (master of ceremonies) at these events.

The name of the dead was never said in public, and words that sounded like the name might be changed at the insistence of the family. Years later, the name would be revived and handed on. Rob Choke's grandmother did this for a relative named "noon" so everyone used the English word.

After her husband died, a widow used a sweat house for 10 days, scouring her body with sweet smelling hemlock. She avoided fresh meat for three months or so because the blood might settle in her liver or other organs, causing her to spit up blood later.

After a hunter's wife died he had to be very careful to sweat and fast for 10 days to keep his luck. Lastly, he rubbed his face with punk from a rotten log.

A long-married pair was especially close, and the survivor was vulnerable, so dicta was said to break the bond. After a year of mourning, the surviving spouse was expected to re-wed into the same family.

The ghosts of the dead come closest to the living during the winter, when it is summer in the afterworld. If they took someone's soul, doctors had to go after it. If they touched someone, that person went crazy. Only doctors can see the dead with the help of their spirit ghost ally, but ghosts always smell moldy to anyone.

The dead person's spirit power would look over the survivors to locate the person who would inherit it, unless this was settled before the death.

Chehalis

Newborn babies were treated differently because they came from the east and went back to the place of the unborn. After they were a year or two old, and capable of "sin," babies were buried with their families in the tree graveyard.

Slaves were dumped into the sea or under a log, without any ceremony at all.

Burial Examples

When Lucy Heck, Silas's wife, died after a long illness, he burned down their house with everything in it, due to his sorrow {98 ph}. His wife had set aside $15,000 for her funeral. Her coffin cost $800.

Mary Iley knew of children who had taken beads and a copper bracelet from a moss covered-canoe burial. That night the ghost came in a dream, so they threw the beads away {123 ly}.

In 1927, the agent only allowed caskets worth up to $150 so that funerals would not be lavish. Peter Heck often made caskets for people, whether or not they paid him.

Suicide was rare, usually an angry act by a rejected spouse {101 ph}. Few people became crazy, and the Shakers cured them before they caused trouble. Some were crazy from being touched by ghosts; others from meeting *silatko* (wild men, sasquatches) who were tall, whistled in the woods, came from the north, and had a dope [used a drug] to make people crazy {106 ph}.

Reburial

If the graves of a family were falling apart or threatened with erosion, the family had the remains removed, cleaned, redressed, and buried. Sometimes, an old person will arrange such a reburial as a gesture to ancestors before they meet again {77 ph?}.

INTERACTIONS

Smoking

Old people merely enjoyed smoking, but some spirit powers insisted on it for doctors, who drew in the smoke "clear to the toes" until he or she passed out {60 md}. After people got tobacco from the traders, they mixed it with kinikinnik [bearberry] leaves. A pipe was called *lapip*, from the French word, and was sometimes passed around a circle.

Some powerful people competed at smoking, drawing in more smoke for longer periods. A man might have the power to light the pipe without using fire, just by willing it so. Young people did not smoke, nor did most women {285 ph}. [Klallam men and women smoked yew leaves in pipes with duck wing bones for stems (Gunther 1927: 279).]

Sweating

Sweat houses were built near a creek, so people could plunge into the cold water when they were too hot. Women used them more than men, especially as M1 when she had to bathe daily for a year {54 md}. A new mother or father sweated for 10 days. Water was sprinkled on hot rocks in a basin-like depression to create the steam. Soothing those hurt, sore, or tired, a few vomited in the sweat house to force a cure {260 ph}.

Crimes

A murderer had to sweat, fast, thirst, and pray for 10 days while his relatives negotiated a settlement or payment. Then he could eat sparingly using a pointed stick or drink from a skunk cabbage leaf. Any plate or cup he used had a hole in it. For about three months, he could not directly touch food or water {5 mi}. Like the M1, they could not touch things with their fingers until the blood was "wiped from their hands."

Unless purified, all the murderer's family will die and brush will grow over their houses {204 mh?}. At Satsop, the family of Stout, who killed Tenas Pete [who reburied graves and so had ghost power {77 ph?}], died out because the murder was not settled with payment and a feast.

Certain doctors had the power to stick a knife or probe into the footprints of a thief, who then would be identified by a foot injury and confess {244 ph}. [Klallam had shamans who could find lost or stolen goods (Gunther 1927: 299).]

Hospitality

Guests were always welcome. Good hosts fed and entertained them well. Indians never had hobos {84 ph}. Meals were served morning and afternoon, with snacks throughout the day.

Upper Cowlitz visited the Taitnapams to fish for smelt or pick huckleberries {125 ly}. Smelt came twice a year, in February and late March.

Trading

Ocean foods were traded for land foods, coastal for interior. Blankets were much in demand {105 ph}. Upper Chehalis traded with the Quinault, Nisqually, Puyallup, Muckleshoot, Squaxin, Cowlitz, Yakama, and many others.

Warfare

Warriors prepared by sweating, then plunging into freezing water. Sometimes, they stood in such water for half a day until numb. A warrior was driven by a fierce spirit who demanded a short life in return for great fame {256 js}. Successful warriors could marry into the royalty. Some warriors picked fights for the fun of it. He had fighting "in his heart like Teddy Roosevelt."

They trained for stamina, endurance, and strength by running, suffering cold, and holding mock battles. They ran through snow-filled trees and dove into ice water.

Strong warrior powers were Wolf, Fox, Coyote, Otter, Cougar, Bear, Eel, Pygmy Owl, Condor, Eagle, and Snake or Lizard, to get through tight places. The greatest of all was Thunder, like Kitsap, Jonas Secena's grandfather, had at Suquamish. A warrior never ate the animal form of his power.

Chehalis

One power, an antlered snake, was so strong that it twisted the unready bodies of those who encountered it. If a lucky boy of good family found it, however, he would always win at war, though his life would be short. Jeff Secena saw it and his life became golden until he died in an accident {259 js}.

Women might get some of these powers, but never at full strength. It only enabled them to be brave enough to carry weapons and serve behind the battle lines {259 js}.

Local warriors never scalped like Satsop and Nisqually. They cut off the whole head and stuck it on a pole in front of the town. The Snohomish did this to Peter Heck's great grandfather's son {243 ph}. The Snohomish came to Mud Bay to counterattack for an Upper Chehalis raid and found this boy courting a sweetheart there.

The Squaxins at Mud Bay had been warned by the sounds of cranes flying at night and fled their homes, but this boy was found close by. A Snohomish who had been a slave recognized who the boy was and they killed him, taking his head away.

Once, at Grand Mound, someone threw a bone into the brush and knocked senseless an enemy wearing buckskin clothes and white paint around his eyes like an Owl {257 js}. Using pitch torches, they found his body and burned him up.

Upper Chehalis would fight the Westports or Skokomish. Mostly warriors wanted children to sell or keep as slaves, many from Grays Harbor. Good families would try to locate and ransom their captured relatives as soon as possible.

A woman and her son were taken from Black River to the Columbia River. Her husband asked his relatives at the mouth of the Cowlitz to watch for his son, who had a scar on his cheek. These relatives found him and ransomed him, after some bickering, for a slave and a fur blanket, itself worth a slave. Thus, the warrior doubled his loot and the boy was freed.

His mother was taken to Oregon, where she worked hard. Everyday, she saved some food until she had enough to escape. They searched for her with the chief's dog, but she hid in a log and fed the dog dried salmon. Near Centralia, she met two men, but one was an enemy. The other man used lip gestures to warn her to stay off the main trails. At Black River, she waited for her son to come to the well and made sure he was safe. Then she went back to Jamestown because she was born a Klallam. She never wanted to see her husband again because he gave up on her.

Upper and Lower Chehalis fought 300 years ago after the Lowers raped and pillaged upriver {145 sh}. The decisive battle was fought at Oakville and thereafter their common boundary line was set at the Satsop River. [sh told Dale Kinkade this boundary was Cloquallam Creek near Elma.]

Gaming

Girls always had dolls and cradleboards, then younger siblings, while boys had tiny tools. A favorite children's game involved placing a shell on a pole on the beach and having members of each team walk up to take it while the other side used words and gestures to try to make him or her laugh. Sometimes, a member of one team was supposed to carry the shell across to the other side, withstanding jeers and taunts. The game taught self control, dignity, and coping with public recognition, but most children broke down, laughed, and ran back.

Chehalis

Children also tested their stamina by hopping in place {111 ph, 188 md}. The winner was able to do this the longest. Boys ran far as part of their training. Before dawn, a royal boy should swim and then run from Rochester to Lequito and back.

Guessing Games used verbal clues to find something hidden.

String Figures or Cat's Cradle were made using cattail strings. Peter Heck could name 11 such figures {330 ph}.

Teams formed for a tug of war using a long pole {261 ph}. Sometimes adult women pulled against adult men, or different tribes, or towns. The women's trick was to sit down so they could not be budged. Sometimes two men sat across from each other holding a stick until one of them was pulled up.

Boys staged mock battles using stump grass arrows and small bows {201 mh?}. Popguns were made, probably as a recent idea. Before a sneak attack, each boy told what his pretended power was in case they needed help along the way. Seeking girls for slaves, the boys rushed an encampment, whose campers fled into hiding. Any captured girls were ransomed by their families and the boys feasted on the proceeds.

When geese passed overhead in the fall, children ran outside, clapping, dancing, and singing "Leave me some backbone!" to change the weather.

All gambling was a contest about the relative strengths of the powers involved or invoked. The side that won had the greater power.

Slahal was played with a pair of tubes made of horse bones, just long enough to hide inside of the palms. One was plain, called woman, and one had a middle black band, called man. Two people each have a pair of bones. Teams and sides would match bets so a winner got double. On the ground, a fire burned in the middle and long poles along each side marked where the teams sit. People used sticks to pound on the poles when they sang lively bone game songs. Leaders sat in the middle of each line and took turns guessing the location of the plain bones. [Klallams said that the game was originally played with only a single plain bone (Gunther 1927: 274).] Swaying, two hiders on each side moved their arms with fists clenched. Every correct guess earns one of the 10 counter sticks, but a game usually goes to 30.

Slahal players were mostly men, but one woman at Chehalis had power (from a large Crane) to do this and people came from all over to play against her. It was wonderful to watch her play when "she was in business" {109 ph}.

Cheaters could effect the outcome of a game by hiring a recent widower or a M1 to stand near the other side and make them unlucky {188 md}. This work was done in secret, or the other team took offense and kept the bets. In more severe cases, a doctor was hired to hex a team or a race horse.

Hoop Disks was played at night with lots of betting before the two sides sat on mats. These disks were eight black and red, one black, and one white. Each side had five and hid them inside shredded cedar bark. They play to a count of 40, using split sticks for tallies, guessing for the solid color.

Beaver Teeth, used like dice only by women or children, were decorated with circles and dots on a side. Those with double rows were called "man," while the others were "woman." One of these "woman teeth" also had a black middle band. Various combination and arrangements of patterns were scored differently. For example, when all four teeth were decorated-face up, it was called "all are laughing" and counted two tally sticks. When all four red backs showed, that was another two sticks.

Chehalis

A hoop made of hazelwood was rolled by boys, who tried to thrust spears through it as it reached a specific spot. Sometimes teams formed. One side rolled the hoop and the other threw spears until it matched a certain agreed upon count and the sides changed. The winners took away [won] all the spears. Sometimes they threw the hoop up and tried to catch it on an arm.

Arrows were used in shooting matches with a large fungus target set in two opposite directions {187 md}. Players shot at one, turn, and shoot at the other. The winner gets all the arrows used. Arrows were also shot for distance, the one that went farthest won.

Ball Game or Shinny was played with a carved white fir sphere and hooked sticks [like field hockey] to get the ball across a goal. Games were held at gatherings where teams could be recruited during dry weather since play was rough and wet ground made it dangerous.

Horse Races were held after these animals were traded from east of the mountains {110 ph}. Both horse and rider fasted and thirsted for a few days before a race. Heavy bets were made, including slaves and clothes. There was a race track near Centralia {297 ph}. People rode bareback, but they did use a homemade pack saddle of crooked roots for transport.

Prairies were deliberately burned over in the spring so the horses would have fresh grass. In the winter, horses knew how to dig under the snow for grass. If winter conditions were severe, an owner might cut fresh reeds or rushes to feed his horses.

Strong men wrestled, grabbing the hair if they were from Quinault or Grays Harbor. Mostly men used the back hold.

In the Myth Age, Animals gambled among themselves. Bear, Cougar, Wolf, and other meat eaters played against Elk, Deer, Beaver, Fisher, Rabbit, and other plant eaters. Of course, the meat eaters usually won {91 jw}.

Medicines

Vomiting was induced with an infusion boiled from the bark of the red wood used to make lal [slahal] gambling disks {38 ph}. Sometimes the white flowers of death camas were used. Vomiting relieved heartburn or internal disorders by ejecting black hard blood. While used as a home remedy, a doctor will also administer it early in the morning and press on the patient's forehead and belly to make sure all of it was expelled.

Roots and leaves were used for sore eyes, along with a nursing mother's milk. A plant with little white balls [snowberries ?] or water lily seeds were also used as a eye wash {183 md, 371 ds}.

Love medicine attracted and held a spouse {109 ph}, especially if used with dicta.

Cuts and wounds were washed with the water of boiled white fir boughs {154 md}. Red fir pitch was mixed with bear oil and taken in a dose of 5 tablespoons a day over 6 weeks for consumption [TB]. Boiled hemlock inner bark, mixed with dogwood or bearberry, gave strength for recovery. Pitch was used as a salve.

Colds were treated with ferns, cedar boughs, mint leaves, bear grease, and inhaling strong smells.

Broken bones were set with splints and a poultice of smashed red elderberry stems.

Powdered, year-old ironberry blossoms healed burns, while boiled red elderberry bark helped bruises, such as the backside of someone thrown from a horse.

Something like bearberry, with pinkish fall blossoms, was boiled and drunk to cure smallpox and worked for Mary Heck.

Chehalis

Inner cedar bark, raw thimbleberry sprouts, and nettles relieved monthlies {155 md}.

Wild Rosebush medicines of Puget Sound were learned by Marion Davis's mother, who paid a horse for them. Mostly they helped women and babies.

Honeysuckle, as boiled scrapings, was used to treat a baby's sore tongue. The boiled roots or flowers were a hair tonic {371 ds}.

Eel oil was used for chapped hands, sores, and scabs.

Bear grease mixed with spruce needles was a good cough medicine.

Gunshots had to be treated by a specialized doctor or shaman. Spirit-caused illnesses also could only be treated by specialists. White doctors could do nothing with spirits, they could only treat smallpox, scarlet fever, measles, and other European diseases.

Dicta

Compelling words or formulas were known in certain families, jealously guarded, and used in a variety of situations (such as love affairs, childbirth, illness, or grief) to determine a favorable outcome. [Other Salishans also passed down such dicta, but not much is known about them. ThA was confused by Erna Gunther (1927: 247), who worked among the Klallams and mistook such forms of "mind control" for a kind of wishing.] Though usually transmitted through family members, training in dicta had to be paid for to make it legitimate. To be effective it had to be very secret and very expensive, but using it "could make a person in New York change their minds" {253 js}.

For example, a jilted woman could use dicta to either lure back or harm her husband or lover {51 md}, reciting it as the sun rose to attract him, or at sun down to kill him {145 sh}.

When used to cure, dicta were said while hands rubbed with bear grease touched the afflicted part of the patient {247 ph}. Other kinds of dicta were used with red paint. The woman who cut the hair of mourners used dicta to lessen their grief.

When gathering medicines in nature, dicta was used to talk to the spirits of these plants and places. Someone who learned a great many dicta quickly was sure to live to a great age. One who had trouble remembering any of the lessons was doomed to an early death.

People could influence the weather {276 ph}. It would rain if the father of a newborn looked at the mountains or waded in a creek. Playing with a shuttlecock made of arrowbush stuck with white duck feathers caused snow. Working strings for cat's cradle or a bullroarer caused bad storms. Teasing tiny fish in a stream near Gate City caused rain. It was expected to rain after a funeral to wash away the dead person's tracks. A hard wind blew after someone drowned in the ocean {373 js}. Pointing at a new moon caused rain {151 sh}. Pointing at the moon in winter caused snow {170 md}.

Dicta used a special vocabulary and power given by Moon to his royal relatives when he remade the world.

Chehalis

RELIGION

Origins

In the beginning of the world, when someone tried to steal a hoop, a fog was made and all the beings got lost. This was a time when all animals were people, just like humans. These beings made a home wherever they got lost and became the **tahmanawas** or spirit powers that give help to humans {45 ph, 41 sh}. After a human died, its spirit would try to join up with another member of that family. All of these spirits, therefore, belong to the earth. They live in this world, but in places that are remote and unsullied by humans. Spirits were around all the time, but ghosts mostly came in the winter since it was summer then in the land of the dead {339 js}. Shaman's curing spirits were always near, but ordinary career spirits were strongest in winter, when visionaries met to sing their songs in large houses like that at Rochester, which was large enough to hold foot races inside {340 js, 195 md}.

Some people got more than one spirit ally, questing until they were satisfied. Spirits gave success either for ordinary careers such as that of leader, fisher, hunter, gambler, singer, and so on; or for curing as a shaman, although this work did not start until much later in life. A shaman was not paid for the first few cures until people were confident in his or her success {219 mh}. Any power could be used either to help or to harm someone, so people were careful how they treated those with spirit powers.

Quest Stages

A spirit ally is acquired through the stages {170 md, 142 sh, 219 mh} of trance, dream, vision, and song, when the personal link between a spirit and human is confirmed by a special tune. Each of the first three stages can occur several times before the song is ultimately given once and for all.

Sometimes, a spirit will send a messenger to make sure the quester is nice, clean, pure, and willing before it comes itself {393 ph}. The spirit chief helps decide if the boy or girl will get an ordinary or a special spirit. If the youngster is satisfied and does not object, that will happen, otherwise another spirit will come. The quester will act according to the power wanted. If he or she behaved like a doctor, a curing spirit appeared. If he used a bow and arrow, a hunting spirit came to help.

Dreaming

Spirit dreams provided access to powers. They were never forgotten. Common dreams did not come true, only spirit dreams did because a tahmanawas talked to the person {131 js}. Every native was born with such a dream to be shaped by life and training to come out well. In a spirit dream, the person was semi-conscious or aware of the special circumstances because his soul is involved. Even day dreams might come from spirits, especially if someone got into the mood by smoking a pipe. A shaman would both smoke and drink alcohol to get in touch with his spirit dreams. A dream might reoccur several times until it led to a vision, when the youngster actively sought contact with the spirit and received a song.

Chehalis

From the time she was eight years old, Mary Heck had a dream of living poles painted black or with red and white strips {396 ph}. She would sleep walk when the dream came and awake in a canoe beached along the river. Once two men came to her, one all black and the other in broad red and white stripes, holding a snake. He thrust the snake toward her and said to take it as her "food." She escaped from the dream by sleep walking. Finally, her father took the dream away.

Some dreams are premonitions. To dream of dead relatives means that you are getting closer to them, especially if you are old. Spirit dreams mostly come to the young, although an old man at Gate City did dream of the arrival of Europeans and their goods, especially kitchen utensils.

Peter Heck {79 ph?} dreamed that one of his sons was dying from a broken leg, so he hit him with an ax to end his misery. A week later, that same son was hit at the exact same place by a sweep [metal cable] while pulling stumps. Just before Peter gets sick, he dreams of being in the boarding school with severe indigestion.

Silas Heck {137 sh} dreamed of a pond among cottonwoods and the sound of a flute made of a thistle stalk. He felt a buzz in his head and became dizzy. Looking into the pond, he saw a deer looking back from the bottom. Then he awoke. Some days, he would wander to that pond, hearing the sounds of someone chopping out a canoe, but there never was anyone there. He finally told his mother, but she scolded him for thus forsaking a potential power for carpentry. In another dream, he was wading out toward a shark he could not see but he knew was there.

Marion Davis {157 md} dreamed that a shaman was coming to make him sick and thus was prepared for the spiritual attack when it came, as from Squally Jim. Davis dreamed that he hid on the bottom of the Nisqually River and so was saved. Such dreams were a protection. Another time, he dreamed how to win a bone game at Puyallup. An unusual dream came when he was coming from Centralia and took refuge in the James family barn. It was late and he was wet and cold. He went to sleep but was awakened by a song. He went to find out who was singing and saw a rooster jumping on the ground and singing. He learned the song and went back to bed. Another night, he listened to a pig speaking in the Grays Harbor or Lower Chehalis language about Davis being a carpenter {161 md}. His gambling song came to him when he dreamed he was riding on the back of a Wolf.

Mrs Davis was once so sick that only a shaman from Hoquiam could cure her. He found that her soul had been hidden in her stepfather's coffin. Later, when she went to the industrial school in Forest Grove, Oregon, [forerunner of Chemawa federal Indian boarding school] her mother married that same shaman, but when they divorced, he took revenge on the daughter. After local physicians had given up on her, she dreamed what was making her ill and thwarted the attack. Soon after, the man burned to death in his home while smoking in bed.

A man at the mouth of Scatter Creek predicted the location of a deer that was hunted to feast everyone {343 js}.

Visions

Training for a quest in earnest, a youngster of about 10 years old applied paint and fasted in preparation for entering a trance [477], fainting or passing out to become as though dead. In a dream, the souls showed him or her their kingdom, often a house inside a lake or mountains, until a spirit decided to stay with that person, giving him or her a song to use before undertaking the activity of their successful career. In this vision, the spirit appeared as a human but left in the outer shape of its animal or other form of being. Thus, for example, a woman was visited by a man who gave her a song and then left as a Bear.

In Mary Heck's father's vision, a doctor spirit took him on a tour of "the other side," always moving higher to get more power. The spirit explained how he would cure and gave him two sticks for his first child, who would be a daughter, to hold when he had a difficult case. He was also given songs while going up a river in a canoe toward the spirit's house. The audience sang along with these songs, "like frogs." He had another vision and song near Satsop, in addition to a spirit ghost who took him to the land of the dead.

Spirits best liked young and clean youngsters, before marriage. A young man may start to get a spirit ally near a trail only to have it go away if an old person comes near. Sometimes, the ally will meet the boy again at another place. Sometimes, it never returned. Spirit powers could still be inherited after marriage when a relative died.

After getting the first power, others were easier to lure. Most powers were acquired before marriage, while the youngster was chaste.

A man could only begin using a career power at about the age of 20 when he showed maturity by handling a canoe, hunting deer, and starting a family {342 js}. Warrior power was something special, but apparently a kind of # 4 [below]. It can only be used to defend the town or tribe, never to benefit that person. Gambling power was a kind of # 6, usually with a fine song. Warrior and chiefs were often the gamblers.

Other spirits could become attached to that person later, either inherited from a deceased relative or attracted by the grief caused by the loss of a baby. Often the spirit of that infant itself would offer to help the father while he was in the sweat house or bathing in a cold creek for 10 days {163 md}. The spirit promised to be reborn into another child, provided the father followed instructions. A miscarriage will sometimes come to the mother as a spirit and offer the same help. The person had no control when a spirit came. He or she got more and more sleepy until the dream began that ended with the vision.

At the least, a close relative will try to lift the grief of the parents by teaching them the use of certain dicta, compelling magic words, to improve their lives.

A human acted as master to his or her spirit allies. Any spirit could be sent to harm someone else, but the danger of this malice was that it could always ricochet back to hurt a weaker member of the person's family {162 md}. Sometimes, the intended victim was so strong that the power reverberated back to kill the sender.

Whatever happened to the power also happened to the human. If a spirit was maimed or weakened, so was the human master, only the spirit could recover but the human might not survive. For example, two spirits once fought too near a fire and that of Peter Heck's wife's father got burned. Later his daughter got sore red eyes from this, not her father, and had to be cured by Queen Susan to overcome partial blindness {278 ph}.

If a family strongly suspected that a person had sent his own spirit, or hired someone else to send one, to kill one or more of its members, they might hire a shaman to send a spirit, a warrior to waylay the person, or add poison to his food {79 ph?}. The choice was up to the family, not the chief.

Chehalis

A doctor had stronger spirits than an ordinary person. He or she could hide someone's soul under a roof to lure a rival shaman {277 ph} to their death when attempting a cure. Only a native doctor could cure soul or spirit sickness.

Inheriting Spirits

When a person died, their spirit tried to reconnect with a younger member of the family. If the child did not know what to do, the spirit poisoned it to death. Sometimes, many children died in the same family until either the spirit was sent away or a youngster accepted the power.

For example, a boy met his grandfather's spirit ally but ran from it. That tahmanawas became like poison inside the body. He could not think right and never got over it, but how could he accept it when he did not already have a power of his own. He was an orphan, though, and such are favored by the spirits. The old people said that the world took pity on orphans and protected them {141 sh, 170 md, 264 ph}. The boy was about 25 in 1927, but he had disappeared two years before.

In important families, children were carefully told not to be afraid of anything strange. It might be a spirit power they could get. Sometimes, a father or uncle will deliberately forget something in a remote place and send a child there to retrieve it. Though afraid, the child went in hopes of meeting a spirit. The proof that they went was to return with the object.

Such children were clean and had "pure hearts" because they were related to chiefs. They did not have to go far to find a spirit.

Insignia (Manifestations)

Sometimes, the spirit ally specified an emblem for the human to make and use. Silas Heck's great grandfather had a cane that helped him get wealth {145 sh}. Questing in the hills behind Gate City, another uncle got a cane to symbolize long life if he had lived by the rules {137 sh}.

Peter Heck {46 ph} recalled a slave who got axayus and made a figure 7 feet tall to represent it during a potlatch at Elma, where it was unwrapped from blankets after everyone was seated. Other people painted images of their spirits on boards or parts of a house, such as planks that the beams rested upon.

Every winter, people with spirit powers gathered in a house to help each other sing their songs. A special repeater made sure they got the words correct. Afterwards, the singers gave gifts to everyone. First time singers in public had to be very careful that no shaman stole their spirit or mixed up their song to cause them pain.

Spirits could also be summoned up briefly. Jonas Secena's mother's stepfather went over the mountains toward the Yakamas and prayed to see a rattlesnake {339 js}. Three came to the trail and then left. This man was a Nisqually and they, like the Puyallups and Yakamas, have a special relationship with snakes.

Personal Encounters

People also have personal encounters with spirits. Mary Iley, as a girl of about 11, was lost picking strawberries. A white woman came and showed her the way home. The woman told her to put on all new clothes once a year. Again, just before she became M1, she met a boy wearing pretty clothes, who said she would have a son just like him. When she turned back to look, there was a snake where the boy had been {6 mi}.

Marion Davis's stepfather, who was a shaman and odyssey doctor, died in Olympia and the agent sent his body home. Marion's mother and older brother wanted to put some things in the coffin, so Marion opened it and threw them inside. The man had been dead for some time. A native doctor stood behind him and willed Marion's soul inside the coffin too. It got buried inside. Marion got very sick. No one could cure him. Finally, his mother took him to Cedarville where her own doctor was, but he said the situation was bad and Marion was beginning to smell like a ghost. He suggested the doctor from Hoquiam, and Marion's brother brought him back three days later. The Hoquiam doctor had a spirit ghost ally who went after the soul in the coffin. Marion got well and the doctor was paid a horse {56 md}.

A man predicted that whites would come with tame elks (cows), metal fires (stoves), pots that did not burn (kettles), and things to ride in (wagons). People called him crazy, but he was right {47 ph}.

In 1927, most Chehalis were Shakers, members of the Indian Shaker Church. [Peter Heck was the elected bishop for the entire region from California to British Columbia. At that time, Shakers were expected to reject their tribal traditions. Whatever spirit powers and other possessions they had were believed to convert to Shakerism at the moment they themselves did. Nonetheless, Heck provided ThA with a wide range of important information.]

Today, spirits have been hurt and taken away from the people by the combined actions of slaves, those of low class, and white governments {339 js}. Instead, they gave people bad blood and disease like tuberculosis. Mary Heck {219 mh} thought that the spirits had been driven away because books and schools have made children forget. [cf Suquamish data later herein where social disruption led elders to emphasize the negative aspects of shamanism during the recent century.]

Specific Powers

Peter Heck {42 ph} listed these types of tahmanawas abilities:

- 1) doctoring the sick, both men and women
- 2) dancing, including the ghost familiar, more women than men
- 3) going to the land of the dead, mostly men
- 4) hunting, mostly men but at least one Cowlitz woman
- 5) fishing, gifted from something of the water, mostly men
- 6) owning property and attracting more, mostly men
- 7) inheriting from a close relative, mostly men
- 8) borrowing from an ancestor {245 ph}, perhaps a ghost, mostly women

[It was on the strength of such astounding details from this Shaker Bishop that Adamson proposed fieldwork on this Church, but it was never funded.]

Chehalis

Spirit Examples

Thunderbird {46 ph}. When a storm moved from east to west, people said it was Thunderbird going to hunt whales in the ocean. People used to find whale bones on White Mountain, so that was a place where he ate his catch. Lighting belongs to Thunder, shooting out of its mouth. When thrown at a tree, an agate could be found at the base to bring good luck.

Yelm Jim, a Nisqually, had Thunder power. When he got hurt, he prayed to Thunder to cool things off so he could not get a fever. After he fought in the Stevens Treaty War of 1856, he was set to be hanged, but a thunder storm scared everyone away and he escaped {46 ph, 184 md}.

Warrior power came from Otter, Mink, Cougar, or Wolf, who often fathered twins. Mary Heck's husband had Wolf power that came to him in the form of a woman {100 ph.}

Leschi, war leader at Nisqually, had power from bees called yellowjackets that also made him a marksman {76 ph?}.

Hummingbird gave power to doctors and to warriors and gamblers. Though tiny, he was strong because he moved so quickly because of the power that was in his mind.

Fishing power came from Fishhawk, Kingfisher, Otter, Raccoon, and Mink {343 js}.

Gambling power was given by Bluejay, Flying Squirrel, Wolf, Coyote, Chicken Hawk, or Hoot Owl.

Sharks were put in a certain place in Puget Sound by *Xwane*. Anyone seeking them as a power went into the woods, cut a two-foot length of hardwood, and sharpened both ends. When they dove into the Sound, holding on to a basket full of rocks, this stick was held in the teeth. As a shark came for him with open mouth, the boy used this stick to hold the jaws open {73 ph}. The shark's wife came next and asked him not to hurt her husband. The boy passed out, gained power, and revived safely out of the water. Sometimes, as proof, people found the dead shark on the beach with is mouth propped open with a sharpened stick.

Recovery power gave ability to go to the land of the dead and retrieve souls. It could be anything associated with the dead, such as a rotten canoe, old bones, or a graveyard {41 ph}. Queen Susan, sister of Yawnish, had this power {75 ph}. Hers was called "moldy face." Women's ability was exactly the same as men's for this. When these shamans went together to the land of the dead, they did not look at each other because they were afraid that their spirits would fight each other.

Humans would contest with each other using their powers {81 ph}. The one who lost got sick and died unless someone with a stronger power cured him or her. Shamans were very jealous and so fought each other through their spirits.

Only women, such as Elsie [?], had Bear spirit {249 ph}.

Sqeip, looking like a person painted on the chin and each shoulder, lived on the Earth, but flew and gave a good song to partially heal {56 md}.

A very powerful spirit for a shaman was *ayaxos*, which had a body like a snake and a head like a deer with antlers {256 ph}. Men away in the mountains to hunt deer or elk would see five ayaxos go in profile along the slope. A man who wanted this power would chase after them to the other side of the ridge and have them go, one at a time, in front of him. They got smaller every time he saw them because the smaller they got, the more power he received. If one of them opened its jaws like a crocodile and showed the red inside, a boy could get great power by shoving his arm down its throat. Sometimes, a man will catch and kill the smallest one, taking

Chehalis

the ribs and hide off to keep for luck. No one must know about his having this power. It must be a secret. Syk'amen was a man who had this power.

Other powerful spirits looked like a tall man or like a woman with huge breasts who raped men and covered them with slime {256 ph}. She lived in the dark timber near the town of Chehalis. In a swamp near Montesano, a spirit woman lived with a crying baby that scared people. Certain families were visited by a crying, old, grey-haired lady just before a member died. Spirits in the hills confused people so they would get lost. Many remote locations at mountains and lakes also had **psa** (dangers in human form) who killed people.

A Sturgeon power lived in a lake across from Independence, but not many young men could endure the ordeal of encountering it to receive fishing success {258 ph}. A woman spirit with long hair lived in the Black River. A whale lived in a crooked-shaped lake near the town of Chehalis.

Siyikwwvlx was the power to be well off without much effort. It was like whites who go to college, set up an office, and live well off half an hour of work {264 ph}.

Little Earths lived near water sources and made people crazy. People alone had to be careful when they took a drink. They had to ask these Little Earths for permission. To be safe, they blew out puffs of breath and squirted out some of the mouthful. Their power helped doctors go to the land of the dead.

The journey to the land of the dead involved different kinds of spirits. A doctor needed a spirit ghost ally to take him or her there, along with a ghost familiar (literally called "stays there") who lived with the dead and "told out" [revealed] where the patient's soul, spirit, or essence was. Marion Davis {195 md} said the familiar "kind of phoned" the shaman with this information, perhaps by telepathy. Sometimes the familiar will bring it part way back ("like from one stage stop to another") to make it easier for the doctors to retrieve, particularly in earth's summer time when the land of the dead has winter snow.

NATIVE DOCTORS (Shamans)

Parents would send their children out to some remote location before puberty to fast, pray, swim, and suffer to attract a spirit ally. Cougar, Mink, Shark were good for doctoring {73 pb}. If a child got power at 10, he or she could not bring it out in public to doctor until 25 years old or more.

First time the song is sung, a repeater, someone with the special ability to catch the words and tune, said them out loud for others to learn. The singer started out crying and sobbing until the repeater could make out what was said, clapped his hands, and sang aloud for other to follow and help the singer {74 ph}.

Most people want tahmanawas for hunting so as to eat well or wealth to live well. Getting doctor power was dangerous because other doctors wanted to kill you or, if your patients died, their families took revenge.

Women doctors got power to help with childbirth. George Sander's aunt, a Scatter Creek raised at Nisqually, would dip her open hand into a basket of water and sling it across a big room without splashing any of it {113 gs}. Then the baby came easy.

Each doctor had a specialty, such as birth, wounds, or gun shots. Some sucked out bad blood, diseases, or intrusive objects.

Chehalis

The Cowlitz came to Chehalis to gamble. The Chehalis sent a messenger to a young man, Mary Heck's grandfather **silac?**, with great power who was still a virgin. He came and watched the game all morning until two boys were sent up to the roof to move some boards to let in more light. Suddenly the man looked up and his power was unleashed. Many people passed out and blood ran from their noses {220 mh}. The game ended. The man was concerned because the probation period set by his spirit was not yet over and already he had abused its power. He recalled a woman who was menstruating and very sick. He went to look at her. He plucked a hair from his head, tied one end to a pole, and attached a bead to the other end. Using it like a fishing pole, he caught her sickness and used it to weaken his own power. The woman was suddenly well, so the man knew he could now safely go among people.

When his aunt became ill, the man decided to begin his public career as a curer. He called people together to pound on boards and help him sing. He doctored his aunt twice, then she recovered. His great power had been weakened enough to help people stay alive. After he cured a few more people, he accepted pay and became rich. This man had the second greatest power. If he also had had the highest one, he could have brought the dead back to life, like the story of Bluejay's wife [below]. He was kind and good, never using this power to kill anyone.

Doctors who kill can also call the rain {245 ph}, like Yelm Jim did with thunder storms. Peter Heck's father once "borrowed" this power to make it rain so Peter would get well from a bad illness.

When a doctor killed someone, he or she sat up just before dying and spoke like their own killer, sometimes gloating over achieving revenge. That was how mean doctors claimed their own. Of course, then the family knew and hired someone to get the doctor, or a warrior would feel sorry for the family and do it for them.

If another doctor got to the patient with stronger power, however, he or she could lift off, remove, or kill the mean spirit and so kill the other shaman. The removed spirit could be drowned, put into a gun and shot, or burned up. Then the owner would suffer a fatal accident.

Once, while men were building a potlatch house, a Wynoochee doctor took an Elma man's soul and stuck it into a tree. The man was proud, loud, and boastful. Another doctor found that soul before the tree was cut down to kill that man.

Sometimes, an ordinary person would get hair or clothes from an enemy and place them with a dead person, in the mouth, on the body, or in the coffin. The enemy will then sicken and slowly die, unless the objects could be removed.

A doctor could project or "shoot" sharp objects into a person to make them sick or die. These had to be sucked out by a more powerful doctor in order for the patient to live.

A doctor could send his soul on the trail to the land of the dead to see who was there and predict the coming deaths of people. A Quinault doctor even knew when a famous race horse would die. He sat, closed his eyes, and sang while his soul went along the trail for four or five days, resting in a soft bed every midnight. When he met someone singing, he knew their body was on the way to death. When he came back, he warned the family and tried to cure the person before they took sick.

Even though a doctor is called to cure someone, he or she might decide to worsen them instead by inflicting a grudge disease [1920].

Chehalis

Odyssey to the Land of the Dead

Sometimes, a person's soul or pulse would wander off or be stolen to the land of the dead. While the human fainted, its soul walked along a marked trail, crossing a river along a foot log. Once there, the person's body will die unless a doctor went to get the soul. It was really his or her spirits that made the journey, but the doctor went through the motions of imitating ("mocked") the actions of each spirit inside a specially prepared house, showing an audience what and how the spirits were doing {44 ph}. Sometimes a doctor would pick something up from a perfectly clean floor and show it to everyone, indicating what the spirits had found along the trail {217 mh}. It might be grass from a basket being made by a woman in the audience. Then they knew her soul was gone, too.

A doctor found out that someone's soul had gone to the afterworld by shaking in a trance. He sang and danced while a carved wooden effigy of his spirit ghost ally went to the land of the dead to find out who was there. Whenever this effigy was near someone with a lost soul, it shook violently. To recover the soul, a doctor simulated the journey.

If confident, only one doctor would go, but, usually, a group went for greater safety. A single doctor might distract the ghosts by turning into a Wolf, Bluejay, or other spirit animal. He or she would howl or act like the animal, then snatch back the soul.

Every doctor who went to the land of the dead had three spirit helpers. These were a curing spirit, a spirit ghost, and a ghost familiar who actually lived among the dead. Mrs Heck's father had this power. His three spirits included a little woman, a man represented by a hide cutout, and another man carved in the form of a wooden cane. He always held the cane at the top, above a necklace of shredded cedarbark.

To start the journey, the doctors faced west and jumped into a hole or loosened soil because the dead went underground. Then they came to the foot log across a raging river. Mrs Heck's father used his cane to vault over the log foot bridge. All of the doctors were very vulnerable to spiritual attack as they crossed this bridge. The next obstacle was a log fastened only at one end and moving up and down to crush travelers. This levering log was along the river bank. Beyond was a crooked prairie where two sisters, who were like Cranes, watched constantly. The spirits spoke well to them and the women let them pass. A huge headless snake might block their path, but the doctors used dicta (powerful words) to strike its heart and make it disappear. They met a perpetual M1 and used dicta to make her forget their arrival.

In time, they hear the sounds of the village in the land of the dead, beside a second bubbling river. (When a preacher came and talked of the "beautiful river," Chehalis thought he meant this one.) Hidden by the sounds of water, these spirits stop to confer and decide to made a deer or elk decoy, telling it to run in front of the village.

One of the dead saw the deer and called out so everyone ran after it. If it were night, the familiar sang to make the dead sleep more soundly.

The spirits peeked through cracks and went into the abandoned houses until they found the waylaid soul and any others. As Mary Heck said, all the ghosts looked the same so the souls, who looked like their humans, stood out {217 mh}.

The spirits and doctors now faced east and took the souls back to this world, returning from the land of the dead by a "short cut" that took less than a day. The spirits and shamans rejoined early in the morning. They sang and danced in the house, returning the souls to the people who had lost them. In preparation, these people had washed and cleaned themselves.

Chehalis

During the moments before the soul was restored, patients had to stand still. If they looked back, their soul would rush away forever. These patients gave gifts and money to the doctors in gratitude. Otherwise, a patient would shortly die or suffer an accident.

Doctors also made predictions about the coming year, based on what they (their spirits) saw in the land of the dead.

When ghosts died in the land of the dead, they went across to the "other side" of the river (or town) where they were forgotten by the living. Anyone who died by falling out of a tree went immediately to the second land of the dead. [Like the bones from an abandoned tree burial) {397 ph]. If a grave burned, that ghost also went across and moved upside down from then on. They walked on their heads. Some said those who were long dead went to the end of the town, not across the river {142 sh}. No one ever revived from this second land of the dead.

Dead babies went east not west back to their home, waiting to be reborn with a sun rise. In ancient times, dead infants were placed in trees in the mountains so their souls can return. These unborn babies walk head down so they can be born more easily.

Ghosts exist around the living. They are very close whenever a fire goes out for no reason. To drive them away, people sing with a drum of elk or deer skin.

In the land of the dead, time and circumstances were reversed from the ordinary. Winter here was summer there, low tide was high tide, and broken vessels were whole {144 sh}. This made an odyssey in the summer especially difficult.

In ordinary summer, the trail to the land of the dead was frosty and deep in snow. A doctor learned that a soul was there because his or her spirit ghost or ghost familiar "phoned" a warning {195 md}. When the doctors were ready to leave, the familiar managed to get the soul part of the way back along the trail. Then the spirit ghost will help, but only if it is not too cold. The doctors came the rest of the way, took the soul, and restored it to its human body.

Among Lushootseed doctors, power from a Little Earth was also required to be able to safely go to the land of the dead, but Chehalis believed that Little Earths were afraid of the ghost familiars {258 ph}. Power to go to land of the dead came from Raven, a black beetle, a post from an abandoned house, bones, Bluejay, or any scavengers {342 js}.

Growlers (xidxidib in Lushootseed, xinxinim in Straits Salish)

Important families had their members, particularly children, initiated into this secret cult organization for lots of money, but it was humbug from top to bottom {144 sh}. Members stuck the back of the mouth to make it bleed. Upper Chehalis had it along with other tribes around Puget Sound. (Marion Davis said Chehalis did not have it, but a woman initiate did live among them {151 md}.) It was not nature's gift, but made up by people. It was very secret. You were killed if you told about it.

When a wealthy family wants a child initiated, they call a meeting. The child is "shot," blood pours out of the nose and mouth, and he or she falls "senseless" to the ground for several days before coming to life with this new power, shouting like dogs in a spiritual way. They act like a fierce tahmanawas, singing and growling like crazy and crawling on hands and knees. They are painted black.

The power was stronger than one boy, half Skokomish and half Squaxin, so he revived with crossed eyes. Another initiate really died until his uncle blew into the top of his head through a closed fist. It is strong with Klallams and Skokomishes. A lavish potlatch always was held at the end.

Membership was used as a defensive power by people along the coast, by "sea warriors along the water front" {377 js}. In preparation for war, young members might slash their bodies. Sometimes they held a sham battle with knives. Other people watched from afar, often in canoes safely off the beach. Chief Yawnish once watched from a ship anchored in the Sound and attracted too much attention. So initiates in canoes chased the ship, brandishing wooden knives that accidentally killed some boys for whom Yawnish had to pay compensation.

Lummi members came to Squaxin Island as a flotilla, the crews standing up and holding seagulls [ducks] that flapped their wings.

Shakers

The Indian Shaker Church was founded when John Slocum, at the head of Skookum Bay, died and revived in 1882. Slocum went into a trance and visited God, who sent him back to reform his own life and others {47 ph}. He taught people to kneel and ask for a blessing. A few days later, people in a room began to get the shake {170 md}. A woman (John's wife Mary) gave them this medicine for getting well.

Mrs Heck joined it at Mud Bay, the mother church, in 1883 and Peter Heck joined in 1884. He came to believe in Shakers when he envisioned a woman with 5 duck feathers in her hair. He was made to see his own father's power. In 1911, he became the Shaker Bishop {47 ph}.

Shakers now find lost spirits, like doctors used to do, but they see ghosts as lighter and better dressed than the doctors did {218 mh}. Shakers believe that candles help out. Five candles were as good as 20 people curing {91 msc}. Bell ringing also helps. Shakers forbid sin, lying, killing, adultery, stealing, and badness.

A young man joined the Shakers and tried to be a missionary, but he "got back on the powwow way" with his tahmanawas. His family had to keep him tied up so he would not fly away {399 ph}.

Luck

The left shoulder, hand, or side of the body will twitch or shake when a relative dies or gets bad news. The back part of the arm will indicate that it was a distant relation {61 md}.

If you find a snake eating a toad and kill the snake, the rescued toad will give you good luck {256 js}. Two boys abused their power by using it to keep a snake from giving birth {255 js}. When thousands of snakes came to bite her, these mean boys laughed. Then a toad came and the snake gave birth. As the boys turned to go, they fell over dead. They were too free with their tahmanawas and used it wrongly on animals.

An agate found at the base of a tree struck by lightning was secretly carried for luck. Tiny fungus from the salmonberry is also kept for luck, not carried around. A hummingbird nest kept in a bullet pouch brought good luck when hunting {262 ph}.

Chehalis

POTLATCH

Reasons for hosting a potlatch included a) raising a social position, b) giving names, c) saving face (removing disgrace), such as after being thrown in a wrestling match, d) piercing the ears of a girl, and e) returning a favor {147 sh}.

People with spirit power hold small potlatches every winter when they sing in public. At big gatherings, 4 men and 4 women were appointed to help, and a special repeater (song catcher) made sure that the words and tunes of each song were correct. At a big winter spirit dance, communities would come in groups with a leader who came in backwards when he danced them in. The best kind of leader was painted in stripes and acted funny like a clown. The women who followed him each had a painted face, wore 5 white duck feathers stuck on top of her head, was wrapped in a shawl, and shook bunches of deer dew claws hung from a stout cane. Everyone there helped a person sing his or her own song, like at gospel hymn sings.

The dancing paused at midnight so everyone could be fed, often salmon skins stuffed with salmon eggs. Some were boiled and some baked nice and crispy. Hosts passed out spoons, with important people getting bigger ones traded from the Chinooks. After several nights of dancing, gifts were given out before all departed.

Important or royal families held small potlatches when their first child was born and a daughter became M1.

Gifts were always given at a funeral. The more important the deceased, the more elaborate the potlatch. These were also held at reburials (renewing graves) and for memorials. The person, known for this special power and strong lungs [to hold his breath], who moved the bones was paid with many gifts {368 ds}.

A person could advance their social position by saving and hosting a potlatch. A Lower Chehalis woman, "of no known family and a long ways from being pretty," gave a potlatch to earn more respect than most people of royal blood.

If a royal boy or man had a baby with a slave, the family hosted a potlatch to make the infant into a "person." Even so, that individual was always regarded as tainted and at least half slave {14 mi}.

Upper Chehalis had different words for giving things away with or without spirit powers involved [61, 624, 149, 426, 524]. Intertribal potlatches were held rarely because they were so expensive. A special large house had to be built, and people fed for 5 to 10 days.

The most famous historic potlatch, about 1870, was hosted by Chief John Heyden, half Oakville and half Tenino, helped by Jim Walker, a second chief of Oakville, by Charley Walker of Oakville, and by *Ulipanx*[w], half Quinault and half Upper Chehalis. It was held in the oak grove about 70 yards from Secena's house {14 mi}. People were invited from Gray's Harbor, Cowlitz, Skokomish, Puget Sound, and all over. It was held to have a good time, but the formal reason was to mark Heyden's daughter as M1. Jim Walker took the name *swtwpc*, from a Puget Sound ancestor.

Messengers were sent out ahead with sticks to invite important guests, who used the sticks to count the days until they were due to arrive. Invitations were serious business because someone might be left out, offended, and take revenge through sorcery or hostility.

At a Nisqually 4th of July gathering, Marion Davis was once denied food and took his revenge by killing his biggest Durham steer and feeding everyone. John Smith, an Upper Chehalis Shaker leader, reminded everyone never to get Davis mad at them {193 md}.

Chehalis

At Taholah potlatches, everyone was fed blueback salmon until they could eat no more. A chief with eat-all power could do this without ill effects. Sometimes, they fed guests whale grease or poured it into a fire. This grease was very valuable. Such conspicuousness was important at a potlatch.

At Centralia, women were given shiny tin plates that they waved around to attract light {202 mh?}. This potlatch was held to pierce the ears of a young girl. It was held in a potlatch house built by 2 men. Mary Heck's father held the girl's head, singing a spirit song twice, while 4 holes were put in each of her ears.

Another big potlatch was held at Westport, just this side of Damon's Point, so everyone could meet the dying son of the host. The family was royal and wanted everyone to remember this boy. So many people came that they overflowed the house. People, especially children, who performed were given clothing as gifts which had been piled around the boy. The Westports were rich in silk and cloth because so many ships and steamers went aground there. Old Secena got a bolt of ribbon, pinned one end to his hat, and let the rest stream behind him as he rode horseback. The ribbon flew far behind him and was very pretty. The boy died after everyone left.

While at public feasts men ate first, then the women. At a potlatch, people ate by community, both men and women together. The host ate last of all, along with everyone in his family who helped serve {294 ph}.

Chehalis

TALES

Background

Stories were told mostly in the winter, to forget the weather during long wet nights. A story teller usually started after supper, and might go until after midnight. Everyone had to lie flat on their back and listen. Only the fireman would get up to tend the flames. When he did, the listeners said "*ososos*" [158] to keep him and themselves from getting a hump back {387 js}. One formal ending was to say "black salmon" [691] {390 js}.

Story tellers would visit widely to expand their repertoire, making a business of it. Of course, stories got borrowed and changed this way. Star Husband belonged to the Upper Chehalis, but the Snoqualmie put it together with their own version. Spider told the girls they were married to Stars and helped them escape back to earth when one of them gave birth to the Moon at Lequito {345 js}.

Old people could support themselves as story tellers, getting food and gifts from their hosts. Most people learned stories from older relatives. Peter Heck was being taught by his uncle until he fell asleep one night and his uncle refused to continue {148 sh}.

Chief Yawnish held a "class" [school] to tell stories to boys, who took good care of him to show their respect and eagerness. Anyone with a good memory and a dramatic sense could become a story teller, even slaves.

Children had to swim before or after hearing a story to express their continuing interest. A child who could not remember stories had bad luck all the time.

Mary Iley's aunty used to say that when she asked her father for a story, he would say, "Run to the river and get it." Then she would rush to the river, dip her hand in, and bring up a stick or stone. She brought this back and her father told half the story until she got sleepy, then he would say, "Go run and put it away. You will get it again tomorrow." The next day, she asked and he would say, "Run to the creek and get it where you put it away." She would run and get something from the water and then bring it back to her father, who finished the story {327 mi}.

Origin stories were few. The Teninos traced themselves back to marriage of the royal daughter and a Wolf. A vague story suggested that Spilyai [Coyote] made the Taitnapam from elderberry sticks and then let his daughters eat fresh salmon and meat so the Taitnapam people would be this way {325 mi}.

Some stories explained how things got to be. Mary Iley told one about how a **psa** scratched chipmunk to make the stripes along the back of all of these animals {267 ph}.

The Mink story took all night. You had to lie flat and not move. If you sat up, you would get a crooked back. You had to pay attention and keep saying **hamukʷi** [540], a word like "amen" {50 md}.

Other families used the word "*hshemo'qi*" [548] while everyone laid flat on their backs to convey the idea that soon the dried salmon would be all gone, and there would be more to dry, the next time {165 md}. The word was also used as the nickname of an old lady [p 336 B20] who lived in a block {166 md} house at Cedarville because she had lots of dried salmon all the time.

Chehalis

Major characters were Xwane, who was smart, and Bluejay, who was smart and good, something like a fortune teller who knew things ahead of time. Old people used to pay close attention to bluejays when they were around. If they said "kash, kash" that meant good luck soon, but if they said "katsh, katsh" it meant you or someone close was going to die {50 md}.

Bluejay had a sister, called either Naw or Yui, who married among the dead.

"Drift people" referred to those who survived the Flood by casting off and floating away. Some people think they include the whites.

French stories were learned from early traders. Peter Heck thought that such stories were distinguished by the presence of "devils" {48 ph}. [Such tales seem to have more to do with royalty, fancy trade goods, monsters, and heros named john, jack, or jean.]

Short Stories

[Stick Indians, Wild Men] {53 md}. ThA verbatim. *s'iatkotq* = wild men [374 ćiatkʷ], whistle in the night time, go from place to place at night time. Never seen or it made a person crazy. Comes from the north, [has] a place there. They live right close to the mt [mountains, Cascades ?], very close to a large mt. Somewhere far above, near a river which leads to the mt. Up at the source, there are lots living there. [A power called] *stol&qwabc* [is] the reason a person who hears one will get crazy "tranced" or something like that. They say they are persons, but rather different. Tall and slim. When the Indians hear them whistle, they talk to them very kindly. Half of the people at Puyallup or White River tell of the siatoko. "I am from your place," so they would be kind to them and not harm them. Also came to Chehalis, last fall when I was fishing, my paint [partner], did not come. I had my tent and fire. Part[ner] said, "Siatko here." I said, "Oh, I am not afraid. I will talk to them." Well, I was awake still, and was coming from my canoe. He (siatko) whistled. My hair stood up. I said, "I am part Duwmch [Duwamish]. You must not do anything to me or try to hurt me, or anything like that." I heard this: L! L! L! L!. The people at Puyallup say that to young people to please them. So the siatko said that to me. The last time I heard him whistle, and I guess he went back. So I believe that if I had thrown stone[s] and said bad words, he might make me crazy, but did not want to do that! *smolokwitsal&m* = anyone who gets crazy. *ltmolokwit&n ltsiatoko* = if someone makes me crazy, or anything makes a person crazy.

Flood story (requested) {63 md}. Published, p. 3 # 4, as "The Flood," Upper Chehalis. Everyone drowned except Pheasant on the tallest tree on the highest hill, though his tail was forever marked by the cresting water.

[River Clams]. Story 1 {227 md}. Published, p. 132 # 64, as "Origin of the Fresh-Water Clams," Upper Chehalis. Two villages across from each other on the Chehalis River decided to join but the canoes of those crossing over capsized and the people sank to become local clams.

Boil and Excrement. Story 2 {228 md}. Published, pp. 131-2 # 63, as "Boil and Excrement," Upper Chehalis. Two elders living together decided to bathe and get firewood, dividing these tasks so Boil burst while pulling off bark and Excrement melted into the river. A variant of Boil and Hammer told by Charlie Anderson.

Robin {238 MD}. Published, p. 30 # 16, as "Robin," Upper Chehalis. Robin's wife dug camas all day, peeling them away to nothing. Angry when he found out such waste, he pushed her face into the fire. For relief, she rolled into the water, acquiring a coating of pebbles to become the periwinkle. In regret, Robin sits on the bank lamenting his act in song.

Thrush. Little Brown Bird {326 mi}. [An unpublished variant of the Flood Story given as ThA verbatim. "Thrush had five brothers-in-law who used to tell him, wash your face, he never minded, was dirty face all the time. Then after long time, his brother-in-law whip him. "Go wash your face." Brother-in-law repeat. "I am going to wash my face." repeat. Danced, just dipped himself, water shook, as jumped, the water rose and rose, sang, danced. "Brothers I'm going to wash my face. I'm bathing now, water come up all the time. Sister said, "Now you whipped him and made him bathe, now we'll float." Brother told him, "You can stop." "But you told me to bathe." Water rose, rose, *spitsx[+u]* flew away, and others flew away. Turned into birds and animals. Went far off into the woods. Spit[sxu] flew, all flew away as birds. Everything all over, water came down, all turned into birds when made Spit[sxu] wash his face."

Cowlitz story. July 7, 1927. (Asked for moral story, this is what got.) {327 mi}. Published, pp. 233-35 # 37, as "Grizzly Bear and His Sons," Cowlitz. A father had five sons and a grandfather had one grandson. The sons were sent far in quest of guardian spirits, but the grandson stayed nearby. Nevertheless, all were killed after the first son stole someone else's wife, the second some property, the third a horse, the fourth slipped on ice and drowned, and the fifth married Grizzly, who ate him. The grandson saw and reported all these happenings. After weeping uncontrollably, the father was revealed to be a Grizzly, who married his own daughter-in-law, and they moved far into the woods. Strenuous questing must be based on good morality to be successful.

Bear. August 3 {377 ph}. ThA verbatim. 40 years ago happened. Fellow went up in canoe to fish. Pretty soon saw Bear go across on river. Canoe just went, middle of river when got to bear, met [meant] to drown him. Land canoe just on bear's back, and would manage to drown him, when the canoe land on bear, bear cut [got] hold on canoe. The fellow stared. Just went back and sat down on the bow side. Was going to walk toward the man, man jumped in the water. Was holding on [to] canoe while under water. Dived under, and held to bow of canoe. Bear, repeat. Dived again. Kept going and going, finally canoe land on shore. Bear went off and left him.

Appearance of the Whites {381 js}. ThA verbatim. My grandfather said, when he was a boy, this was the Spanish or the Hudson Bay, that either the Squaxin or Mud Bay were camping one time. Big crowd of Indians camping on the shore. People came who were white. That is, a ghost. When came closer, the Indians said, "They smell strong like ghosts." The Indians were so clean, as went on, someone said, that must be people, others said, "No, ghosts." Others decided that the ghosts shouldn't come again. That would cause people to die. Indians watched them in white's camp, had boat, made fire, had something in their mouth to smoke. Some said ghosts are different that they come back from land of the dead. One warrior said, "What shell [shall] we do with them?" Someone suggested, "Shall be no ghosts here. We'll get rid of them." The chief agreed. When the whites went to sleep, hit him [them] on the head. One squealed, hit the others. Burned them up and everything they had. Thought they were really ghosts. Didn't kill them from meanness, but were really afraid.

Chehalis

Stockade. Published, pp. 11-12 #8, as "Bluejay and Crane," Upper Chehalis. Given to illustrate a use similar to a stockade {388 js}. Bluejay asked Crane for some salmon from his trap but could not understand Crane's reply and struck him. Crane promised attack so Bluejay made allies of Nettle, Bull-Thistle, Slipperiest Mud, Rotten Meat, and Skunk, who became the leader. Crane's crowd eventually trampled down the defending plants, but Skunk sprayed Crane in the eyes to win. The next day, Bluejay and Crane made up. Here is what the notes say about this engagement.

ThA verbatim. Enemies trample on the "enemies" about the house, would fall, but not hurt. Bluejay helpers were now tramped on. His git [hit] player was close to the door, Skunk, Crane couldn't stand the odor. Bluejay saw he was going to get him. Crane was trying to get him. Skunk had hind quarters turned toward Crane, let go and hit Crane in the eyes. Crane announced would retreat. Next day Bluejay and Crane made peace, Bluejay was whipped badly, except for Skunk, who saved him, his whole arm was crushed to death. End. This is a chapt[er] of a Bluejay story {389 js}.

Bluejay

Bluejay As Bungling Host {67 pb}. Published, pp. 6-9 #6, as Bungling Host (Second Version), Upper Chehalis. Bluejay was a widower with four children living with his grandmother. All went to visit Bear for breakfast, who cut meat from his thigh and roasted it for them. Bear had a rocking chair and also served fresh bread, coffee, potatoes, cake, and pie. The next morning when Bear visited with his wife and two children, Bluejay imitated each of Bear's actions but he almost bled to death until Bear fixed him up and provided more of his meat. Next, Bluejay visited Fish Duck, who had a wife and six children. His sons dove for fish to feed the visitors. When Fish Duck visited the next day, Bluejay's children nearly drowned until the other youngsters dove for fish successfully. Bluejay visited Seal, who had a wife and six children. Seal killed his youngest son to feed everyone breakfast, then the boy revived. When Seal visited Bluejay, that youngest son died forever. Bluejay went to Beaver's the following day and his family was served willow branches and black mud, but they could not eat it. When Beaver visited, Bluejay served that family the same and they much enjoyed it. Lastly, Bluejay visited Shadow, failed to steal some beads, and was served a salmon egg in a bucket of water that vastly increased. If Shadow returned the visit remains unknown.

Bluejay {88 msc}. Published, pp. 348-49 V # 2, as "Bungling Host," Satsop Tales. Bluejay and his sister Yu'i visited Bear, who fed them meat cut from his thigh. When Bear visited, Bluejay's five children dove for trout but the youngest drowned. Bear left them some of his thigh meat before restoring the cut and going home.

Bluejay {92 jw}. Published, pp. 343-44 IV # 1, 344-45 IV # 2, as "Xwane"" and "Bungling Host," Wynoochee Tales. Xwane broke up the fishtrap of an old woman to release the salmon. Starving and marooned on a bluff, he ate his own eyes, then prayed for new ones until he strangled Owl and took those eyes and wings to escape. He met an old woman packing baskets full of camas (lacamas) and offered her a slave in exchange for one of them, but there was no slave. Later in revenge, the woman traded Xwane a basket filled with mean bees and told him to open it only in a sealed up hollow tree where they nearly killed him so he had to eat his own eyes again to survive. Yellowhammer pecked through the stump and Xwane came out and wandered blindly, except for some dim help from flowers in his eye sockets, until he got to the home of Snail and exchanged her sharp eyes for the blossoms that soon wilted. Bluejay visited Fish Duck to eat Chinook salmon. When Fish Duck came as a guest, Bluejay struck his own head on a rock while diving and Fish Duck had to provide another salmon to eat. Bluejay visited Bear, who fed meat cut from his own feet, but when Bluejay tried this he became crippled and had to be cured by Bear.

Bluejay and Girl {207 mh}. Published, p. 20 # 11, as "Bluejay and the Young Woman," Upper Chehalis. A beautiful girl died and five days later Bluejay stole her body and searched for a powerful shaman to restore her. The fifth one did so and Bluejay had a wife until her parents visited twice and then took her back. Since then the dead have not revived.

Bluejay. Story 3 {229 md}. Published, pp. 15-20 # 10, as "The Contests (Second Version)," Upper Chehalis. A chief told his people to make a trip across the ocean to get a kind of bead. His sister Nau sent Bluejay with a string of beads to put around the head of a host to exchange for food. She told him to put branches on the bottom of the canoe to keep dry, but he heard her to say that he should hide between these bushes and the canoe. After some time, the paddlers heard five noises beneath them and so discovered an almost crushed Bluejay. After traveling five days, they got to the base of the icy trail leading to the hilltop home of their host. Bluejay jumped out and promptly stunned his head in a fall. Then the chief led the way up, his feet melting the ice for everyone to follow in his steps. At the door stood two huge dogs who greeted this visiting leader. The host chief was abed in a cold house, but he called his slave to kindle a fire from a tiny stick while Bluejay rudely complained. The stick became three cords of wood to feed a large fire. The house filled with dense smoke until another slave sucked it all in. Bluejay got too hot and complained about that. A tiny piece of whale meat produced a vast quantity that had to be consumed, but their chief had given all his people hollow elderwood sticks to put into their throats and out the other side. Only when a small amount of food was left did they remove these and eat normally. The chief called for a diving contest, with Seal as champion for the hosts. Bluejay dove for the visitors, but he arranged a pile of brush beside the canoe in the ocean so he could sneak breaths there and so he won. The next day the contest was to shoot at nimble human targets, either Beaver or Bluejay, who won on the fifth shot. The next day, he competed against Squirrel at tree climbing, clubbing him to death to win. The visitors had won consistently and were set to leave. Exchanges were made for food, but Bluejay put his beads around a pile of his own excrement because that is what he thought his sister said. She was very disappointed when he got home.

Bluejay. Story 4 {235 md}. Published, pp. 24-27 # 13, as "Bluejay Goes To The Land of the Dead (Second Version)," Upper Chehalis. Bluejay lived with his sister Nau and seemed to grow very sick. He asked her to step over his eyes, but she refused to expose herself until Bluejay got even worse. Then she jumped over his face, but he insisted she slow down until she stood over him the fifth time. Bluejay decided to marry her to a ghost who had asked to do so and they had a huge wedding. Later, Bluejay decided to visit her, crossing five prairies. He stood across from the city and shouted five times but no one came. Very tied, he yawned and a canoe came for him immediately. It had a hole in the middle and pile of bones at one end that was the brother-in-law. During the day, the dead were only bones, but at night they took on

Chehalis

flesh. What seemed a floating tree was a beached whale to them. After many differences of perspective, Bluejay left, carrying five buckets of water to put out five flaming prairies, but he misjudged and so burned up on the third prairie. When he got back to the city of the dead, everything seemed to him as nice as it should be. Because he burned to death, he soon went on the Second Death land where everyone sits head down. Later the dead go to the Children's City in preparation for the Return to Life. Babies are born head down because that is how they existed in the afterworld. The everyday bluejay was created from the sparks from this burned-up Bluejay.

Xwane

Xwane. Note "P" [Pike Ben] is "coached" by his wife, this may influence the type of story, ThA {71 pb}. Published, pp. 151-52 # 82, as "Xwane and the Fish," Upper Chehalis. Xwane put nice trout into the Satsop, blueback sockeye into the Tahola [Quinault], and into the Chehalis, black, silverside, and dog salmon to come every year. He also left a large falls [Rainbow] where eels stop, after they jump ten feet high, sometimes to fall back into baskets with a long handle.

Crane and Xwane. Always tell 2 stories before they stop {177 mh}. Published, pp. 145-46 #78, as "Xwan and Crane (Second Version)," Upper Chehalis. Xwane, Crane, and three others stayed at Scatter Creek. One day after gorging on blackberries, they all went to sleep on a sandbar until Xwane woke them up yelling the Qwa'qʷ are coming, four times. Then he too fell asleep and the Basket Ogress (Sqwaqwsma'ikk) came the fifth time and put them all in her basket. The other three escaped as she went under tree branches where they could lift themselves out. At her home, Xwane and Crane were treated well to fatten them up. Xwane planned to have Crane fall ill to sing his tahmanawus song after the house was entirely clean and plugged with moss and pitch. Her four sisters were to be invited. Crane put a tongue-flicking snake around his head, singing about it. Then Xwane took sick, spitting chewed bark onto his chest to look like he was spitting up blood. They danced continuously for four nights and the sisters fell into a deep sleep. Then Crane and Xwane set fire to the house so all the women exploded and burned up. Later these men ground up all the ashes to protect the future world. [The sense is that by eating berries straight from the bushes, they had no defense from the Basket Ogress.]

Xwane. 2 August {180 mh}. Published, pp. 148-50 # 80, as "Xwan Loses His Eyes (Second Version)," Upper Chehalis. Xwane got lonesome and went on a trail, meeting a woman with a basketful of steelhead salmon eggs. Four times he fooled her into thinking he was five brothers and so got four helpings of eggs, but for the fifth she put a hornet's nest in the basket and told Xwane to eat them inside a closed up tree stump. The hornets nearly killed him. Woodpecker made a hole in the trunk, and Xwane took himself apart to get out, starting with his eyes and anus, which were stolen. Claiming there were lice on her blanket, Xwane fooled Snail out of her eyes. At a Newaukum Prairie house where they were gambling with his eyes and anus, he stole them back.

Xwane and the Girl. Upper Chehalis Q'wayaił Story. 28 July {199 md}. Published, p. 152 # 83, as "Xwan and the Girl," Upper Chehalis. A girl remained tiny for five years, never growing. Xwane buried himself in a sandbar with his "organ" protruding and she "sat" on it, growing quickly from them on. {Distinct break in the overall manuscript, a gap after 200}

Animals

[Steelhead 1473]. Story (Requested) {134 js}. Published pp. 72-74 # 36, #37, as "Steelhead and Spring Salmon," Upper Chehalis (First, Second Versions). Spring Salmon had an enormous head and his younger brother was Silver Eel. Steelhead and his brother Trout always came into the Chehalis River from the ocean for the winter. Steelhead's power was that he would always revive after any death. One early spring, while Steelhead and Trout were going downriver, they met Spring Salmon and Silver Eel coming up, seeming to be a man and a boy. Spring asked the way to the falls at the head of the river, but Steelhead picked a fight, insulting his head, looks, and character. They fought all day, with Trout shouting so much that his mouth enlarged. Steelhead was killed, but Trout gathered up his bones and revived him. Spring Salmon took Steelhead's flesh and fat, while Silver Eel took the oil. Steelhead revived but some bones were too badly crushed so Trout got blossoms and limbs of vine maple to make replacements. In version two, he reused a shed snake's skin for his own outside covering. Hence Spring Salmon now comes to the Chehalis where Steelhead always belonged.

Walking Fish. Steelhead is the only one who goes to the ocean in the summer, about the month of May. Will walk about early in the morning, put his hands over his eyes and peep out over the prairie. Looks about to see who is there {136 js}.

[Steelhead] Story {266 ph}. ThA verbatim. Had fish trap here, Upper Chehalis. Clear across river. Steelhead can't get through. Steelhead went out on shore, on the prairie. Pretty soon people say something stick his head up, then down again. People excited, could it be a ghost? Pretty soon, up, again, went to look. Saw salmon on prairie, to see where he was and if going to the river. (Doesn't believe this.) Heck does not know anything about making fun of sockeye salmon or of any kind of salmon.

[Steelhead, Unpublished]. {239 md}. Steelhead Story. ThA verbatim. Steelhead came up and used himself here, spawning and so on. And now time to go back down home, was fat. He met Spring Salmon and Eel coming up. They met Steelhead and captured him, finally get best of him, and take all his fat away. Spring Salmon took some of the fat and took and gave it to Eel then let him go. Steelhead, somehow got some ironwood to make his backbone. How to make his skin, he found a shed snake skin. He thought, "This will be my skin now. This will be my skin." That's why Steelhead has tough backbone. Old people used to cook the backbones and chew the juice out, but Steelhead they couldn't chew.

Now Steelhead [Spring Salmon] and Eel has his fat. "Guess that is the reason he gets poor when he goes down." If not for that, would be fat. When hunt for Steelhead riffle in spring time, the fisherman hit the rock with his spear, pole, on bottom of river, then Steelhead comes toward fisherman. {239 md end}

Skunk. Upper Chehalis Qwayai-t Story {172 md}. Published, pp. 46-52 # 27, as "Skunk," Upper Chehalis. A chief warned his two daughters going to pick berries to take only the right trail sprinkled with red paint but never the left one sprinkled with feathers. The elder took the feathered trail and the younger went home. In a clearing she saw a big house and a little one, where a handsome young man lived. She married him, though he was Skunk, slave to the master in the big house. Through proximity to Skunk's odor, the girl became thin, yellowish, and unhealthy. Soon she gave birth to many tiny Skunks. Then the master rescued and married her himself. Skunk searched for them, thinking they were inside a spring that was reflecting them from their sky abode. He sprayed the spring, but they remained in view. After five times, he lay on the ground and, looking up, saw them. They told him to climb up backside first and rolled hot rocks into his anus, which pushed out through his mouth like a hoop and fell into the middle of the river. Skunk had to get it back, going down river. At each town, he asked after "his property" and was either insulted by a blunt reference to his anus or pleased by discrete directions. Far downriver people were playing with a hoop that shot out fiery red flashes. Changing himself into an old man with a cane, Skunk got his anus back and blasted all the players to death. Then he went upriver, blasting those towns who insulted him by having them seal up a house before hearing his "important news" but sparing those who were kind. He found a precious blanket covered with maggots, a camouflaged Whistlebird. Cleaning it off, Skunk took it as a gift for his former wife. Suddenly, the pack began to whistle and scare Skunk, who died so Skunks can no longer kill people with their musk.

Spear. {208 mh} Published, pp. 87-94 # 45, as "Spear," Upper Chehalis. Spear's sister would go out for fern roots to feed them, but Spear never shared what he got from his fishtrap. During meals, he ate salmon eggs hidden on his wrist. Doubting her brother, she married the chief of the Silverside Salmon living where earth and sky join. Spear went to visit. An old man called an Elk, who came beside him to be killed, skinned, butchered, and revived from the intact skin, head, and legs. Spear ate the elk meat and huckleberries from an inexhaustible tiny basket. At night, the house residents return howling, dancing inside holding broken fishing gear, which were their treasures. First came Black Salmon, then Silversides, Dogs, Springs (with sparse property), and Steelhead, These five species shared the house of their father Sqwe'lius and his daughter World's End. They slept and were gone the next day before dawn. World's End cooked his nephew for Spear's breakfast, and the father revived him from the bones. On the fifth day of this, however, Spear left a bit of meat and the boy died permanently. His sister told Spear to leave, so he returned through the air instead of the water. Inside a big house, he fell in love with a daughter of Thunder. After five days, Thunder tried to teach Spear to use wings and act like him, but he failed and fled. At another winter house, he briefly married a Pitch woman. In another house, an old man warned him to seek refuge in a dead white fir when attacked by another old man who owned the trail. He killed and burned up that elder so no one could ever own a trail again. He crossed a river over a fishtrap and married a Giant woman. He killed her father and another fighting over their fishtraps and decreed that these traps be far apart in the future so all had to share from the local one. He restored the sight of a middle aged woman, who warned him how to kill Cougar, an old man with a murderous long tail. He burned the body and modern cougars came from the ashes. In another house, an old woman warned Spear that people were gathering in a prairie to kill him but he changed them into a cluster of wild rhubarb plants. Finally, he found his own house with his returned sister inside, but, instead, he decided to become a May flowering plant that children could use as a toy. The sister also transformed into something useful.

Chehalis

Raven. July 14. (Heck can't remember all the story) Siyoyuw-n was a great hunter {336 ph}. Published, pp. 41-43 # 23, as "*Syuyu'wen*," Upper Chehalis. A great hunter shot an elk but did not track it. Raven found and claimed the meat. The hunter let him have it, though he lied. He butchered and carried it home to his five sons, but it was moss and wood when unpacked. Another time the hunter wounded an elk that Pheasant found and truthfully did not claim, so when packed home to his five children remained meat and rich fat because he was worthy. Raven discovered the bounty when a Pheasant child choked and alerted everyone. Ever kind, Pheasant gave Raven meat and half the hide. Raven put one hair from it on each of his children on a cold winter night and they all froze to death, but Raven insisted they died of getting too hot.

Urine. 7 August 1927 {324 mi}. Published, p 226 # 33, as Urine Boy, Cowlitz Tales. Urine danced every day on a rock, looking around. Five times, he killed a Danger pursuing a man, put the man under his single braid, and married him to one of his five sisters. The eldest had many children, but a son and daughter (brother and sister) fell in love and ran away. Their mother followed them and rubbed their mats together to revenge the shame. This couple had a boy who sang five times a day, "My mother is my aunty and my father is my uncle," until his father killed him. Finally, Xwane came and married them off to strangers, forbidding incest from then on.

Boogey [**Psa**] Story {10 mi}. Published, pp. 218-20 # 28, as "Chipmunk and the Dangerous Woman," Cowlitz. (See last year's story, when she offered him a salmon head [Reference is to another version, p 217-18 # 25.] Chipmunk was an orphan living with his grandmother Roe. While he was eating serviceberries, a dangerous woman attacked him and scratched his back. He escaped and his grandmother hid him under a basket. The woman wanted to know how the grandmother got so pretty white and so was tricked into letting herself be stabbed to peal off her skin. Her four sisters were killed by overeating meat, but Coyote had to find and kill their children, advised by his own "sisters" to first cut down their souls hanging from a tree.

Beaver **Psa** {182 mh}. Published, pp. 128-131, # 61, as "The Dangerous Beaver Being," Upper Chehalis. [A distinct break occurs here in the overall manuscript, which seems to switch to Marion Davis. Thus, the story began as {182 mh} and ended as {401 ph}.] Five brothers lived together. The eldest went hunting, shot a pheasant, hung it in a tree, and went on to find a shack where an old man asked him to kill a Beaver bothering people in the river. The old man gave him a phony spear and the hunter was killed by the old man, then changed into the Beaver, who ate the brother's heart. The other brothers were killed in turn, but the youngest (smartest) killed the Beaverman, aided by an informative dream. He burned up the corpse and modern beavers came from the ashes.

Mink. Oakville. This side of Little Rock, big prairie with "rolling waves" {65 pb}. Published, pp. 133-36 # 69, as "Mink Kills Whale (Second Version)," Upper Chehalis. A first paragraph about Noah was removed:

Noah, who had a big boat, same time he travel, all s[alt] water, not land at all, just s[alt] water and same time prairie, waves on the salt water. Used to be waves and first white man comes to this country, he came on this prairie. What is dis [this]? One, one, two, three, men perhaps. Trees to find. Three men got a shovel, mattock, dig in little hill to find what under.

Chehalis

Maybe gold think of. One little hill find one little flounder, wasn't det [dead] at all. So white man and Indians together excited. Indian man proved used to have waves there. Flounders inside and you can go on prairie. Whale in that prairie today. West from Olympia, cart half by railroad, look east, near Gate City. Whale get dry there, too. Whale's head east of prairie, stretched out. On the brush, his hand in a little hole. Tail to the west. Can't get out anywhere. So on the ground, kicking now. Think he'd like salt water.

Mink saw a Whale digging clams in a bay, cut his way inside, and cut off the heart to kill "it." He gave meat away to his villagers and sold some for a love medicine to attract a high class girl whose parents did not approve of him. Soon they had a baby Mink, went out for sea eggs [urchins], and Mink disgraced himself as a glutton so he and his son were abandoned on watery tree roots.

Mink. 25 July. Nisqually, White River, my mother's story {171 md}. Published, p. 361 VI # 1, as "Mink Kills A Chief's Son," White River. Mink confessed to the murder of the son of a chief, singing a song five times while Frogs and Crane chorused "Wa'a." Then Mink was butchered and his body parts shot off like fireworks with a bow.

Mink and Cougar. 6 August 1927 {298 mi}. Published, p. 209-211 II # 19, as "Cougar and Mink," Cowlitz. Cougar and his brother Mink went to visit one of his wives after a three year absence. His father-in-law Thunder planned to kill him, but Mink stayed awake to warn his brother when Thunder came with a knife. The next morning Cougar went out hunting, but stepped on Lark's leg. He mended her with beads and she warned him of danger. His wife was Grizzly Bear, and he was sent off with a phony bow and arrows, but he also kept his own. He made a dummy of rotten wood and dressed it in his own clothing. As Grizzly lunged for it, he shot her with all his arrows. Many slaves had been sent with him to pack the meat, but he fed the udder to his father-in-law. Mink got White Agate and Blue Rock and threw them into the house, where they fought until all was destroyed. Thunder and the slaves changed into birds. Mink agreed to stay near creek and lake water, while Cougar went into the trees. Xwane decreed that only like members of a species would mate thereafter, never mixing like Cougar and Grizzly.

Crow's Son. Mother's Story. 20 July {197 md}. Published, pp. 361-64 VI # 2, as "Crow Doctors Her Daughter," White River, Puget Sound, Song on p. 427. Crow was the mother of a son and a daughter. She went to dig clams on the bay and told the son to cook some clams for his sister if she woke up. Instead, he roasted his sister, thinking that is what she said. The fifth time, the son admitted his mistake and retrieved her body from the gooseberry bushes. Crow prepared to doctor her daughter, holding her right forearm against her forehead, and revived the girl. After digging clams five times, Crow clubbed a Seal and invited everyone to a feast except her brother Raven. She had sent her son with fat to invite his uncle, but the boy ate the gift. Raven disemboweled the boy, ate the fat, and threw the body in the river. The boy was still alive "in his heart" and asked the fall leaves to heal him. After resting on the shore, he got lots of lake fish with a gooseberry hook, took them home, roasted them, and fed Raven until the bones stuck in his throat and he died.

Chehalis

"French Stories"

All but the last two were from Mary Iley and freely mixed native and European motifs, often ending with an explanation of how the world was everafter changed in some way by these events.

[Obstacles] {17 mi}

A king had a daughter he promised to any man who could get him a drink from the ocean. Jack went to try. Along the way, he variously met a strong man twisting out an oak tree by its roots, a man shooting eyes out of mice, a man with long legs bound up, a man with a powerful sneeze, and a man carrying 5000 pounds of rocks. They all agreed to help Jack.

He got to the king and was given a cup like a sieve. He gave it to the man with long legs, who stretched to the ocean and back in an instant, filling the cup, and Jack won. Everyone danced all night.

The king gave him 5000 pounds of gold, which the rock man carried away. The couple left in a buggy. The bride warned that her father would send an army to take everything back. When the soldiers came, the crack shot held them off until the other man sneezed to "mash them to nothing."

At their new home, the tree man had cleared trees from 10 acres and built a house.

[Gifts] {19 mi}

A boy worked for a rich man for 10 years until he was 25 years old. The man gave him a tiny white pony with a fancy bridle and saddle. He showed the boy how to clap so the pony "pooped" silver, then gold. The man told the boy never to let anyone else touch the pony.

Along the way, the boy stopped at a little house overnight with a old woman he called "grandmother." The next morning, he rode into town, where the pony only produced "manures." He went back to the rich man, who said the real pony had been stolen. He gave the boy a box that fulfilled wishes.

The boy wandered and eventually came back to the old woman's house, where his box was stolen. He went to the rich man, who gave him a whip that struck on command. It whipped the "grandmother" until she was bloody to get back the pony, then to the bone to get back the box.

The boy started a rich farm and store. He married, but his wife ran off with the box and the hired man. The boy went looking for her and found 2 men fighting over a pair of shoes that could go anywhere. He outfitted both men, took the shoes, and used them to get back the box, leaving the wife and hired man to starve on a height. He married again and got richer.

[Marriage] {23 mi}

A mean couple kept a boy, apparently wanting to marry him off to get the many presents [dowry] provided that the wife "stayed until her bones rot." [Taitnapam not French marriage procedures were described.]

Chehalis

Handless Girl {300 mi}

A farm had a full smokehouse, then a ham began to disappear every day. The farmer caught the thief and locked him up, but the only daughter released him. Enraged, the father cut off her hands and sent her away with her dog.

Five women tried to attract the dog, who seemed to be a stray, by leaving food out. In time, their brother Peter [the thief ?] came home, found the hiding girl, and married her. He gave his sisters many things to take good care of her while he was away "at his store." The bride soon had a baby, but the sisters sent her away, with the baby tied to her back, and wrote their brother that the infant looked like the dog.

The girl was helpless and cried. Then she prayed to God, who gave her new hands. She found work on a farm. Her husband came home and yelled at his sisters. He advertised to find the handless girl, but she had hands now. After 3 years, the husband saw the dog and found his wife and son. The farmer gave her $500 for all her work. The man sent his sisters away with nothing.

Boy Wins King's Daughter. {303 mi}

A thief stole from a farmer and was locked up, but the son freed him. The father banished the son, who found work herding pigs for the king. In the forest, the boy met the thief, who took him to his secluded home where they fought until the boy killed the thief and his wife, taking over all their loot.

The king went to war. The boy fought as a brave soldier [knight], each day with a horse and clothes of a different color (black, red, bay, gray, and spotted). At last, he was wounded on the knee and identified as the swine herder. He became a hero and married the king's daughter. His parents forgave him, but lying and stealing remain in the world.

Bull {309 mi}

A lonely woman worked her farm all the time. In the garden, she wished aloud for a mate to work outside so she would only have to do house chores. That night a handsome man (her own bull) came to her bed. He fooled her for four days, on the fifth, she found and burned up his horns and hide so he stayed a man. They made money, but he took up with another girl in town. On the street, the wife reminded him that he was a bull, who then rampaged until he was shot dead.

Seven Heads {311 mi}

A man (seven-headed monster) ate only teenagers, including all of the king's children except a young girl. A soldier wanted to marry her, so he killed the man. His dog helped by biting the legs and distracting the heads. Later, when a blacksmith claimed to have done the killing and was about to marry the girl, the dog broke up the wedding banquet. Then the soldier showed the king all 7 tongues and married the girl. The blacksmith was nailed to the wall, but later released.

Chehalis

Little Jean (Johnnie) {314 mi}

Three brothers, who were 15, 13, and 10, went to work for the king, who had daughters of 14 and 12. The older brothers grew to hate the youngest, named Jean, because he worked in the kitchen with the girls and got lots of kisses and hugs. The jealous brothers told the king that Jean could steal the cow of Pelatcoke [a monster], wanting that man to eat him.

An old lady, whose children had been eaten by the monster man, helped Jean. Delighted with the cow, the king sent him back several more times for the horse, moon, fiddle, and clock. By the end, he had killed the monster's wife, got fine clothes, married a daughter, and become king.

King and Two Queens {321 mi}

The king went to war and met a young girl. He wanted to divorce his queen and marry the girl. His wife loved him and refused a divorce. Her pure white skin bled in grief. She pretended to be a maid to the girl. Everything she washed came out the whitest possible because she was pure and good. She stopped the wedding and made the king stay with her. The law was that both husband and wife had to agree to a divorce and then wait six months before marrying again.

Little Jack 1 {382 js}

A boy got luck from tiny things to become a gambler. He got involved in a crooked game and lost everything, even his clothes and his body. He fled to the farm of a sister and brother, who had hard times because their only crop, crab apples, kept disappearing. No one could stay awake to watch. Jack made hoops filled with sharp nails so when he fell asleep they jabbed him awake. He saw tiny birds taking the crab apples down a hole, followed them, killed them, and went on to Hell, where he won Satan's daughter in a card game. After 30 years, he went back to France.

Little Jack 2 {385 js}

When he was younger, Jack's sister sent him to the store for butter. On the way back, he saw his shadow for the first time and tried to rub it with butter to even it out. Since he gambled all night and slept all day, he never had gone out in the sun to see any shadows.

Chehalis

Appendix: Other Sources

A classmate and colleague of Adamson, Melville Jacobs (1934, hereafter MJ) worked with Mary Iley (Eyley in his spelling) and her family, providing more details on her life. She also gave him the evocative image of a myth being like a canoe, tied up each night during a long telling or drifting away during lengthy asides (MJ: x). In 1934, William Elmendorf (1993, hereafter WE), a graduate student at the University of Washington, began his masterful research with Frank and Henry Allen, who lived at Skokomish and had Klallam, Twana, and other ancestry as befit members of the high class. Together, they provide fascinating accounts of Upper Cowlitz and Lower Chehalis life and rituals.

Reports from Sahaptin Upper Cowlitz

In June and July of 1927, Jacobs collected texts in Morton, including 12 (1 European) from the father (Sam Eyley), 5 from the mother (Mary Eyley), and 10 tales (2 European) from their son (Sam N. Eyley, Jr.).

Sam N. Eyley, Jr., was about 30, lived in Morton, Washington and spoke English and Taitnapam, as did his wife (MJ: 102). 107 # 3 Rock and Boil.

Sam Eyley, Sr, (**a'ihili, i'lsxtxalikt**), was about 70 or 80, a Yakama who lived among the Cowlitz for over 40 years, suggesting to Jacobs that his stories were "Salish Cowlitz, told by a Yakima, and having ta'iDnapam traces" (MJ: 125).

Mary Eyley (**kiya'itani**), "she is over sixty and a far abler person and better versed in native -- especially Salish -- lore than her husband; she is partly upper Cowlitz Taitnapam, mainly lower Cowlitz Coast Salish (tLkwi'lipam, as the upper Cowlitz say) in tribal identification" (MJ: 125) her Taitnapam had a slight accent. She was the sister of Sophie Smith, worked in 1926 and 1927 with Thelma Adamson, her father was Lower or Salish Cowlitz (MJ: 168).

Mary Eyley also supplied an account (MJ: 223) of the quests of **kaLxa'yim** (Minnie Case's mother and Mary's aunt). As a girl, her father's sister sent her into the mountains, where she stayed two nights. While crossing along a fallen log, she met an old man with white hair, who took her into his home, saying, "I am your grandfather, you too will have white hair like me. You will have a son who will be a courageous fighter and a daughter who will be a shaman. He gave her "penis power."

Later, her father's sister sent her to a lake near Cinnabar Mountain at the head of the Chehalis River, where she swam out to a rock and spent the night. In the morning, she awoke on shore, with blood on her nose and mouth, because that spirit was hostile to her prior spirit. She went home and slept for two days until a shaman came and "fixed" both her soul and her power (MJ: 224).

Later, she went to pick blackberries and met a seated old woman, who said she would never pick blackberries again (because she would shortly be dead.) Then the old woman turned around and became a blackberry. She was doctored by her mate, however, and recovered to live a long time.

Lower Cowlitz Ethnographic Notes by Mary Eyley indicated there were ten families in a longhouse, which also held winter food of dried chinook salmon, roots, berries, nuts, and meat

Chehalis

(MJ: 225). Women wore short skirts of woven cedarbark. Travel was by canoe, and some drowned. They caught smelts, sometimes at Cowlitz Prairie, but "they were always fearful of the smelts, because a great many died from smelts." Lower Cowlitz traded with Upper for huckleberries, and intermarried to receive elk and deer meat from Taitnapam hunting husbands. Though Lower Cowlitz "were ashamed of it. They gave a man or woman to the ta'iDnapam for food." A slow match of a cottonwood root was carried to make fire (MJ: 226).

During winter, Cowlitz gathered to sing tahmanawas songs, using "poking sticks" (five or six foot staffs) to drum on the floor or ceiling. Sometimes, a staff danced by itself. Men were on one side, women on the other. When they danced, women followed behind the men. At intervals, they feasted on salmon eggs, camas, fern roots, and dried fish.

Upper class marriages were arranged through messengers. At the wedding, bride and groom, sitting across from each other, were dressed in finery and their families exchanged gifts and slaves. The mother of the groom tossed unfinished moccasins as a path between the couple and two men led the groom half way across, where he sat down (MJ: 227). The bride, richly dressed, was led to sit beside the groom. As long as the pair stayed married, the families gave gifts to each other.

Boys (and girls) were sent to seek power so "everything will go on by, everything moves aside and is open to him, valuables come to him, the boy's body will be bright and light with it...." In the mountains or somewhere, he met a person who told him what his life would be before that person turned and changed into something, maybe an animal like a deer. A girl took work, often an unfinished basket, along on her quest so she would never be idle. When the person who empowered her turned to go, it often was a plant like a water lily.

Mrs Dan Secena (**wa'x-mlut**), a pshwa'nwapam, northernmost Sahaptin band near Ellensburg. "Mrs Secena is a dignified, energetic, social active woman of about sixty years of age; she speaks several Washington coast Salish dialects about as well as the pshwa'nwapam (Kittitas) Sahaptin speech of her childhood. She is now a well-traveled and respected shaman and is married to a Chehalis (Coast Salish) Indian. Her blind son Jonas was Chehalis informant and interpreter for Dr. Adamson and Dr. Boas in 1926 and 1927" (MJ: 213), and dictated texts for Jacobs in August of 1927. She provided a family history of her great grandfather *t'saya'ix*, his daughter *wa'x-mluD* (her namesake grandmother), younger son *wiya'ipax*, and their marriages and descendants. Her own grandfather was *kuyu'pqan* and her father was named *kt`sa'p* and *saya'mxan*. Her namesake grandmother led women's activities like berrying and rooting (MJ: 270). An old man served as a whipper to discipline children and make them grow up strong (MJ: 271). Upper class people had small feet, while commoners had big feet. A chief served the people and spoke to and for them to "take good care of things" (MJ: 272). After whites came and settled Kittitas Valley, the pshwanwapams divided, some going to Nespelem on the Colville Reservation, where they vanished [untrue, as witnessed by the family of Ida Nason], and many more to the Yakama Reservation, where they left offspring.

Reports from the Twana of Hood Canal

The Skokomish, Nisqually, and Upper Chehalis gambled at horse races and disk games, about 1860, between Skokomish and Elma at Carstairs Prairie, where strawberries and camas grew. Secena raced his horse against that of a Nisqually and won. Undaunted, the Nisqually went home, got a second horse, raced that, and lost again to Secena.

Chehalis

Then they switched to disk game. That Secena's wife was half Skokomish, related to the Allen family, so the Skokomish joined Secena's team. That night, they played, but Secena pointed wrong five times, so the Skokomish took the lead. Secena had met his Robin power on that prairie so he sang for help, took the disks, and the Nisqually missed [misguessed] him twice. All night, they alternated pointing. In the morning, Secena asked for a new man, Jim Allen (father of Frank and Henry), to point and won half the counters (30 of 60). Many people now gathered to bet and rally until the pile of bets was soon taller than a man. The game went on for a day and two nights until Secena had 57 counters and the other three were paused in the middle. Secena took over, sang his second song, and won the game.

The Nisqually asked for a second chance, so their request was honored. They bet 12 horses, but Secena soon won half the counters. Jim Allen took over, called on his White Owl power, and won most of the counters. When the Nisqually got the disks, a man knelt down and took off his shirt to show many scars where he had cut himself [in supplication]. He won back three sticks, but then Secena's side won them all. The Nisqually lost two games in four days and many walked home broke, although Secena and other winners gave each of the best Nisqually gamblers a horse (WE: 22-26).

At Westport, a Lower Chehalis man was training his son for wealth power, there called **stk'e`lcomis** [Lushootseed, Twana **tiyuɫbax̌ʷ**]. The son went up a big bluff near Aberdeen carrying a big rock to weight him down when he dove off. Eventually, he was taken into the underwater house where this spirit lived after they were sure he had only high class blood. He was shown all the women and slaves he would have, then woke up on the beach. Whenever people came from all over to bet him slaves, women, and goods in disk games; he won them all. The wealth power had demanded his first and oldest wife in return, but the boy did not want to give her up. He dressed up a pretty slave and threw her from the bluff, but she would not sink. After she was retrieved, he covered himself with a goat wool blanket, and had his slaves paddle home. When they got to Westport, the boy had vanished. Wealth had taken him instead of the wife (WE: 167-168).

Frank Allen's great grandfather was half Westport Lower Chehalis. This man and his brother both had four wives, each with a slave. Their uncle was the Westport chief. When a nephew, a great Twana hunter, visited, he was married to a Westport relative to keep him there. The day after his wedding, he killed five elk. The slaves packed back the meat for a feast (WE: 168-169).

Frank Allen's grandfather's uncle's father was the Westport chief and had the power to land whales. He sang "To the beach, to the beach, Whale" for two days, then had his slaves watch the beach. A few days later, a whale beached and was cut up by the slaves into long strips. He kept those near the head and gave away those near the tail to his own tribe and neighbors. People came from all over. Foreigners had to buy whale meat with gifts and women. Nothing was wasted. This chief brought whales to beaches as long as he lived, then his son became chief but he never got that Wealth power for whales. Once, when the slaves were cutting up a whale, they found it was full of dentalia money. He gave everyone in the huge Westport town five shells. Another time, many sea otters washed up on the beach and the valuable pelts were used to make seats for his wives and children. The Quinault went out in canoes to hunt whales, but they just drifted to the Lower Chehalis (WE: 169-170).

About 1870, a Lower Chehalis named Lighthouse Charley lived at Georgetown on Shoalwater (Willapa) Bay and had three or four thousand dollars when he left his wife for another woman. The jilted wife hid all his money, burying it in place after place until she died. Charley hired a woman shaman with Little Earth power represented by a four foot effigy with a handle on the back. A big fire was built inside Charley's house while two men retrieved the effigy, wrapped in cedarbark, from the woods. Charley picked a middle-aged man to hold the effigy, and the man asked for oil to grease his hands so they would not be burned from touching the rushing-about wooden carving. The woman sat at one end and sang, while the man knelt beside the fire, facing her and holding the figure in front with both hands.

The effigy was cold from being out in the woods, so it had to warm up. Suddenly, it shook and danced before it made for the door and into the house next door, which had belonged to the jilted wife. The woman shaman followed, along with everyone else beating sticks and singing. The effigy left the house and went into the woods to a windfall, where they found evidence that the money had once been buried there. By then both the woman and the handler were sweating profusely. They went to the beach and a canoe, where the woman sat, until the figure pointed across the bay. As it was noon, they cooled off by having a lunch of sturgeon.

They decided to ask Old Man George Kanoodle from Oakville to join them with his own Little Earth figure. Kanoodle was fishing on the Columbia River so Charley was gone all afternoon fetching him. That night they ate again, sang for hours to alert the spirits, and ate again before going to sleep. The next morning a man went into the woods to get Kanoodle's effigy. He came back with it, but his fingers were blistered because it was so hot. They sang while the figure rested by the fire, then variously led them next door, to the windfall, and back into her house. There Kanoodle confronted Big Jim, her brother, who admitted she had given him $20 before she died. He offered it back to Charley but was allowed to keep it.

Next, both effigies went across the bay, where the wife had been born and raised. Little Earths do not work on water [since they belong to the land], so they rested quietly in the canoes going over. The wife had another house over there, where they built a fire to heat the effigies before they went around together inside the house. Finally, at the right rear post, they both shook violently. Men dug down three feet and there was a can wrapped up in a rag. Inside were five twenties in gold and two fathoms of dentalia. "Now that is an Indian way. When you know you are going to die you put something where you were raised." Next the effigies ran into the woods to a big tree, where they dug between two roots to find her hatchet, mat needle, and mat creaser. Then they went back to Charley's for a meal.

The next morning they began again since they had found only $120 of thousands. They warmed the effigies at the fire before each rushed off, rose up high, and shook. That meant something far off, pointing toward Westport where the wife had lived as a girl. Everyone got horses and rode there. The effigies followed the trail of the woman to the beach, where she (and they) cried, washed, trotted to the middle of where the town had been, and sat down. They dug three feet to find $100 and 2 horn spoons wrapped in gunny sacks and rags. The effigies went up a hill, down to the shore, and pointed back to Georgetown. Everyone rode back and ate. The figures were warmed, put into a big canoe, landed a quarter mile down the beach, then paddled into the bay, where they pointed down into deep water.

The next morning, Charley got a long drag net that a white man had given to him and put it into that deep water, but all they got were a few fish and crabs. The second time, they went out farther and hauled in flounders, crabs, and the big rag that had been wrapped around the money. Then they gave up. Charley paid blankets and guns to the shamans and handlers. They only got

$220 that she had given as presents to the places where she was raised, so her ghost could retrieve the value and spirits of these objects to take into the afterworld.

Only the Chehalis had those single Little Earths with handles. The Duwamish used painted boards, and the Twana had canes and a rope to go to the ghost land (WE: 242-249).

Other incidents mentioning the Oakvilles or Upper Chehalis include Skokomish selling them whale meat for dentalia -- a chunk for 10-20 shells (WE: 27); declining to join Kitsap's Lushootseed expedition, about 1845, against the Lekwiltok because they had never been bothered or attacked by these Kwakwaka'wakw (Kwakiutl), although a Cowlitz warrior did join because his people had been attached once (WE: 146); coming to the falls of the Skokomish River to eat herring provided by a Fish Boss power (WE: 193, 194); and giving a wife to a Skokomish shaman for curing a sick man (WE: 204).

During a Skokomish potlatch at Enatai in 1878, the Nisqually "advertised" an elite girl who had been carefully secluded and chaperoned, eating only every second day. She had yet to marry because no one could match her worth until a Cowlitz man named *Ayel* gave 50 horses to marry her (WE: 33).

BIBLIOGRAPHY

Adamson, Thelma 1934 Folk-Tales of the Coast Salish. New York: Memoir of the American Folk-lore Society, Volume XXVII. 430pp.

Boas, Franz 1901 Kathlamet Texts. Bureau of American Ethnology, Bulletin 26.

Curtis, Edward 1913 North American Indians. Salishan Tribes of the Coast, Chimakum, Quileute, and Willapa. Volume 9. New York.

Elmendorf, William W 1993. Twana Narratives. Native Historical Accounts of a Coast Salish Culture. Seattle: University of Washington Press.

Fried, Jacob 1974 The Territorial Distribution of Some of the Aboriginal Population of Western Washington State and the Economic and Political Aspects of Their Culture. Coast Salish and Western Washington Indians III: 193-243. American Indian Ethnohistory. Indians of the Northwest. David Agee Horr, ed. New York: Garland Publishing.

Gunther, Erna 1925 Klallam Folk Tales. University of Washington Publications in Anthropology 1 (4): 113-170. August.

1927 Klallam Ethnography. University of Washington Publications in Anthropology 1 (5): 171-314. January.

Harrington, John Peabody 1942 Chehalis Notes. DC: National Anthropological Archives. Microfilm Reels 17, 18.

Hajda, Yvonne 1990 Southwestern Coast Salish. Northwest Coast. Wayne Suttles, ed. Handbook of North American Indians, Volume 7: 503-517.

Jacobs, Melville 1934 Northwest Sahaptin Texts, Columbia University Contributions to Anthropology 19, Part I (English).

Kinkade, M Dale 1963 "Phonology and Morphology of Upper Chehalis: I." International Journal of American Linguistics 29 (3): 181-195.

1963 "Phonology and Morphology of Upper Chehalis: II." International Journal of American Linguistics 29 (4): 345-356.

1964 "Phonology and Morphology of Upper Chehalis: III." <u>International Journal of American Linguistics</u> 30 (1): 32-61.

1964 "Phonology and Morphology of Upper Chehalis: IV." <u>International Journal of American Linguistics</u> 30 (3): 251-260.

1966 "Vowel Alternation in Upper Chehalis." <u>International Journal of American Linguistics</u> 32 (4): 343-349.

1967 "Prefix-Suffix Constructions in Upper Chehalis. "<u>Anthropological Linguistics</u> 9 (2): 1-4.

1991 <u>Upper Chehalis Dictionary</u>. University of Montana Occasional Papers in Linguistics 7. 378pp.

1992 "Kinship Terminology in Upper Chehalis in a Historical Framework." <u>Anthropological Linguistics</u> 34 (1-4): 84-103.

Laird, Carobeth 1975 <u>Encounter with an Angry God</u>. Banning, CA: Malki Museum Press.

Miller, Jay 1988 <u>Shamanic Odyssey</u>. The Lushootseed Salish Journey to the Land of the Dead. Menlo Park, CA: Ballena Press Anthropological Papers 32. 215pp.

1999 <u>Lushootseed Culture and the Shamanic Odyssey</u>. Lincoln: University of Nebraska Press.

Palmer, Katherine Van Winkle 1925 <u>Honne, Spirit of the Chehalis</u>. The Indian Interpretation of the Origin of the People and Animals. As Narrated by George Saunders. Geneva, NY: Press of W.F. Humphrey.

Ray, Verne 1938 Lower Chinook Ethnographic Notes. University of Washington Publications in Anthropology 7: 29-165.

1974 Handbook of the Cowlitz Indians. <u>Coast Salish and Western Washington Indians</u> III: 245-315. American Indian Ethnohistory. Indians of the Northwest. Edited by David Agee Horr. New York: Garland Publishing.

Taylor, Herbert C., Jr 1974a Anthropological Investigations of the Chehalis Indians. <u>Coast Salish and Western Washington Indians</u> III: 117-157. American Indian Ethnohistory. Indians of the Northwest. David Agee Horr, ed. New York: Garland Publishing.

1974b John Work on the Chehalis Indians. <u>Coast Salish and Western Washington Indians</u> III: 159-191.

Van Syckle, Edwin 1982 <u>The River Pioneers</u>. Early Days on Gray's Harbor. Pacific Search Press. 423pp.

Work, John 1912 Journal, November and December 1824. TC Elliott, ed. Washington Historical Quarterly 3: 198-228.

Suquamish Contents

169 Introduction   167   Research 172   Editing 173

174 ECONOMY   Julia Jacobs   Drying   Deer and Elk   Salmon   ;Ellen and Wilson George   Moons   Dog Salmon Eggs   Potatoes ~ Ed Sigo   Salmon Trolling   Deer ~ John Adams   Specialization   Moons   Plants   Fish   Hunting

178 TECHNOLOGY   Julia Jacobs   Fibers   Duck Nets   Canoes   Cooking Pits; Ellen George   Dog Yarn   Basketry Hats   Combs   Dishes   Stone ~ Wilson George   Weirs   Digging Sticks   Bone   Sweatlodges ~ Ed Sigo   Burning Down A Tree   Wood   Tools ~ John Adams   Fibers   Nets   Tools   Canoes   Mat Houses

186 SOCIETY   Ranks   Leadership   Wilson George   Chiefs   Ellen George   Speakers   John Adams; Slavery   Ellen George   Wilson George   John Adams

192 AGE AND GENDER   Julia Jacobs   First Menstruation   Marriage   Child Care   Death   Burial ~ Ellen George   Division Of Labor   Training   First Menstruation   Marriage   Child Care ~ Wilson George   Naming   Training   Divorce   Ghosts ~ John Adams   Marriage   Difficult Childbirth   Burial   Games

204 INTERTRIBAL RELATIONS   John Adams   Ed Sigo

204 MEDICINE   Julia Jacobs   Ellen George   John Adams

205 RITUAL   Salmon Ceremony   Ellen George   Power, Questing, and Spirit Allies ~ Wilson George   John Adams   Wilson George   Secret Society   Odyssey Ceremony   Potlatch

218 FOLKLORE   Julia Jacobs   Changer   Dog Husband   Star Husband   Ellen and Wilson George; Ellen George   Little Wild Men; Wilson George   Wolf and Winter Salmon; John Adams   Star Husband   Mink and Devilfish   Mink   Wolf and Elk   Steelhead and Rainbow Trout   Raccoon   Five Brothers   Girl With Long Fingernails   Chipmunk and Basket Ogress   Little Wild Men

227 WAR TALES   Wilson George; John Adams   Kitsap In Battle   Klallam Attack   Skykomish Raids   Leschi   A Kitsap Raid   Wilson George

231 APPENDIX   Kitsap Raid

234 Bibliography 235

JOURNAL OF NORTHWEST ANTHROPOLOGY

VOLUME 33	Spring 1999	NUMBER 1

SUQUAMISH TRADITIONS

Jay Miller, with Warren Snyder

Abstract

Ethnographic materials on the aboriginal inhabitants of Suquamish on the Kitsap Peninsula across from the city of Seattle are assembled herein from rechecked 1952-54 notes by Warren Snyder to include the topics of Economy, Technology, Society by Rank, Age and Gender, Intertribal Relations, Medicine, Ritual, Folklore, and War Tales. An appendix adds another battle account and a finding aid lists elders and subtopics.

INTRODUCTION

As preparation for my book-length overview of Puget Sound ethnography, following up a prior study of its major ritual -- the shamanic odyssey to the land of the dead (Miller 1988, 1999), the 1952-54 fieldnotes of Dr Warren Snyder were typed into a computer and edited into this ethnography. Copies of it have been in the keeping of the Suquamish Tribe for over two decades, but this publication now makes it available for peer review and scholarly evaluation. A similar effort was made with the 1927 Chehalis area materials from Thelma Adamson, only there her notes had to be condensed and here his had to be fleshed out and articulated. Strongly motivating these contributions has been increasing despair that anthropologists, especially in the Northwest, have been actively denying their own founders, both women and men, even as local native peoples constantly remind each other not to forget their elders. This growing contrast only adds to the larger sense of loss.

Named for the important leader prior to Chief Seattle, the Kitsap Peninsula is the western edge of the Lushootseed (Puget Sound) peoples. Their language and traditions place them within the southern dialect chain, distinguished from the northern one by some important vocabulary differences and respective accents on the first or second vowel of the basic word stem ~ root.

Throughout Lushootseed territory, each "tribal" group is closely associated with its own river drainage, which provided cohesion and identity to an otherwise diverse collection of autonomous communities and camps. On the east and west sides of Puget Sound, however, were exceptions to this dendritic Y-branching pattern. On the east, the drainage of the Duwamish had a complex outlet with an H or trellis pattern, fostering an important population concentration on the interconnecting Black River, since diverted and filled. On the west, the Suquamish ancestral territory is located between the Sound and Hood Canal, a salt-water hook. Significantly, this homeland lacked any major rivers, so their subsistence adaptation required extensive travel to collect supplies needed for winter, in addition to the harvesting of local foods from sheltered bays and local small streams.

Suquamish

Their usual and accustomed (U&A, UnA, U and A) fishery, therefore, was judged by the Federal Court to have extended from the Fraser River mouth and Puget Sound to Hood Canal, of necessity. Barbara Lane (1974: 4) specifically noted "The Suquamish often traveled to Hood Canal and to upper Puget Sound as well as in other directions to harvest natural resources or to visit with relatives in other areas." Local resources, moreover, were also utilized, as these were available. "Shrimp were taken near Indianola and near Holly on the east shore of Hood Canal" (Lane 1974: 20).

Most recently, before aggregating on their present reservation, the people now known as the Suquamish (Riddell 1932), occupied about six winter towns, located on inland bays on the east side of the peninsula. The west side of the peninsula along Hood Canal was too windy, cold, and unprotected to allow for anything but camping during mild weather or for enduring privations necessary for religious devotions. All of their villages and camps represented central locations giving ready access to diverse nearby resources, to Puget Sound, and to interior forests. Those in the inland bays also had the advantage of access to the shores of both the Sound and the Canal via canoes, trails, and game tracks.

Modern elders recall going with parents and grandparents to the Edmonds area to gather blackberries and basketry materials. In alternate years, they camped at Mosier near Mukilteo to take advantage of the biennial run of "pinks" (chum salmon) there.

Suquamish tacitly approved the settlement of Port Gamble (Little Boston) on the northeast side of the Canal by S'Klallams who were working at the Pope and Talbot Mill started there in 1852. A similar situation also applies to the Klallam colony at Seabeck near the Washington Mill.

Important trails across the Kitsap Peninsula included those from Dye Inlet, from the villages at Chico - Erland Point to Seabeck, from Poulsbo (known to Suquamish as Mapleville), from the village at Suquamish to Port Gamble. That from Silverdale on Dye Inlet was so useful it is now paved as the Anderson Hill Road. Martha George (Indian Claims Commission 1952: 44) explicitly testified to the use of these trails.

The occasion for the return of the Snyder note cards to the tribe was a 1982 fishing rights trial requested by the Skokomish, acting as successors in interest to the nine aboriginal Twana winter communities, which were located along the western and the lower portions of Hood Canal. Their request was intended to establish their primary right to fish in the Canal and to exclude other tribes as this became necessary to guarantee profits from commercial salmon fishing. As judicially determined, Skokomish were given exclusive rights to fish the canal, but, to their credit, sent shellfish to the Suquamish museum dedication and allow Suquamish to fish in the canal during good runs.

Since ancient times, Suquamish came to Hood Canal because of signals from nature, not invitations or permission. Many people went there when the basketry materials were ready, or the shrimp, or the oysters, or passed through on their way to hunt in the Olympics. The fall run of dog salmon was announced by the ripening of the salmonberries, much as the spring runs coincided with the blooming of the dogwood.

As they finished the processing of dog salmon for winter use, the guardian spirits of the most inexperienced visionaries came to them while they were still at the Canal. Older, more experienced visionaries knew their spirits well enough to have them arrive after they were safely settled in the winter villages. People helped the new singers, by gathering around to help with these songs while they were still in the camps. Later in the winter villages, shamans and other professionals would give them better help at controlling their powers.

Research

Located close to a major city, much material exists relating to Suquamish, but little of it has been published. Early converts to Catholicism -- Chief Seattle was baptized with the name of Noah -- much relevant data is located in the Seattle Catholic archives. Records from the trading post run by William Deshaw [De Shaw], son-in-law to Chief Seattle, are now stored on the campus of the University of Washington.

Active fieldworkers have included Edward S Curtis (1913), who collected another version of the Lushootseed battle in Canada at ends of these notes and singular materials from Jacob Wahelchu, a famous leader who lived for over a century. In 1910, John Peabody Harrington collected linguistic data and place names from Chief William Rogers, hereditary leader of the Duwamish but living on Miller Bay among the Suquamish, who regarded him as one of their subchiefs. In 1942, Harrington returned to nearby Port Gamble and coastal Washington.

Just before his tragic death, the young Herman Haeberlin worked among the residents of the Tulalip Reservation in 1916-17. After resuming her position at the University of Washington, Erna Gunther edited his notes and translated his 1924 German text to provide the classic summary of Lushootseed tribes, concentrating on the Snohomish, Snoqualmie, and Nisqually.

In 1918, Thomas Talbot Waterman, continuing efforts by Harrington and Haeberlin, worked closely with Arthur Ballard in the collection of folklore and developed close ties at Suquamish, particularly with Jack Adams and family.

During the early 1930s, pleas by Lushootseed and neighboring tribes were heard to demand compensation and recognition for inequities from the loss of their lands and resources. These issues were raised again during the 1950s when the federal government established the Indian Claims Commission allowing tribes to sue for compensation for the loss of land, property, and improvements. Warren Snyder testified for Suquamish (Indian Claims Commission 1952: 94-97), but that fall testified again on the basis of a compelling document and map that clarified his earlier testimony. While this is good academic practice, it is deadly in a court of law, where any change of opinion is ruthlessly discredited, and Dr Snyder became an object lesson for expert witnesses who have come after him.

Some time after her 1935-36 fieldwork among the Puyallup-Nisqually, Marian Smith, a kindly woman crippled by polio, visited on the Port Madison Reservation with Sam Wilson. Her notes (Folder Four), now in London, detail family histories of Wilson, Kitsap, and Seattle; religious and spiritual topics; mythic and personal happenings; and technology (Amoss 1975). Smith remained in correspondence between 1939-47 with an amateur archaeologist named Ernest Bertelson living at Suquamish. Copies of his letters and his artifact collection, particularly from Old Man House, are now respectively in the Archives and the Burke Museum at the University of Washington, or on loan to the Suquamish Tribal Museum.

Before and after his testimony for Suquamish land claims, Dr. Warren Snyder worked in the Suquamish area from 1952-55. He began as an archaeologist testing the site of Old Man House, but, during the claims litigation, he collected ethnographic information to testify on 13, 16 June 1952 and 4, 5 August 1953. Then, at the encouragement of Dr Melville Jacobs, he turned to linguistics, producing a grammar of Suquamish Lushootseed. While his ethnographic note cards remained in storage, these linguistic materials were published (1968) in two volumes of grammar and of texts, place names, and dictionary interesting for its sweeping diversity of camps, resource areas, graveyards, forts, and places mentioned in mythology.

Lastly, according to a late, great Suquamish leader, while the locations of ancestral Suquamish villages are scattered in all prior sources, an important feature for determining residences, whether camp or village, is proximity to fresh water. For example, Blake Island lacked any water source. Overnight campers had to carry water with them, though now that it is a public park, drinkable water is provided by the state.

Lawrence Webster, past tribal chairman and grandson of Jacob Wahelchu, said that good water was only available at a few locations on the Kitsap Peninsula. On the East Side were Grovers Creek and others in Miller Bay, Indianola -- a spring in the sand flats to the east, Kingston Bay -- at its head, Manzanita, Eagle Harbor at Winslow -- a small but good water supply, Liberty Bay near Scandia and Sherman, Dyes Inlet at Clear and Chico Creeks, Gorst Creek on the Port Orchard side, Blackjack Creek, Colby, Ollala, and Wilson Creeks. On the West Side were Creeks on Port Gamble Bay, and Big and Little Beef Creeks near Seabeck on Hood Canal.

Editing

Based on these note cards by Snyder, a basic Suquamish ethnography can be presented. The breath, scope, and purpose of his three field research are rare for the Northwest or anywhere else, making it all the more valuable. The cards which are presented below were given to Jay Miller in September 1982 during a meeting in the Sacramento home of Warren and Grace Snyder. Miller was then preparing to serve as the expert witness for the Suquamish in the case adjudicating Skokomish claims to a primary fishing right in Hood Canal. When the notes reached Seattle, Miller reviewed and edited them in anticipation of this publication, before turning the originals over to the Suquamish Tribal Archives.

The notes consist of 5x8 inch cards, each devoted to a particular topic and elder, with long entries numbered sequentially. They were arranged in a file box according to conventional headings like land, material culture, economy, society, religion, and folklore. Miller undertook to write out the sketchy phrases and sentences, relying on his own fieldwork among Suquamish. Any comments he introduced into the narrative are marked by [brackets]. Topics are arranged from the most to the least voluminous, noting in curved brackets { } the initials of the person who provided the information to facilitate comparative work in the future. Linguistic terms that have not been verified are in *italic* while those confirmed by Vi Hilbert are in **bold**.

Because data from women have been relatively scarce, each topic begins with material supplied by Julia Jacobs, who lived at Indianola until her death. She was the mother of the former tribal chairman, Lawrence Webster (1899-1991, thus 83 in 1982), and the adopted daughter of the long-lived Chief Jacob Wahelchu, who died at the age of 112 in 1911 (cf Miller 1999: 11-13). Other material was provided by Wilson George, living at Tulalip, Ellen Sigo George, his double first cousin (two brothers married sisters) living among the Port Gamble Klallam, and Ed Sigo, living at Shelton in 1952 before he moved to Squaxon Island where he died in 1982, and John Adams, about 80 in 1952 and living near Poulsbo (known to the Suquamish as Mapleville), until he died just short of his 90th birthday in July 1961. He was the son of Jack Adams (**hadᶻius**), who died at the age of 75 in 1931 and was a major source for the information collected by John Peabody Harrington about 1910 and by T T Waterman about 1920.

Suquamish Traditions

ECONOMY

Year {jj}

The year was divided into different seasons. There was a time of the year when the wind blew a lot, around March or April. This was called spopohəgʷd. There was a time in the fall when the salmon fishing and berry picking first started. It was called patalos [pəd "time of" + tˈalos = "sliced salmon"]. A cold winter was called stəs = "cold", while winter in general was called pats [pədtəs = "time of cold"]. Summer had two names, shadab [warmth] and **padhadab** ["time of warmth"].

Drying {jj}

Berries were treated in the same way meat was cooked. They laid fern on sticks and then put the berries (huckle, black, salmon) on top. They turned the berries over every so often until they were thoroughly dry. Then they were stored in hard baskets for winter use. When they wanted to use some dried berries, they soaked them in water and smashed them in a hard basket with a piece of wood used just for this purpose.

Horse Clams were shelled and the inside muscle put on sticks about 2 1/2 feet long, pointed at one end. They made a long fire and put a frame across one or both sides. The clam sticks were leaned against this frame and turned often to dry and cook. When they were done, women strung them on cedar bark strings and dried them further in the sun.

Butter Clams were steamed and dried. They gathered rocks together and made a fire on top of them until the rocks were red hot. Then they took the fire off and made the rocks level. The clams were left in the shells, put on the rocks, and covered with mats. They cooked for about 20 minutes. When they were cooler, they were shelled and put on sticks like horse clams. They were roasted, put on cedar strings, and put in the sun. Butter and horse were the only two kinds of clams that were dried. They were eaten after being soaked in water, boiled, or chewed as they were. Sometimes the clams were slightly smoked to give them a different flavor.

Deer and Elk {jj}

The meat was sliced thin and laid on sticks over a fire to cure and dry.

Salmon {jj}

Soup. Fresh salmon was boiled. It was cut up, put in water, and boiled. Then they added small roots that looked like onions and were called ċabəd. They had a sweet taste and used to grow over near Seattle. The Yakama still dig and use them [camas?]. They also put in another plant that looks like macaroni and was called **piyaxe** [bitter root]. They put the soup in a big, hard basket. They had certain baskets for eating soups, usually round and 3 feet wide. Julia's father had one. Everyone sat around the same basket to eat the soup. They used wooden spoons, big around with a short handle. Each person had their own spoon to dip into the soup.

Suquamish

Smoking. Salmon was butchered with a special bone knife Julia heard about but never saw them. She can't describe them exactly. They put sharp sticks into the strips of flesh to make it stretch and stiffen. They hung these up, with a fire under them. They used fir bark for the fire, sometimes alder, but fir was best. The fish were left there for a few days, less then a week, until they were dry. They used a smokehouse for this after the whites came. Before that they used their living quarters in a plank house.

They only dried salmon and herring. Julia never heard of them drying sole or halibut [?]. Herring was dried like salmon except that the bodies weren't spread out with sticks. They were strung on sticks and hung over a fire to smoke. Dried fish was eaten boiled or as it was.

Seasons {eg, wg}

Ellen remembered that her father had different names for the "moons" of the year, but she didn't recall them. Wilson said that the coldest part of the year was called xa?xa?. Following was elsoqwa [iłsoq̓ʷa = "has a younger brother"]. It was called this because it wasn't as cold and the weather was milder. The word xa?xa? means "sacred, forbidden, taboo." It refereed to all the words to live by, like telling someone not to lie, talk back to a parent, or show disrespect for someone older. Or *xa?xa? gʷadsyabukʷ*, "Don't ever fight." Early December before xa?xa? was called **sičalwas**, meaning "put away [sheath] your paddles." This was the time when they stopped hunting and fishing. Other terms for the seasons included **paƛkole**, meaning the change of weather to the spring time following **spopohəgʷəd** = "winds inside," and **waq̓ʷaq̓us** = "frog's face,", referring to the frogs that come out in February to sing, following "younger brother time."

Each "moon" or month was devoted to a particular activity, with approximate Western calendar months,

- July was spent drying clams, catching early salmon, and picking blackberries, blackcaps, red huckleberries, and red elderberries;
- August involved continuing to dry clams, pick salalberries, eat fresh summer dog and humpy salmon (not good for drying), and hunt for fattened deer;
- September to October saw much activity with the fall salmon runs, the beginning of duck-hunting, and the picking of huckleberries;
- November had things winding down except for taking ducks;
- December was the start of the sacred season, the first games and ceremonies, although they still dug some clams and took bottom fish from canoe heated with fires inside;
- January to February were spent at ceremonies and visiting;
- March was the beginning of the salmon return;
- May was for salmonberries and red elderberries, with some camas dug on Smith Island, steamed or kept dry in a basket;
- June to July brought salmon trout, with some dried after it was cooked.

Wilson said they started making their canoes in the spring and tried to finish them during the summer. The purpose was to have them done by the time the salmon started to run. Ellen said a Klallam told her that when you worked on a dugout canoe, it shortened your life unless you washed and kept the cedar smell off your body. Wilson said it only shortened your life if you worked on cedar after dark.

Suquamish

Dog Salmon Eggs {eg, wg}

These fish eggs were dried and smoked in deer guts. The gut was turned inside out, cleaned, blown out, and filled with the eggs. They ate it like cheese and it tasted something like it, too. They ate it mixed with salmonberry sprouts or potatoes. They never dried silver salmon eggs because they had too much fat and soon spoiled.

Potatoes {eg, wg}

Ellen said the Klallam got their first potatoes from the Chehalis. Ellen's Klallam father in law's grandfather got them and planted them at Port Discovery Bay. They were growing there when the first ship came in and the whites bought some of the potatoes for the crew. Ellen believed that the Suquamish got their potatoes from the Chehalis at about the same time.

Salmon Trolling {es}

They gathered and dried kelp, tied strands of it together, and used this for trolling. They made partly curved hooks from a hardwood like ironwood or dogwood and attached them to the kelp ropes. These were baited it with clams, especially cockles, and used it in the Sound where there were salmon for most of the year. The creeks had salmon only during the spawning season. At other times they had to troll for them in the Sound.

Deer {es}

Deer came down to the beach only during the summer (June, July, and August) when the flies were bothering them in the woods. The rest of the year they were back in the forests. After a kill, the animal was butchered and the meat sliced to be dried over hot coals. The deer had regular trails through the woods. Ed had heard of traps being set into these. They tied a rope from a tree with a hoop hanging at head height over the trail. When a deer ran down the trail, it caught its neck in the loop and strangled itself. Hunters used these animal runs to travel back into the woods everywhere. Ed has used them on Squaxin Island. He believed that the underbrush of the past was quite similar to what it is now.

Specialization {ja}

There were special men to do the different tasks, like whites have carpenters, blacksmiths, painters, and so on. Each of them had "something" [power] to help made him or her do that job. A hunter might have Wolf [power]: **stəqayo**. Specialists could also do other things. A hunter might have "something else" for fishing, but he was not as good at being a fisher as being a hunter. A few men might be good at all of them, depending on what they have.

They had names for the different times of the year: **ƙaqʷlab** means everything was nice and quiet now, about May; **əɬska** meant older brother and was December, followed by **əɬsoqʷa**, younger brother; **waqʼaqos** was when the frogs started in February or March; **paƛxʷay** was dog salmon time in October; **paƛkole** was in the fall when they started to dry salmon and pick huckleberries; and **pədhədəb** was the summer months of June, July, and August when they picked berries.

The yearly cycle by approximate month ran as follows:

June to July = picking and drying blackberries, traveling to the areas where they were found and
    living in summer camps. There was little fishing then but they hunted. Women went

berrying and men went hunting. Women dried the berries and the meat, along with cockles, horse clams, and butter clams.

August = picking and drying salalberries, storing them in deer intestines. Men went hunting, started getting ducks.

September = fall salmon runs, silver and tyee (king). They moved to the streams the salmon were going up to build dams [weirs] across them and spear fish to be sliced and smoke-dried. The body was split and held open with cedar sticks. There were no berries now. Women were busy drying salmon, also getting and drying clams. Men were hunting ducks, eaten fresh, not preserved.

October = ate fresh huckleberries. They worked hard catching and drying dog salmon. Men started fishing for smelt and continued through early December.

December = There was little doing then, cold weather and snow brought the people back to the winter villages for ceremonies.

January to February = herring started to run in late January and continued into early March. They were caught and dried, together with spring salmon, **yubač** when fresh and **talop** when dried.

March to April = no particular fishing, mostly hunting. People still in the permanent winter villages.

May = left the winter villages and went to various camping areas. The salmon berries were ripe, eaten fresh and not dried. Salmonberry sprouts eaten with dried salmon eggs. Only went for bottom fish (flounder, sole, and skate), available year around. It was a bad month for doe because fawns were on the way, so they only killed bucks.

All year long, they took clams, seal, porpoise, and used torchlight fishing for flounder. In the fall and spring, they used to camp near creeks on Port Orchard Bay for the salmon runs. The camping places were located according to what they were after, going to different spots according to the season and what was ready to be caught, dug, or gathered; then prepared, boiled, or smoke-dried it for storage and winter use.

Plants {ja}

Fern roots were dug and warmed on the fire before being eaten. Salmonberry sprouts were pealed and eaten raw. Blackberries were picked, put in deer gut, and placed on a platform over a fire to dry. They kept a long time in this way, and were soaked in water before they were used in food. They did the same thing with cranberries.

Fish {ja}

Herring. When these spawned on seaweed they would collect the eggs and eat them raw. They shook water grass to get the eggs off. Then they washed and ate them. They also took branches and little trees three to four feet high and put them in the water off the beach. When the tide came in, the herring spawned on the branches, which the Indians collected for the eggs, washed off and eaten raw. They dried some over a fire to preserve them for later use.

Smelt. They split cedar limbs and wove them into a "dip" net [more like a seine] about a foot wide and six feet long. The smelt spawned on the beach. People dug a hole there to hold the smelt after people dipped them up from the shallow water. Someone else then took them from the hole and put them in baskets, usually women and children. They cooked the smelt by sticking them crossways through the middle onto hardwood slats. Each one could hold a lot of fish that way. They placed the slats in the ground leaning toward the fire, turning them several times to cook thoroughly.

Hunting {ja}

John saw some of the original forest when he was young. There wasn't nearly as much underbrush then as there is now that the forests have been cut down and second growth has come up. In the old days it was easy to get through the forest. They had to do this to hunt deer, among other reasons. John said there used to be elk in the Suquamish area, but that was before his time. He knows it was true because he once found some elk horns in the woods. The old people said that the elk used to come into the area [from the Olympics ?].

John never heard of running deer or elk down with dogs. The old way was for several men to spread out and go through the woods. It was easy to detect the trail of a deer by the trampled bushes and grass. When they scared up a deer, they shot it with bows and arrows. They also used traps. John never saw one, but the old people said they were made of wood, but he wasn't sure if it were a deadfall or some other technique.

When the deer was butchered and the meat sliced, it was hung way up over the fire, not close to the heat but in the smoke coming up from the fire. When they wanted to use the dried meat, they hammered it to soften it up. Since it was already cooked, they could also eat it as it was. Their hammer was a stone pestle shaped like an elongated dumb bell. They also used it to break the bones to get the marrow out after the old people had eaten the meat off the bones.

John hunted with his uncle [John] Curly around Poulsbo and Keysport, going back into the timber for grouse, pheasant, deer, and elk. People always considered it a good hunting place. John hunted there in 1896. They also fished in the area. There were no separate fishing grounds that John knew of. They didn't use traps there, but John heard that they had before the whites came.

TECHNOLOGY

Fibers {jj}

Soft Baskets. These were made of dried cattails. They started weaving them at the base. When they had finished a flat bottom, they turned the cattails up and continued the weaving for the walls. The top was finished in a different way, braided around the edge. These over one/under one twill-woven containers were made in different shapes, for different purposes, mostly storage since they did not hold water. They were decorated by dyeing the cattails. Wild Oregon grape gave a yellow color, and wild cherry bark a brown one. These ingredients were boiled to bring out the color.

Clam Baskets. These were made of cedar boughs, with a checkerboard weave on the bottom. The boughs were then brought up the side and two stripes were woven around them, every inch or so, to give the basket shape. It was a very loose weave to let out the water and grit from the clams. Julia made hers with a handle like a shopping basket.

Hard Baskets. These were water proof and made of cedar roots split into long, even stripes. These were the easiest to use. They were dried in the sun to season them. To make the foundation, a number of them were bunched together. An awl or another sharp point was used to make holes in this long bundle to be able to sew on the outside covering and designs. This sewing also held the bundles together to form the basket. In modern times they have used a punch with an iron needle as the point to make the holes. Before this the awl was of bone. The sewing made the bundles coil around to make a flat bottom before they were piled on top of each other to make the sides. The shape of the bottom determined the shape of the basket, oblong or round.

The sewing alternatively went through the bundles and then over them to fasten the basket together. The finished outer coating was a nice, even pattern of stitches. The decoration used colored stitches woven into the exterior. Colors used were red of wild cherry bark, white of a dried mountain grass, and yellow of Oregon grape roots. All these were boiled in water. Designs were usually geometrical and sometimes intricate. These baskets were used to carry and store water, make salmon soup, and stone boil food.

Mats. Cattails [*olal*] were sewn together with a long wooden needle about 2 1/2 feet long and called pacad. It had a hole in one end and was sharp on the other. They were made from the branch of a bush called qacaqʷac, ironwood. Julia had the one used by her foster mother. It had a triangular cross section and was slightly bent, 1/2 inch thick in the middle and 3/4 inch wide. [The mat creaser is called x̌ədalusəd = "push over the face of it" + instrument suffix, "something for."]

The cattails were gathered in the fall, about September. They were best then because they were strong and stiff. They grew at Jefferson Head, at Indianola just west of Julia's, at Richmond Beach [**stubus**], at Edmonds, and at the mouth of the Duwamish where they were best of all. All of these places were also Suquamish territory and they harvested cattails there from their canoes. They were spread and dried in the sun. When dry, they were split into strings. They took a cattail, doubled it, and then rubbed it on the thigh under a hand. This string was tied into the hole in the needle. The other dried cattails were laid side by side on the ground. They used string to tie the ends of the cattails together. When these were secured, they ran the needle through rows of cattails and pulled the thread through. They used several needles to make holes at even intervals along each cattail. When all of the needles were in place, they turned the mat over and sewed it on the other side. They used the mats for beds, piled several layers thick to about six inches. They rolled up mats to make pillows.

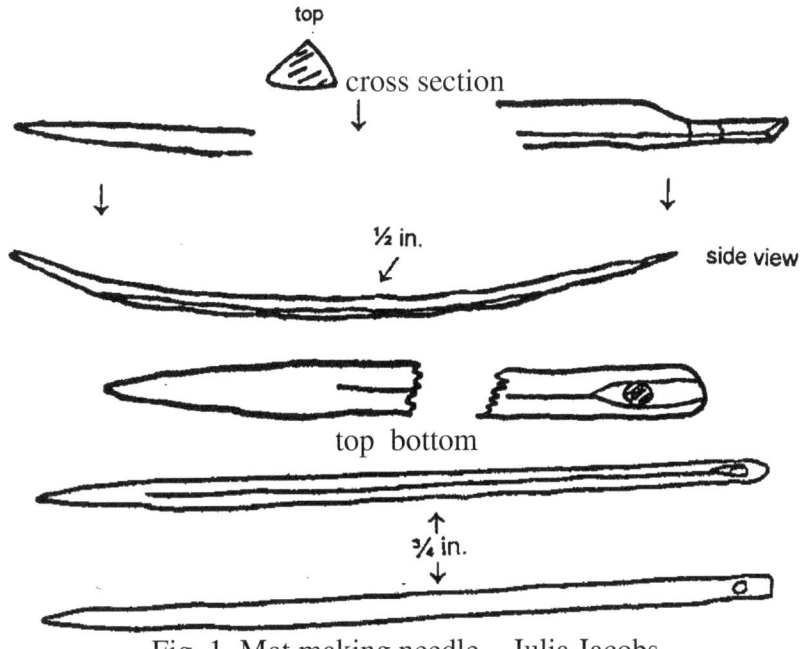

Fig. 1 Mat making needle ~ Julia Jacobs

Duck Nets {jj}

There were aerial nets made of string, stretched across a narrows, like Agate Pass, with a man on each side. When the ducks were coming, they pulled up the net for the ducks to fly into. They were also put up along shore out in the water or on poles where ducks would be feeding on herring eggs. When the ducks got behind the net, people on shore started making noise to scare them. The ducks flew off in the opposite direction and hit the net. They got their necks caught and couldn't get away, if they didn't break them. As a girl, Julia hunted ducks this way with her parents. There were lots of ducks then, but no more.

Canoes {jj}

They used a small hand adze to dig into a carefully selected cedar log to turn it into a canoe. Julia saw lots of them made, but the adze had an iron blade in her day. It took about half a year to make a canoe. When all carved out, they burned the bottoms, then scraped off the char and rubbed the surface until it was smooth and hard.

Cooking Pits {jj}

There were two cooking pits on the sandspit at Miller Bay. To make one, they gathered rocks and made a fire on top of them. This got the rocks hot. Then they cleaned off the remains of the fire. They leveled out the rocks and put food on top of them. The food was clams, mussels, potatoes, or a root [sčadə] that looked like onion. They covered the food with a cattail mat and left it for hours. When it was cooked, they gathered around the big open pit and ate it.

Dog Yarn {eg}

They used dog hair and the "cotton" from pink fire flowers [fireweed] to make a yarn for blankets. The dog had long hair. Ellen's grandfather said the dog was black with [woolly] long hair. When finished, the yarn looked gray. Ellen did not know how the hair was taken off the dog.

Basketry Hats {eg}

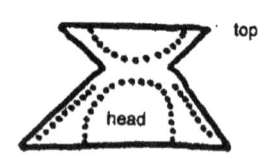

These hats were used for protection from rain or sunshine, woven of cedar root like a hard basket. Women wore them, maybe men, too, but Ellen and Wilson were not sure. The hat had the shape of an hourglass or an X. Ellen's half-sister, a Suquamish, had such a hat.

Combs {eg}

Before the whites, women used combs made of yew wood with long teeth, "like a Chinese comb." Ellen's grandmother had one made by her own father. It was as wide as a hand. Ellen thought that men used them, too, but she wasn't sure.

Dishes {eg}

They used to make large spoons out of wood and horn. Ellen had one used by her grandmother, made of horn. The bowl of the spoon was 120 mm long, 75 mm at the widest, and 16 mm deep. The handle was 80 mm long, 30 mm at the widest, and 7 mm thick. Ellen also had an old Klallam spoon. The bowl was 130 mm long, 117 mm wide, 23 mm deep. The handle was 85 mm long, 35 mm wide at the base, and 7 mm thick. It was hooked at the end and perforated.

To make these horn spoons, they took a horn, wrapped it in weeds, and put it in hot water. When it was soft, they split it and opened it out. Whenever it started to get hard, they put it back into the hot water. When it was most soft, they bent it into shape. They kept bending and putting it in hot water until it had the right shape. Then they cut and trimmed it so it had even edges. Ellen didn't know what they used to cut it. When it was finished, they let it harden for good. Then they used dog fish skin to sandpaper the surface smooth. Such spoons were used for eating and for stirring cooking food.

Ellen's grandmother also had wooden spoons made of maple and alder, similar in shape to the horn ones. All of them were plain, no carving or decorations. Her grandmother also had large wooden platters. These were 2 to 2 1/2 feet long, rectangular with four corners, almost square. The ends were 2 or 3 inches high, sloped slightly outward. The inside was a basin, like baking pans. These platters were used for communal meals.

Fig.2 Eating Spoons, top & side views ~ Ellen George

Stone {eg}

Ellen said there was a big rock just south from Johnson's, up from the beach, where people used to go and get stone for making tools.

Weirs {wg}

Wilson never saw these closely. They were made of poles driven into the ground on two sides, with split cedar pounded between them making porous walls. These stretched out into the water from the beach, as far out as the tide went. At low tide fish were caught inside, but they swam out at the high one. Therefore, the fish, herring and cod, were gathered up every low tide when the trap was dry.

Digging Sticks (Dibbles) {wg}

It was used for clams and roots, tapered to a fire tempered and hardened point. Each woman had two or three of different lengths, for different purposes, made of ironwood. All of them were big enough around to be comfortable in her hand, and slightly curved for better thrust. The longer ones were for horse clams and other deep foods, while shorter ones were for little neck clams and anything else requiring shallow or fast digging.

Suquamish

Bone {wg}

Wilson's father worked with bone, cutting and grounding it with a rough stone, mostly to make knitting needles. There was a Duwamish who made bone barbs and put them in a metal point to make salmon spears. He tied two barbs together with a string and put pitch over all of it. This was Henry Moses, a young man about fifty [at Renton].

Sweatlodges (sxʷcićabi) [*swuxtəd*] {wg}

Wilson saw and used one at Point Glover. They were always built by a stream where there was running fresh water. They were built of fir or cedar saplings, against the wall of a bank. The earthen bank became the back wall, after they dug it out and squared it off. They stood the poles together as close as they could, about three thick, to make the walls and stuffed the cracks with moss, which eventually took hold there and grew on the walls. Split cedar was put across the top for the roof, the split side up and the bark one down. Another row was laid over the cracks with the split side down and the bark up. Then dirt was put over the roof to seal it tight. When done, the lodge had a square shape with an entrance in the middle of the front wall, open to the roof and about 18 inches wide.

The door was made of split cedar, just big enough for a person to get through. Usually, there was room enough for only one or two people. The inside walls also had moss stuffed in the cracks and were about five feet high, so people had to stoop slightly in there. There were no seats, only cedar limbs on the floor.

The fire was built outside to heat the rocks, which were taken inside. If you had dry bark that didn't make much smoke, you could use it to build a fire inside on top of the rocks, but you had to brush the coals off when the rocks were hot. It was cleaner to heat the rocks outside. Once they came inside, a little water was thrown on the rocks to create steam. When the steam got too light, they added more water. They stayed inside for as long as they possibly could.

When you had enough, you went to the creek to throw cold water on yourself. Then you could go back to sweat again. This procedure could be repeated several times during one session. When you were all done, you rubbed yourself with soft, shredded cedar bark. The used rocks were safely stored in the back against the dirt wall.

Wilson never heard that the sweatlodge was used in connection with the guardian spirit quest, any ceremony, nor had any other special meaning. It was just supposed to be good for a person to do this.

Burning Down A Tree {es}

Ed watched his grandfather do this. First his grandfather determined the direction that the tree was leaning and built a fire on the opposite side. After the fire was started, he piled rocks against the place where the fire was burning the tree. The rocks kept the heat focused on that spot. It took three or four days to burn a tree down, though four or five feet thick. He came to tend the fire a couple of times a day and add more fuel.

Wood {es}

In the old days, the bow was held horizontally. The end of the arrow was grabbed between the thumb and first joint of the index finger. They grabbed the arrow not the string.

Suquamish

Bows were about four feet long, made of yew. They were flat, not rounded in cross section, and narrowed at the middle for an easier grip. Some were all straight, others curved at the end. He watched his uncle curve the ends once. He wrapped a piece of blanket soaked in water around the end, buried it slightly in the ground, and moved some of the fire to the spot. When it was baked soft, he took it out, scorched it with a heated nail in three places on the inside, convex side, and then bent the end back. He did the same to the other side. Ed did not believe that the Suquamish ever put rawhide on the back of the bow. He felt that only "Eastern" Washington [Plateau] Indians made sinew backed bows.

The fire drill was rubbed between the hands to ignite some fine kindling to start a fire. They didn't use a bow to twirl it.

Salmon spears usually had two points, made out of ironwood or of bone barbs rubbed smooth on rough stone. The points were mounted in a Y shape with the barbs held on each tip with wrapping and a covering of pitch. If they had no rawhide for the wrapping, they used wild cherry bark.

The cod lure was used in the San Juans [by Klallam ?], but not in Puget Sound. It was carved of light wood, four inches long, in a pattern of notches along a point. They pushed it down to the bottom on the end of a spear, then pulled up the spear. The lure slowly came up, slowly revolving so cod would follow it up to be speared.

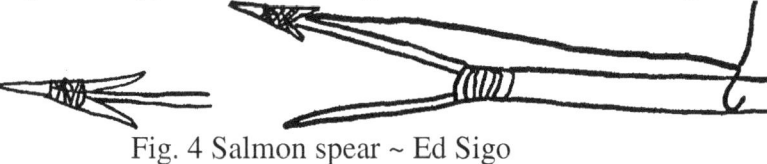

Fig. 4 Salmon spear ~ Ed Sigo

Tools {es}

Arrow points were made of bone without barbs. Ed once found a chipped one at Erland Point so he knew that kind was used in the past. Ed never saw the bone points either, but they were described to him as made of two pieces of bone, tied together, and covered with pitch on the shaft. They didn't use feathers very much.

They used flint from Erland Point to make tools like chisels, adzes, and points. The chisels were unhafted and struck with pieces of wood to plane down wood. They used elk horn for wedges. Stones pestles were used to pound meat, break clams, and work wood.

Fibers {ja}

Cattail mats. They had a long stick of hardwood with a hole in one end for a needle. It was about 30 inches long. They put a string in it. They had another piece of wood with an angled groove along the bottom to crease the mats along the line of the string to make the mat stronger. The mat creaser was called *kadalwacat* [x̌ədalusəd].

They got cattails and dried them in the sun. They got them from east of John's home near Poulsbo and the spit near Indianola. They used to go over from Point No Point to Edmonds where there were two marshes.

Then they took two stripes off a cattail, rubbed them on the thigh, and twisted the two strings that resulted into a thread. They pulled this through the hole in the needle *q̓laqtəd* [λ̓akʷtəd]. They put the cattails down on a flat place side by side. They made two layers of them by tying the edges together. They took the needle and pushed it through each of the cattails in one of the layers, through as much of the row as they wanted. When one layer was all threaded, the cattails were turned over and the thread was put through the other layer. Then it was turned over to put another thread through about four inches from the first. This way the thread went back and forth through a series of rows along each cattail.

The mats were used in houses to sleep on or serve food. John used a small one as a boy over his lap when riding in a canoe. Other things were covered with mats during a canoe trip to keep them dry.

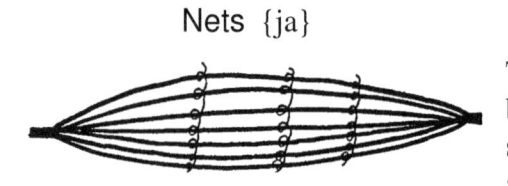

Nets {ja}

To make the dip or drag net for smelt, they got cedar boughs and bit through them with the teeth to start splitting them. They held on to one end with the teeth and grabbed the other with the hands to split it. They did the same with cedar roots. The boughs made strips six feet long. They lined them up until they were about a foot wide and then wove the cedar root twine through them to hold the net together. The net was widest in the middle and tapered to the ends where the boughs were all bunched together. They held the net at these ends and pulled it through the water.

Smaller nets were made out of cedar limbs steamed over a fire so they were easy to work. They twisted the limbs together to make a rope and wove this into a net.

Tools {ja}

A fire drill was used to start fires with a fine cedar bark kindling. This was placed on a hearth board with notches in it to hold the point of the drill and cause the friction that started the fire. The drill was rotated between the palms of the hands until sparks began to burn the cedar dust. They blew on it until it started to flame and then added the fine bark. When they moved from place to place, they carried fire in the canoe, just like that used for night fishing. They put a board with mud over it into the canoe bottom and moved the fire in on top of it. This kept it safe and contained. They didn't use the fire drill often, just when their fire went out. This fire drill was the only method known to John. They did not strike fire from flint.

Spoons were made of wood, some of cattle horn, after the whites came. They were made locally. One man used to come from the north and bring big plates made out of rock [argillite ?] to trade. That was in the 1860s. John's great grandfather had a wooden plate. Everyone ate out of this one dish, about two feet long, one foot wide, and five inches deep, made of maple. Such plates varied in size, but all were smooth and undecorated.

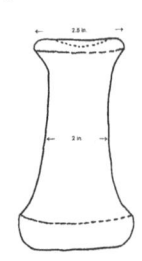

John heard that the ancient people had rock mortars to pound food, such as dried horse clams to get the tough skin off, deer meat to soften it to eat, and hazel nuts to crack the shells.

A herring rake was about 12 feet long with sharp pieces of hardwood stuck in along one side about half an inch apart for about two feet or more. Sometimes the points were made of bone. The pole itself was fir or cedar. They used it like a paddle from a canoe. They put the rake in the water in front of them, drew it back, and shook the impaled fish off into the canoe behind them. After whites came they started using nails for the teeth of the rake. They hammered these in, but in the old days they had to drill a hole for each board with a sharp bone rotated between the palms.

Bows were made by John's father out of yew wood. He never put sinew on the back of the bow. His bows were short, about 30 inches and he bent the ends in a curve by steaming them. This gave the bow more power and made it easy to carry. At the middle grip, the bow was rounded but the rest was flat. John watched his father's father make such bows seventy years ago. The bow string was elk sinew. Arrows had two or three eagle feathers attached with a twist to make the arrow spin. They had metal points and cedar shafts. Arrows were used to kill ducks, deer, elk, and men.

Harpoons were used for seal and porpoise. John had seen the outfit of Old Joe. His spear [harpoon] had a back that was cut to fit the fingers and string tied to it. Bladders for air floats were attached way back on this string. The front of the string was tied to the detachable point with barbs to hold it inside the prey. When they speared a mammal, the pole came out but the head stayed in while it ran away with the line. They threw the bladders overboard to slow it down. When the animal tired, they hauled it close and killed it. They got it in the canoe before it sank.

Fish spears [ƛagʷəcəd, ƛakʷ + icəd = insertion instrument] were used for bottom fish like flounder at night. They built a fire in the middle of a canoe upon a mud coated board or gravel and used this to attract fish and game. A rainy night was the best time to catch ducks because they were blinded by the light. These fires burned pitch wood because it gave a bright, clean fire.

The spears were made of hardwood or bone. Later the points were made out of a metal file. The points were tied on with wild cherry bark. Some spears had two prongs like a Y and others had three like a leister. Bone points averaged about 10 inches long, some longer. The plain tapered bone point was a little rounded but sharp, and the other end was flat. There didn't seem to be foreshafts or barbs.

Duck spears were similar to fish spears, except they had a string attached so they could be thrown and retrieved. They were more like harpoons but the head did not detach because ducks were not strong enough to break the pole, which was 10 feet long.

Canoes {ja}

John made canoes with metal tools. In the old days, they used stone and horn. He roughed out the canoe and put water inside. He heated it with rocks to make the walls soft. Then he stretched the canoe to the shape he wanted and held it there with sticks and supports. He started with little sticks, but as he threw hot water around the insides with a clam shell and got it softer, he changed to longer sticks to widen it. If he did this too much, it would all split. Jack made a few small cedar canoes in this way. He made the last one 50 years ago. He didn't make others because there was no good cedar left in the area. He said Stevens promised in the treaty that Indians could always make canoes. He named three styles of canoe: shovel nose [ƛlay], women's [stəwatɬ, all purpose], and racing.

Mat Houses [x̌ix̌qalgʷiɬ] {ja}

John lived in these around Port Orchard when he was little. They were started with four fir poles dug into the ground. Cross poles were added to steady them and roof boards were put over these. The roof had a gradual slope. The boards were made of hollowed out cedar boards about a foot and a half wide. They were laid in alternation so the grooves interlocked because one board was up and the next one was down, forming troughs to drain off the rain. If they weren't traveling with these roof boards from the plank houses, they used bark from a dead cedar tree, because this stripped off wide and hard. These were also laid in alternating overlaps.

Cattail mats were put all along the sides, with the long side parallel to the ground, and tied to the poles. Several were used so they overlapped and kept out the rain. When they wanted light, they pushed boards or mats aside with a pole. There would be as many fires as there were families, arranged down the center. They used mats and boughs as flooring. When they broke camp, the roof boards and mats went in the cargo canoe. If there were a lot of these, the big canoe was towed behind the family one.

SOCIETY

Ranks

Leadership {wg}

Status depended to a large extent on ancestry. They would speak of their genealogy and point out the weak spot if they were finding fault with someone. But if someone ran you down, you would point out to them where their own "blood" was weak, according to Ellen. In an argument, they might spit on their little finger, hold it up, and say "That's what you are." [Implying a weak, defiled, and puny ancestry.]

Weak blooded people did not have as much "say" as did a higher ranked person. Low class people were not allowed to mingle with high class ones.

The leader of the high class people only suggested what he wanted done. He let others know so they could help him decide. If the other people decided it was all right to do so, then it would be done. What the majority of them wanted was what they would do.

If a camp was going to move, the chief would suggest it and tell everyone to decide on the date If all agreed, then they would move on the day selected. Wilson told the story of a man who sometimes wouldn't camp among the other people. He would always be going off away from the camp to stay by himself. Once when the group moved camp, the chief said, "He always wants to be alone. He is only one person and we are a group. We'll just leave him here. The man was making a new canoe in the woods. When he finished, he went to his people but they were gone. He followed them to the new camp and from then on he camped right in the midst of the encampment. Wilson said, "He found out it was wrong to act so stubborn."

This was also how Jim Seattle lost the chiefship of the Suquamish when they voted in Chief Jacob Wahelchu. The head chief was always supposed to have the "first say" on things. He did the suggesting and then let the people vote on it. Jim Seattle had inherited the chiefship, but he was quick tempered and easily offended. The people didn't like that, so they voted for Chief Jacob to be the head man. The people would get together, then each man got up and said his part about what would be a good thing to do. Then the people would decide what was the best thing to do. The people did not want Jim Seattle because they didn't want someone who would "go all to pieces like that." Jim Seattle still had some "say," but Chief Jacobs had the "first say." In fact, everybody had a "say."

There would be a headman for the different areas where people were living. For example, Wilson remembered that there was a headman in the Port Washington area. His name was sq̓axʷtəd. This was before the white people came that he was headman there. The people of this area would listen to him. Such positions of leadership had a strong tendency to run in family lines.] As honorary Suquamish chief, Bill Kitsap's father's grandfather had been the old chief Kitsap.

A low class man, if he were very smart and good, could become the headman if the people chose him. Then he would be chief until he died unless he did things that people didn't like. Then they would replace him with someone else. There were headmen in different villages or areas who would have the "first say" in each. They were always chosen by the agreement of all the people. A low class person had the right to get up and make a suggestion. If the others agreed that it was a good idea, they accepted it.

The headman of a band would choose who he wanted to be the leader of a war party. Or he could be the leader of a war party himself if he so chose. Chief Kitsap was like that. He always led the war parties. When a raid was planned, it was necessary to talk it over and for each person to have a "say." They would have to approve or disapprove the whole plan. A headman could not do anything that importantly effected his people before he had their approval.

A village would usually be made up of two or three families. They would always camp close together. Sometimes a family would adopt a person into their kindred. This would be a friend of theirs who didn't have a family or who just wanted to live with them. One man was the head of each family. Age did not matter in this. If he were smart and had good ideas, the family would recognize him as headman. He would suggest to the family what he thought they should do, "if it was all right, they would use his idea." Where there were several families in a village, they would all have to agree on one person to "have the first say" in the community. When the head of a family died, it sometimes happened that a son of his became the head, but this was not always the rule. They wanted someone who was smart and whose ideas were good. This was the most important consideration in selecting a new headman.

The entire tribe would get together under one head when some trouble arose. This would be when they were attacked by someone else, or something like that. Kitsap [q̓c̓ap] was the earliest chief of the tribe that Wilson recalled. They had him for chief because he was such a good war leader. An arrow never got through his skin. It just glanced off and away. It never stuck in his body. {wg}

After Kitsap died, **walak** took over for a short time. He was a good speaker. That was why the people chose him to be headman. He led until treaty times. At the treaty, he was an interpreter. He could talk Chinook Jargon and Seattle couldn't. Wilson didn't know how walak was related to Kitsap or to Seattle, Kitsap did not chose anyone when he died to succeed him.

Seattle [syaɬ, siʔaɬ] was chosen headman at the time of the treaty. He was chosen to make the treaty. Ellen believed that Seattle was born among the Duwamish, but she didn't know whom he married. His son was married to the sister of Ellen's grandmother. When Seattle was old, the mother of Ellen and Wilson took care of him until he died. They were living at the old village at Suquamish, at Oldman House. That was where their mother took care of him. She was related to him, but not closely. She called him sapa [tsapa = grand father-uncle]. She used to cook his food and take it over to him. His mother used to say, "Chief siʔaɬ has got lots of relations, but here I am taking care of him until he dies." Sam Snyder used to carry water to the old chief when Sam was a little boy. Seattle remained a chief until his death.

Jim Seattle was chief then for a little while. He was something like old Kitsap. He was good in war. The people listened to him for a time. But he got so that he talked rough to the people. So they told him they were going to replace him. They chose Jacob then to be the chief.

Suquamish

In those days, the whole tribe moved together so they didn't have to send for anyone to come in for the meeting to ask their opinion about changing the chief. They were all together. [Jacob Wahelchu was chief until he died 2 October 1911, at the age of 112.]

Kitsap was only chief of the Suquamish. It was only after Chief Seattle that the Suquamish and Duwamish had the same chief. Seattle could be the chief over both tribes because he was related over there.

After the treaty, the Duwamish had a head chief named **kabsəd**. After Seattle signed the treaty, William, the brother of kabsəd, wanted a separate treaty so that they wouldn't have to move away from the Duwamish River. They didn't get it because of trouble with other Indians [the 1855-56 Treaty War]. The government moved Governor Stevens [he went back to fight and die in the Civil War Between the States] so he didn't settle with the Duwamish. After that, the Duwamish were moved all over.

One of Seattle's parents [his mother] was Duwamish, but Wilson was not sure which. This was what made it possible for him to speak for both peoples. As Kitsap was just chief of the Suquamish, Wilson thought that before the time of Seattle the two tribes had separate chiefs.

Sometimes a chief might name his successor. If he didn't, the people had to choose one. He was not necessarily from the family of the old chief. But the people had to agree on the person selected by the dying chief, at least for a time. If he were not acceptable, they chose someone else. The head chief never owned any hunting or fishing grounds for his exclusive use.

If a hunter killed more than he needed, he might take some of it to the head chief, but this was nothing special. A hunter always cut up his meat and distributed it to other people. He just kept as much as he could use for his own family. A hunter or fisher would give part of what he got to the chief first. If it were the village chief, he was given his portion first of all. Often the whole village would eat together and share what they had. They always gave the chief a piece of whatever they caught, no matter how little it was [to show their appreciation for his looking out for their welfare.]

But if a family had very little, the chief would also share what he had with that family. That was how a good chief looked after his people. A family might have a good hunter or more than one, but no good fishers. Another family might have good fishers but no good hunters. So they would share the various types of food that they had so everyone got a range of things to eat.

For example, one family might have caught a porpoise and another a seal. They would cook them on different fires and, which ever one was done first, everyone in the village gathered there to share in it. The man that caught the animal would give portions to each person. If a young man caught it, his parents were the ones to pass it out, showing what their boy could do. Sometimes, someone was chosen to hand out the meat. This person was selected by the head of the family. After the feast, if any was left, it was divided among the people to take home.

Sometimes a family lost a child or adult member to death. The hunters and fishers would bring the family food to eat because they could not get their own meals during mourning. The head of the family would choose someone to butcher the deer or fix the fish. What was left over after the family and everyone had eaten was divided by the head of the family, or someone he selected, to give to people outside of the family. The family that lost a child would not keep what was left of the food. People who received the food were then supposed to take it home and divide it with others who could not make it to the wake and feast. Wilson saw this happen in his family when he was about 20.

Once Wilson was at a feast in La Conner [Swinomish]. He had some fish of his own. When he left he took his fish back without dividing it among the people there. That night he dreamed. Someone asked him, "Why didn't you divide those fish with some of the people there?" Someone else said to the first voice, "Why didn't you tell him when he was still up there?" The next morning, Wilson's wife said he had talked all night long in his sleep. That day they went to eat with the Sneatlams, some of his relations in Tulalip. He took some of his fish there to give to them so as to clear himself of his trouble. He was not feeling well and kept shouting out on the way there. His wife told him to pray for help. He took his rosary and did so. He couldn't eat much, but later he did feel better.

That was the first time he found out that there was a spirit, like those in the smokehouse, following him wherever he went. One of his old people had had this spirit and so he had inherited it. It followed him like a dog wherever he went. Wilson was not sure just what kind of a power it was. Its song kept ringing in his ears, even while he was in the Sneatlam house. Yet he did not know what it was. He did not want the power, so he refused to sing it. By giving this salmon to others, he was able to clear himself partly. Also, he thought his prayers to God kept it away from him. Whatever the cause, he has not been sick because of this spirit any more.

When Warren Snyder asked him if a chief could demand food from others or what would happen if a chief had more food than he needed and still demanded food from others who did not have much, Wilson said that if the chief had a lot of food and the others did not, the chief always divided it among the people. By the same token, people "naturally" gave part of their food to the chief first. If a person did have food and refused to divide it with others, the likelihood was that he would become sick, or anything bad could happen to him [for he was offending spirits as well as neighbors.]

The chief usually did not go out to hunt and fish. His wives went out gathering berries and clams. His slaves went out to fish and hunt. Only young slaves went hunting. The chief directed his slaves and told them what to do. He would tell his slaves when to go hunting and where. He told them what to do to the game after they got it. Sometimes, it was divided among the people, either cooked or uncooked depending on his "say." Most chiefs also had slaves make their canoes and other utensils. The chief was expected to spend his time directing the activities of his slaves and advising the community. This was equally true of the high blooded people as well as the chief.

If a chief sent for a relative and gave him something, such as a canoe, the relative brought back something to give to the chief in exchange, such as a blanket. If what he gave was less than the relative thought the canoe was worth, then, at some later time, when the relative gave a potlatch, he would give this chief something more to make up for the value of the canoe. The speaker would announce that this was in payment for the gift of a canoe. [Then their sharing was balanced and even.]

Some people had only one or two slaves. Chiefs always had more than two. People who had few slaves had to do a lot of work themselves. But the slaves always had to do as much work as their masters were doing, so these slaves worked long and hard. The master and slave sometimes worked together, like hunting and fishing as a pair. The master was the boss, though, and the slave did somewhat more work than the master, usually, in these cases.

When they lived in the big plank smokehouses, the slaves had a certain section of the house where they stayed [usually nearest the door, the most vulnerable spot.] The slaves did all of the cleaning, and they got the water and wood. When people were camping, however, and using the smaller mat houses, the slaves had a separate mat house of their own to stay in.

For very important meetings, women were not allowed to speak, only at less important ones could they personally voice an opinion. A woman could not become a chief. If she were smart, she might be allowed to speak informally. Women could not speak at a war meeting either. That was strictly men's business. Only those going into the fight could speak at such meetings. Mostly, women spoke at meetings where their own marriage or something else of keen interest to them was under discussion. Even then only very smart women were listened to. A woman had to be older and more experienced before she was heard. A woman who had gone through the change of life did not have any more right to speak than any other female. As in the case of a headman, the important consideration was the level of intelligence, ability, experience, and oratorical fluency

Chiefs {eg}

People took their troubles to the chief. He had two or three others, subchiefs, under him. They would straighten out family troubles or whatever came before them. The chief was the head of the tribe and he had to be smart. If anyone wanted to know anything, they would go to him for the answer or for advice. A man who became chief had to be high blooded. He couldn't be a commoner or ordinary. Usually the chiefship was inherited.

Speakers {ja}

John's grandfather was a speaker. He was a spokesman. During a potlatch, he would do the talking until he was hoarse. He spoke for Chief Kitsap. They used a long potlatch house that stood where the light house is now. His job was to forward what the chief said. The chief told him what to talk about, but not exactly what to say. Mostly he described what was going on, especially when the chief was passing things out. He gave away to and fed the people. It was called cgʷəgʷə [sgʷigʷi] (potlatching or inviting).

Slavery {eg, wg}

High class people had slaves who did work for them like getting wood, digging clams, and so forth. Ellen's grandmother had slaves. When the slaves were freed in 1865, she tried to get them to leave her, but they didn't want to go. Finally, they did leave her, but when they went picking berries or digging clams, they would always bring some to her. They continued to help her even after they were free. {eg}

Most of the slaves were good so they didn't have to be punished. The master would beat them if they were not dutiful and good. Some masters might be mean to their slaves, but others would advise him not to punish his slave too much. Scolding was usually considered to be enough to get a slave back into line. But if a slave were very bad, he'd be punished by making him work longer and harder. Most people knew that slaves worked harder and minded better when they were well treated.

A slave might ask a man who was good to his own slaves to buy him because his present master was too harsh. Wilson said that his own grandfather got more than one slave in this way. His uncle helped to buy one of them.

Slaves ate after the others were through. They ate by themselves. People ate off a mat and there was a separate one for slaves. Slaves could marry, but any children belonged to the master of the [slave] parents. They were allowed to be present at a meeting to discuss important matters. A master might even allow a good, smart slave to talk at such a gathering and to give his opinion on some question.

Suquamish

When the cousin of Wilson's grandfather died, they killed one of his slaves and buried him underneath his master. It was not done outright, but by trickery. They were taking the body in a canoe to the burial place. Wilson's father's father pulled a knot out of the bottom of the canoe so the water started to leak in. The slave had a knife so the man asked to use it to stop the leak. When they got to shore, Wilson's relative kicked the slave in the shin and then stabbed him when he bent over. They buried him under the body.

Wilson never heard of burying a slave in a post hole when building a house or of killing slaves at a potlatch. They might give them away, but more often they sold them at such large gatherings. When a boy got married, his father might give him a slave. His won grandfather bought a young slave about 14 or 16 to care for Wilson while he was young. His name was **saya** and he was supposed to help Wilson's mother take care of the boy. He used to carry wood, get water, and perform other duties around the house. He was from Alaska. His own uncle, his father's brother, sold him. He was from high blood, but still his uncle sold him. He died while Wilson was yet a baby.

The West Coast Indians around Fort Rupert used to sell slaves a lot cheaper than did the people around Olympia and the southern part of the Sound. They used to get them cheap from the **yəłuiłtx** [Ucluelet] across from Neah Bay on Vancouver Island. That was where John Kettle's wife came from. John and his wife were the last slaves left around Suquamish. Kettle was first owned by Chief Jacob, then by Alfred, who was the son of Chief Jacob's brother and that way inherited the slave.

They bought most of their slaves from the north, but they did buy some in the area of Puget Sound. In the generation of Kitsap, they used to go out and raid for slaves, but Wilson wasn't sure where they went for them. {eg}

The grandmother of Curly way back was captured by people from the north. They took her and made her a slave. That is why people around here look down on John, because he had slave ancestry. Yet Curly became a great man, a speaker, any way.

They had slaves right here in Suquamish. John Kettle was one. He was from the north. Slaves got wood, clams, and packed water. The owner didn't do this. Anybody could capture someone and then make them work. The slave lived with the person who captured him. They had to marry other slaves. A free man could marry a slave, but the people looked down on such a person afterward. The children were considered as slaves and the people would look down on them too. When they traveled in a canoe, the slave did the paddling. Slaves could have power if they trained for it, then went out and got it.

The master could kill his slave if he got mad enough. Kitsap had a slave who had a daughter Kitsap went after. His wife said "Don't do it," but Kitsap persisted anyway. The daughter scratched his face, so he took a weapon and split open her head. The mother of the girl used to go into the woods to sit and cry. She must have had something [power] because shortly afterwards Kitsap died. It must have been she who did it. She had something.

There was a Suquamish who was a kidnapper. He made slaves of children. An old man here who died about 50 years ago was kidnapped by that man and taken to Skokomish where he was used as a bet on the outcome of a horse race and thus the boy was lost.

John never heard of killing a slave at a ceremony or anything similar. They were pretty much well treated, it was just that they were slaves. If Suquamish were kidnapped by northern Indians but came back later, they were still considered slaves. {ja}

Suquamish

AGE AND GENDER

M1 (First Menstruation) {jj}

A girl was not allowed to stay in the house at this time. They made a little tent [hut] for her up in the woods somewhere near their home. This was a great disgrace [concern ?] for the family. [Good families were especially determined to seclude their daughters at this time to protect others from the great power she was soon to learn to control.] They didn't want the girl to look at anybody. If she did, the person would become sick. They didn't visit her, except for one old woman who attended her. This might be her great grandmother or her grandmother. If they were not alive, then it was some other old related woman. She told the girl what she was supposed to do.

She couldn't eat for a few days. She was away from her folks for a month, but it was only for a few days of this that they starved her. They starved her for the first few days that she went out. She had to clean herself every morning. She had a certain place to go to clean herself. This would be at a stream but not in the Sound. This was a special place for her. Others were not supposed to go there. Then they took her back home.

While she was there, she worked on baskets and other tasks. If she didn't do this during the change in her life, she would always be lazy and not want to work. The tent she was in was a hut made of branches from fir trees. They also made her a bed in the inside from a special type of fir tree branches because they smelled so sweet. The girl was also given a dry weed like nettle to rub over her body to clean and toughen it.

They were told they could not use their fingernails to scratch themselves with. If they itched, they had to use the dried nettles. Their fingernails were like a poison to them if they used them to scratch their own bodies [short-circuiting their raw power].

Girls were allowed to eat only special foods, none associated with men. She could not eat salmon because if she did, salmon would disappear from the Sound. It was a long time after she had left the hut that she was finally allowed to eat salmon again. Also, during her later monthly periods a woman was not allowed to eat salmon.

A girl ate roots from the forest, such as fern root. She also could eat clams. She couldn't eat meat such as deer or elk while she was in the hut because then these animals would become scarce. Julia was not sure if they could eat berries. There were no other ceremonies or public events. There were no feasts.

Marriage {jj}

When a boy was interested in a girl, his parents gave belongings to the girl's folks. After that, half a year to a year later, the girl's parents would bring presents back to those of the boy. They would return as much as they had received. Julia saw this done when she was a girl. There was just this one exchange of presents. If a boy were the son of a chief, then he had to look for the daughter of a chief to marry so his children would be high born. If he married a lower girl, his children would not be high blooded.

A long way back it was a little different. There would be a dance. The girls would be standing around. One boy would dance around. He would have long strings tied around his waist. If a girl wanted to marry him, she would grab hold of a string. Then the boy had to marry her. Several girls could grab the string of one boy and he would have to marry them. They didn't exchange gifts at the dance. [This practice was diffused from the Plateau Prophet Cults active almost two centuries ago.]

A man could have several wives if he could support them. This was done before the time of buying a wife. The boy took the girl to his home. The girl was supposed to work for the boy's parents. She was supposed to do the housekeeping for them. If she didn't, she was lazy and the boy's parents might take her back to her home.

A person could never marry relatives, unless they were at least five times removed in the genealogy. He wasn't allowed to marry any closer than this, otherwise all of his children would die.

Wife buying involved marrying someone outside of the tribe or community. The Suquamish married into any tribe around the area, Port Gamble, Muckleshoot, Snohomish, and so on. Marrying outside of the tribe was thought to be the best kind of marriage. When the granddaughter [Agatha] of Julia's foster father [Jacob Wahelchu] got married, they had a feast afterwards. They invited lots of people and had dances. Chief Jacob gave away clothes, food, and dishes at the feast. They used to do it this way before the whites came. They did not feast when the gifts were exchanged before the marriage.

The couple could go to live with either set of folks, those of the boy or of the girl. When they went to live with the boy's folks, the girl had to help the boy's parents and be good to them. The boy's parents could send the girl back if she were not acceptable. Nothing was done about the gifts already exchanged if that happened.

They were most likely to go to live with the boy's parents, unless there were more than one wife. Before the whites came, they could have more than one wife. People said that the wives used to fight. Julia knew a man in Port Gamble who had two wives.

If a man's wife died and she had a younger sister who was not married, then this girl had to marry the man and take her sister's place. This practice was called balocit [sbalotsid]. In English this would mean something like sister-in-law [more accurately, potential wife according to the sororate]. It meant more than just that. All of the deceased wife's relatives would be balocid to the husband after her death, but not before. The wife was łaha [sxaʔxaʔ] to the boy's parents.

If the man died, his wife went home to her parents. It was expected that the deceased's brother would marry her, but he did not have to unless his parents wanted him to do so. Also, a cousin of the dead husband could marry her if he wanted to, but the brother had first preference. A man had a choice in this kind of marriage, but a woman did not if the man wanted her.

In either of these cases, there would be no gift exchanges after the initial alliance. If a boy from Suquamish married a girl from another tribe like the Snohomish and the boy brought the girl home to live with his parents, they would give a feast for the new couple, inviting a lot of people to come. If they went to live with the girl's parents, then the boy was supposed to help his inlaws. If he did not hunt and fish for them, he was called lazy, but the girl's parents couldn't send the boy home. The girl's parents could only criticize him and try to make him work.

Parents always wanted their children to marry as high blooded a person as they possibly could because the social position of the children depended on this. Rank was inherited. When lower blooded children grew up and had children, others would say to these children that they were low down people. So the parents always wanted their children to marry high up, so others couldn't later call their grandchildren low class. This was important because grandparents had special rights and duties in the training of their grandchildren.

Suquamish

Julia's foster father was young when his parents negotiated with another family to arrange his marriage. He was about 13 and so was the girl. He and the girl had played together. So when they got older, they were well acquainted with each other and willingly married. It was common for important marriages to be arranged when the children were this age. Sometime, the boy and girl were even younger, about 5 or 6, when the parents made the arrangements for a later marriage. They didn't do this when the children were the first born because "they didn't know whether they would live or die. [See the tale of Five Brothers by John Adams for the mythic justification for this.]

Child Care {jj}

When a baby was born, they cut off the afterbirth and wrapped it up, took it into the woods, and buried it. They washed the baby in the Sound as soon as it was born, placed it on a thin board, and wrapped it up. As the baby grew, they made longer boards for it. They packed the baby on the board, hanging down the back, when they went any where. They held it on the back with a blanket wrapped around the shoulders. Now younger Indians use shawls.

A new mother cooked [heated] her breasts before nursing to increase the flow of milk. She warmed white shells and placed them against her breasts. This made good, plentiful milk.

They had a hammock to put the baby on when they were busy. The hammock swayed and kept the baby happy. They used cedar skin [cambium] like a diaper. Cedar skin was found underneath the bark. It came off in sheets and dried nice and crisp. Some sheets were big enough to use as a hammock. Babies were weaned when they were about three or four years old. Julia saw older ones, big kids, playing around when all of a sudden they would run to their mother to nurse. To help with weaning, women put something on the nipple to make it taste bad. They started feeding babies solid food when they had teeth to chew with.

Children were punished by whipping them with a little stick, not the hand, just enough to make them learn they had done wrong. Sometimes, they would make fast food for a while.

When children were old enough to help, the parents gave them small tasks, saying "Go, get me this." If a child said he was tired and didn't want to go, they would call him lazy and give him a slight whipping. Children were not supposed to talk back to grown ups. If the adult said something mean, and the child answered back, he or she would still be whipped.

Once, years ago there was a famine for three or four years. They wouldn't clean the heads of the children and they had lice. So did their parents. When they got hungry, they would pick their heads and eat the lice. They gave each child one louse. If the child cried for more, they said "You've had one, that's enough."

A child was not allowed to play with any part of a salmon. Julia used to do this but they stopped her. They said she would get sick from this and that the salmon would take her back home with them to teach her a lesson.

Death {jj}

If anyone died in a family, the survivors gave the dead's belongings away after the funeral. They gave them to people who came to the funeral. They gave everything away. Then other people had to give them things to use because all that they had was given away. They did this in memory of the dead and because they did not want to see things that belonged to the dead person. It reminded everyone of the loss. They had to start all over getting things to use.

After a person died, it was a disgrace [disrespectful] to mention their name again. They did not want to talk about or mention people who had died. Women cried when a close relative died. They wailed just like singing. The men may cry but not loudly.

Burial {jj}

When a person died, they would get a good canoe and split it on the bottom. Then they put the body in it. They took all of this back into the thick brush and trees, where they hung up the canoe. The body was inside covered with blankets. They put favorite belongings, tools and utensils, in with the body. Sometimes, they laid it on the ground and put boards over it like an A-frame tent. When this got old and worn, they made another one for the body. They called this tent səlawtxʷ [**silaltxʷ** = cloth house]. There was a burial ground with these at the place where Suquamish is now. Another one was at the end of Bainbridge Island.

Division of Labor {eg}

Men and women had different ways of dressing and different tasks to do. Women parted their hair in the middle and braided it on both sides. Men had long hair but they didn't braid it. It was allowed to hang around the shoulders.

The different jobs included the following:
- drying = women did all berries, meat, and fish
- cooking = women did it all
- weaving = women made the blankets of dog wool and the mats, cutting the cattails for them
- baskets = women made them and got their own material like cedar boughs, bark, grasses, and roots [men made the open work clamming baskets]
- canoes = made by men
- clams = women dug them and dried them, but men sometimes watched the clams drying over a fire to see they did not burn
- berries = picked and dried by women
- fishing = men did it
- hunting = men
- paddling canoes = both men and women

In addition, men put up houses for curing meat and fish, built fire places for cooking, made cradle boards, speared ducks, woodworked planks and carvings, got fire wood, made long wooden needles for mats, and prepared ironwood stakes for cooking salmon and clams.

Ellen said the Neah Bay [Makah] people made the women get the fire wood. Ellen's father wouldn't let her marry a man from Neah Bay because he didn't want his daughter going out and hauling wood in a basket while her husband sat around a warm fire. The Neah Bay people were not very good to their women.

Suquamish

Training {eg}

Boys were made to swim when they were young. They made them fast for a certain number of days. The grandfather would give them a token or a marker, a board, stick, or something. He'd tell the boy where to take it and tell him how to place it. Then the boy did this and came back. As he got older, he was sent further and further away up a mountain or to a lake. This was what they did when boys were seeking their Tamanamus [**tahmanawas**, Chinook Jargon word for spirit or supernatural, from **tah**, power]. Some of them used to use this to doctor sick people.

During these cures, they used to get down in the middle of the floor and all the other people would sit around the edges and hit on boards with little sticks to sing with the doctor. Some had little men carved with faces on them. When they were singing, these cedar figures would come out of a corner and dance around and then go back to sit in the corner again. These cedar men had spirits in them.

Ellen said that when she was young these carvings would bump and make a noise if anyone tried to take anything in the house. This happened to her when she was a little girl.

Very few girls had spirits, but they all went out to seek them. They were sent to a creek to bathe. They had to rub themselves with rotten pieces of wood [to remove their human odor.] Some said it was to smooth their skin. [Girls were trained for work that did not require strong spirits.] They would show girls how to make yarn from dog wool and duck down. Then they would show them how to weave. Such finished material was used for girl's skirts. They taught girls how to cut fish, dry it, and cure it. They learned how to make baskets and mats. They went with older women to dig roots.

Mostly men got power. As soon as a man was 14 or 16, he would get married. They would start training boys to hunt and fish when they were four or five. They gave them little bows and arrows, also slings. These were like toys but, at the same time, they were meant to teach the boys how to use such things. The men showed them how to care for and use them. Boys went out hunting in earnest, able to get food for the people when they were older. By the time they were ready for marriage, they were skillful at hunting and fishing.

M1 First Menstruation {eg}

They put a girl out of sight when this happened. At night they took her to a creek and made her bathe and scrub with a sponge made of rotten cedar to clean herself. During the day, she was given something to work on like weaving mats, blankets, making yarn, or doing baskets. This was to make her familiar with constant activity so she would be a good wife later.

The second night they would make her bathe again. She was put on a strict diet. They cooked the food, but they waited until it was cold to feed it to her. They gave her very little to eat, no fruit, nothing warm. She could eat roots. Toward the end of the seclusion, the grandmother would invite other old women to join them. They would gather to sing, dance, and eat, although the girl could not join in this [lifting her spirits].

The girl was not allowed to touch her own hair. Someone else had to comb and braid it for her. They braided it tightly in two braids and tied them on either side of her ears. Then they wrapped her head up so that none of her hair showed. Ellen believed the cedar bark was used to wrap it, but she was not sure. They gave her a piece of ironwood sharp on one end and flat on the other. She was supposed to use it to scratch herself if she had an itch.

The girl had to eat and drink from her own dishes. She couldn't go picking berries, nor was she allowed on the beach. If a hunter came down with a deer, she must never look at it.

During this period, the girl was instructed in how to conduct herself when she was married. She was given instructions in drying fish, picking berries, digging clams, and keeping a household. If she married a man with a family, she was told to be good to her mother-in-law and other inlaws. She was told not to talk back to them even if they abused her verbally.

Children were not to talk back to anyone older than themselves. They were told to help anyone who was in trouble and needed a hand. This sort of instruction came down to Ellen and her sisters from their own grandmother. Ellen said she went through seclusion, but it was hard, with a harder time with her mother-in-law, who was mean.

Ordinarily, it was permitted to talk to parents in law, but if they were mad at you or mean, you were not supposed to say anything back.

When the girl was well, the grandmother would give each woman there part of the cloth or mat that the girl was secluded behind. Then she was ready to be married. An unmarried girl was not allowed to speak to any man, not even her cousins. She was to be quiet around men, even her own brother(s). She was not to talk foolishly or play or act rowdy. There were no men nor male kin that a girl could joke with.

Marriage {eg}

Usually a girl married an old man first. When he died, then she married a younger man. Ellen's grandmother married an old man, but he didn't last long. He died. She did not marry any relative of his. She married into another family. After her second husband died, she married her stepson. In those days, a woman could even marry her brother-in-law. She was expected to. Her second husband told his son to marry his stepmother. This was an acceptable form of marriage.

In the old days there was something called a marriage dance. An unmarried man's people would announce the dance. This was his father or grandfather. They invited lots of people. The boy tied some string, probably buckskin, around his waist. Then his relatives started a song. The boy sang too. The others joined in. Any girl who wanted to marry the boy would come up to him while he was dancing and take hold of the string. Several girls might grab hold of the string. The son of a chief got lots of girls. The boy married all the girls who held on to his string. The girls held on to the string and followed him dancing until he was through. Ellen said that the end of the dance marked the marriage. Ellen did not know whether any gifts were given to the girl's parents in this kind of marriage. They did have a big feast, but she didn't know if gifts were exchanged.

The gift exchange was another form of marriage. The boy's parents took him along when they went to see the parents of the girl about a marriage. He was left outside sitting by the door, saying nothing, until he was called in. The girl could not be around during the discussions. When he was called in, then he was considered married to the girl and they ate together. The boy's parents had brought the food for a feast to the girl's home and they ate there. The boy's parents also brought gifts, but these were left in the canoe. If the boy were accepted, they went to the canoe and unloaded the food and gifts.

Sometimes boys would sit at the door a long time. At night he would come just inside the doorway and lie there to get warm. The boy had to be silent. If he were in the way, the members of the household just stepped over him, ignoring him. He might have to sit there for days before they finally accepted [or rejected] him.

They used to have valuable shell beads that they gave to the girl as a necklace. Abalone shells were used, broken up into pieces, and rubbed [abraded] into the shape of beads with a stone. Then they were strung into a necklace. Other pretty shells were also used. Dentalia was a favorite ornament. Anyone with any shell ornaments was looked up to because these were considered very valuable. They would use these shells to trade for other goods, such as blankets and shawls. Chiefs used them to decorate their clothing.

In most cases, the young married couple would go to live with his parents. They would go to visit hers, but mostly they lived with his. When a man got game, such as a deer, he might take part of it to his inlaws. He would treat them first of all. Even when a girl's parents had lots of food, they treated their in laws first. If a man wanted to go and live with his wife's people, this was acceptable, but it was not usual. [Among tribes of Northern California, this was called half-marriage when a groom lived with his inlaws.]

They preferred to marry into other tribes. There were low class and high class people. So a high class person from the Suquamish would rather marry a high class person from another tribe than marry someone from the low class of his own tribe. Low class people married others of the low class, so they were much more likely to marry into their own tribe. So, marrying into your own tribe was not considered desirable.

As soon after a marriage as they could, the parents of the girl would take presents to the boy's parents. They also brought food to hold a feast there. There was no other marriage ceremony outside of these constant feasts and gift exchanges.

After the Catholic priests came in, they tried to make the men with many wives give up all of them but one. Ellen said that even then some women stayed. Ellen knew a man with two wives, who were sisters, as recently as 1919, when he died. The last of his wives died in 1942.

If a woman did not like her husband, she could leave him. Also, if a man did not want his wife, he could tell her to leave. The girl's parents would take her back and tried to get her married again. Ellen said that this usually didn't take too long.

Child Care {eg}

When a man and wife were expecting a baby, the man would go out and get some cedar bark. He took off the outside bark and went for the thin underbark or cambium skin. He brought it home and they rubbed it between their hands to make it soft. Then they cut it into sizes large enough for diapers. They rendered dog fish livers and stored the oil. They cooked it over a fire to get the oil out. Then they strained it through some cedar skin. Sometimes they made the oil from ratfish liver.

When the woman was six months along, they got some medicine, some leaves, for her to chew and swallow or boil like a tea to shortened her labor. She chewed a plant called squirrel tail, *skəkazohop,* or made a tea out of wild cherry bark.

When a woman got sick, she wasn't supposed to tell anyone, not even her husband that she was ready to deliver. She was not to groan or cry or make any noise. She had the baby by herself. She went away from the others when she knew the time was close and had the child by herself. When it came, the others would hear it cry. Her mother, grandmother, mother-in-law, or other older woman would go and help her then. Only a woman could help because it was a disgrace for a man to be around when a baby was born.

When the baby was first born, they rubbed it with this fish oil all over the body. Then they put dogfish, never ratfish, oil in a clam shell and warmed it by the fire. They dipped a feather in the warm oil and let it drop into the mouth of the baby to feed it. They fed the baby only this oil for seven days directly after it was born before a mother started nursing.

Suquamish

Ellen was brought up this way by her grandmother, who claimed they fed babies dogfish oil because it kept them well -- it cleaned them out so they didn't get sick as easily. This oil was used as a medicine for adults as well as children. It was used for fevers, colds, burns, purges, and almost anything else.

The afterbirth was wrapped up. It was taken into the woods and put up in a tree. People said that if it were put in a maple, the child would be good-natured.

The baby had to be seven to ten days old before it got a first bath. When they bathed it, the mother laid it on her thighs and bathed it with soft cedar bark like a sponge. They did not wash it in the Sound. In the summer, they warmed the bath water in the sunshine. In the winter, they dropped hot rocks in water held in a hollowed out cedar log and bathed the baby with that.

Mothers made a little fire and heated rocks. Ellen saw her own mother do this. They got some weeds growing in clusters on logs out on the beach. These snap when you squeeze them. They are brown and called stoċ [toċ, tots means "to shoot"). The weeds were put in a basket and the hot rocks were placed on top, so as not to scorch the basket. Then the woman bend over it with a blanket around her neck to keep the steam out of her face. They sprinkled water on the rocks. This was the way she cooked or steamed her breasts for about an hour to increase milk production. Ellen's mother did this twice to cook her milk for a new baby. If this weren't done, the baby would have colic all of the time. Another way of cooking the breasts was to rub them with warmed clam shells. Because the shell was white, it was emblematic of a wish for thick milk.

Nursing could go on until the child was three or four. Even if she had a tiny baby, she still nursed an older one along with the baby. Ellen knows one case where a boy nursed until he was old enough to play ball with the other boys. She never heard of a mother who was unable to nurse. A baby nursed on demand or when the mother thought it was time. If the baby cried from hunger, it was always nursed then.

They ate solid foods along with the nursing. When babies were about a year old, they used to give them bear or seal fat to suck on. Also, they took dried clams, soaked them in water, and let the baby suck on them. Gradually, they went on to solid food.

To wean them some mothers took flounder gall, which was bitter, and put it on the nipples to discourage the baby.

When a baby soiled its cedar skin diapers, they weren't thrown away. They were wrapped up and saved until the child was old enough to chew and eat, only then were they thrown away. If they threw them away before the baby stopped nursing, the baby would have loose bowels. A baby that was passing all of the time was considered to be "no good." The urine of little children was gathered and put away where the rain would never touch it. When it thickened up, it was used as a shampoo. Men and women both used it to wash their hair in the creek.

The cradle boards for a child were made by the father. He took a piece of cedar about eight to ten inches wide and two feet long and bored holes along each side. Then he took soft buckskin and sewed it onto the board through these holes. He put the inner bark or skin of cedar inside. These were blankets just big enough to cover the baby, made especially for it of dog hair wool and fern cotton, twisted into a string and woven.

The baby was wrapped in cedar skin first, then in a blanket. It was laced into the buckskin on the board with leather strips. A stick was put over the cradle at night to hold the baby in.

They had a way of making a baby rocker. Two pieces of yew wood six feet long were planted in the ground. The cradle board [sxaltəd] was suspended from these by thongs. A string was tied to the top of the poles and the mother made them bob up and down by pushing on the string with her foot. She could sit and do her own work while also rocking the baby.

In the old days, they used to flatten the baby's head in the cradle board. They used to take a small board and place it with paddling on the baby's forehead and lace it down on each side. A baby used a cradle board for a year, but it didn't learn to walk or crawl until out of it. They were not walking as early as children do now a days.

The board was carried on the back by the mother. A strap came over each shoulder and was attached to a strap around the upper part of her chest. When not being carried, or in the rocker hammock, the cradle board leaned against a wall, post, or tree.

Naming

Children were named at about 12 years of age. The father or uncle would suggest a name; then the family had to decide on it. If the family objected, they picked out another name. If it were accepted and agreed upon, the child was given the name. After they got older they might change this name for another one. Names "went down in" a family, they passing through the generations.

When a person died, there would be a period of time when they couldn't speak the name for a year or so. But the name would stay in the family and it would used again afterward. The family had to agree that the time was right to bring it out again. A family could never use the names of another one, except under exceptional circumstances of friendship.

A name could come from either the family of the father or of the mother. As a person got older, they remained entitled to names from each side. Some people of high blood had several names. If the family could afford it, a potlatch was given when the name was passed on. The quantity of gifts distributed reflected on the prestige that went with the name. At a big potlatch, people announced they were going to take another name, but they also kept their previous names.

When the name of a dead ancestor was given to a child or an adult took a new name, they would show to the public something that used to belong to the dead person who had the name previously. They announced that from now on the name could be mentioned and used. Then they destroyed the article of clothing from the last holder of the name. A "high" name would be known to all around because so many people would have heard it used at the potlatch.

Training {wg}

Boys and girls of 10 to 14 were sent out when it was hailing to run naked facing into the storm. This made them able to face anything when they grew up, and not be afraid, nervous, or excited. They would not be upset or afraid when someone talked rough to them.

Divorce {wg}

Wilson said that Angeline [daughter of Chief Seattle] was lazy when she was married to her first husband. She would lay in bed until late in the morning. Finally, her Skagit husband **daxʷsəb** told her "There is a canoe. Take it and go home to your people." He didn't want her because he was ashamed she slept too much.

Ghosts {wg}

The land where the spirits of the dead live was far away. Wilson and Ellen did not have a clear idea where it was supposed to be. The dead lived in houses, just like the old plank smokehouses. They slept in them and the shamans visiting on the Soul Odyssey were careful when looking around not to wake them.

When evening came, children were told to come inside because the ghosts of the dead might steal them at night. Dark nights were the most dangerous. Moonlit nights were not as bad. Clothes were never left out at night, otherwise the spirits would steal the warmth-spirit from them. If this happened, the owner sickened or died. If any leftover food was thrown outside at night, ghosts might eat it making someone in the house sick.

There were two roads to this afterworld. One was short. Anyone who went on this one could not come back. This happened if a person died suddenly by accident or being killed. The long way was more leisurely. It was taken by the odyssey shamans when visiting the ghost land. A person's soul could start along this way and they would still be alive.

Wilson told of his uncle Sam Snyder who was not feeling well. Later a shaman found his soul along the way to the afterworld. He just happened on it on the way to recover another soul during one of the annual winter trips. The leader heard someone singing, so he repeated the song. This was the song given to Sam by his spirit ally. When they began to sing the song, Sam started to cry. The shaman turned the soul back. The reason that the soul was on the long road was that someone had badly hurt Sam's feelings. He got to feeling that he wished he were dead. That's why his soul started to drift down the road to the afterworld.

When someone in the family died, close relatives might be hurt so badly that they wished they were dead, too. Their souls might go astray like that of Sam. If a person was accused of something they didn't do, they might be hurt badly and their soul would start on its way. Every year the souls of such people were found on the way to the land of the dead.

When someone died, the rest of the family was afraid that if any belongings were left around, the dead would come back for them. Thus, when people were buried in canoes, their favorite things were put into the wrapping of the body. The other stuff was given to people who came to the wake, burial, and feast and who were not closely related. Sometimes pieces of cloth were torn into sections large enough for a shawl and these were given to visiting women. Anything that might attract the dead back was given away. They did not want the dead to return and take other members of the family back with them.

Marriage {ja}

When someone married out of the tribe, the parents of the boy would take presents to those of the girl. Then later the girl's family would reciprocate and pay them back. When John was young, his parents tried to make an arrangement like this with a Skokomish family, but she died before they could be married. This gift exchange at marriage was called *oloɬ*.

When a man's wife died, her unmarried sisters were considered balocid to him and they called each other by this term. If he decided that he wanted to marry one of them, he had an option to *obalocidəb*, to take her as his new wife. While the wife was living, these same unmarried sisters were called **čabas** and they used this term for each other. The families of a married pair were siuxsiaya [six^{w}syaya] to each other. This included all of the families except the parents. The fathers and mothers were **sxaʔxaʔ** to the young couple.

Suquamish

Most couples lived with his family, but even if they went to live with the family of the bride this was still called okʷiłyoʔ [ʔokʷiłiw]. The same term is used for living with the either family. They used the same word for both without distinction. The boy or the girl belonged to the tribe of the other one as a result of their marriage [cemented by the birth of children]. When living with the boy's parents, the girl was supposed to work for her parents-in-law and be good to them. If the girl had to be sent home for being lazy, it might cause hard feelings and start a feud between the families. It was considered an insult to the girl.

If a man had a brother and the man's wife or both of them died, then the children they had together were sklazotał [sqəladzutał] to the brother. When neither parent was dead, then the children were **stalał** (singular) or **staltalał** (plural) to the brother.

When the husband died, his brother or other close male relative had a claim on the widow. Her family decided which of these men would be the new husband based on his abilities. If they could not decide, then the woman could make up her own mind. Once her family had selected someone, however, she was obligated to go through with the marriage. If none of the male relatives wanted to marry her, they did not have to.

If a man were forced to marry her by his family, he might run away. They might not get along or start quarreling and fighting. Such fighting between a man and his wife was called **x̌acab**. A girl might also run away from such a marriage. The exchange presents were not returned. Although they were lost to the givers, this was never the cause of a fight.

Sometimes, in the case of a fight between two tribes, the chief might give a daughter to the chief or a member of his family in the other tribe. This brought a halt to the fighting. Then the tribes were connected through marriage and children. The daughter was treated as an important wife, not a slave.

In the old days, they would sometimes get married when the couple were still young, about 12 or 13 years old. This was not usual. Usually, a first marriage happened about 15 or 16. A boy could not get spirit power after he was married for then he wasn't clean [and innocent]. He had to get it before he married; although, even if a boy were married, he could still inherit power from a relative. Anyone who died could leave power for him. Then the boy would get sick and have to have the power "fixed" in him by a shaman so he could handle it. If he did not have it "fixed," it might follow him around and even give him help, but he would not know how to handle it. Once a person had three sets of power, no one could do anything to harm him.

Difficult Childbirth {ja}

A white woman was having a baby assisted by white doctors. The woman was suffering but they couldn't do anything. Someone told her husband, "We have an Indian man who could make the child come out all right." His name was x̌akəytəd. The husband said to go and get him. The Indian doctor arrived and explained that the Indian custom was to give the healer what you wanted to pay him in advance and tell him "This is what I am calling you for." The shaman was given money and accepted it.

He came close and looked at the woman. He just looked and said, "The reason that the child hasn't come is that he is tangled up." He told them the sex of the child and what was wrong. Then he went through the motions of untangling the child in front of the woman. He told the white doctors, "Now watch the child come safely." He went outside. The child was born just as he said. The husband went out to thank the shaman and asked "What do I owe you." The doctor said "Nothing". The man made him take a horse, anyway. This happened in the 1850s. Later the other Indians killed that doctor. John didn't know why.

Burial {ja}

A long time ago they wrapped the body in mats and put it up in a tree. Later they put what [bones] remained in the ground. Those high born were put into canoes.

One man died here, was wrapped in a mat, and put in a tree. His wife used to go and cry to him. One day she was crying and she heard him say "Is that you? Is that you? Take me down from here. Take me down." She said, "I'm going home to tell the people my husband is talking to me." This happened long before John's grandfather was born. She told her people and they got him down and unwrapped him. He was still alive. He lived for four generations [?] after that.

They only started to bury people in the ground after whites arrived and insisted on it. When they buried in trees, they put tools and other things with them. They wrapped up their favorites in the mat. They buried all over. John has found skulls a quarter of a mile from his place and they found a skeleton at Keyport wrapped in cattail mats when they were building the torpedo station there. In the 1850s a man died at Chico and was buried with all of his gold in his coffin. A boy dug up his body and took the money.

Games {ja}

There was a gambling game played with two bones. It was called **slahal**. One bone was plain and the other had two stripes, one around each end of the bone. There were two teams. The two leaders chose who they wanted on their team. A leader passed the bones to the men [or women] he wanted to hide them. Each team had two men who did this, each with a pair of bones. They would put their hand beneath a covering, like a blanket, and mix up the bones. When they brought their hands out, they might move them around or switch the bones from one hand to another so fast that they couldn't be seen.

The leader on the other side was supposed to guess which hand held the plain bone. If you looked into the eyes of the man holding the bones, you could sometimes tell which hand the bone was in [because his eyes darted in that direction]. Score was kept with pointed sticks of equal number stuck in the ground in front of each team. There were usually a couple dozen sticks, but the numbers varied. If the hand was correctly guessed, the winning side got one of the sticks from in front of the other side. If he guessed the marked bone, his side had to give up both a stick and a set of bones if they had them.

They guessed only one bone holder at a time, or, if he saw a pattern to the two pairs, he used hand signals to guess both sets. To indicate that he thought that the plain bones were on the outside, he pointed outward. To guess they were both in the middle, he pointed straight and down. To guess they were on the left or the right ends, he pointed in the appropriate direction. [These were the basic moves, but actually there was a great range of personal variation and style during the games.] When a side lost all of their sticks, they lost the game.

Sometimes a player would cheat by switching the bones after the other side had guessed. If he were caught, he was warned to stop. This was a very hard thing to accomplish because so many people were always watching. If a person ever cheated, other people would discover it eventually and watch him ever more closely.

Another game was called **slahaləb**. It was played with a number of different colored wooden disks about two or three inches in diameter. John's father had a set of these, but, even so, he doesn't remember the exact colors used. There were two teams. One of them had two piles of these disks. They were put inside a big ball of shredded cedar bark. Cattail mats were placed on the ground between the two teams. A roll of mats was placed in the center. One of the disks was marked with grooves. John did not recall the nature of the markings.

One player put his hands inside the shredded bark ball and mixed up the disks. He kept track of which pile had the marked disk. The other side guessed one of the piles. The disk holder then threw all of the disks in that pile, one by one, against the rolled up mat. If the marked disk came out, his side lost and he had to give the disks and one stick to the other side. If the marked disk did not come out, his side kept the disks and got a stick from the other side. When all of the sticks from one team were gone, that side lost.

In this game, the sticks were not pointed. They were just plain and laid side by side on the ground. The sticks had different names that indicated how much of the pile had gone. Women danced and sang behind the players. Sometimes the players tried to cheat by slipping the marked disk beneath the mats.

There was a hockey or shinny game called q̓ʷaq̓ʷtəlc. Curly was a good player of it. It was played on the beach with two sides. Many men made up each team; there were no set numbers. Each player had a crooked stick made like a long wooden spoon about 3 feet long. At one end it was flat and bent like a spoon. The handle was round. They were used to hit a round wooden sphere, called sbkʷ, the size of a golf ball.

Two players started the game, standing on either side of the ball. Each tried to hit the ball to one of the players on his own team. The other side tried to block. The field was half a mile or more along the beach. One side tried to get the ball across the goal line of the other. This goal was just a line drawn in the beach sand. Hitting the ball involved scooping it up, not striking it. The other side tried to prevent this by hooking the stick of the ball carrier. Sometimes they hit each other with these sticks, but it was considered accidental. The game ended with the first goal. Different tribes would visit each other and play this game. Suquamish and Snohomish played it a lot. Told 8/2/52.

INTERTRIBAL RELATIONS

Because of intertribal marriages, families could go back and forth between different tribes where they had relations. The Suquamish and Duwamish did not feel they were separate tribes, while the Snohomish was a different one, although the Snohomish and Suquamish were always good friends. The Suquamish married as far north as Lummi and throughout Puget Sound. The Skykomish fought with the Suquamish all of the time.

There was never any trouble with the Snohomish. The Skokomish were not always friendly, but the Snohomish were welcome. {ja}

Ed's mother, who was about 83 in 1925, could remember a white man coming to the beach somewhere near Suquamish to talk about the treaty. He filled a plug hat with gravel and put it in front of the people to try and show them that each was to get a lot of gold. She recalled that people were scared of the first ship to come into the harbor near Suquamish. {es}

MEDICINE

Plants {jj}

The root of hemlock stopped diarrhea. The roots were smashed, put in water, and warmed. They did not boil it because then it got too strong. They drank the warm tea.

Cedar bark healed cuts. It was boiled in water, strained, and used to wash the cut.

Suquamish

A fern root [sax̌olč] smashed, boiled, strained, and drunk was good to heal any soreness inside someone.

Rickrish [sƛ̓owilxʷ, licorice root, sqaycq] was used to get sick people to eat, to restore their appetite. It grew on the moss of a tree, was green, and looked like little roots about the size of fingers. If anyone was sick and wouldn't eat, they made them chew this so they would get hungry and eat.

Wild cherry [plilac, **playlaʔac**] was good for sore eyes. The second skin was peeled off, mashed, and soaked in water. They wrapped the bark in a rag and put it on the eyes. {jj}

In her father's house when she was young, the whole place got smallpox. One of his slaves told him that when his people got smallpox, they used skunk as a cure. They would bring a skunk into the house and tease it until it put out juice. So her father had them go out and get some skunks. They got a couple and tied them to the house posts before teasing them. Ellen's grandmother said the stink was terrible, but it worked. None of the family died of smallpox. Other families who didn't use skunks died. The Suquamish hadn't used skunk before this, but this started them doing so. Ellen didn't recall where the slave was from. {eg}

Boiled salt water was used to induce vomiting. Willow bark steeped in water and drunk was good for anything wrong inside and to wash sores. John once skinned a toe during a canoe race and they used this as a wash. It cleared it right up. For sore eyes and cuts they used a plant about a foot high with white flowers on top that looked like cauliflower and with droopy leaves like a squirrel tail. In 1947, a man gave John some to chew and wrap on a cut. Sometimes it was steeped and put on the eyes. {ja}

RITUAL

Salmon Ceremony {eg}

The ceremony was held in honor of a dog salmon with a deformed jaw, called **yabos**. They'd gather little sticks and cook pieces of it on the sticks. Then each little kid was supposed to go and swim. They had to gather up all the bones of the salmon and put them in one place in the water where they were swimming. This was to let the salmon know they wanted them to come back again the next year. This salmon was higher than the other salmon. It was like a chief. It was any salmon with a crooked face. Usually, though, it was a dog salmon.

Each one of the children would be given one of the sticks with salmon on it. Then one of the children took the bones out and dumped them in one place in the water. Then all of the children went out there to that place with the empty sticks in their hands. They throw the sticks away before they start to dive, swim, and have a good time.

Ellen has never heard that this was done when the first salmon of the season was caught. This would happen whenever they caught a salmon with a deformed head.

It was only the children who ate these fish. When the children swam this way, they wore mats around the waist.

This was the custom. Ellen doesn't know why they used these mats, but she says that they also put the fish on these mats. This was a special way of eating. Usually, they used large wooden bowls.

Both Ellen and Wilson know about the [First Salmon] ceremony held at La Conner [Swinomish] and among the Lummi, but they have never heard it mentioned or heard any old people talk about a ceremony like this for the Suquamish. However, Wilson confirmed the rite as described by Ellen above. He says you could always get some salmon in the Sound, so it wasn't like the river people who had to wait for the runs of salmon to arrive.

John Adams did not know of any first salmon ceremony. {ja}

Power, Questing, and Spirit Allies {wg}

At a certain time in the fall of the year (about November), when all of the dog salmon were gone and what had been caught was dried, the spirit powers of some of the young men would return for the first time since they had found them. People would be invited. The father of the person who received the Power would do the inviting. The man hit by the power would be repeating the spirit song he received, but otherwise he couldn't talk. The father placed guests in the house where they belonged, according to locales and status. This was in a regular home, not in a big potlatch house. They invited just what the house could hold.

The power only comes at this time of the year. When the power comes, the man has to sing it. The first time the power comes the people are not specifically invited, but anyone comes who wants to hear the song and learn it. Certain people, who know the power and are able to do it, would come and sing to help out. This would help the boy who was sick. The young man could not start singing until someone else sang the song to open his mouth. Wilson says there was one man that had a song no one could sing correctly. The power he had came to him. But no one could hit the song that would start off the sick man singing. They tried but all of them failed. This was a young man who came from up near Shelton [Skokomish Reservation]. He was married to a Suquamish. This man was having a hard time since no one could start his song for him.

There was a young man from Up Sound who could understand the power, yet he couldn't get out and start the song before someone announced that if anyone in the crowd knew the power, he should come out of the crowd to help. [It was not polite or "high class" to volunteer help unless it was asked for.] Finally the man from Up Sound was asked by one of the sick man's parents and he agreed. He started, got up and talked. Afterward, he started to repeat this man's power song.

The sick man was in bed. When the Up Sound man started to sing, he got up, repeated his song and started to dance. Then everyone joined in. The sick man was out on the floor dancing then. He went around the house just as if he hadn't been sick. He was strong again.

There was another young man named šəgʷap, according to a story told to Wilson by Jim dapsotał. It happened long before Wilson's time. A young man was going from house to house in the village. He was singing. They were just "playing and singing for fun." While he was doing this, his power hit him. He became "helpless," like fainting. Some of the people went to the father of the boy and told him to clean up his house. They wanted him to take everything out of the house to make room for a crowd to come and see his son sing and dance the power.

This man didn't want to do this. He thought that his son was just acting foolish. He said, "Why don't you have him in you're house?" He was told, "No, you have to do it because you are his father." Finally, he agreed and prepared his house for the gathering. The people were to sit around the house on the sleeping benches. Sometimes the spectators would sleep there if events went on for a long time. Often, a new singer like this one sang all night. The minimum first time was about four days.

They brought him to the house and his father invited certain of the people inside. In addition to these, others came in just to watch without an invitation. The people invited by the

Suquamish

father were the ones the father thought could help sing for his son. It was up to the father to find someone to help his son sing when the boy got sick in this way.

The father appointed someone to take care of the guests and to show them where they were to sit in the house. For four or five nights, they helped this young man. He didn't go to bed to sleep during the entire time. He just went to sit in a corner for awhile and remain quiet. This is how he rested after he started singing and dancing. He quit dancing for a while and sat in a corner every so often. He might sing to himself while sitting there, but it was just for his own benefit. Nobody repeated the song after him, like they did in public.

When he started to sing the song, a man chosen by his father, someone who understood the power, repeated the song as the young man sang it. When the song ended, the repeater started it over again and then the rest all joined in. When they all started singing, the young man did his dance for the first time.

When he was ready to quit, he made a sign. Then he changed his song to other words. The repeater copied this and the same routine as above was followed. The second dance might be different from the first. There might be two or three of these songs and dances. If he changed three times, when the third verse ended, he'd sing the first one again. He would go through each one of them three times during the four days that he was singing.

After he was through with the three songs sung three times, he might start another, different song. He might even go on to a fifth or sixth. When morning came, it was time for him to rest. He sat in the corner and might sing for himself, but he didn't sleep. The other people ate and then slept. But the singer never ate. Some of them lasted as long as 8 days without eating or sleeping. This was the longest they could go. Most of them go for four days.

At the end of all of these activities, the gathering broke up. Some went home, some stayed on a little longer because some of the older people started to sing after the young boy was done. An elder got out on the floor to sing and dance his song. This was to "clear himself [or herself] from getting sick."

When the full series of days was completed, a boy could, eat, sleep, and rest. Then he had to go back to work: fishing, hunting, making canoes, or whatever he did with his power.

The next year about this same time, the spirit would come back for the second time. The next year, the father was prepared for it, as the father of šəgʷap. Sometimes, the father himself got a spirit. Then it was up to the son to take care of him. He chose a repeater to get him started. The second year the same repeater might come back or the father or son might select another one. That time, the repeater did not have to actually sing to start the boy off. The boy sang the same song as the year before and now he understood it better. The entire process of the previous year was repeated again. After the second year, they could sing for themselves. They might have a repeater to help out, but they could sing for themselves. The older a person got, the more he had to do for himself in the singing. Whoever happened to be near when the power hit helped a singer through the sickness.

[Power was conveyed by many different kinds of spirits. Many more than can be named here.] There was a particular spirit which made it necessary for a person to give things away in order to "get clear of it." This power was called **sqayap**.

Another type of spirit power was q̓ʷax̌ʷq̓. When it hit a person, he'd sing it. Then he'll ask for the poles and someone else used them to keep time by bouncing them against the roof while he sang. Others would beat with sticks on boards laid flat. Some people asked for these poles to be used and also for cedar bark to be tied around the pole near the top. When they used it, the cedar bark flopped in time with the song. Not everyone used this cedar bark. It wasn't a helping (curing) power, but it was a "help" to the person who has it. [In other words, it brought benefits only to its human ally, not for helping others.]

The power called **sgʷədiləč** did not occur among the Suquamish, but they knew about it for other tribes. Wilson's mother had this power and sang it at Suquamish. She was a Lower Skagit. She was the only one here who had this kind of power. This happened before Wilson was born. She inherited it from some of her people. Wilson says that no Suquamish tried to get it. It belonged Up Sound way. If anyone here got it, they would have a hard time getting it started for it was unknown to the local repeaters. Wilson's father was the repeater for his wife. He had a special power that helped him understand strange powers. He was good as a repeater. He helped lots of people. The name of the power that helped him be a good repeater was **sƛ̕alkəb** [monster]

[Power could be used both to hurt and to help, the human ally had to decide.] The whites put a stop to Indian doctoring and that gave a clear path to the bad doctors [shamans]. They started killing all the Indians. The good doctors couldn't do anything about it because the whites had stopped them from doctoring, but they did not stop the bad ones, so they had a free hand and they killed off a lot of the Indians.

Questing {ja}

As soon as the boys were old enough, they started training. They were told to go into the salt water every morning and night. They had to stay in it until their bodies didn't steam when they came out. There was a fire ready for them to warm themselves beside when they got out. John does not know of any restrictions on conduct or the eating of certain foods during this period of training. The boys were not sent out to get power right a way for they had first to train for a long time. They were told when and where to go at the time when they were ready. They were sent to places where the spirits were known to be [for that family].

This might be up on top of a mountain. There was a mountain over by Mission Lake named **babdət** (Mt Green ?). Some of them were sent there. When a boy was sent there, he was given some sticks to take up to the top of the mountain. He was supposed to leave them there to show that he had actually been up there. Later, older men would go up to see whether the sticks were really there. If they weren't, the boy would be punished.

They might be told to walk all the way around Bainbridge Island along the beach. They would find power there, like John Bull. It was a rock so he was very strong. They used to hit him and beat him and shoot him, but they couldn't kill him. He was hard to kill. He was shot once, but it didn't kill him. While he was in bed, they shot him with a shotgun and blew him in two. This was how they finally killed him.

Some were sent to Point No Point. There were a lot of snakes there, and they would get Snake power. It isn't very strong, though.

When the boys were sent out to seek their power, they had to be clean or the powers wouldn't come to them. They were given physics [emetics] to clean them out. Their finger and toe nails had to be clean. While they were out, they were not supposed to eat or drink. John thinks that sometimes they did not eat or drink for up to 30 days.

John related that one time when he was a boy, he was running home on the beach after sundown when it was dark. Suddenly, he saw an old, stooped-over woman with a blanket over her shoulders walking on the beach and leaning on a wooden staff. He looked at her and said, "What is that? There's nothing in camp like that." He was young then and didn't know about such encounters and so he ran on. The old people told him that she was a power. If he had grabbed her, she would have knocked him out, and both of them would have fallen on the beach and lain side by side for a long time -- maybe as long as 10 hours. This old woman represented a number of powers. You couldn't tell which one you would get. She represented a group of powers called ceyod [**siyod**]. John did not recall the specifics of these powers.

Instead, his thoughts turned to the story of how his grand uncle Tom or **wəlpəkad** tried to cure a little girl. The girl had been eating bread when her mother hit her on the back and made some of the bread go up her nose. She got sick and her parents called Tom to cure her. But they had waited too long. Tom told the father that it was too late, but the father told him to go ahead because she was going to die anyway. So Tom sucked out the bread, but she died just as he had told them she would. He should have been called sooner. This grand uncle was later killed by a Suquamish, but John did not want to talk about the details.

Another time, John said that this man was John Curly, his maternal uncle. Curly was born a Duwamish and lived there most of his life, although he did visit Suquamish often. At the time when Leschi (a Duwamish [Nisqually-Puyallup] whose grandmother was part Yakama) was going to attack the whites at Seattle (1856), Curly went to the whites and warned them about it. Leschi had threatened anyone who would tell the whites, but nothing ever happened to Curly because he told. John and Curly often hunted together.

Curly had Rattlesnake power. When he was a boy, he had been in the Okanogan country. His mother had spanked him and he went out into the mountains to cry. Snake appeared to him there. John said that this was like stealing it from the Okanogan. Curly gave it to John, who had the Indian name of **satabsoq** [**sk̓idk̓ʷ**] meaning "little devil, or rattlesnake." This spirit followed John around all over, but he never had a doctor [shaman] "fix it to him." Eventually, he had it taken way because he was afraid that he might be accidentally responsible for killing someone with it.

Power was sometimes inherited in this way. For example, a father might pass his power(s) on to his son. After the father died, the son would get sick because he had inherited the power(s). Then a doctor would have to "fix" the power in him. That means he would "straighten it out". But the son would not be able to use the power for a long time -- maybe 10 or 15 years. Sometimes, one man could steal another man's power, but if it was too strong for him, he would die [because it would overpower him to death].

John says that when he was a boy, a lot of children who were sent to government schools got sick and died. Some of the people thought that the teachers were doing it, but John says it was bad doctors at home who were sending the sickness to them. People who had Bear power could do this. One of his people way back [long ago] killed lots of people with this power.

Someone was working on John when he was a boy in mission school. It hurt him on his left side at the bottom of his chest and made him stop growing. He didn't know who was doing it to him. Another Indian doctor came to work on him. This doctor wasn't called. He just knew about it. He sucked at the place where it hurt. His power was Loon. It isn't a very strong power and he couldn't get it all out. John's parents took him to Dr Morgan at Port Madison, who gave him cod liver oil mixed with port wine. His parents gave this white doctor the credit for helping him, but John says it was the Indian doctor who really helped him the most. It was because of him that he grew up. Even so, he didn't grow as strong as he should have been. The pain came back again later in the same place. John says that it has really been there all the time and that that is what is wrong with him now, late in life.

The general name for all power(s) is **sqəlalitut**. A shaman doctor had to have three sets of them to be any good. If he had three sets, no one could do anything to him. John says that that is why his father could stand up and talk and no one could do anything to him. He was a very good speaker.

Chief Kitsap had lots of powers. Eagle was one of them. The snow is called the "lice of the eagle." If an arrow was shot at him, it would go right through his hair and not hurt him, no matter where you aimed at him. A little red canoe was another of his powers.

John knew a woman called Julia Nappie, **sləqalca**, who had Dog Salmon for a power. She would never eat dog salmon. From this and other cases, John thinks there was a general taboo against anyone eating members of the species of their own power.

People who had the Blackfish (Killerwhale, Orca) for power were good fishers because the Blackfish eats other fish. Anyone who had Thunderbird for power could make it thunder whenever they wanted to. John knew a man who had Cloud for a power. This was Wind who could blow away anything that bothered him. John also remembered Seal, Sea Lion, and Porpoise as power(s). He said anything could be a power. All living things could have power.

Girls could get power too. They could get the same kinds of power that men got. There were many different kinds in all.

John says that a place called Devil's Hole by the whites is located near a sandspit between Bangor and Vinland on the eastern side of Hood Canal. It is a pool of water. The Klallam got power there, but the Suquamish knew there were bad, mean spirits there. If they got too near it, they would back away to make sure it did not get them from behind. They always backed away.

Half way between Charleston and Gorst at the head of Port Orchard Bay there was a rocky place that was used for meetings and sports that included gambling, jumping, and other games. The gambling used two bone pieces and was part of the ancient traditions, long before the whites came. There were smokehouses and camps there on different sides of the bay. Everyone would come there from all over to play games when there was plenty of food. John didn't associate it with any particular time, just whenever there was enough food to get them all together. There was no big potlatch house there. They just had cedar bark houses. The bark was in strips with cattail mats around the whole house.

John was born near Charleston. Indians used to camp there where the Navy is now. That was in 1872 when John was born. He knows this is right because Pete Fowler was born the same year in September and John was born in October. He felt this was important because some places have recorded his birth date in error. The allotment patent has him two years older and this is wrong. His mother was from the Duwamish and named Mary. The father of his father was from the Skokomish, but his father went to live at Mapleville (in the Poulsbo-Keysport area) after marriage because it was a good place to hunt. Because of his marriage, he could go back and forth between Skokomish and Suquamish. His wife was a Suquamish so "This was his home too."

He used to hunt around that area, way back in the timber. Deer were all he hunted there. He used a bow and arrows when small, but a gun when he was older. There were no camps back in the timber because they were always along the shore. They just traveled into the woods to hunt.

Before the whites came, there was a man and his wife who lived back on Mission Creek. His name was **sxʷatkadə** and he was the father of Steve Wilson. He was a Suquamish. He didn't know why he lived way back there [as a holy caretaker]. He lived on the southwest side of the mountain where the stream is. Boys in training had to take sticks up to the top of this mountain. Later this old man or others would go up to see if the sticks were there. If they weren't, the boy was punished.

Suquamish

A smokehouse was near the head of Mission Creek, at Mission Lake near the mountain. The man just went into the timber in the fall when the salmon were running in the creek. He'd catch them there and cure them in the smokehouse. Then he would bring them back for storage in the main camp on the shore.

East of the mountain where the sticks were taken, there was a swamp. Once, Jack's father, John Bull, and several others were hunting deer there. They camped there at night. Vapor rose from the pond. When it got high up, thunder started. A young man could go there and get this power. Then he could make it thunder any time he wanted to. A white man asked several Indian doctors around Yakama if any of them could make it thunder. One of the Yakama doctors did it.

Some whites believed in Indian doctors and used them to cure diseases. The whites used to have one Duwamish doctor come to the back of a store and work on them there by sucking out diseases. He had Mosquito for power. It was part of Thunder and showed up in the Rainbow.

Bluejay was a power that allowed a person to talk any language. John says it was here long ago, before the whites. He does not know of any power used to locate the bodies of drowned people.

The Suquamish did not use the "boom, boom" (drum) like the Yakama do. When they were singing in a house, they would take a long pole and hit it on the roof to keep time with the singing. Anyone could keep time with the pole.

This was a long pole about 8 or 10 feet tall. John saw one when he was about 10 years old about 70 years ago. The pole was painted red. These poles were always kept out in the woods. You couldn't keep them in the house because they were part of what a doctor had, and, thus, too powerful for encounters with ordinary mortals. Some doctors did not have them, it depended on what the spirit told his ally at the first meeting. They were kept out in the woods up in a tree or in the hollow of a cedar. The sticks belonged to the doctor, but anyone could beat time with them while the doctor sang.

John says that at certain times, during certain parts of the song, the pole would come to life. Once an Indian doubted this. So they told him to hold a cedar man. It was a figurine, not a pole, a man made of cedar about four-foot high [cf Chehalis]. These figures had handles on the back to hold them. They held them up in front of them when they danced. At a certain point in the song, the figure would come to life. This represented part of the power of a doctor. So they gave this man the carved man of cedar. He danced with it. When they got to that certain part, the carving came to life and took the person through the roof and drowned him in the water. These figures were given up a long time ago. John never saw one, but the old people told him about them.

Near the end of some of the poles, a two foot piece of cedar bark was sometimes tied. Just a single piece. The pole itself was cedar, about as thick as a baseball bat, 3 inches in diameter. Because it was cedar it wasn't heavy. This power of the pole was called təstəd, a sibling of the power boards.

Curly saw some of these poles come out of the water at the southern end of Bainbridge Island. This was a place where this power could be gotten. You would keep going into the water to get this one. When the poles came up, you would build a raft and go out to get them. When you got hold of one, it would take you down into the water. You would stay down there for 3 days and nights. You could do this because you were with the power. This power could be used to kill with, also to cure people. After you understood it, you came up and floated on the water, drifting to shore. You would be weak. Sometimes they came home on their hands and knees they were so exhausted.

While in the water, the thing told you what you're going to be. It gave you songs to sing. It also gave you a dance different from that of anyone else. It would be as long as 30 years before the power could be used. You couldn't doctor with it when you were still a boy. You had to grow up first. It had to be "fixed" in a person only when it was inherited. A person who inherited power would get sick. Then an Indian doctor would be called to "fix" it on him or her. If a man went out and got power himself, it wouldn't have to be "fixed" on him. Sometimes after a person had gotten power, he became sick. This was because the power did not stay with you all of the time. When you called it back, you might get sick. Then a doctor would have to help you.

John's father was hunting near Bainbridge Island at night. Doctor Peters was coming along, half drunk, and saying "He thinks he's a big Indian doctor, but he'll find out. Just watch!" Curly was there, too, and he heard someone singing way off, like crying. It turned out to signify that Dr Peters had got Dr Bob. Dr Peters got the power of Dr Bob and that killed him. Dr Bob was the person who received the poles at Sandy Hook. Dr Peters was a bad man. Forty-seven years ago, Indians were burying three and four people every week. Dr Peters was doing that.

Secret Society ~ Guild {wg}

The secret society of Dog Eaters [sx̌ədx̌ədəb, sx̌idx̌idəb] had certain songs they used to sing. It was a kind of secret power. When they sang the song and got under the influence of the power, they acted silly [crazy]. If a dog were around them, they got it and tore it to pieces with their teeth. They were supposed to eat it, but they really didn't. They made the people believe that they did, though.

They used to make people not belonging to it think that they were doing things that they weren't. They would take a young person, lay him down, put him to sleep, and then one of them sucked on his body. Then he spit out blood supposedly from the young man. Actually, the man had cut his tongue underneath. This was not part of the initiation into the group. It was only part of what they showed others, their showing off to other people what they could do.

Once, Wilson's mother was sick and supposed to be asleep. A couple of members were planning something and she overheard them. It was only in the middle of winter when they would perform. In the performance they made people believe that they could make something move without anyone doing this. They used to make noise with a rattle, a piece of wood hollowed out to hold stones. It was the size and shape of a duck. They would shake it in time with the singing. It was made of two pieces of wood tied together, made in the shape of a bird, and tied around the small end. It was called **yobax̌ʷačatab**.

While they were singing they made the people believe they could make the rattle move without someone doing it. While singing the song, they'd lay it on the ground. But first, they scattered some feather down [q̓ʷəq̓ʷalc] on the ground. This covered the string tied to the rattle. There were two people in the middle of the smokehouse. They were opposite each other. First one pulled it toward him in a jerking way. He had a blanket over himself, covering his head. He could not be seen clearly. This made the bird rattle look as if it were alive. Then the other man pulled it the other way. All of the time, they were singing a song that were supposed to make the bird move. If the down should get thin or become pulled away, they kept watch and ran out to pick up the rattle. They started to use it as a rattle again before anyone could see the string.

Suquamish

The well-to-do people were entitled to join this society. The group itself had a choice as to who was to become a member. If anyone overheard any of the secrets, they had to join. Even a low class person would be taken in if they learned any of the secrets. This forced membership kept everything secret. Women of the high class were also taken in.

When a young man was about 14 years old, he "kind of felt big." Teenagers felt that they knew it all. To keep them modest, they made them join the society because there he had to listen and learn from the older people. They would take a young man away to where the others could not see the initiation. They worked over the initiate and put a spirit power into him. This would put him to sleep. He was helpless then. To wake him up, two people went on either side of him to raise him. Then they let him down again. They did this three or four times, probably three. At first, he was face down. After lifting him, they turned him over on his back and lifted him up and down again, three or four times. When they let him down the last time, they sat him up. That was when they woke him. When he was able, they stood him upright.

Then they take him to a special room where they start him singing. They tell him what power he was to have by singing it to him first. He was in a special room from which he could emerge into the public. They also taught him a dance. When he was trained and ready, he came out before the people at a public gathering to sing and dance. He had a special repeater to help him get started and to followed him around the smokehouse. The boy sang part of the song and then stopped while the repeater echoed it. Then the boy started again, stopped, and the repeater followed. This continued until the song was finished.

Then they had another boy come out and sing. The second boy would have a different power with a slightly different song and dance. The same procedure was pretty much followed in every case. No one else was allowed to sing exactly the same song. The tune might even be the same, but then the words were different. There are many powers that have almost the same song, but each remains distinct within about eight kinds of music.

The public gathering was attended by anyone who wanted to come. They were not told any stories or anything else about what was happening to the initiates when they were training in the special room. Other tribes had the same society so their initiates could join in during rites at other tribes. Wilson was never able to see an initiation because in his day the Catholics were very strong and they forbid these ceremonies.

When a boy received a song, it was his until death. Then the song might be inherited by someone else, but it stayed within the family. When someone died, the spirit ally was "just like a dog" and went to another member of the family who was familiar to it. It could go to any member, not necessarily the son. Membership in the society tended to pass along family lines, so when a boy was initiated, he might be given the song that belonged to some deceased member of his family. A person outside of the family was not allowed to take such a song, unless the family approved it under very unusually circumstances.

These inherited powers or the ones from the secret society did not require a power quest. They helped the boy, however, to get other powers for himself. Thus, once a boy had joined the secret society, he often went out to seek power for himself. They only went out in the winter, never in the summer.

A low class person who didn't belong to the society could go out in quest of power for him/herself. This power then could be passed on in this family at death [but it was almost never a strong one].

Power that was passed on by the secret society was not the property of the society as such. The members of the society decided what power belonged to the family of a boy (or girl) so it could be passed on to him. It was the family members already in the society who decided this.

The instruction in the special room also included what to do if you meet a power at any time. Sometimes, an animal would be a power. Should you meet it, you were supposed to act in a certain way toward it until it talked to you in your language and gave you its power. Sometimes it was in dreams that you saw the animal. The secret society told what to do in a dream of this kind. When the animal spoke to a boy in his own language, then that was his power for life.

Besides an animal, you might meet a person who was not human. These powers will show up as a living person or animal, yet it wasn't what it seemed. After they spoke, then the animal or person disappeared. Then you were to go home, tell no one, and keep it to yourself until it hit as a power and you became ill. When it hit, it was a day during the fall of the year. If you couldn't sing it, it was the place of your father to call for help. The voice of the spirit sank into your body. When it came back, you needed a repeater to help sing it out initially.

In dreams when a person met a spirit, it said "My father sent me to tell you to come out and meet me." Yet the animal or person talking was the power itself. The power told you to meet his father at a certain place. This place might be a spring, or a big stream. Then you must go and swim in this certain place early in the morning until you meet the power there. While the power spoke of "its father," it was really the power itself that was doing this. It really didn't have a father.

If a boy kept clean enough, he finally got power. If he had courage enough to go there and swim every day early in the morning, he eventually got power. After a boy received power, the spring of water might go dry but break out in some place else, or go dry entirely. Wilson denied that the boy was required to dive a certain number of times, although people often went to lakes and mountains to get power and diving was a practice during quests. {wg}

Ellen said they used to go to Island Lake near Silverdale to get power. The common people who didn't belong to the society could also go out and look for power. Women also sought power. They usually just got common things like birds, and so forth. They usually didn't get any strong power like those that came to men, but they could. Ellen remembers hearing of a woman who got a strong power just like a man's. {eg}

Wilson believed that slaves could get power too. There were many possible ways and kinds of power. Wilson said his family on the side of his father did not have to go out searching for power the way most others did. They could get power even if they never left home, provided that they were clean.

Wilson provided an example of one of his dreams. He saw a bear coming down the creek on all four feet. When it got close, it stood up and its hair [fur] was gone. It was like a human. It told Wilson that its father wanted to see him. But Wilson decided not to go up to that creek. He was afraid. So he wouldn't go to this creek unless someone else went with him for then the spirit would never come. You had to be alone at such meetings to get power.

John Adams didn't know much about the secret society. His father told him that it was a lot of faking. Anyway, it was before his time; he hadn't heard much about it. {ja}

Odyssey Ceremony {wg}

Wilson actually saw this done. It required shamans, generally known as **daxʷdaʔab**, who had a special kind of power. We are out here alive and when the dead come here they look for sick people. Then the dead person's spirit will find the clothes of the sick person lying outside.

Suquamish

What they find from these clothes, they take back with them. It was the warmth of that sick person's body that had soaked into the clothes. The dead took this out of the clothes and took it with them to the spirit land. Every time they did this, it weakened the sick person. Then the shaman needed to get over into the spirit land to get the warmth away from the power of the dead people. In that way, he helped the sick person and sometimes this enabled him to get well.

The first shaman asked to cure the sick person chooses another shaman or two to help him. When they were doctoring, they use the verb **opəgʷəd** [spigʷəd]. This was when they performed, singing and dancing to fulfill their power to help the sick. Each shaman had a cedar board representing a power. The Suquamish called this **sptadax̣** [spəɬtədaq] and the Duwamish called it **spəgʷəd** [spigʷəd]. Each shaman had only one. Sometimes they were in the shape of a human. On the board they would mark their power: Lizard, Snake, some kind of beast, and so on. They painted on the board a picture of the power. Such boards were from six to eight inches wide, and four to five feet high. They were carved and painted. The background was painted white with the other colors over the white.

When they worked on a sick person, they could either use the boards by themselves or they could use a simulated canoe outlined in cedar bark, with the boards set up inside. When they used the boards alone, they would shake when handled, but in the canoe they stood steady and did not move.

The canoe was made of strands of inner cedar bark pounded so that they were soft and pliable, about 10 to 12 feet long. The boards were put in the canoe, but they were dug down into the ground so that they stood up straight. The shamans would be in the canoe making dancing motions, but keeping their feet on the ground so as not to tip the imaginary canoe.

Many shamans made the trip to the spirit land. Usually three was the minimum. When they got out of the canoe, they were supposed to be there. They danced around very carefully, looking for the spirits. They lifted their feet up high and crossed their legs as they walked, moving slowly and carefully. [In this way they were imitating the motions of the dead so as not to attract undo attention to themselves.] All this time, they were looking for the spirit. Sometimes they would find the warm stuff on the clothing of some of the dead.

One or two of the shamans might have a piece of cedar bark draped around his shoulders like a scarf reaching to about the waist. When they found the spirit, they put it on this cedar bark to take it back safely. If they were not using cedar bark, they put the warmth to the breast. When they had the spirit-warmth, they brought it back to the sick person. The shaman pulled off the warmth with two hands and held it toward the patient. Then he put it back on that body with a motion of the two hands brushing the person with the palms out.

If the sick person got well, he might start singing his own spirit song, getting up to dance and sing after only half an hour. If he did not get well, the shamans may have had to repeat the trip because, "There was something else they did not get." While they were doing this, they were all singing constantly.

They usually started for the spirit land in the morning. The trip took from 6 to 12 hours. If the sick person did not get better, then they made another trip, this one their third. If the patient then showed signs of getting well, they don't make any more trips. If he didn't show any improvement, there was nothing left to do. It was seldom that even two trips were necessary.

If they didn't use the canoe, they just stood their boards up on the plain ground so they were straight. When they were coming home from the spirit land, they shook the boards, to speed up the trip back, in time with their singing, moving them forward and back instead of side to side for that might tip the canoe. The people sitting around the house kept time with the music, singing during the trip out and the return. While the shamans were in the spirit land all noise stopped. It had to be very quiet. Even the shamans spoke only in whispers. Everyone was afraid of being heard by the spirits.

The actual trip involved tracing in cedar bark strips the outline of a canoe big enough to surround all the shamans going along. At the start, they got down on their knees to sing. The spectators beat time to the song, hitting sticks on boards about a foot long. Usually, it was a cedar board from a house. That sounded the loudest.

Later they stood up and danced, but they never moved their feet around to keep from tipping over. Going, they had poles that they used like paddles. The stroke was long and slow. When they came to a stream of water in the spirit land, they left the canoe to cross a bridge. They go one at a time. The leader at the bow went first. Then all of them entered the camp of the spirit people.

On the trip back, they did not pass the bridge because they took another way back, depending on where they found the spirit. Then they wanted to travel very fast and they shook the boards. In the canoe, they used the poles to make paddling motions that were faster than they used going. They sang and beat time a little faster, also. When they got back, they sank down on their knees in the canoe until they landed and got out.

Then they knelt again and sang some more. Each doctor sang his song. When all of them were done, the leader delivered "what they brought back" to the sick person. The leader went first, but then the others went in turn, each singing and delivering some part of the spirit. They were singing then because the personal power of each of them was coming to them from the place were they initially encountered it. When all had given their parts, the patient sang his own song if he felt revived or cured. They might be working on more than one sick person at a time, if so, they repeated this procedure separately for each one.

Potlatch {wg}

Wilson said the smoke house [plank dwelling] was divided into sections for groups coming from different areas. When a man gave a potlatch, he would send word to the headmen of different areas, so that what was given away went to the leaders of these different bands.

Wilson went to many potlatches as a boy. The last one he went to was given by John Seattle at Green River. John was not related to the old chief, he just took the name.

When a leader came, he brought some of his family. This group was seated in a special part of the gathering. The man giving the potlatch would announce the names as people came in. Or he might have a speaker do this. They would have men like ushers who showed each group where to sit and whom to stay with. The people brought gift food with them when they came.

When all the people were there, the leader started, singing his power song. Then he spoke to the people, saying "so and so has come in. That is the last of the people I have invited." Then he changed to another tune of his song and kept singing until he got to the end. Then he started to give away what he had collected together, saying "The first person invited was so and so." Then that tribal leader was given presents, and so on until they got to the last one to come in. Then his helper started his own song, finished it, and gave out his own gifts in the same order. The giver usually called on his relatives to help him. He gave only to the leading members of other communities. After the gifts had been given to the chiefs, and the feasting was over, there was a Scramble. Everyone was allowed in this event [but the high class thought it too crass to behave in so undignified a manner]. A platform was made on the roof and blankets were piled on it. Then the people would crowd around below it. A man would throw the blankets down at them, one at a time. Everyone tried to get ahold of one of these. They didn't pull or tear it. One of them who had a firm grip would claim it. Then he had to pay the others also hanging on to it for their share. Sometimes an old man would get hold of a blanket and a strong young man would pull it away from the others until he could give it to the old man for his own. [This showed respect and regard for the elders.] Poles were also thrown down and people would try to take hold of them for each represented one canoe. The person left holding the stick had to pay the others for their share.

During the first part of a potlatch, when the gifts were given out to the invited leaders, these headmen could either keep all that they received or they could give some of it to members of their group. It was up to them, but a wise leader shared what he had.

The reasons for holding a potlatch included 1) Naming -- this was the most important, whether giving a name to a child or changing one later in life; 2) Remove Stigma -- for a daughter sent home by her husband, the father would announce what had happened and say he didn't know why his daughter had been sent home, this cleared her name so she could marry honorably again; 3) Status Changes -- mark the death of one chief and the elevation of his heir.

John Adams said they would invite people from all over, tribes friendly to them. They wouldn't invite enemies. It was always a chief who gave the potlatch, but he had other men go out and do the inviting. The name for a potlatch gʷəgʷə [gʷigʷi] means "to gather people from all over, to invite [call, ask]."

The guests arrived singing their own songs. Chief Seattle had a potlatch at Old Man House around the 1850s. He went to Victoria for some blankets. When he left, he told the people, "When I leave Victoria, you will hear Thunder and then you will know I am on my way back." This happened. Curly was the speaker for Chief Seattle at this potlatch.

Sometimes a chief would deliberately stigmatize himself to have an excuse for a potlatch. salq̓b, the second chief after Kitsap and the one ahead of young Seattle, was fixing the fire in his hearth. He wanted his blanket to catch on fire. He went slowly around the flames until his blanket ignited.. Then he held a potlatch.. Having his clothing catch fire gave him the excuse he needed to hold a potlatch.

Suquamish

FOLKLORE

The Changer [dokʷibəɫ] {jj}

Around Squaxin Island towards Olympia, the Changer was going there. He wanted to change this land into something else, but the land would throw itself to one side every time he tried to change it. It would say, "I am old land, I'm old land, I'll stay the way I want." Then the Changer left it. Now this land is very hilly. It is up and down all over. This was from the way it was throwing itself to one side.

There is a rock with lots of little rocks around it south of Sandy Hood. This was a person, a man. He and his dogs were chasing a elk. The dogs were barking [too loudly]. All at once, the Changer came along and turned them all into rocks. The little rocks are the dogs. The big rocks are the elk and the man.

The Changer was always going around turning things into something else. One rock at Poulsbo was a person. He was filing a bone to make it into a knife. He was singing about cutting up the Changer when he came along. The Changer heard this and sneaked up behind him. All at once he said: "What are you singing now, Deer?" He called him Deer to turn him into a deer. The Changer took the knife and put it on the back part of his leg above the hoof. Then the deer turned into the rock. They call the rock *halils*. It has a white mark like a collar around it.

Dog Husband {jj}

There was a girl who had a little puppy. The puppy always slept with her. It began to grow up and it still slept with her. Pretty soon the girl gave birth to a lot of little puppies. The father of the girl was so ashamed of her he left her with her puppies. The father, mother, and all the people left the girl alone.

The puppies got older and older. All she gave them to eat was clams. There was one little girl and four boys. The girl was half and half, a person on one side and a dog on the other.

All at once, they were getting older and she [the mother] used to hear lots of noise in her home when she was out on the beach digging clams. She decided to see what they were doing. So she sneaked up on the house. She peeped through a little hole. She saw them. They had taken off their dog skins and they were handsome looking boys. She went to the little girl. The little girl was always with her. She went back to the beach to dig. She made a plan and told it to her daughter. They took their clamming sticks and stuck them in the sand and put some of their clothes on them. Then they sneaked up to the house because they heard a noise.

(Before she had gone down to the beach again, she had made a big fire in the house, but the boys did not know what she made the fire for.)

She told her daughter they would grab the furs (hides) and throw them into the fire. Her little girl and she went in quickly. They grabbed the hide coats and threw them into the fire. Then the boys were ashamed and became still. The mother said "Why didn't you be like this before. You have made me ashamed. My family left because you wore clothes like a dog."

The boys grew up to be big, handsome hunters. Two went up to hunt for deer and elk; two went out into the Sound to fish. The mother went picking berries. The boys got all kinds of nice meat and fish. They dried the meats, salmon, and berries. They did this every day and were getting lots to eat.

The father and mother could see the smoke when they were drying all the time and they said, "What are they doing over there?" So they said, "We'd better go over and see." So they went, got there, and saw that there was lots to eat. So the girl was good to her folks. She gave them bundles of meat and other things she had.

They went back to their new home and told the people. The father was so proud of his daughter. She told her father, when he came, about her boys and how they really were.

Then he told his people, "Get ready, we're going back to our old home, my daughter's children are hunters." So they all went back. The boys hunted and fed these people that came back to them. The people were sorry for what they had done before. The father and mother asked for forgiveness. They said that she and her boys would be the leaders of the tribe from then on.

The daughter got married and had other children. They weren't too bad. The grandchildren were better. They didn't show so much hair on the face, just a little brown where it had been in the previous generation.

Star Story (Star Husband) {jj}

This is a story the Suquamish got from the Snoqualmie.

Two girls used to go camping. They would be lying on their bed facing the sky. They were sisters.

One of the girls said, "Oh, that is a nice white star. I would like to have it for a boy friend." The other girl said, "I'd like to have that pink star for my boy friend." They went to sleep.

When they woke up, they both had men lying with them. They were afraid of the men, but one of them said, "You wanted me when you saw me up in the sky."

Then these men put the girls to sleep so they wouldn't know which way they were going. They took them up into the sky, the girls didn't know where they were going. They took them to their home.

The girls went out camping again in their new home and dug some fern roots to eat. They did this every day.

Not long after, the older girl had a baby boy by her husband, the white star who had matter in his eyes. The pink star, though, was a handsome young fellow.

The baby was getting older. They went digging fern roots every day and came home every evening. One night they came home and didn't have any fern roots. Their husbands asked, "Why don't you get any anymore." They answered, "Oh, the baby cries so much we can't do anything else but take care of him. The baby didn't actually cry. They just fooled their husbands.

Instead, when they were out every day, they kept digging deeper until all at once wind came up through the hole. They said, "This wind acts like where we came from." So they blocked up the hole. They started to plan what they would do.

They gathered cedar boughs. Then they wove the cedar boughs, warmed them and twisted them to make them soft. When they got home, they'd have no fern roots. They'd tell their husbands the same story, "The baby cries and we can't dig roots." All of the time, they were working these cedar boughs to make a rope. They tied them together until they thought they were long enough.

Then they opened the hole and put the rope through to see if it would touch the land where they had come up from. They let it down, down, down -- until it stopped. They thought,

"Well, I guess it has gotten to where we came from. They pulled it up. They tied it around the waist of the younger one. They tied the other end to a tree. Then they made the hole big enough for her body to go through.

The younger sister said, "If I get to the bottom, I'll pull on the rope and then you'll know I'm down. When she got down she did this. Then her sister pulled the rope up. She tied her baby next and let him down. At the bottom, his aunt untied the baby and pulled on the rope to let her sister know it was ready to go up again.

Then she pulled the rope up and tied herself. Then she let herself down. When she left, she fixed the hole so that their husbands wouldn't find it. She got down all right. Then they pulled the rope down. She let it come down and pile up there. This is still at Snoqualmie. It looks like a little mountain.

They went home. Their mothers told them they had been looking for them. The girls told their mother the story.

The baby grew up to be a big, nice looking boy. He got married and had children. Their children got big and got married. This was the beginning of the Snoqualmie. They are descended from the stars.

[The mother of Chief Jacob was part Snoqualmie, but even so this story is very different from the way it was told there. The older sister was killed on the way down and the rope remained affixed to the sky so everyone could use it as a swing until mouse {Rat} gnawed through it and it fell into a rocky heap near Mount Si.]

Responses {eg, wg}

The people listening to a story were supposed to say **haboki** occasionally while they were listening to show their continued attention and to keep from getting hunchbacked.

Little Wild Men [ċyatko] {eg}

These little wild men were like animals. They weren't as big as real men. Ellen's grandmother told a story about them.

She was a little girl at the mouth of the Duwamish. One night they were sleeping in their house. One of the woman who had a small baby woke up when her baby started to cry. She saw some men standing inside the house while the residents were asleep. They had a fire right in the middle of the house and they were sleeping on both sides of the house on wooden platforms along the edges.

The next morning she told about what she saw. They looked around and saw that some of the smoked fish were missing. The grandfather of my grandmother said, "They'll be back. We can catch them when they do because they are not very big men."

The next night, they came back and the men were waiting for them. They came in and started stealing more dried salmon. The men jumped them but they all got away except for one. This one they kept. He used to go hunting and in a short time he would come back with a deer with its neck broken. He didn't have any weapons.

They kept him for a while and then they let him go. After that, they would, every once in a while, find a deer or two with broken necks lying in front of their door in the morning. Then they would hang dried fish outside and the wild man would take it at night. So they never had to worry about their coming back to rob them again.

The Wolf and The Winter Salmon {wg}

There were five Wolves and they were brothers. The Wolves and Salmon were friends, but the Wolves killed a King Salmon near a creek. One of the scales of the Salmon got away from them and fell into a crack of a stone. The Wolves tried to get it out with their tongues, but they couldn't reach it. The oldest Wolf failed. The second one tried it and failed. The third also failed. The fourth and fifth ones also failed. So they quit trying to get the scale and went out hunting.

When they got back, they came to the creek to get a drink. The scale had grown into another King Salmon. He waited for the Wolves at the head of that creek. The Wolves came down to take a drink. The oldest one smelled the Salmon in the creek. He stooped down once and the smell was too strong -- he got up without drinking. He stooped three times to drink and each time the smell was too strong. The fourth time, he took a drink. When he got up from drinking, Mr King Salmon hit him through the heart with an arrow and killed him.

His second brother came down to drink. He also smelled the Salmon. He got scared during each of the three times he stooped to drink. He always got scared. The fourth time he drank. When he got up, he was also shot through the heart and died.

The third brother did the same. He stooped three times and didn't drink. The fourth time, he drank and, when he got up, he was shot and killed.

The fourth Wolf did the same. He did the same thing, and was finally killed when he drank the fourth time.

The fifth one, the youngest, knew his brothers were all killed but he had to have a drink. He also stooped three times to drink. He would sip a little water and bound back to try to keep from being killed. But he finally drank and then he was also killed like the others. The End

Star Husband {ja}

Two girls were sleeping. They were lying down to sleep. They were looking up at the sky. One said, "I wish that bright star belonged to my sister, and that that red one would be mine." The other sister said, "What else are you going to say? You say everything [and are likely to get us into trouble with your talk.]"

They woke up and didn't know where they were. One of the girls found out that the bright star was an old, old man with matter all over his eyes. The red star they found out was a nice looking young man.

It came to pass that the one talking all the time had a baby. Each day they went and dug fern roots. These men, the Stars, told them "Don't follow any of the roots that go deep into the soil," but the girls asked themselves, "Why did they tell us that about not following a root that goes deep?" So they followed one that went way down. Air came up out of the hole they dug. "Oh, so that's why they didn't want us to follow that root down. We're up in the sky, that's where we are."

So they decided to make a ladder out of cedar limbs, a rope. The Star men asked them, "Why is it you don't get anymore fern roots and you are gone all day?" They said, "Oh, the baby cries too much. We're taking care of the baby all of the time we are out. We can't dig fern roots any more. The baby cries all of the time." This was not so, they were just busy making the rope ladder. When they thought it was long enough to make it to the ground, they opened the hole and put the ladder down. They used a digging stick to put across the opening and hold the ladder up.

They went down, the three of them, on the rope ladder. They got home and the people gathered around. They used the ladder now as a swing. The people would swing back and forth on the rope. They gave the baby to their old, blind grandfather to take care of. They were having a lot of fun swinging on the ladder. Then they noticed that the baby was not crying any more. They asked, "What's the matter that the baby isn't crying any more?" They went to the old man and he was singing "My grandchild is a piece of wood now." Sure enough, it was true. They went to see what the grandfather was singing about and the real baby was gone now. The father of the child had come down and taken the child with him up to the sky again.

In the meantime, Rat chewed the ladder off of the stick. It came down, all piled up in one place. The people wanted to find out where that child went but now nobody could go up to the sky. Bluejay was the only one that could fly up there. But he couldn't get through the hole, he got caught in the opening. That is why the head of bluejay is flat now.

There is a rock over in Snoqualmie that looks just like the ladder piled up. That is where the ladder came down [and it shows the eternal truth of this story.]

Mink and Devilfish (Octopus) {ja}

The people were all gathered in one place, meeting. There was a Devilfish (Octopus) lying by the door. Mink said, "What is this thing here lying in the way? I'll take you and throw you out in the bay." Devilfish said, "Who's stopping you from throwing me out in the bay? Go ahead !" "Do you think I can't do it?," said Mink, and he took the Devilfish by the head and dragged him into the water.

The Devilfish said, "Take me out in the deep. Don't throw me here close to the beach. Take me way out." When they were deep enough, he grabbed hold of Mr. Mink, who said, "I was just playing with you. I don't mean anything, I don't mean anything." The Devilfish took him down and didn't let him go until he was nearly drowned.

Mink

A child was born and the people gathered around to see who was the father of it. The baby looked at the people and said, "No, my dad isn't here."

Mink told his grandmother, "I'm going over there where the people are gathered. That baby might say. "That's my dad now." His grandmother told him, "You don't want to go there. What do you want to go for?" He went anyhow for Mink was full of tricks.

He got to where the people were gathered and stood outside on one side of the door. He crossed over to the other side of the door. The baby said, "There's dad!" The people looked around to see who the person was that the baby called dad.

He crossed by the door again. This time he walked slowly. So, again, the baby called, "That's Dad! Daddy, Daddy, Daddy, Daddy!" So he took his baby and the woman home with him.

One day they went out riding in a canoe, all three of them. While they were out, the woman saw sea eggs (sea urchins) down on the bottom. He told his wife, "I'll go down and get you some." He went down, gathered some up for his wife, and took them up. She opened them and started to eat them. Each time he went down, he'd be gone longer. The last time, he was gone a very long time. His wife looked down and there he was busy eating all of the eggs by himself down there.

She got mad and threw the baby overboard. Then she went home. When Mink came up, his wife was gone and his baby was swimming around on the water. He told his son, "You swim to those roots over there, to that stump on the beach." That is the reason we still find minks around those stumps on the beaches [and the underside of sea urchins look as they do].

Wolf and Elk {ja}

There are two rocks on Bolen's Point that used to be people, Wolf and Elk. Wolf was chasing Elk and they landed on that point. This was during the universal change and flood. Now there are two rocks where they were at that moment. One is a Wolf and one an Elk. They were turned to stone.

Steelhead and Rainbow Trout {ja}

Steelhead and Rainbow were coming down the river. A big Jack Salmon was going upstream. They met. The big Salmon said, "How is the river? How deep is the river?" There was no answer. Salmon repeated his question. Then Steelhead said, "Oh, it's high enough now for a big-headed fish to go up." In reply to this insult, the Salmon went to the Steelhead and the Rainbow and took away all of their paddles. He gave them yew wood ones instead. That is why the bones of steelhead and rainbow trout are now so hard. [The implication is that these modern fish began as humanoids in canoes. At the change, everything (body, canoe, and paddles) became a distinct species and King Salmon benefited from the fat and bones (as paddles) he took from Steelhead and Rainbow Trout.]

Raccoon {ja}

The Coon and his family lived out in the woods. The old man stayed home all of the time. The children always went down on the beach, singing like the Chipmunk about what they were going to get. Instead, a thing would catch them and eat their hearts. This kept on until a girl had a baby coming and the father begged her "Don't go down on the beach! Your brothers and sisters went down and never came back."

She went down anyway. They liked little crabs and she went for some. That thing killed her. The old man went down and said, "I told that girl not to go down but she must have gone anyway for she has disappeared." He found his girl on the beach and he took out of her body the baby that was coming. He took it home and raised it.

When the baby was grown up, he was running around the cedar trees. He said, "Grandpa, you had better make me a bow and arrows because that one with big ears and big eyes (Rabbit) is close by. Better make me a bow and arrows so I can shoot that." The little Raccoon was getting bigger. His grandfather said, "Don't go down to the beach. Your people all died, were killed, when they went down there. Don't go! Don't go!"

The boy got curious. "Why doesn't Grandpa want me to go down on the beach?" He got curious, so he went down and his old grandpa didn't know anything about it. He sang the song his family always used when they were going out for a particular food. Here came that thing! Little coon took his bow and arrows and shot him. He killed the monster.

When the old man missed his grandson, he said, "Where did that boy go. I told him not to go down to the beach, but he must have gone down there." On his way to the beach, he met his grandson returning. The boy had gathered a lot of little crabs and packed them up to his grandfather. He laid them down in front of the old man, who said, "I told you not to go down there." The boy said, "I know you told me not to go down there, but I killed him. He is dead now."

They slept well that night. They had a good feed of crabs and went to sleep. The next morning, the boy went out to the cedar trees he played around. There were lots of people there, relatives of the thing he had killed down on the beach. He was ready and took a something he had made of wood [a staff ?]. When he swung it at them, all his enemies on one side died. Then he did the same on the other side. The same thing happened.

He went back home and told his grandfather. "Come out now and take all of the blankets they left. I've killed them now." The old fellow went out and took all the blankets. (A long time ago, the old Indians had a blanket over them instead of a coat.)

The old man, when the grandson got to be a man, went away with him to find a wife for him. People started to sing, "Old man Raccoon must be traveling now. The land is foggy now. It's a nice quiet day but its foggy." [The implication is the Raccoon had such great power he could affect the weather, taking it out of the ordinary to let everyone know he was on the move.]

Five Brothers {ja}

There were five brothers. One went out some place and never came back. He got to a cedar tree at night and had to camp there. Something hollered then, "Are you awake?" He said, "Yes, I'm awake." The voice kept this up until there was no answer and the voice knew he was asleep now. It came down and took out his heart, ate it, and threw the body away.

The next brother came. It kept up like that, for all five of the brothers. He'd ask them the same question every night when they camped by that tree.

When the fifth and youngest came, he said, "What kind of thing is killing my brothers?" He took his bow and arrows, following the way they went. He came to the same tree and laid down at the foot of it. The thing up in it asked, "Are you awake yet?" He said, "Yes, I'm awake yet." He made a dummy to look like himself lying down there and he got to one side. The thing asked, "Are you asleep now?" But he did not answer. So the thing came down to take out his heart. The boy shot it with an arrow and killed it.

Then he opened it up and took out the fourth brother's heart and put it back into his body. Then he jumped over his brother back and forth until his brother came back to life and got up. He did the same for the third brother, and for the second one. Finally he got to the oldest brother, but he could only briefly hold up his head before it fell back again. The youngest kept stepping back and forth, but he could never get the oldest one back. He was too far gone. He said, "The oldest brother of the people to come will always die."

The Girl With Long Sharp Fingernails {ja}

A girl had long, sharp fingernails. When she got mad at other children, she hooked them in the stomach and killed them. So they decided to take her away.

The Crows were going to take her away in a canoe. They put her on board it. They were paddling with the edge instead of the flat of the paddles so the canoe wasn't going very fast. Someone turned a paddle sideways and then the canoe started to go quickly. All of them started to paddle that way and they went fast now. When they got way out, the Crows flew away and left her alone in the canoe. She drifted and landed where a young man and his grandmother were. He was away. The Grandma took the girl ashore and hid her.

When the young man (his wife was made of wood) came back and started to fight with his wife, the grandmother motioned for the girl not to laugh. She had warned her before, "Don't laugh. It's comical what you are going to see."

The next day, the grandmother and girl went out digging roots. The young man came down after fighting with his wooden wife, and said, "Grandmother, there's someone here." She asked him, "What makes you think so?" He said, "Because the roots you're getting now are good ones. You couldn't get those deep ones by yourself before. There has to be someone here with you now." She said, "No, there's no one here. You know I'm here alone all the time." They left it at that.

So, one day, he went up to hunt in the woods. He came back in the evening and started to fight with his wooden wife. They fought and talked. The young girl couldn't stand it anymore and she started to laugh. The boy looked over and saw the girl. He left the house to throw his wooden wife in the water and came back to take this girl for his real wife. [Cowichan on Vancouver Island regard this as an origin epic.]

Chipmunk and the Basket Ogress {ja}

A Chipmunk went out to pick berries and his grandmother warned him, "When you go berry picking, don't sing." But when he got to the blackberries, he started to sing anyway, "The ripe ones I'm going to eat here and the unripe ones I'm going to save for my grandmother."

The Basket Ogress [skale] was a wild woman who used to chase children. She heard Chipmunk and chased him. (If you go where there are black berries, you'll still hear the chipmunks singing this song, going chunk, chunk, and so on.) She was going to eat the boy. Before he knew anyone was around, she grabbed and got him at the back of the head. But he ran up a tree and slipped out of her hands. She scratched him from head to tail and that is why chipmunks now have those stripes along the back.

She was at the foot of the tree watching for him when he came down. So, he took a cone from the tree and threw it a ways from the tree. She went after this and Chipmunk got away. When she realized she had gone the wrong way, she looked for traces and saw him going. She chased him.

He got home to his grandmother all tired out. He pleaded, "You hide me. Hide me! She is right behind me!" Grandmother covered him with a clam shell. She scolded him, "I told you not to sing when you go berry picking. Now she's come after you."

When she came, she too was tired and said, "I can smell that boy. He's here! He's here!" But the grandmother said, "He's not here." So the Ogress went away.

Little Wild Men {ja}

The little wild men came from the Fraser River. They were people but wild ones. When the berries are ripe, they come down this way. They were men, but they were wild. There are two tribes of them. The stətał and the ċyətko. They were the same kind of people, but different tribes. They were wild men. They stayed in the woods all of the time. Both kinds of these stole food from Indians. John Adams knows a story about the stətał stealing a girl from the Snohomish. But they were usually good to people and didn't harm them.

Suquamish

There was a girl picking cranberries in a marsh. She heard the ċyatko talking. They didn't talk like other Indians. They were wild. She saw two men coming after her. (A long time ago, the girls were trained, like the boys, to go out, swim and run, to make them strong.) They caught up to her. One of them took the girl. The other said, "No, you can't have her." And they started fighting over her. The girl got away. They ran after her and got her again. Then they started fighting again. This time they fought for good, to settle it. The second man decided that if he couldn't have her, then he wouldn't let the other one have her. So he kept fighting the other one until the girl got away completely.

In another story, a woman was out in the woods seeking power. She heard ċyatko talking, making noise. She found a hollow cedar. She crawled in backwards and pulled in a block of wood behind her. They were looking for her all over. They had long sticks. They poked into the hollow log, and felt the sticks stop. They said, "No, she's not there. There's a block in there. The pole doesn't go in very far." That's the way she got away.

When she thought they were gone, she came out. She was good and hungry. She had been there for days with nothing to eat. But she found the bones of deer and elk killed by a cougar. So, she split them and ate the marrow. She would take a rock and crack them, then eat the marrow inside. Marrow is called **dadawšəd**. Finally, she got home.

If a person looked at one of these ċyatko, it was like taking a drug. You went to sleep. Sometimes you would know what was going on, but you couldn't do anything. Once, they captured some ċyatko who said, "What we put on our face so we can see in the night, you can't stand. That's what makes you unconscious when you look at us."

A young man was going from the Duwamish to Snoqualmie to see a girl there. Night overtook him half way. He built a big fire. He had his bow and arrows. While at the fire, some ċyatko came. He was lying there. He couldn't move but he knew they were there with him before he passed out. They were laughing at him, tying him up, and playing tricks on him. They took his clothes off. When he came to, there was one going into the brush. The Indian shot him in the back. He went back toward the Duwamish again. On the way, he heard them crying when they found the dead one. They were people, but they were wild.

Another time on the Duwamish River, they weren't getting any salmon at night from the place where they had a dam. What was happening to the salmon, they wondered? So, they wandered along the bank and found human tracks. They followed them. They found him. He was an old man. He lived in a hollow cedar. He was drying salmon there. He was sound asleep just then. He awoke and got scared. He wanted to feed the people who had come there. Instead, they took him down to their homes. They didn't harm him. He would go with them when they were spearing fish at night in the river. He would always take a small salmon and cook it. They kept him a long time until they finally let him go. They gave him back all the possessions he had, but they didn't give him back his fire drill. He would not leave and they wondered why he wouldn't go. Finally, they understood he wanted his fire making equipment. They gave it to him and then he went away. He had to have it to make fire. He was a human being just like anyone, but he was wild.

The uncle of John Adam's father was hunting around Keysport and Poulsbo. He heard these things around so he called his dogs. The dogs wouldn't sleep. He heard them all around his log house. They shoved a stick in from the outside and hit him. Next day he got out of there. On the way, he found where they had their fires and cooked fish.

A white logger was going into the woods one morning while it was still dark. He stumbled over someone lying on the skid road, and the logger fell asleep right there. Another man came along and asked the sleeping logger what the matter with him was. He stood up and told what had happened. After that, he wouldn't go into the woods by himself. It was a ċyatko, but he never knew what it was.

They go around at night better than in the day because of their special paint. Sam Wilson, cousin to John Adams, was on a creek in Port Orchard Bay waiting for bear to come and eat salmon. It was getting dark. He pointed his gun toward a place still lighted to see if he could see things through his sights. He proved that he could. Then he turned them on a dark place. Suddenly, a feeling came over his face. It worked down his body to his knees. He jumped down off the log and almost fell right there. He took off his clothes and went into the creek. He had Bullhead for his power. That's why he went into the bay. At night, when the tide was out, he'd use a torch -- you could hear the dog salmon going up the creek -- and go down to the shore and hook them in with a gaff. He knew those waters.

Another time, he heard a run of fish coming. He was lying by the fire, but he didn't go and get the fish. He let it go. A dog salmon did not go far before someone else hooked it. While he was lying there, somebody started to open the mat door. His mother whispered to him, "Someone is opening that mat to shoot you." He took his rifle and shot right through the mat, but, even so, he missed the wild man. He heard someone trip on a cedar rail in their hurry to get away. The next day, his whole family got out of there. There were too many wild men.

From their tracks it is known they have long feet, longer than those of most people.

An old Suquamish who was a boy in the 1840s was sent one night to another tribe to deliver a message. He went along a little trail with a small mat as a rain hat over his head to keep himself dry. On the way, he stepped on someone lying across the trail. He immediately fell asleep right there. There were other wild men. They played tricks on him and tied him up. It was raining. When he came to, he got up and started to go on his way. He didn't get far before he found his mat hanging beside the trail. He went a little further and found more of his things hanging along the way. This was how they played. They would never harm you unless you did something mean to them. Usually, they were only interested in coming into the smokehouse at night to steal prepared fish.

There aren't any left now. They weren't killed off, it's just that they all became civilized. Some of our own people had them as ancestors. One cousin of John Adams had a sharp face and was a terrible man; that was because he was part wild man.

WAR TALES

The Suquamish did not take heads when they raided. Kitsap didn't believe in hanging the heads of enemies in front of the village or camp. That was too much like showing off. They knew that the northern tribes did it, but the Suquamish thought it too crass and didn't believe in it.

There were special men who did the fighting. The leader was especially selected. He was not usually the same as the chief in peace time. The leader had the right to order his men about, to tell them what to do. {wg} [He was in charge of all their lives.]

When an enemy tribe would attack, the women and children would go back into the woods for safety, away from the beach and camp. {ja}

Suquamish

Kitsap In Battle {ja}

Curly told this story about the Puget Sound tribes attacking northern peoples about 1840 or maybe before. There were several leaders, but Kitsap [q̓c̓ap] was Suquamish chief and war leader both. The tribes involved included those from Oakville [staq̓tabš, "Inland/Upland People") [Chehalis] from the other side of Tacoma, who got in trouble because they didn't know how to handle a canoe in war, the Nisqually [sq̓ʷali] from near Tacoma and the other side of Steilacoom, and the Mud Bay [sq̓ʷaqcət, Squaxin Island] from near Olympia. These three groups planned the raid before coming to Kitsap to ask the Suquamish to go. Kitsap took 10 canoe loads, with 30 to 40 men in each canoe. The Duwamish weren't asked and didn't go. The reason for the raid is not known now, probably someone was killed, as always went on.

They met these enemies on a sandspit. They were Canadians always coming down to fight with the Skagits on Whidbey Island. They wanted to clean up the Skagits, but they met the tribes from the Sound going the other way. The Canadian leader said "If you call off the fight, we'll give you as many women as you want as wives." They started negotiating, but, meanwhile, people from Up Sound started taking stray arrow shots into the air above the Canadians and managed to hit one of them. So, before Kitsap had a chance to say anything, the battle was on. The arrow shooters got what they wanted.

The sandspit was up on the other side of Victoria. Canadians tried to tip over the American canoes. This was a deliberate strategy of theirs. They tried to do this to the canoe with Kitsap, but he took a spear and tipped them over. Then he speared them like fish in the water. The Suquamish knew how to fight from canoes. The warriors at the bow and stern did all of the shooting, while the others paddled and protected the canoe. Kitsap and his brother [talibot] did the shooting from their canoe. The other tribes from Tacoma did not do this. Everyone in a canoe would drop their paddles and shoot. They got the worst of it because the Canadians were able to come along side and shove them over. The Suquamish were always able to out maneuver the Canadians.

Talibot fought bravely. A Canadian came at him from one side, but he plucked his bow string and the Canadian ducked down in a canoe. When he came up again, Talibot had an arrow ready and shot him. The Canadian pulled it out, saying he was a great man, but the point was barbed so it stayed in the body when the shaft came out. Pretty soon, the man dropped dead. Later Talibot was shot in the eye. He pulled the arrow out, but the eye came with it. He continued fighting with one eye until Kitsap said he was asking to be killed. Then Talibot got down into the bottom of the canoe and stayed there.

Sam Wilson heard that the Canadians had Kitsap surrounded with their canoes, yet he came out without a scratch. He had great power from Eagle. After the battle, all of the arrows shot at him shook out of his hair. He had several sets of powers and they all helped him.

A man from Mud Bay had great power, but he had been forewarned that he would be great but his bones would be way off. He fought well at the battle, but his canoe capsized. He came out of the water with his bow at the ready, but he was killed. That was what was meant by the phrase his bones would be far off.

After everyone else in the canoe was dead, another man from Mud Bay spread out his arms and said "kahk" and flew like a bird to another canoe. His power was Raven, probably.

One Suquamish had a coonskin sack full of arrows but he never used them. When they asked him for arrows, he said, "No, you might waste them." When the battle was over, he had the only arrows left. The warriors only had spears, but they were too far apart. Kitsap and the leader of the Canadians were going to fight it out {one on one} and were coming toward each

Suquamish

other. Someone in the canoe with Kitsap handed him a long spear on the sly. The Canadian saw it and backed away. Kitsap was the stronger and so never lost a man.

Four men from Up Sound were left on shore after the battle. Their canoe was tipped over by the Canadians but they had Fish power and swam under water safely to shore, walking to Victoria. When Canadian Indians came along, they hid in trees with tops flat due to the heavy winds. They found some drift logs and made a raft tied together with twisted cedar branches rope. They drifted around until they asked each other to identify their power, but the first three were of no help. The fourth only said, "I've got nothing, but watch those clouds moving." As soon as he finished speaking, the wind came up and blew them to the American side around Port Angeles.

While they were in Canadian waters, they stayed flat and tried to look like some floating logs. That last foggy morning, the Americans looked out and said to one another, "Those look like logs, leave them alone." The four men started jumping around on the raft and the Americans said, "Those are seals, let them alone." Finally, they stuck the sticks they were using for paddles into knot holes and the people on shore said, "That didn't have limbs a while ago. Now it has." So they went out, captured them, and brought them to shore. They locked them up in a house.

People decided to go across the straits because they thought there was trouble on the other side. The village was mostly deserted. A woman visiting from somewhere else started to talk to the prisoners. She spoke their language and maybe was a relative. That night she went around to all the houses and stole one bow and one arrow from each. She gave them to the prisoners and said, "Here's your equipment." She gave them a clam stick because it was sharp on one end. She gave them a big clam shell and said, "Now you crawl under the bench beds when you think all are asleep and dig out a hole with the clam shell." They did this and when the hole was big enough, they crawled out and ran. They came along the shores of Hood Canal to their homes.

One man was crying because his son was lost at the battle. He kept saying, "I thought my son was well brought up and trained. Sometimes I see his face." One day they were out in the sun talking and saw someone coming up the beach over a log. It was the missing boy, so they all finally got home safely.

Because of this, people felt confident and a boy from Duwamish wandered to Victoria. He wanted to get home and asked some Canadian Indians to take him back when they left to pick hops in the Sound. They went toward Port Townsend and half way across the straits, they threw the boy over. That was how they got their revenge, but it was a long time later in the 1870s.

Sometime around 1850 there was a big potlatch at Mud Bay and John's father went. Canadian Indians came to it and asked to see the man who flew during the battle. They took the visitors to him. He was old then. They agreed they had seen him fly like a bird, but the Canadians didn't show off any of their stunts.

Kitsap was a good general. He had men posted at each point to warn if anyone came. No one could get in if they were dangerous. It was after Kitsap was gone that Klallams made a raid on a Suquamish group, but didn't do much damage. The chief at that time was named čalqəb. The Suquamish got together a party to revenge the raid but the chief found out and asked where they were going. They wanted to get even with the Klallams, but the chief would not let them. He wasn't afraid of the Klallam, he just didn't want any more trouble. They obeyed the chief; he was good and didn't want trouble.

Suquamish

Klallam Attack {ja}

John heard of the raid from his parents, but it happened in the days of his grandparents. Several times, Klallams raided a small group in the bay where Keyport is now. They killed the people by catching them asleep. The chief was ćalqəb, the one after Kitsap and before Seattle. He made the Suquamish raiders stay home to prevent even more trouble.

Skykomish Raids {ja}

The Skykomish [sqayhabš] were mean. They wanted to fight all of the time, and thought they were better than everyone else. Now there are hardly any left. John did not know why they wanted to fight so much.

The Suquamish were camping at Point No Point, probably in the 1850s or 60s. They were there all of the time because it was a good fishing place. The Skykomish had muskets then and attacked the Suquamish. They fought on the beach in the day time. A man named qəlaywap was sent to fight them, but he was a lesser warrior. The main ones stayed in camp eating dried clams because they didn't consider the enemy very strong.

The warrior took some men and hid behind rocks on the beach to shoot at the enemy. A Suquamish was hit in the knee by a glancing bullet, but he was the only one hurt. They drove back the Skykomish, who gave up and left in their canoes. John didn't know if any enemy were killed or hurt.

The Skykomish came to Point No Point another time, saying they were going to take [steal] some canoes. "Instead of making them, we're going to get them from the Suquamish. They came to the beach and were sizing up the canoes. An old man had a pole stuck in the beach and was sitting in his canoe. Meanwhile, the enemy were shaking canoes and deciding which were the good ones. When they shook the canoe of the old man and said it was a good one, he replied "Will you please get off." He repeated it louder a few more times and said, "Did you hear me." Then the old man took his pole and hit them over the head. The Skykomish couldn't do anything because they were on the beach and were an easy musket shot from the Suquamish camp on the bluff. That ended it and the enemies left.

Later still, the Skykomish came to present Suquamish and took women to make them slaves. When the white man came and said there would be no more slavery, they were released. This was the last time the enemy came, probably in the 1860s.

Leschi {ja}

The whites took the pastures for their stock. Leschi [ləšxiʔ, ləšxi(x̣)] started fighting over this. One Indian was a traitor to the white side and scouted for them. He was William Rogers. The soldiers were marching to the sound of fife and drum. Then Leschi knew where they were and told his men to shoot first "the one who hollers" (gives the commands). The rest would be easy because soldiers didn't know what to do with their leader gone.

The Indians cut a tree across the foot path along the White River. They hid in the willow trees on one side of the river. They caught the soldiers. One Indian stuck his hat over a log on a stick. When a soldier got up to shoot at the hat, the Indian killed him. Only two Indians were shooting, the others were loading for them. Some whites tried to get across on a foot log, but they were shot. One did get across, but they shot him on the other side. One Indian left his gun and the soldiers killed him when he went back for it. The whites were defeated and afterwards the place was called Slaughter. Now it is called Auburn.

Suquamish

The whites got Leschi's father. Leschi said, "Let the old man go. I'll die in his place." So Leschi came in and the whites took a rope and hanged him. He was strung up for a long time before he was taken down and pronounced dead. The rope was cut off his neck. As he lay on the ground, he started to come to life again. The Duwamish said, "If he comes to life again, he'll only kill us [get us killed]." So they killed him again there. They never got what they were fighting for and the whites still took possession anyhow.

Moses was a Yakama and a bad man. [Moses was a Columbia Salishan who died on the Colville reservation.] He came over the mountains to help his uncle Leschi but he didn't stay long. He told his uncle that the ground was too soft and he might be shot. He went home. He had seen the bounty of the country and he came back with Yakamas to attack the Nisqually and kill their cattle. If people tried to shoot Moses with a bullet, it couldn't hit him. He had a belt around his waist, and the bullets went into his belt instead of hitting him when he was shot at.

Finally, a Nisqually took a piece of iron, heated it in a fire, and hammered it like a knife that would fit into the barrel of his gun. He waited until Moses was coming at him on a horse and he shot Moses. The iron went right through his body, but it didn't kill him. He only fell off the horse. Moses had black powder pistols tied all over his body. When the Yakama saw him fall, they left all the cattle to make their get away. Moses kept fighting, using his pistols until he was out of ammunition. Then the Nisqually used spears to kill him dead. They cut him open to see what made him so mean. Inside of him they found a little man all covered with hair. That was what made him so mean.

APPENDIX

To compare with John Adam's account of Kitsap's fight, apparently directed against the Cowichan of Vancouver Island during the 1830s, here is a version Wilson George gave to Leon Metcalf, a Seattle musician who visited among the natives of Puget Sound in the early 1950s with a bulky tape recorder, preserving texts, messages, and conversations to be played back to other native speakers. He donated these to the Burke Museum at the University of Washington. Other versions of this or similar battles appear in Curtis (1913: 14) and Elmendorf (1993: 132, 136, 145).

By the best of circumstances, Violet Anderson Hilbert [taqʷšəblu] took on the job of transcribing and translating these tapes, many of which involved her relatives. As a native speaker of Skagit and a university instructor, Mrs. Hilbert was especially gifted for this task. She is most comfortable with northern Lushootseed (Puget Salish), but the southern dialect differs only in minor features of vocabulary, agreement, and accent. These dialects are mutually intelligible, as shown by her translation of the southern Lushootseed saga of Fly (Hilbert 1985: 33-41).

Dr Vi Hilbert's work on the text of the Kitsap raid, as told at the Tulalip Reservation on 20 February 1952, has been rephrased by Jay Miller, with his explanations marked by brackets [].

The place name ʔəhiw̓ is prominent in this text. It has been translated as Portage because it marked the one between Puget Sound and the tip of Hood Canal. As such it was an important passage among the tribes allied with Kitsap.

Suquamish

A Kitsap Raid {wg}

My elders were visited by people from Portage. They were not just from one tribe. There were many different people who arrived and said to these old timers, "Let us go now to war on those people from the West [over there?]." [My elders responded,] "Let us all gather ourselves together so we can join on a raid, if that is what is on your mind, noble sir [siʔab].

Kitsap said, "Yes, I understand you. I hear what you folks are saying about raiding those well-known people. The ones who think that they should be important everywhere, although that is not so. We also have something that we want for ourselves. If any one of you thinks that they want to fight us about this, then we will fight them. [He wanted to be recognized as a leader on this expedition.] If this raid is on your minds, then I will go. I shall go along with you and I shall fight just as your other leaders fight while I am with you. I shall go. I shall go and I shall fight."

[All was settled and the Suquamish joined.] The people went by canoe. They arrived at the place where Klallams lived and crossed over the water [Strait of Juan de Fuca] from there [to the southern tip of Vancouver Island.]

They visited the people at scukʷs [Sooke ?] and invited them to join. They were addressed, "It is best for you to accompany us, we go to the mean people across the water, way over there [up island]. This was at what they now call Vancouver Island at the present time and that was the name of the whole area. That was Vancouver Island.

[As an aside, Wilson said. "Its native name is different, but I can't recall its real name just now. My memory is getting short. It's particularly short now. I do not remember things very well. And I do not remember the native names for a lot of places and things. Yet they were raiding them [on the island]. They were the ones that many were going to [in order to fight.]

Then they found out that they did not have to go all the way to the land of the enemy to accomplish the raid. The mean ones from across the water were on the way to raid the Klallams.

Then the two forces met each other. The ones from across the water on Vancouver Island said, "Oh, we are not going to fight. We are too far away from our own land and you are far from yours. It is best not to fight. It is best that you just... If you folks give a man, one of your young ones, to us, that would be acceptable [to form an alliance through marriage]. If you provide a woman instead, it would be up to us to give you a young man."

All of those from Portage said, "No, we don't want anything like that. We are on our way to fight. We intend to fight you folks. Therefore, if you are willing, then we will fight now. It is best we just fight. We shall fight on the salt water. Offshore."

Kitsap said [to his allies], "Oh, the people from around here are skillful on the salt water. We won't be able to beat them if we fight them on the ocean."

[The allies responded,] "However, those of us from Portage have come here to fight and we can not just return home without a battle. That would belittle and disgrace our name [reputation]. That is why I think that we should intend to fight as long as you wish to fight."

So! The people from Vancouver Island had it settled now. They said, "All right. The mind of your leader is good. We are also ready to fight. And when he decides to fight, then we are ready."

So! They fought. The people gathered from Portage were bested because they were unsure of the water and their spears were short.

[In an aside, Wilson comments, "Spear is what the whites call this weapon. Theirs were short and those of the people from across the water were long.]

They were way short, those belonging to the people from Portage and they were capsized by the people from across the water. They were capsized and killed.

Suquamish

Kitsap, however, fought with a bow and arrow. [That was the style of the Suquamish. He fought bravely with arrows.] When he had used up all of his arrows, he just went to where there was a riptide and gathered up the arrows floating there until he had lots of them again. When he got back to the thick of the battle, he put them into his quiver. That was the way Kitsap got ahead of them and they could not beat him.

He would retreat, moving backwards. When they would advance, he would retreat. As he moved back and they moved closer, he would shoot the leader [sternman, steersman] who would tumble out of the canoe. The canoe would lose direction and veer sideways. When it was broadside of him, he shot across the rim at other members of the crew. His arrow would go right through the hull of the other canoe. [This way,] he managed to shoot the paddler sitting in the other seat, who died. Kitsap continued to kill [the enemy]. His people did not die [in the fight]. No!

One of them was shot, however. He was shot right in the eye by the sternman of an enemy canoe. He took the arrow and pulled it out. His eye came out with it. Talibot was his name. Talibot was the name of the man whose eye came out. He only paddled a little way before he collapsed in his canoe. He capsized. Someone nearby pulled him out and loaded him safely [into a canoe]. He had no eye now. He died now. Someone took his place in the canoe as captain [sternman]. Another warrior took the place of Talibot.

Kitsap fought on. He was chased. He would retreat so they thought he was going away. However, he just wanted to be chased [to have an advantage.] As those following came nearer, he would shoot their captain, who would flip out and die. As the canoe meandered, he would continue shooting until all [the crew] was finished off.

When he ran out of arrows, he would go after lots of them floating nearby in eddies and gather them up. By now, he was only using enemy arrows for his killing.

Suddenly, one of the allies made note aloud [of what Kitsap was doing]. "Kitsap is being chased by those from across the water. He does not retreat in order to get away from the raiders. He just wants to be chased so then he can shoot the one in the stern and kill him. When the canoe is broadside, he shoots again until everyone in the canoe is finished off.

Then another canoe chases him because they want to get Kitsap. That is what he wants! That is how he gets at those from across the water. Then he kills them until they are all gone. Until everyone in the enemy canoe quit shooting. After one canoe is finished off, another one arrives. But Kitsap kills all of them. They can not take Kitsap. Still he wants them to chase him. He isn't retreating in order to get away. NO! [He is luring them on.] He wants to be chased by those from across the water.

By the end of the battle, his strategy dawned on one of the enemy, who announced his observation. He said, "Kitsap is not running away from us. NO! He just wants us to chase after him, but I will not. I am finished, my friends. All of you folks stop now. No one chase Kitsap now. No one. He wants to be chased. He wants this [to happen]. That is the way he is killing your friends. You folks stop now. You folks stop right now. No one can kill him. The spirit power of Kitsap is mighty. It is special.

You folks see how he is shot [by our warriors] but he just deflects these arrows. They do not go into his body. They only go into his hair where they are available for him to use. He takes those which have been shot at him and he shoots them back, killing those who shot the arrows at him [intentionally]. Do not shoot at his head. You are giving him arrows. You folks stop now. My people, you must stop now. Stop this instant! "We have been beaten by Kitsap.

Stop now. I am finished. You folks stop now, members of my tribe. I urge all of you, my people, to stop now. Then Kitsap will also stop and go home."

[And so it must have happened since Wilson George next said, "This is the end of my story."]

BIBLIOGRAPHY

Amoss, Pamela
  1975 Catalogue of the Marian Smith Collection of Fieldnotes, Manuscripts, and Photographs in the Library of the Royal Anthropological Institute of Great Britain and Ireland.

Blalock, Susan
  1979 List of Suquamish Settlements. Suquamish Tribal Library And Archives.

Curtis, Edward
  1913 The North American Indian, being a series of volumes picturing and describing the Indians of the United States, the Dominion of Canada, and Alaska. Written, Illustrated, and Published By Edward S. Curtis. Frederick Webb Hodge, ed. Volume 9 of 20.

Elmendorf, William
  1982 Deposition of February 25 and 26. Davis, California. Civil # 9213 - Phase I.
  1993 Twana Narratives. Native Historical Accounts of a Coast Salish Culture. Seattle: University of Washington Press.

Harrington, John P.
  1910 Lummi/Duwamish. Microfilm of Fieldnotes. (Cited by frame in the text).
    1942 Chemakum /Clallam /Makah /Quileute fieldnotes.

Indian Claims Commission
  1952 Suquamish Tribe of Indians vs. The United States of America. Docket 132.

Lane, Barbara
  c1974 Anthropological Report on the Identity, Treaty Status, and Fisheries of the Skokomish Tribe of Indians. 86pp.
  1974 Identity, Treaty Status and Fisheries of the Suquamish Tribe of the Port Madison Reservation. 52pp.

Maclachlan, Morag
  1998 The Fort Langley Journals, 1827-30. Vancouver: University of British Columbia Press.

Miller, Jay
  1988 Shamanic Odyssey: The Lushootseed Salish Journey to the Land of the Dead. Menlo Park: Ballena Press.
  1999 Lushootseed Culture and the Shamanic Odyssey: An Anchored Radiance. Lincoln: University of Nebraska Press.

Riddell, E. E.
  1932 History of Suquamish. Kitsap County Herald. Poulsbo, Washington. Friday, October 14.

Ruby, Robert, and John A Brown
  1996 John Slocum and the Indian Shaker Church. Norman: Unviersity of Oklahoma Press.

Snyder, Warren
  1968 Southern Puget Sound Salish: Phonology and Morphology. Sacramento Anthropological Society, Paper 8. 83pp.

1968   Southern Puget Sound Salish: Texts, Place Names, and Dictionary. <u>Sacramento Anthropological Society, Paper</u> 9. 199pp.

Walls, Robert
1987   <u>Bibliography Of Washington State Folklore And Folklife</u>. Seattle: University of Washington Press. 301pp.

Waterman, T.T.
1922 "The Geographical Names Used by the Indians of the Pacific Coast." <u>The Geographical Review</u> 12 (2): 175-194.

Ethnozoology of the Snoqualmie
Second Edition, revised
Harriet Turner, edited by Jay Miller

Contents

237	Preface
238	Phonetic Symbols
239	Introduction
241	Indian Country: The River and Its People
246	Annotated List of Animals

Invertebrates Arthropoda Crustacea [Crayfish Barnacle Crab Centipede] Insecta [Grasshopper Earwig Termite Louse Leaf Hopper Stinkbug Water strider Dragonfly Lacewing Caddis Fly ~ Periwinkle Butterfly Moth Housefly Horsefly Mosquito Metallic Wood-borer Ant Hornet Western Bumblebee Yellow Jacket] Arachnoidea [Spider] Mollusca [Limpet Lewis Moon Snail Garden Snail Dentalium Bay Mussel Pacific Pink Scallop Olympia Oyster Basket Cockle Bent Nose Clam Native Littleneck Butter Clam Goeduc Horse Clam Razor Clam Pacific Octopus]

250 Fish

Shark Dogfish Shark Skate Humpback salmon Dog salmon King salmon Silver salmon Sockeye salmon Cutthroat trout Steelhead trout Rainbow trout Bull trout Sucker Bullhead Halibut Flounder Sole Rock Cod Black Cod Night Fishing 2

254 Amphibians and Reptiles

Northwestern Salamander Long-toed Salamander Pacific Giant Salamander Rough-skinned Newt Western Red-backed Salamander Enstina Frog, Toad Painted Turtle Northwestern Fence Lizard Western Skink Garter Snake Northern Pacific Rattlesnake

257 Birds

Loons Grebes Cormorants Herons Bitterns Swans, Geese & Ducks Vultures Grouse Coots Shorebirds Pigeons Owls Goatsuckers & Allies Hummingbirds Kingfishers Woodpeckers Flycatchers Swallows Jays Magpies Crows Chickadees Dippers Wrens Robins Thrushes Warblers Conclusions

277 Mammals

Trowbridge Shrew Shrew Mole Townsend's Mole Little Brown Bat Pika Snowshoe Hare Townsend Chipmunk Mountain Beaver Hoary Marmot Douglas's Squirrel Northern Flying Squirrel Beaver Mouse Muskrat Pacific Jumping Mouse Coyote Gray Wolf Domestic Dog Black Bear Grizzly Bear Raccoon Marten Fisher Long-tailed Weasel Mink Striped Skunk River Otter Cougar Bobcat Elk Black-tailed Deer Cascade Mountain Goat

290	Summary
292	Bibliography 297

Snoqualmi

PREFACE

The information upon which this study is based was obtained in Carnation, Washington, during the course of field work from the fall of 1946 to 1948, the funds for which were supplied by the University of Washington Department of Anthropology.[1]

The only available informant with a knowledge of his faunal environment was Chief Jerry Kanim of the Snoqualmie tribe, living in Carnation (Tolt). He was a professional trapper, about 75 years of age. Chief Kanim's [purported] uncle Patkanim represented the Snoqualmie people at Point Elliott during the signing of the Treat in 1855. [Saniwa, chief of the Upper Snoqualmies, boycotted the treaty council, and his people remained in the uplands.]

Chief Kanim's mother and father were both Snoqualmie {??}, and he spoke the language fluently. He has always lived in Snoqualmie territory, and is thus familiar with two wildlife regions, the Cascade mountain area and the Pacific Coast. Visits to the eastern part of Washington state have provided the opportunity to observe the fauna of the Yakima valley.

Additional information was obtained from Betsy Losier, about 70 years of age, who was living at the Muckleshoot reservation near Auburn, Washington. Betsy was the sister of Jack Stillman, who was Arthur Ballard's principal Snoqualmie informant.

Phillip Starr, a man of about 75 years old, lived at Muckleshoot reservation. He was a Muckleshoot married to Emma Charlie, a Snoqualmie. Phillip was most helpful in identification of shells and insects.

From 1973 to 1975 additional information was obtained from Ed Davis, a Snoqualmie – Duwamish Indian, presently enrolled in the Snoqualmie tribe. Mr. Davis is about 88 years of age, and is a member of the Snoqualmie Tribal Council.

Ed Davis was born near Cedar Mountain, several miles east of Renton, Washington. He moved to Lake Sammamish when he was a young boy, and lived at Inglewood, on the east shore of Lake Sammamish. In 1911 he moved to Fall City. Mr Davis was employed as a logger in Grays Harbor and in the Snoqualmie Valley. When he was a young man in his twenties, he learned myths and folk tales from his Snoqualmie mother-in-law, Lucy Johnnie. Mr Davis speaks the southern Puget Sound dialect of [Coast] Salish [Lushootseed].

---

[1] In 2013, HT explained that she and Richard Daugherty received these teaching assistantships paying $100 a month. In addition, she had research funds to pay 50 cents an hour during fieldwork. At the time of this award, she had been out of school for five years, with a two-year old daughter and a marriage that was soon to end. Her original graduate school plans crumbled when her father died suddenly on her 21st birthday. Though intended to be her MA thesis, HT did not write up the material until thirty years had passed. Dr. Erna Gunther, her advisor, was still alive to receive a copy and add comments. HT taught elementary grades at Enumclaw and Elma before retiring to the family home near Green Lake.

For price comparison, in 1954, HT herself worked at a candy store (Boehms) for 90 cents an hour. Since she promised Jerry she would never accept money for this work, she has donated many hours of volunteer labor to the Snoqualmies. Between her research and writeup, the Snoqualmie Tribal Organization (STO) was dropped from federal BIA funding in 1953, and had to petition for federal rerecognition, which was granted in 1999 after a challenge from Tulalip lawyers, as the Snoqualmie Indian Nation (SIN).

Snoqualmi

The author was also privileged to work with Willy Martin, age 93, in August, 1973. Willy lived at Goldbar, Washington on the Skykomish river. Willy was a cousin of Mrs Jerry Kanim.

I wish to express my gratitude to Dr Erna Gunther for encouragement and assistance. I am also indebted to the late Arthur Ballard, Research Associate, University of Washington, who permitted me to use unpublished data. Dr Arthur Svihla loaned me Amphibian and Reptile specimens.

The author gratefully acknowledges the assistance of many friends who have helped in the preparation of this paper.

Mary Ferrell, President of the Snoqualmie Valley Historical Society, has loaned me valuable manuscript material.

Thank you to Delmar Nordquist and John Putnam of the Washington Archaeological Society for technical assistance [though their plans to publish this work fell through].

Thank you, Dr Thom Hess, University of Washington [University of Victoria], and Professor Earl Larrison, University of Idaho, who corrected inaccuracies in the first draft.

I wish to acknowledge the Seattle-based Baruch the Scribe company's help with the typing of the Bird chapter.

To my friends in the Snoqualmie tribe, especially to cəldʔax̌ad I thank you for inspiration and encouragement.

A very special Thank You to Archie Jones who read the final draft.

Finally I wish to thank my Mother, Stella Turner, and brother Charles. This paper would have been impossible without their infinite patience and understanding.   Harriet Turner

Phonetic Symbols

Vowels

a   as in father
e   between a of cake and e of set
I   between ee of feet and I of fit
o   as in pole
u   between oo of boot and u of but
ə   the a of comma, sofa

Consonants

c   ts as in gets
č   ch as in change
ł   between l and the
š   sh as in shell
x   ch of German ich
x̌   ch if German ach is made back in the throat (~ x)
x^w as in English wh with the lips rounded
k^w qu as in quit
q   the sound resembles k, made farther back in the throat
q^w same sound with lips rounded
'   pronounced with more force glottal stop
'   accent mark, written after a stressed syllable

b d g h l m n p s t w y z   as in English

The term Snoqualmie is the English version of sdokʷalbixʷ, the term used by the Snoqualmie Indians to refer to their own people, who lived on the river sdokʷalbixʷ stolaqʷ and its tributaries.

They spoke a dialect of Coast Salish, and were surrounded by other Salish speaking tribes, who shared a similar culture. The Skykomish and Snohomish people bounded them on the north, the Duwamish, on the north and west. Snoqualmie territory extended eastward to the summit of the Cascades.

The term "Salish" refers to both the language and the people (Smith 1949: 4). The Coast Salish are the people of the river and coastal areas of Washington, Oregon, and western BC speaking related languages of the Salish linguistic stock.

The Interior Salish are the people of the Plateau areas of Washington, Oregon, and BC who spoke related languages of the Salish linguistic stock.

Salish refers to an entire group of related languages. This term is used for both the people and their language.

Warren Snyder (1968a: 1) writes:

The southern Puget Sound dialect of Salish was spoken by a number of tribes along the shores of Puget Sound and inland. The language was spoken from just north of Seattle southward to the end of the Sound, and then northward to the end of the Kitsap peninsula of the western side of the Sound. An exception was a group speaking Upper Chehalis at Mud Bay at the southern tip of Puget Sound.

People who spoke the southern Puget Salish dialect included the Duwamish, Snoqualmie, Muckleshoot, Puyallup, Nisqually, and Suquamish.

The recent work of Dr Thomas M Hess suggests that Snohomish and Skagit, north of Seattle, are also closely related to these dialects (Hess 1976). He proposes the term "Puget Salish" [most recently Lushootseed] for all of these dialects.

Snyder's informants were from the Suquamish, Duwamish, and Snoqualmie. They said that all the people in the southern Sound area who spoke this dialect could understand each other, although there are slight linguistic differences between the tribes.

INTRODUCTION

Animals have always played a significant role in the world of man. They have not only furnished materials for our food, clothing, and shelter, but their amusing behavior has also enriched our lives, providing companionship as well as entertainment.

In western culture, the relationship of man and animals may often reflect our own ambivalent feelings – sentimental, reverent, or even brutal. Dembeck (1965: 30) has indicated that man's friendly alliance with the ancestor of the dog began in southern France within the last 12,000 years. In Ancient Egypt, the cat was a sacred animal worshipped as a symbol of the animal god Bastet (Mery 1968: 29).

Man's cruelty toward living creatures has been written in the history of the fur trade, beginning in the Old World in 800 AD, when wholesale slaughter of fur bearing animals including sable, ermine, and beaver, creating wealth for the fur merchants of northern Europe and Asia (Dembeck 1965: 123-127).

What is the relationship between animal and man among pre-contact people.

Henderson and Harrington (1914) have indicated that animal life within a particular area is closely related to the culture of its human inhabitants.

In the study of ethnobiology, several problems may be considered:

1. What specific attributes of a particular animal receive special attention within a culture? Which animals are not used?

2. Does abundance determine the use of an animal?

3. How are human emotional needs related to animal behavior?

4. Is the animal kingdom contemplated from the humanistic point of view with a feeling of kinship toward other creatures? Or are animals created to serve man?

What is ethnozoology, and what is its meaning?

The science of ethnozoology is concerned with the study of the cultural significance of animal life within a pre-contact society. The term " cultural significance" refers to the animal's relationship to man; how a specific creature is used.

It is hoped that the material presented in this paper may provide a basis for further study of the rich heritage of animal lore among the Coast Salish Indians.

This report includes the following Invertebrate classes: Crustaceans, Insects, Spiders, and Mollusca. The Vertebrate classes include Fish, Amphibians, Reptiles, Birds, and Mammals.

Those species recognized by my principal informant Chief Jerry Kanim, have been arranged in zoological order according to current check-lists. Nearly all of the Snoqualmie names have been obtained directly from Jerry; fortunately, Ed Davis could recall the native terms for the fish, a few amphibians, the reptiles, several birds, and all the mammals listed in the original manuscript.

In the annotated list of animals, the Snoqualmie name is followed by a description of the animal's behavior, as observed by the informants. This material is arranged according to use as food, clothing, materials, charms, or pets. The creature's role in folklore and religious life is summarized at the end of each section. In many instances, the full cultural significance of an animal cannot be determined, as the data are either too fragmentary, or not available.

Preserved specimens, skins, and colored plates were used in identification of the animals, amphibians, birds, and fish could have been more accurately identified if Jerry or Ed had observed them alive in the natural environment. Drainage of swamps will disrupt the nesting sites of waterfowl. Or a sand and gravel company will destroy a good fish run, according to Ed Davis.

It must be emphasized that there has been no active participation in the native culture for at least 75 years. Furthermore, cultural change has affected aboriginal vocabulary and animal habitats.

Nature lore is particularly vulnerable when traditional hunting and fishing grounds are lost.

INDIEN COUNTRY
The River and Its People

Aboriginal explorers out of Asia discovered the Pacific Northwest, a naturalist's paradise supporting an amazing variety of animal life. This vast wilderness included present-day western Washington – a land of striking contrasts; towing ice-covered peaks, colorful alpine meadows and lakes, and a unique river landscape bordered by deep forests, swamps, and grassy prairies.

James Cooper (1859, XII: 38) writes

To a traveler approaching the coast from the sea, the whole country appears mountainous and densely clothed with dark green forests from the water level to the limits of perpetual snow. On nearing land this noble scenery is found to be accompanied by a proportionately gigantic vegetation, and, indeed, everything seems planned on a gigantic scale of twice the dimensions to which we have been accustomed.

According to James Tilton (F 275: 402), Surveyor-General of Washington territory:

The general character of the country is unbroken forests of the greatest magnitude of vegetation. Firs, admirably adapted for masts and spars; cedars frequently ten feet in diameter, and two hundred feet high, and an undergrowth of shrubs bearing edible and not unfrequently delicious berries, which constitute a considerable part of the food of the aborigines. The ferns, lacamas, and other plants produce edible roots, and the numerous rivers, taking their rise upon the western slope of the Cascades and flowing westward to Puget Sound, abound in excellent salmon.

The Snoqualmie river, draining 475 square miles, is located mostly in King County, and descends in a northwest direction, where it connects with the Skykomish river near Monroe in Snohomish County. Here the two rivers join to form the Snohomish, which eventually finds its way to the saltwater, north of Everett.

The North, Middle, and South forks of the Snoqualmie river rise from mountain streams in the snow meadows of the Cascade mountains. These three tributaries of the Snoqualmie river join the main channel several miles north of North Bend.

Howard Coombs writes:

The Snoqualmie river formerly drained the area west of Mount Si and north of the present Falls. As the continental glacier extended into the North Bend area and left a thick deposit of glacial drift, the Snoqualmie river was deflected southward along the line of the present Milwaukee railroad.

When the ice melted, the river tried to resume its former course, but instead flowed on the new glacial silt and gravel. The river selected the lowest part of the drift and soon cut into the old rock below.

At the site of Snoqualmie Falls, the river encountered a thick resistant layer of lava (andesite), and now the river is "hung up" at the falls. It will be a long time before the Snoqualmie can carve out its channel through the lava.[2]

The Snoqualmie falls are located two miles north of the town of Snoqualmie. Today the cataract plunges 268 feet into a pool 65 feet deep.

In 1850, Samuel Hancock (1927: 120) explored the Snoqualmie valley. Hancock writes

The Snoqualmie river above the Falls was as wide and as deep as below the falls, with occasional snags.

A canoe could be hauled up a steep and rugged trail to the river above the falls, a three mile trip which took several hours.

John Muir (1918: 256-60) has described the beautiful scenery near the Falls.

From the hotel at the ranch village the road to the Falls leads down the right bank of the river through the magnificent maple woods. I have mentioned elsewhere a fine view of the Falls may be had on that side both from above and below. It is situated on the main river, where it plunges over a sheer precipice, about two hundred and forty feet high, in leaving the level meadows of the ancient lake basin.

In a general way it resembles the well known Nevada Falls in Yosemite, having the same twisted appearance at the top and the free plunge in numberless comet-shaped masses into a deep pool seventy-five or eighty yards in diameter.

The pool is of considerable depth as is shown by the radiating well-beaten foam and mist which is of a beautiful rose color at times, of exquisite fineness of tone, and by the heavy waves that lash the rocks in front of it. Though to a Californian, the height of this fall would not seem great, the volume of water is heavy, and all the surroundings are delightful.

The upper fall is about seventy-five feet high with bouncing rapids at head and foot set in a romantic dell thatched with dripping mosses, ferns, and embowered in dense evergreens and blooming bushes, the distance to it from the upper end of the meadows being about eight miles. The road leads through majestic woods with ferns ten feet high beneath some of the thickets and across a gravelly plain deforested by fire many years ago.

The origin of the Snoqualmie Falls is explained in the Star Husband story. Two sisters Yeselbc and Tapaltx^w married stars, and returned to earth on a ladder made of twisted cedar twigs.

According to Henry Sicade (Haeberlin 1924: 375-376),

The years passed and the ladder finally fell down from the sky, and was turned into Snoqualmie Falls.

---

[2] Written to Mrs. Marge Quall by Howard Coombs (Professor Emeritus, formerly Chairman, Departmetn of Geological Sciences, University of Washington), this letter is quoted by permission of Mary Ferrell (Director, Snoqualmie Valley Historical Society, North Bend, Washington).

Snoqualmi

Near Mount Si in the middle of the Snoqualmie valley, there is a large rock about forty feet high. This rock, called *idoad*, was also formed when the cedar twig ladder fell to the ground.

In Skookum George's version of the Star Husband (Haeberlin 1924: 374),

Rat had been swinging, and he gnawed at the swing, and it dropped down into a pile, and formed a large round rock in the Snoqualmie valley.

Mount Si, located several miles east of North Bend, was a spectacular landmark long ago during the mythological era.

The following story was told by Ed Davis:

Mount Si was all people during the time they had that swing. They were sitting there watching this ladder swing. Then it turned into rock. That ladder turned into rock when this Rat got up there and chewed it off, and it come down and hit the soil, and it turned into rock. That's why that little rock is there, sitting on that meadow prairie.

In those days, when the earth was young, trees were scarce; the land at large was open and easy to go over; there was no moon, no sun, and the people lived in a kind of perpetual twilight. They mingled with the animals: birds, beasts, and men having a common tongue" (Henry Sicade in Haeberlin 1924: 375).

Long ago, the Snoqualmie lived in fishing villages along the sdok"albix" stolaq" (Snoqualmie River), and its tributaries. There were at least four permanent villages located near Edmonds, Tolt, Fall City, and two miles below the mouth of Tokul creek. Scattered permanent settlements still existed at the turn of the century on the east shore of Lake Sammamish.

According to Ed Davis,

They (the Snoqualmie) came to Lake Sammamish for a red fish feed. That's how they came to settle there. That was before my time. They stayed there and they all died away, and they had a cemetery there. That was years ago.

In early June, before the berries ripened, the people went to the saltwater to dig clams. Here they dried clams, and fished for halibut, sole, skate, and flounder. The Snoqualmie lived in temporary camps for nearly one month, returning inland to the foothills for berry picking and hunting. Animals taken in summer included chipmunk, mountain beaver, deer, and mountain goat.

Beginning in the 1860s, over fifty acres of hops were grown in the Sqawx̌ (Lake Sammamish) valley.

According to Ed Davis,

We started to pick hops around September tenth. If there was a good crop, the season lasted for six weeks.

Hop fields were also located at the south end of Lake Sammamish, west of the present site of the Issaquah shopping center. John Muir has described a hop ranch on the upper Snoqualmie, where 300 acres of hop vines were planted in the cleared area, bordered by groves of spruce, alder, and wild roses. About one thousand Indians were employed in Meadowbrook on the upper Snoqualmie, formerly known as Ranger's Prairie (Muir 1918: 256-257).

Hop picking attracted Indians from BC to the Squax valley. They ⸋larkia⸋ in their long dugouts from Elliott Bay up the Duwamish and Black Rivers, through Lake Washington and Sammamish slough to Lake Sammamish.

There was a marsh near Duvall where cranberries were picked. Here the people built temporary camps along the river.

My informant, Ed Davis, had seen two types of houses: the temporary cattail mat house gʷataq́altʷ and the long house made of split cedar boards pəgʷədaltʷ (Haeberlin and Gunther 1930: 15-19).

Ed Davis describes the mat house,

I saw a temporary one out of mats on Lake Sammamish. It was put up like a tipi. It was round, made of fir poles, cedar rope. You could have a fire in the middle. A blanket or canvas or some material for a door. Some of 'em winters in it and they said it kept them warm.

The longhouse in Fall City was located about thirty feet south of Ed Davis's present home. According to Mr Davis, this longhouse was about 40 feet wide and 80 feet long.

In Lake Sammamish, there was a longhouse 40 feet wide and about 90 feet long near Bill Bedzeus's home. Bill Bedzeus was an Indian doctor and Longhouse Speaker.

Teachings of Longhouse Speakers are similar to Shaker beliefs, according to Mr Davis:

Anything in that longhouse, it touches lots of that teaching in the Shaker Church, where they taught the youngster never to accept anything that was not good for them. In the longhouse they will tell you not to take anything that don't belong to you.

Cheyenne Joe, he was a Yakima man, he used to bring it out so plain, "Now something is coming now. Don't ever look at you sisters's husband. You're going to break up that family. Don't ever look at your brother's wife. Because you're going to steal that woman in the later future."

But they get along fine. They obey the teachings, and they live according to the teachings.

The Guardian Spirit Concept was most important in the religious life of the Coast Salish Indians. Snoqualmie children were went out at the time of puberty during the winter without any food in order to find a spirit or power (Haeberlin and Gunther 1930: 68). Hopefully, a child would meet an animal or bird spirit which would promise to help the young person in the future, Chief Kanim said that Loon, Fisher, and Mountain Goat were "good spirits". Children were told to avoid Rat and Mouse because these animals steal.

Chief Kanim describes the search for a Power:

Anyone, rich or poor, girl or boy, could have Power. They said, "You must be clean, must not eat, to get Power." As soon as a spirit spoke to you, you will have been asleep. The spirit took you and moved you. I never received a spirit. It was before my time.

Snoqualmi

Those who got good spirits would be help for people in sickness or war. Any sin committed would prevent you from getting a Power. Even an old person might get one if he was clean, fasted, swam until the spirits come to you.

There are two kinds of spirits: sklaletut is the layman's spirit. It brings good luck in hunting, fishing, gathering clams, or basket making. x̌dab is the Indian doctor's spirit, effective in curing illness.

According to Ed Davis,

You got to quit eating. You got to keep clean. You got to bathe, and then you could find that spirit. Then that spirit would talk to you, and you would talk to them. Your mother and father won't let you eat. You're supposed to be clean and starved out, and nothing in your stomach. Then you could meet that spirit. You could take the sklaletut or you could take the x^{w}dab.

That will be in a dream when you meet him. You don't talk to him in person. Where you come to meet him it will be a fog. They call it sg^{w}əšab. Just like a foggy morning or a foggy night. It gets so thick you couldn't cut it with a razor.

That's between a man and his sklaletut and a woman and her sklaletut.

The transformer Dok^{w}ibəɬ created the world, changing all the people of the mythological era into animal and human forms as we see them today.

Ed Davis speaks,

After the Dok^{w}ibəɬ come along, the people all turned into animals and those that didn't turn into animals, they turned into rock.

What did Dok^{w}ibəɬ look like? According to Ed,

Quite a few of them talk about it and ask their mother. Their mother won't tell. She says, "You already learned what you going to learn about Dok^{w}ibəɬ. You keep still now."

They didn't want it spread what took place. It's sad in a way – you stop and study it and look at it. When you are a person, and you know you are a person. Then you come to be an animal.

So they used to stop them youngsters from talking about Dok^{w}ibəɬ.

In the Transformer myth, the Transformer told his relatives,

Everything is done now. I have changed everything. There will be meat, and there will be berries and all kinds of food. You, my relatives, will be the first of the future people. You will look after the people of the future. Your name will continue on into the future. The people of the future will keep the name of sdok^{w}albix^w forever (Jerry Kanim in Snyder 1968a:)

Snoqualmi

ANNOTATED LIST OF ANIMALS
Invertebrates
Arthropoda

Crustacea

Preserved specimens from the Burke Museum have been used for this report.

Crayfish saẏx̌ The crayfish was not used for food.

Barnacle c̓ubc̓ub no specimen was available for the barnacle. The Snohomish ate barnacles, which were gathered only in certain places where the beach was clean (Haeberlin and Gunther 1930: 21).

Crab busqʷ Crabs were speared at night. A fire was made in the canoe. They are also picked up on the beach at low tide. Jerry could not recall how crabs were prepared [a curious omission given that they were usually steamed or boiled].

Centipede <əə>[3] Jerry had seen this creature, but could not remember its name. [For Chinooks, it represents death.]

Insecta

Grasshopper təc̓t [x̌ix̌iƛič titx̌ələʔ] The grasshopper was used for bait. The legs were removed and the body was tied to the line. This insect was not considered an insect pest until the land was cleared [and planted].

Earwig <əə> The earwig was recognized, but its name was forgotten. Jerry didn't believe that they were seen in the "early days."

Termite <əə> This insect was seen, but Jerry could not recall its name.

Louse bəsčab

Leaf Hopper təc̓ Betsy Losier has seen this insect. The same native term was used for both the grasshopper and the leaf hopper.

Stinkbug c̓əkəɬax This term means "doesn't bathe."

Water strider <əə> This insect was recognized but the name could not be recalled.

---

[3] These double schwa between angle brackets <əə> are space holders waiting for idenfication of the Lushootseed name.

Snoqualmi

Dragonfly bibacay The dragonfly is seen near lakes and swamps. Jerry described the dragonfly as follows:

> "They are quick. They will fight back; or perhaps they are playing. They won't hurt you, but maybe they are teasing."

Lacewing titkays

Caddis Fly or Periwinkle qʷayecʼəqs The larva of the Caddis Fly was tied to a line and used as bait for trout and bullheads.

Butterfly Jerry thought that the old people had names for each kind of butterfly, but he could not recall all of them. The cocoon of any species is called pəpʼidays. It is placed near the baby so he will sleep. The caterpillar is called qʷałoxʷa.
        sasacʼəb = any species
        qʼʷeqʷeklab = cabbage butterfly
        yoyobač ~ xəlxəlyaxad = swallowtail butterfly

Moth sasacʼəb any species. Jerry was not aware of the life history of moths and butterflies.

Housefly xayoxwa The egg is called a'os and the maggot šodza.

Horsefly təbtpʼ

Mosquito čicʼqs Betsy noted that the mosquito is injurious because it bites and sucks blood.

Metallic Wood-borer <əə> None of the informants could recall the name of this beetle. Betsy believed that this insect "brings good luck, money, or anything." The Metallic Woodborer was used for a love charm (pləx). Jerry describes pləx as follows.

> It is used to get a woman. I heard such talk, but I do not know it is true or not. It is killed and pinned toward the sun. In several days it gets dry. You take a piece of grass and dry it. Mash deer fat, bug and grass together. I don't known how it is used, but it does work to get a woman to love you. But if the man doesn't see the woman after a certain length of time, she will kill herself, the medicine is so powerful.
> If you believe in it, it will work; but if you don't believe in it, it won't work. A woman can use this dope on a man.

The following beetles were recognized, although the informants could not recall their names: Ladybug, Carrion Woodboring Beetle, and Ground Beetle.

Ant pčəlola Jerry told the following story about the Ant:

> Bear and Ant had an argument about daylight. Bear said, "It will be dark during winter, and light the rest of the year." Ant said, "It will be day and night."

Snoqualmi

Ant took a string and tied it around her waist. As she danced for several days, she tightened the string. That's why she has a small waist. Bear and Ant jumped up and down. Bear was too slow, so he lost the argument.

Bear said, "I'll sleep during winter." Ant said, "I'll stay awake in the daytime." If Bear had won, we would all sleep during winter. That is why Ant's waist is so small.

Hornet x̣aybəthʷsəbd "A black yellow jacket"

Western Bumblebee bawklš Jerry said that when the bumblebee flies into a house, and buzzes near a woman, he is asking them to make baskets quickly because berries will be ripe soon.

Yellow Jacket hʷšəbd = stinger utotid = "shoot you" honey = blas. In July and August, the Yellowjacket is powerful. At this time of the year, the hives were gathered. After the hive and bees were removed from the trees, they were soaked in a basket together with the arrow heads. Betsy said that the Yellowjacket and Hornet's sting were "worst of all."

Arachnoidea

Spider tupəl any large variety [qʷəsɫaʔ]
       totpl any small variety
       ɫatd web
       topl ɫatd spider web

Mollusca

"In spring clams change and get fat. As soon as the Dogwood tree is white, all clams are good eating." – Jerry

Jerry described clam digging : "Before the berries ripened, the whole tribe went to the saltwater in early June to dig clams. They returned when the clams were dried. Jerry emphasized that only dried clams were kept. Saltwater fish taken by the Snoqualmie included halibut, sole, flounder, and skate. Saltwater fish were caught and eaten fresh. The people remained at the Sound for almost a month. Then they returned inland for berry picking.

The Snoqualmie dug clams in three places: on an island on the East side of Holmes Harbor qoqosədo, at Edmonds stobos, and at Three Tree point sk̓əylab." There was a big low tide every two weeks when one could get large horse clams which were dried and hung on cedar bark. The biggest low tide of the year used to be around the last week of July.

Specimens from the Burke Museum have been used for this report. Shells have been listed according to Rice's <u>Marine Shells of the Pacific North West</u> (1972).

Limpet, Chinese hat, Slipper shell <əə> These shells were seen, although the names could not be recalled.

Lewis Moon Snail kəbadi <u>Polinices lewisii</u> According to Jerry "The large ones used to be eaten by the old people." They were baked together with other clams and roasted in the open fire or boiled. The small snails, called kəkabadi were used only for necklaces and earrings. Phillip Starr mentioned that the moon snail ate clams so it was destroyed by the people. He also said that this snail was roasted in an open fire.

Garden Snail əswax̌ʷiuq̓ʷ = snail and shell   giaglad = snail only, body.

Money Tusk, Wampum   solax   <u>Dentalium pretiosum</u>   These shells were strung in pairs with a round bead between and used for trade. One fathom of solax was equal to one basket (Haeberlin and Gunther 1930: 29). Jerry did not know how this shell was used in trade. He had seen the money tusk used for beads, earrings, and bracelets.

Bay Mussel tulq̓ʷ {LD 322}[4] <u>Mytilus edulis</u> Mussels and clams are poisonous in August and September. Two methods of cooking were used. They could be cooked on top of a fire, or baked in rocks, covered with leaves.

Pacific Pink Scallop sx̌ʷayway <u>Chlamys herica</u> Jerry believed that his mollusk lives in deep water because the entire shell is seldom seen.
 The Pecten is not eaten.

Olympia Oyster ƛ́ux̌ʷƛ́ux̌ʷ <u>Osrea lurida</u> Oysters were roasted on the open fire.

Basket Cockle sxapad sx̌əp̓əd <u>Clinocardium</u> sp This mollusk, also known as Heart shell was roasted on top of the fire, boiled, or baked.

Bent Nose Clam xaxəts haʔəc {LD 299} <u>Macoma nasuta</u> This is considered a young horse clam. It was shelled, dried, and placed on sticks set upright against a log [to dry].

Native Littleneck q̓oxʷdi k̓ʷuxʷdiʔ <u>Venerupis staminea</u> This clam was baked, boiled, boiled in baskets, or roasted in an open fire.

Butter Clam scq̓ʷət c̓q̓ʷət <u>Saxidomus giganteus</u> This clam and the horse clam were considered the "best eating."

Goeduc gʷidəq <u>Panope generosa</u> Jerry did not know if this clam was dried: "It is hard to get and few of them."

Horse Clam xaxəts stəbcəʔ <u>Tresus nuttalli</u> Every two weeks there was a low tide when one could get these clams (full moon tide "swadač"). This was a good eating clam. The shells were used for spoons.

---

[4] **LD** refers to Lushootseed Dictionary by Dawn Bates, Thom Hess, and Vi Hilbert 1994, expanding the earlier dictionary by Hess (1976), following the early efforts of George Gibbs in his Nisqually (Southern Lushootseed) dictionary.

Snoqualmi

Razor Clam <əə> Siliqua patrila This clam is found on ocean beaches. No name was known for this shell. The Razor clam was not used for food [inland yet much favored along the coast].

Pacific Octopus sk̓ibqʷ sqwləč {LD 335} ocotopus + squid = sqibk̓ʷ Octopus dolfleini Devilfish were caught during the first week of July at 11:00 in the morning, because at this time of year, the tide was very low.

    A large piece of ironwood was pushed into the hole in the rocks and pulled out immediately. The heart, which is directly under the head, must be removed instantly or the Devilfish cannot be killed.
    The meat is boiled for a long time. It is also roasted and dried. Jerry said that a bear once drowned after it was pulled into the water by a Devilfish.

Fish

The origin of fish is explained in the following transformer myth told by Little Sam (Haeberlin 1924: 372).[5]

Before the world had changed, five women traveled from the west. They were dog salmon, tyee salmon, silver salmon, steelhead salmon, and rainbow salmon.

The women came to the Snoqualmie river near the Falls where they found an old woman who had fallen asleep holding a baby in a cradle. The women stole the child, left some rotten wood in the cradle, and the five women took the child away to their home in the west where the end of the world was.

Bluejay, the child's grandmother, flew to the west. Here she met a man who made fish nets. This was the stolen boy Dokʷibəł who showed Bluejay all the salmon who were his children. He taught her how to make nets.

Dokʷibəł returned to this world, and he brought all his salmon children with him, so that they could spawn in the rivers. Before Dokʷibəł came, there were no salmon in this world, and when he brought all the salmon, the humpback salmon were forgotten, and so this kind of salmon comes only every second year.

The fish data were obtained primarily from Chief Jerry Kanim. Colored plates were not available for identification. However, two specimens were examined: a dog salmon and a sucker.

Information given by Ed Davis has been added to the original manuscript.[6] Colored plates in a federal chart of <u>Marine Fishes of the North Pacific</u> were most satisfactory for identification of the saltwater species.

Shark sqʷactə   any variety k̓ʷičtəličuʔ

Dogfish Shark   skʷac {LD 306}

Skate k̓ʷiʔk̓ʷił {LD 253} k̓ʷuʔt k̓ʷałaq   The skate was caught and eaten fresh in June, when the people went to the saltwater to dig clams.

Humpback salmon hadu' {LD 348} The humpback or pink salmon migrated into the stream every other year. It is seen near Tolt in September. However, in the last few years, the run has declined because fish are caught before they reach freshwater.

---

[5] Little Sam was principal Snoqualmie informant for Herman Haeberlin (Miller 2005), who died young from diabetes and was a favored student of Franz Boas, founder of academic anthropology in the US, Canada, and Mexico.

[6] HT learned of color plates for a book on freshwater fishes available at UW but she had stopped driving by that time. While arranging for Ed Davis to see them, he said that he preferred instead to buy a good watch in a pawn shop if he was to travel to Seattle from Fall City.

The humpback was taken in September with nets and spears in the Tolt and Snoqualmie rivers. It was roasted over the open fire. This salmon was never smoked. According to Jerry the pink salmon was not very important as a source of food.[7]

Dog salmon λx̌ʷayʔ <u>Oncorhynchus keta</u> The dog or chum salmon begins to migrate in early fall and by December it appears near Tolt. The run is over by the last of December. According to Jerry, a fish shaped like a steelhead formerly came with the dog salmon. This fish goes far up in the canyon of the Tolt river. It is bright in color, and does not get darker with age like steelhead. Jerry called it xubadi. According to Ed Davis, the blueback is xubadi.

This salmon may be recognized by its large front teeth, and red and white bars. As the male reaches freshwater, the bars appear, and the skin is dull in color.

Gill nets made of bear grass (<u>Xerophylum tenax</u>) were set about the first of December when the fish appeared. In the Snoqualmie there were two eddies which were the principal fishing grounds. Nets were laid at night in twelve feet of water around a deep eddy on the up stream side. The net was tied to a single stake on shore. The opposite end, as well as the bottom of the net, was anchored with rocks. The net was watched for several hours during the night. In the morning the net was pulled in. Gill nets were used primarily by older men.

Fish were speared in shallow water, at any time of the day. Spearing was done from canoes, usually by younger men. A gaff was used at night.

All species of salmon were caught by means of a trap sc̓losid built across a stream. Traps were used throughout the year (Haeberlin and Gunther 1930; Ballard 1957).

Dog salmon was most desirable. It was smoked, roasted, or boiled. The eggs were always saved. They were dried and stored in a bag made of a deer stomach. They were eaten with roasted potatoes and berries. Small girls often saved eggs and kept them in an air bladder.

Children were told they should not tease the dog salmon. If the fish is held by the gills, one will be punished; his face will swell and become distorted. Chief Kanim also said that the dog salmon must be held with the head facing up stream. Children were told that they should not play with the dog salmon because it would take away one's soul, and death would follow (Gunther 1928).

Ed Davis said that mourners could not eat salmon

> It's in this way. If you were setting a gill net, and you catch that salmon (especially a [grieving] mother or father), your net will be spoiled and fish won't run for a year.
> They won't eat anything that's killed fresh for 10 or 20 days, especially a mother or a father. They just have to live without that meat or fish. Then after that time, 15 or 20 days, it comes free again.

---

[7] This species enters freshwater not long before spawning, when body changes have already occurred. Food value has deteriorated (Schrenkeisen 1939: 35). My principal informant also mentioned that the color changes when the humpback enters freshwater. The side turns yellow, and the belly, white. The hump appears only after the salmon has entered the stream, according to Jerry.

King salmon yubəč <u>Oncorhynchus tshawytscha</u> This salmon is also known as Spring, Chinook, or Tyee. The salmon run begins about the first of July. Fish are seen in the Skykomish during August. By the last of August, the run is over. This salmon is not as plentiful as the dog or silver salmon. King salmon were never seen in the Tolt river. Therefore the Snoqualmie fished at the mouth of the Skykomish river.

Fish were speared in the Cedar river; gill nets were laid in the Skykomish.

King salmon was eaten fresh or dried. Eggs were placed inside a split stick and roasted. Eggs were also boiled in baskets. "This is primarily the salmon of the larger streams" (Schrenkeisen 1938: 38).

According to Haeberlin and Gunther (1930: 23-24),

> One of the most popular ways of preparing fish was to roast it on a stick over the fire. This method was called   sk!eEm. A stick about two feet long was split in half to about three-fourths of its length. The fish was split on one side and stuck lengthwise into the split stick. Then the stick was tied together just above and below the fish so as to keep the fish in a fixed position. Little sticks were inserted in a crosswise position in order to keep the fish flat so that the heat could get at the whole piece. The long stick was stuck into the ground in a slanting position, and a fire was built under it.
>
> Salmon was split and roasted in the same way. This was called sq!ᵘolEm. Large clams were also roasted in this fashion, and after roasting, they were strung on cedar bark and hung up for winter use.

Silver salmon skʷxʷic {LD 348} sq̓əčqs <u>Oncorhynchus kisutch</u> The silver or Coho salmon migrates into the stream in September. The run lasts until March. Spawning occurs during January and February. Immediately after entering freshwater, the silver color changes to red.

Gill nets were laid in the Skykomish and Snoqualmie. Fish were speared in the Tolt and elsewhere in Snoqualmie territory. The meat was boiled, roasted, dried, and smoked.

Sockeye salmon sc̓uwad <u>Oncorhynchus nerka</u> This fish is also known as Alaska, Red, or Blueback salmon. A few sockeye appear with jack salmon (yoqʷ [??]) during September in the Tolt and Snoqualmie rivers. Gill nets and spears were used to take the sockeye.

Cutthroat trout skʷəspɬ {LD 368} <u>Salmo □larkia</u> Several species of trout were seen in streams. They were caught with a line baited with cylindrical traps, eight feet in length, made of willow strips. Trout were roasted and boiled. They were never dried.

Steelhead trout sq̓ʷawəl q̓iw̓x̌ <u>Salmo gairdneri</u> Steelhead appear annually around the last of December in the Tolt. Spawning occurs for a period of two weeks in March. By the end of March, the run is over. After hatching, fingerlings migrate to saltwater and become salmon. The female also returns to saltwater after spawning.

Rainbow trout qʷəspɬ q̇iw̓x̌ <u>Salmo gairdneri</u> Jerry considered the steelhead and rainbow as separate species. The rainbow and cutthroat were called by the same name, although their differences were recognized.

Bull trout pasač <u>Salvetenus malma</u> The Dolly Varden is seen at a certain time of the day during the Spring. It was speared in the upper end of Cedar lake.
    <u>Folklore</u>: It is believed that Dolly Varden trout turn into Loons if one spears them for any length of time. They may be seen rising to the top of the water, having grown wings.

Sucker skʷuup {LD 312} <u>Catostomus</u> sp Ed Davis describes the sucker's habits as follows:

They run on the rivers. They're even on the lakes, suckers are. I guess where there's fishing, its in deep pools on big body of water like Snoqualmie. And when they run to spawn, why they run up on these small streams, Raging and Snoqualmie rivers and lakes.

Did you ever drive by Snoqualmie Falls Timber Company? Where they dump logs? I used to work there. I put in about thirteen years. Then I come to know these suckers. They spawn in the mud, too. They are in that slough or in that pond. I never believe it, you know, my mother-in-law used to talk about suckers. They even spawn in the mud.

The sucker heads were boiled and eaten. Several bones in the skull resemble birds.[8] A small bone is said to resemble blackberries. Late in the summer, the ends of the bone are red. This means that the blackberries are getting ripe.

Bullhead sx̌ʷədiʔ Children caught bullheads with a line baited with dried salmon eggs or the larvae of a caddis fly.

I have listed the following saltwater fish which were mentioned by Jerry Kanim, and also identified by Ed Davis.

        Halibut sċotx̣
        Flounder p'uəyʔ
        Sole sċəx̌əč
        Rock Cod taɬiqsid
        Black Cod ssi̇tayəb

In the summer the Snoqualmie went to the saltwater to dig clams. Here they caught several varieties of marine fish. Jerry emphasized that all saltwater fish were eaten fresh, never dried.

Ed Davis describes night fishing.

---

[8] See also Osprey and Coot for Sucker head bones in their shapes.

There used to be a pan with handles, a big pan ten inches deep. You fill that with sand. You take and chop up that pitchwood fir čəbidac. You light a little fire on this pan on top of this sand. It will throw a big flame. And then it blinds the fish. They go back and hit the drag net.

Then you got to shore, and you pull that drag net on each end, and well, if you're in the lake, you get lots of different kinds of little fish. You get ducks, you get trout. That's the way they fish down there at Tulalip for salmon.

But them days, what they use in the lake here where I seen it, where I have been with them, it's a short one about sixty to eighty feet long. Then you have a canoe together. Then you paddle that canoe. You land ashore. You get off the canoe there, then you pull it by hand. And you get all that little fishing to the rock bed.

Four men, two on each canoe, and they had a little board, and keep throwing a little pitchwood in that pan there to keep it blazing right along. A pan in each boat.

Then the captain on that boat there, he's hanging on to that web, that net that you're dragging in. If you have a net, say about sixty to eighty feet long, that's just as far apart as your canoes.

Night fishing or torch fishing was called ošəšədəb "dragging the net."

Amphibians and Reptiles

The distribution of amphibians and reptiles varies according to the humidity of the area. Amphibians occur in greatest numbers where there is extensive freshwater; reptiles occur in greatest numbers where freshwater is reduced in amount. Thus, in the territory formerly occupied by the Snoqualmie amphibians are numerous and show great variability, while reptiles are relatively few in number.

A amphibian and reptiles are listed according to Stebbin's Filed Guide to Western Reptiles and Amphibians (1968). Preserved specimens were used in the identification of the forms. Specimens and plates were not available for the Washington salamander (Plethodon vandykei).

Northwestern Salamander   p̓ip̓əq̓yuɬ {LD 348}   Ambystoma gracile   The north western salamander was observed swimming in ponds and lakes. Jerry noted that this species showed considerable variation in size.

Long-toed salamander   p̓ip̓əq̓yuɬ   Ambystoma macrodactylum   This salamander, terrestrial in habitat, was very common in Snoqualmie territory.

Pacific Giant salamander   p̓ip̓əq̓yuɬ   Dicamptodon ensatus   This species is commonly known as the Marbled salamander. Jerry called this salamander a water dog. In several ponds near Cedar lake, salamanders were seen piled along the shore. They were about fourteen inches in length, black or reddish in color, and spotted with white.

Snoqualmi

Rough-skinned Newt gʷəɫqo p̓ip̓əq̓yuɫ <u>Taricha granulosa gr</u> Newts were seen in swamps and lakes. All salamanders and newts were called by the same name; however, several varieties were recognized.[9]

Western Red-backed salamander p̓ip̓əq̓yuɫ <u>Plethodon vehiculum</u> Several specimens, both bleached and unbleached, were observed by the informant. Although this species is recognized, Jerry said that he had never seen the unbleached form.

Enstina bəqats p̓ip̓əq̓yuɫ <u>Ersatina eschscholtzii</u> This salamander was frequently found in rotten logs.

Frog, Toad swaq̓waq̓   All frogs and toads were called by the same name. The following species were recognized as occurring Snoqualmie territory ; Tailed frog (<u>Ascaphus truei</u>) Pacific Tree frog (<u>Hyla regilla</u>), Red Legged frog (<u>Rana aurora</u>), Spotted frog (<u>Rana pretiosa</u>), and Western Toad (<u>Bufo boreas</u>).

The term colswaya was used to designate a "large frog " known to occur commonly. According to Ballard, the term ts'əlsawiya was the name for Toad.[10]
<u>Folklore</u>: The Snoqualmie do not kill the Toad. Jack Stillman said,[11]

Toad, the grandmother of Moon, is to be seen in the moon today. Just that one was taken up when Moon went on his course. The rest were left down here. That is why the Snoqualmie people, when they find Toad, do not kill it.

Chief Kanim mentioned that frogs may be heard singing in March. They are telling the tide to go out so that the people may dig clams. tide goes out = di di swadač tide goes in = či či swadač

Painted Turtle ʔaləšik {LD 368} <u>Crysemys picta</u> Neither Jerry nor Ed had seen this turtle. However, Jerry had heard that this creature was called. According to Suckley (1859, 12: 292), the Nisqually called the turtle El-la-chick.

Northwestern Fence Lizard dədicxayʔ {LD 327} <u>Sceloporus occidentalis</u> According to Jerry, lizards live on land, while salamander are found in water. It is believed that the lizard is vicious and ill-tempered, while the salamander is harmless.[12]
Ed Davis has described the lizard as follows:

---

[9] In 2013, HT recalled that the specimens used had faded in their jars, this loss of natural coloration made identification difficult and Jerry Kanim temporized by calling them "of the water".

[10] Animals are more than mere characters in stories; significant one have personal names which become treasured family property passed down through the generations.

[11] Jack Stillman, brother of Betsy Losier and husband of Annie, said to be sister of Jerry Kanim, was the primary Snoqualmie source for Arthur Ballard.

[12] Also known as Blue-belly or Swift, it is actually a harmless species (Stebbins 1968: 241).

> You see, the color of a lizard, it's dependin' on the place where they are. If it's in a rock place or in a hill soil, that makes the different colors.
>
> I heard some story about the tail. It says, "A tail of a lizard is a poison. If it hits you, it's going to make you awful sick." It will fall off, and then it explained it this way. The lizard got shamed of herself. "oxʷexʷedʔe sdididʔxay" That little animal got shamed of herself because she didn't hit you.
>
> You take a lizard or some other little animal, and you watch it, whenever it comes in sight, like you're in the woods, or any little kind of a lawn like that, and you'll see a lizard there awalkin'. Got that kind of little funny action or movin'. And you know, my Missus, Louisa, in her native tongue, she used to bring it out, telling a story about the lizard. She says, before the come along, "Why," she says, "There's a prettiest woman ever walked, the lizard was."
>
> That's in her story. That's Skagit.

It was known that the Fence lizard could throw its tail. If this animal was touched or killed, the tail would break off. About 1 inch of the tail was lost. It was not known if the tail could be regenerated.[13]

Supernatural Beliefs: This lizard could appear as a shaman's power xʷdab. Powerful doctors had a lizard which they "shot" into people. The dried head was kept in a bag and used in the curing procedure. The head was "shot" into the patient (Haeberlin and Gunther 1930: 79).

It is believed that lizards "try you out and see if you have a sklaletut power." If the tail does not hit, a person evidently has a power. If one has no power, the tail will strike, leaving a permanent scar. As the tail was thrown through the air, humming sounds could be heard.

Folklore: It is said that the lizard goes to the salt water in summer where it changes into a Bullhead. For this reason many people refuse to eat Bullhead eggs.

Western Skink pipəqyuɫ <u>Eumeces skiltonianus</u> This reptile is classified as a salamander.

Garter Snake bəċac {LD 355} <u>Thamnophis sp</u>
    Supernatural Beliefs: The garter snake appeared as a doctor's power. Certain doctors had a dried snake head which they "shot" into the patient (Haeberlin and Gunther 1930: 79).
    Folklore: When a small snake was seen, this was a sign that bad luck would follow. Jerry said

> Once I saw a little snake about six inches long crawling around the house. Two days later Dr Bill Kanim died.

Northern Pacific Rattlesnake sk̓idəkʷ {LD 355} waxpuš <u>Crotalus viridus oreganus</u>
    Rattlesnakes were formerly abundant near Yakima, until they were destroyed by pigs. Today the few that remain are found in the mountains.

---

[13] Many Lizards, when attacked, lose a portion of the tail, which will squirm and wiggle while the lizard escapes (Pickwell 1947: 88).

Jerry believed that before the snake sheds its skin, it is blind. At this time it rattles, warning one not to tough it. Snake bites were treated either by supernatural methods or by removal of the affected parts. According to Jerry,

> My step father said "When you first get bit, cut out the piece of flesh immediately with a sharp knife, and lay it on a rock. If the flesh swells up, the poison has not entered the rest of the body. If the flesh doesn't swell, it is too late; the poison has gone through the rest of the body. When the poison enters the body and gets into the heart, you are gone."

Folklore: According to Jerry, rattlesnakes were formerly members of the Snohomish tribe. Now when a Snoqualmie speaks to a rattlesnake, he introduces himself, informing the snake that he also is a Snohomish. Then the rattlesnake will not harm him.

When rattlesnakes hiss, they are talking. It is said that they understand all dialects west of the Cascades. Long ago they were observed in migration eastward from western Washington.

According to Ed Davis,

> When he is sticking his tongue out, he means "Don't you hurt me." You know the story of that rattlesnake. It's from down here from the coast. But the Indians went up there for something [fire] at that time. And the rattlesnake followed them. Then they got blocked up and they could not get back, but the Indians got back to the coast. We would have a rattlesnake if he didn't get stalled up there and couldn't get back, but the Indians got back.

Birds {LD 291}

The creation of the birds is explained in the following story told by the principal informant:

> Birds were formerly orphans, the children who had been taken away by sxʷayoqʷ Moon słokʷalb changed these children into birds, and they flew in different directions. Then he called them back again, and gathered them together again, turning them loose. He repeated this four times. The fourth time he turned them loose, they all lit on the same tree, which suited Moon.
>
> Then he called them back for the fifth time on a different tree. On the fifth tree, they flew away, and Moon said, "After this šišildš you will always come out before it rains, and give people warning of approaching storms."
>
> The people changed at once into every bird and animal.

Jerry Kanim's observation concerning bird migration might perhaps reflect a critical attitude toward traditional Snoqualmie birdlore.

> There is a place in the North where ducks nest. When they are through, they come here for food. All little birds stay here in winter except sxʷut ([Wood] Thrush Hylocichla). They go way up, because they are Thunder's children. I believe they

go away where it is warm. The old people say they go to their father. I don't believe it; I think they go to a warmer climate.

It is probably that the Snoqualmie recognized that birds are distributed according to ecological niches. Jerry believed that

Certain birds are seen in each locality. Each one has a certain thing to go after.

Skins and colored plates in Taverner's <u>Birds of Western Canada</u> were used in identification of the birds. Chief Kanim visited the Burke Museum where he observed birds and mammals. All species have been listed in zoological order according to Larrison and Sonnenberg's <u>Washington Birds</u>.

Loons Gaviidae <əə>

Common Loon swuqʷəd {LD 327} <u>Gavia immer</u>   This bird was very common in Snoqualmie territory. Loons were seen along rivers the year around, feeding on fish and worms. My principal informant noted that the loon obtains its food by diving. [lesser šukʼʷus]
Loons were hunted in fall, winter, and spring. Loop snares made of bear grass (<u>Xerophyllum tenax</u>) were set in shallow water near the mouth of a stream. A small slip loop was hung on a branch or cattail, and tied to a stake driven into the bottom of a creek. Loops were also set flat on the water directly above a dead fish.

Food: The meat was roasted on a spit over the fire. Jerry said, Some people ate it. I never ate it. The meat doesn't look good to me. It's dark.

Materials: Chief Kanim brother-in-law, Jack Stillman, wore a cap made from a single loon skin. The head of the bird was worn in front and the tail hung down the back. This was the only loon skin cap seen by my informant.

<u>Supernatural Beliefs</u>:   One of the powers received by Bill Kanim, Jerry's uncle, included the loon.

My uncle Doctor Bill received swuqʷad power and became a medicine man. He told me, "When I was a boy, Loon spoke to me." He said, "Look at me, every time I go down, I come out with something. I never come out with nothing. When a sick person lies down, your will dive down and suck the sickness out of him. You will be like me, you will dive into someone's body and come out with the disease. Now I will be your power. When you doctor some sick person, you think of me. I'll be with you."
When Doctor Bill began to cure, he told the people what power he would use. He said, "My power is Loon. When I received the power, Loon brought fish to the surface; so I will use this power. Doctor Bill sang, dived toward the body, and sucked out the disease."
He spit out pus and blood in a basket, half full of water. If a man was bruised, he sucked bad blood. I saw it myself.

The more he was paid, the harder he worked; a horse or two blankets or guns. At first he worked for a little; later he asked for more. If you were a relation and had nothing, the doctor would help you.

<u>Folklore</u>: According to the Snoqualmie, the Loon was once a human being. The old people whipped him and told him to get a power. He began to cry. Now in spring this bird may be heard crying as it flies east to fish. It calls oo-oo-oo.

In Cedar lake, Dolly Varden trout were seen changing into loons. The fish grew wings as they rose to the surface. My principal informant stated that

> The Dolly Varden trout turn into swoq̓ʷad if you keep spearing them. They come to the top of the water with wings, so the people stopped spearing them. If you had kept on spearing, Dolly Varden would have turned into Loons.
> There are two loons at the upper end of the lake and two at the lower end of Cedar lake. When you see them you whistle at them, and they cry oo-oo-oo. They dive down, and each time they come out, one extra comes up. Soon a flock of them appears, and they begin to sing.[14]

Grebes <əə>

Red-necked Grebe xʷətis {LD 317} <u>Podiceps grisegena</u> Grebes were seen near the saltwater. These birds were known to be skillful divers.

Pied-Billed Grebe xoxʷay <u>Podilymbus podiceps</u> This bird, commonly known as helldiver, was observed near the saltwater. According to the informant, it does not dive like a duck, but sinks in the water.

Cormorants <əə>

Cormorant bačus <u>Phalacrocorax sp</u> Cormorants were seen near the saltwater at low tide.

Herons Ardeidea <əə>

Great Blue Heron sbəq̓ʷaʔ {LD 319} <u>Ardea herodias</u> The heron, known locally as the crane, was seen the year around. My informant had observed this bird in shallow water feeding on frogs and bullheads.
  <u>Folklore</u>: The long bill and legs of the heron are explained in the Star Husband story (Ballard 1927: 77-78).

---

[14] Suckley (1859: 279) writes: The distance that this bird will pass under water when endeavoring to escape by diving is wonderful. I think that I have certainly seen them after diving reappear at a distance of nearly half a mile. They use their wings under water, flying in realinty through the aqueous element.

Snoqualmi

Bitterns <əə>

American Bittern sbiq̇o' <u>Botaurus lentiginosus</u> The bittern was seen in marshes near Lake Sammamish, My informant thought that its call sounds as if "someone is driving a stake in the mud" [because only the middle note travels, sounding like a stake being driven with a wooden mallet, Larrison 1968: 63].
<u>Folklore</u>: If you look at this bird while it is flying, you will have bad luck.

Swans, Geese, and Ducks Anatidae <əə>

Whistling Swan sxʷoq̇əd <u>Olor columbianus</u> Swans were observed in migration near Lake Sammamish and Cedar lake. It is believed that this bird flies east in the fall and returns in the spring of the following year. The informant also suggested that the swan nests in the north [These nests are on the Arctic coast and islands west of Hudson Bay, Taverner 1926: 112]. {LD 361 sliʔhib, čuƛ̇qid, č̇əƛ̇qid}

Canada Goose ʔəxəʔ Snow goose {LD 316} <u>Branta canadiensis</u> In the fall and spring, Canada geese migrate from the north to feed in the area formerly occupied by the Snoqualmie. Jerry Kanim observed that flocks were the rule, and single birds the exception. Geese were never used as food.

Brant gilgałdał <u>Branta bernicla</u> [*<u>nigricans</u>] The informant noted that this bird commonly occurs near the saltwater, although he could not recall the name. It is listed by Ballard as gilgałdał. [słulac {LD 291}]

Mallard x̌ətx̌ət <u>Anas platyrhynchos</u> This term is imitative of the bird's call. In fall and winter, mallards were very abundant in Snoqualmie territory. My informant noted that they spend the night out on open water, returning in the early morning and evening to feed near shore.

Ducks were taken in fall and winter. In Lake Sammamish nets were laid near the shore slightly submerged under water. These nets, 12 feet square, were stretched horizontally and fastened to six posts in shallow water, about 10 feet deep.
Ducks were also taken by means of loops snares or were shot with bow and arrow. A slip loop was hung on a branch or cattail, and tied to a stake driven into the mud.

<u>Food</u>: Nearly all fresh water and marine ducks were used as food [except wood ducks]. Freshwater ducks were usually considered palatable, except for a few weeks in December, at which time they were known to feed upon dead dog salmon (łˣʷay). My informant mentioned that saltwater ducks are edible the year around.

Mallards, as well as all other edible varieties of waterfowl, were roasted on a spit over the fire. Ducks were also boiled in baskets. The heart and crop were saved and eaten with the rest of the bird. The liver was never used.

<u>Materials</u>: Dancers sprinkled the down in their hair.

Green-winged Teal xaxətxat skiʔks {LD 363} "small mallard" Anas carilinense The mimetic term   is combined with an infix to form the name of this bird. The green-winged teal, formerly very abundant, was found near freshwater.

American Widgeon wasilka wəciʔ {LD 292} Anas americana *Mareca americana The name may be imitative of the widgeon's call. Jerry Kanim could not identify this duck from either plates or skins; however he had heard a saltwater duck whose call sounded like wasi'lka. Ballard records the widgeon as wasilka.

Shoveller gʷəgʷəqotq̓s Anas clypeata *Spatula clypeata The name refers to the wide spoon-shaped bill of the shoveller. This bird was seen on the saltwater, but no name was known for it. It is listed by Ballard as gwegwigotq̓s.

Wood Duck yeceb Aix sponsa This duck was observed near swamps and rivers. It was never used for food. My informant explained that this duck feeds on snakes, frogs, and fish.

Folklore: When the wood duck is frightened, it sings "I am from way up the river."

Redhead dišəbq̓əd Aythya americana   The redhead was seen on saltwater and along rivers. [small sawbill didšəlqid {LD 291}]

Canvas-back cəkowapcəb Aythya valisineria The canvas-back was very common in Snoqualmie territory, although the informant could not recall the name. Ballard records this duck as tsəkowaptsəb.

Greater Scaup Duck <əə> Aythya marila This bird was observed near streams and saltwater during the summer, but no name was known for it. The canvas back and the greater scaup were classified by the informant as a single species.

Lesser Scaup Duck ələdgʷəs Aythya affinis This name is descriptive of the appearance of the lesser scaup. This duck was seen near the saltwater. It is quite possible that the Snoqualmie considered the two scaups as a single species. According to Taverner (1926: 91-92), these ducks are inseparable in the field.

Common Golden-eye xʷiyəxʷ tq̓ʷəč {LD 291} Bucephala clangula The name is possibly onomatopoetic in origin. This bird calls wəx-wəx-wəx. The Goldeneye or whistler was found near the coast and along rivers in the winter. My informant observed that this duck whistles as it rises from the water. He believed that the whistling sound is made by the bird's wings [correctly, Taverner 1926: 93].

Buffle-head təṫkʷi stəṫtqʷiʔ {LD 295} Bucephala albeola The bufflehead was seen near the saltwater and occasionally in the Tolt and Snoqualmie rivers.

Oldsquaw[k] saagi Clangula hyemalis The term is derived from the notes of the bird's call. Although my informant did not recognize the old squaw, he recalled that he had heard of a saltwater duck named saagi in imitation of its call. This duck cries aagi aagi. According to Ballard the old squaw was called ċagə'.[15]

Harlequin x̌əladʔus from salos "painted, marked face" <u>Histrionicus histrionicus</u> This name is descriptive of the appearance of the harlequin duck. Harlequins were seen near the saltwater.

White-winged Scoter qʷalxʷ <u>Melanitta fusca</u> *<u>Melanitta deglandi</u> White winged scoters, frequently observed near the saltwater, were also very abundant in Snoqualmie territory. These birds are now seldom seen. The meat is considered particularly desirable.

Hooded Merganser šəbq̇əd skəks <u>Mergus cucullatus</u> *<u>Lophodytes cucullatus</u> The hooded merganser occurred commonly in the area formerly occupied by the Snoqualmie. [didšəlqid]

Common Merganser sqoqəbš <u>Mergus merganser</u> This duck was seen near the saltwater in summer.

Red-breasted Merganser swehič <u>Mergus serrator</u> Red breasted mergansers are found along the rivers and near the saltwater. My informant believed that this duck nests near the Snoqualmie and Tolt rivers. In early summer the female and young were known to appear on the river in rafts. The informant observed that the female "teaches the young birds to dive."
It was noted that this bird is a skillful diver; "It can dive under a waterfall and come to the top of the water on the other side."

<u>Supernatural Beliefs</u>: If one had swehič for a power, he could become a shaman or a skillful diver.

<u>Folklore</u>: The origin of the merganser is explained in the Star Husband story (Ballard 1927: 19).

Vultures Cathartidae <əə>

Turkey Vulture ċikawd <u>Cathartes aura</u> The vulture was seen circling high in the air, searching for carrion. The informant believed that scent guides vultures in locating food [but "Eyesight alone is relied upon for locating food" (Taverner 1926: 180)].

California Condor <əə> <u>Vultur californianus</u> *<u>Gymnogyps californianus</u> A large predatory bird, heard only at night, was never actually seen by the informant. He identified it only as hediləbš.[16]

---

[15] Now called Longtail to avoid the older racist and sexist term, or Old Squawk to capture their noisiness, this duck – whose plumages changes by age, gender, and season – is the avatar of the little-known coastal Transformer called Misp^h.

[16] "The appearance of the white man doubtless hastened its withdrawl, for it was last seen in the state of Washington about 1830, and in Oregon about 1913" (Matthiessen 1962: 106-109).

The old people said it could pick up sheep or a large animal. It sounded like a large dog.

Ballard records the California condor as hedᵊlIbc. One of Ballard's informants observed that hədᵊlIbc "broke down the weirs."

Cooper's Hawk x̌ibx̌ib {LD 319} "grabs with the claws" <u>Accipter cooperii</u> This term is descriptive of the predatory habits of the hawk. Cooper's hawk or the "chicken hawk" was seen near chicken yards. It was considered a harmful species as it was known to prey upon small birds.

Red-tailed Hawk piya' <u>Buteo jamaicensis</u> The red tailed hawk was very abundant along the Tolt river where it was seen feeding on dead salmon. The feathers of this bird were not used.

Swainson's Hawk tɬoqʷtɬoqʷ <u>Buteo swainsoni</u> This bird, formerly abundant, was seen along rivers feeding on dead fish. The black pigeon hawk is listed by Ballard as tɬoqtɬoq.

Rough-legged Hawk cecaal <u>Buteo lagopus</u> The rough legged hawk is seen near streams.

Bald Eagle yəxʷəlaʔ <u>Haliaeetus leucocephalus</u> Eagles were formerly seen near Tolt. Now they are rare in Snoqualmie territory.

<u>Materials</u>: Fish hooks were made from the large claws of eagles and hawks. The informants could not recall how such fish hooks were made.

<u>Supernatural beliefs</u>: If a man had yəxʷila for a power, he could look for a lost soul.

Marsh Hawk agsxʷədxʷəb "hawk of medium size" <u>Circus cyaneus</u> The descriptive term xebxeb is combined with a prefixed element to form the name for the marsh hawk. The informant noted that his hawk resembles a small owl. Marsh hawks were seen along sloughs, feeding on frogs. According to Ballard the marsh hawk was called tʼitxʷlus.

Osprey ċix̌ċix̌ "stingy" <u>Pandion haliaetus</u> The name is descriptive of the behavior of the fish hawk.

When this one gets a fish it doesn't give it to any other bird.

The terms is also imitative of the osprey's call. Larrison (1968: 91) describes the call as "whew-whew-whew-whi-whi-whi". The osprey is seen along rivers, preying on fish.

<u>Supernatural Beliefs</u>: If a man had Osprey for a power he would become a good fisherman.

<u>Folklore</u>: The large skull bone of the sucker is said to resemble the osprey.

Snoqualmi

Black Pigeon [Merlin] Hawk xexexeb "small hawk" <u>Falco columbarius suckleyi</u> The descriptive term əast is combined with an infix to form the name of this hawk. It is recorded by Ballard as tɬoqtɬoq. The informant had observed pigeon hawks feeding on snakes.

Grouse Tetraonidae əast

Blue Grouse sbəkʷbəkʷ {LD 317} <u>Dendrogapus obscurus</u> The informant believed that this bird remains in the deep woods throughout the winter, as it was seen only in the spring. Nests were found in early summer. It was noted that the eggs are larger than those of the ruffed grouse; they are white in color, spotted with brown. This bird was hunted with bow and arrow. [stəxʷəb {LD 317}]

<u>Food</u>: Grouse were roasted on a spit over the fire or boiled in baskets. The eggs were also eaten.

Ruffed Grouse sgʷəlub {LD 338} <u>Bonasa umbellus</u> The ruffed grouse, locally called "pheasant," was seen the year around, particularly near crab apple trees. [stəxʷəb]

In summer, it was taken by means of a loop snare or shot with bow and arrow. A decoy of moss was placed on one end of a log where pheasants were seen drumming. A loop snare was hung from the branches above the moss. The bird charged the moss, and was caught in the snare. A similar type of snare has been described by Haeberlin (1924: 413-414).

<u>Food</u>: Grouse were eaten in summer after they had grown fat on a diet of berries. The meat was boiled in baskets or roasted on a spit over the fire.

<u>Material</u>: The wing feathers are used on arrows.

<u>Supernatural Beliefs</u>: A grouse caught by means of a loop snare might speak to a boy and become his power. One who received sgʷəlob for a power would become a skillful hunter or warrior.

<u>Folklore</u>: When Pheasant is drumming, he is fixing his moccasins for the winter.

> Don't eat pheasant when you are young because pheasant is a lazy bird and you will not be industrious. However, you will be able to run fast because pheasant is a runner.

Hancock (1927: 127-128) writes of the Snoqualmie:

> The pheasant they had procured for my special benefit, as these Indians do not eat them, having, I believe, some kind of superstition in regard to them, and I did not attempt to disabuse their minds of this prejudice while eating the richly flavored and delicate birds myself.

"Pheasant" feathers were considered better than those of any other bird, for it was believed that pheasant, a great hunter, also used his wing feathers for arrows.

The use of the snare is explained in the myth, Origin of the Pheasant recorded by Haeberlin (1924: 413-414).

Sharp-tailed Grouse siap miyawəx Ballard says miyawəx is the Sahaptin term for a "high class person." The sharp tailed grouse or prairie chicken was seen in eastern Washington. This bird was clubbed by women. Grouse was eaten by the Yakima.

<u>Folklore</u>: If one calls to this bird, "You are chief," the grouse will nod its head in reply. Then it can be caught easily.

Coots Rallidae <əə>

American Coot habu' <u>Fulica americana</u>   Coots, also known as mud hens, were observed near Lake Sammamish. They were taken in fall by means of loop snares, as noted above.
<u>Food</u>: This bird was boiled in baskets or roasted on a spit over the fire.

<u>Folklore</u>: It is believed that the scallop webbed toes, characteristic of the mud hen, appear in the fall when this bird is seen near the water. In late spring the mud hen is found in the trees; it then "loses" the webs and becomes a "land habo" or pigeon. A man once observed the small webs on immature mud hens; he was therefore convinced that a single bird actually existed.[17]

My informant noted that both the [band-tailed] pigeon (<u>Columba fasciata</u>) and the coot are found in the area occupied by the Snoqualmie; however, the two birds are seen at different times of the year. He believed that if both forms could be observed together, it could be proved that two distinct birds are involved in the apparent "transmutation." The informant mentioned that the problem of the coot changing into a pigeon was the source of many "arguments." The coot cries for berries, particularly elderberries.
A small bone in the sucker's head resembles the coot, according to Jerry.

Shorebirds <əə>

Wilson's [Common] Snipe kiyowⁱya <u>Gallinago gallinago</u> *<u>Capella gallinago</u> This bird, known as the jack snipe, was seen on sand bars and near swamps. The informant regarded the snipe and the long-billed dowitcher (<u>Limnodromus scolopaceus</u> *<u>Limnodromus griseus</u>) as a single species. Both birds were called Kiyowⁱya.

Sandpiper wiłwił   The name is imitative of the bird's call.

The following birds were recognized and considered as one species: spotted sandpiper (<u>Tringa macularis</u> *<u>Actitus macularis</u>), pectoral sandpiper (<u>Calidris melanotos</u> *<u>Erolia melanotos</u>), least sandpiper (<u>Calidris minutilla</u> *<u>Erolia minutilla</u>), and Dunlin red-backed sandpiper (<u>Calidrus alpina</u> *<u>Erolia alpina</u>). [snipe {LD 355}]
Sandpiper were seen near the coast and along streams.

---

[17] A transspecies motif, explanatory of certain zoological phenomena, especially intra and extra species variability, is found across North American (Speck and Witthoft 1947: 345-349).

Snoqualmi

Northern Phalarope šišildš Phalaropus lobatus *Lobipes lobatus This name has reference to the bird's flight. Although the informant had never observed the phalarope at close range, his excellent description of the bird's habits established the identity of this species. Phalarope were seen near the saltwater and along rivers.
They are seen in groups. They twist, and look like mosquitoes on the water.
    Folklore: In the informant's version of the Star Husband story, the characteristics of this bird are explained by the transformer:

    After this, šišildš, you will always come out before it rains and give people warning of storms approaching.

Herring Gull kiyuuq^{w}s {LD 291, 350} kiyo!ks Larus argentatus The herring seagull and glaucous-winged gull (Larus glaucescens) were both called by the same name. The juvenile gull, regarded as a distinct species, is called qpəs. Ballard lists the Black Tern as qpəs. Gulls were occasionally seen feeding on insects and fish, preying on clams.

Pigeon Guillemot sqaq^{w}ič Cepphus columba This bird was found on the saltwater. The nests were located on high bluffs. It was not used as food.

Pigeons Columbidae əast

Band-tailed Pigeon həbu' Columba fasciata fasciata The band-tail pigeon and the coot (Porphyrio americana *Falica americana) were classified as a single species by my informant.

Western Mourning Dove həbu' Zenaidura macroura The Sahaptin term mimim is imitative of the dove's call.

Although the dove, coot, and band-tailed pigeon were all called by the same name habu', the Snoqualmie considered the dove as a separate species, distinct from either the coot or the pigeon. The bird was seen in eastern Washington.

Owls <əə> {LD 336}

According to the informant, all owls live in the deep woods; they are predatory, feeding on chickens, mice, and snakes.

Kennicott's Screech Owl sk^{w}əq^{w}ubš Otus asio The screech owl was heard at night.

Folklore: When this owl hoots, it means he is fixing his house for the winter.

Coast [Northern] Pygmy Owl stɬatɬ^{w}q Glaucidium gnoma These small owls are heard at night.
  [stitəɬ]
    Folklore: When this owl hoots, it means someone will die; it is also a warning that you will have bad luck.

Snoqualmi

The pygmy owl is similar to the saw-whet owl. He utters a series of short staccato notes at night. This owl is seen in the daytime.

Great Gray Owl čiitbixʷ təkʷtəkʷəlus Strix nebulosa The great gray owl is listed by Ballard as həqʷhəqʷ. My informant had never seen either the gray owl or the owl which he identified only as haqʷhaqʷ. However, he recalled that haqʷhaqʷ sounds like a dog barking. həqʷhəqʷ is bigger than the horned owl. It howls like a dog barking. It is seldom seen here.

Short-eared Owl ƛ̓klos Asio flammeus flammeus The short-eared owl "speaks" the Snoqualmie language. The short-eared owl's call is a warning that an old person will die soon.

> Before Mrs Kanim's aunt died, this owl was heard; this was a warning that the old woman would soon leave her family.

Saw-Whet Owl sqoqʷəlbc Aegolius acadicus This small owl is nocturnal in habit. The call sounds like a whistle. Ballard records the saw-whet as stɬatɬaqʷ. [sx̌əƛ̓akʷ xʷupšəd]

> He has more ears and is larger than skokʷəlbc. It is said that he has but one leg.

Goatsuckers and Allies <əə>

Common Nighthawk xexəxʷəb Chordeiles minor hesperis The descriptive term x̌əbx̌əb "grabs with the claws" is combined with an infix to form the name of this bird. It is believed that the nighthawk preys upon snakes, frogs and small birds. Therefore, it was hunted with bow and arrows to protect other birds. [xʷp̓ača?əl {LD 334}]

Hummingbirds Trochilidae <əə>

Rufous Hummingbird tʸəyⁱd Selasphorus rufus Hummingbird's eggs were saved for hunting and gambling charms. [təti?əd {LD 291}]

Kingfishers Alcedinidae <əə>

Belted Kingfisher sčətx̌ Ceryle alcyon *Megaceryle alcyon The kingfisher sits on a limb over the water. It may be seen diving into the water for small trout and bullhead.

Folklore: Long ago, this bird was [a] Kingfisher. The transformer said, "Your name will be sčətx̌. You will be a great fisherman."

Woodpeckers Picidae <əə>

Northern flicker čədʸaqʷ Colaptes auratus *Colaptes cafer. The informant noted that flickers are not as common as other small birds. The northern flicker is seen perched on the house. This bird is hunted with bow and arrow.

Snoqualmi

<u>Materials</u>: The tail feathers were worn in the hair or sewn on skin caps. Feathers were also used as trimming on the shoulders of jackets.

<u>Folklore</u>: This bird is regarded as a doctor who cures trees by removing worms [and these birds are indeed beneficial (Taverner 1926: 226)].

Pileated Woodpecker qataqata <u>Dryocopus pileatus</u> The name is imitative of the woodpecker's call. This bird was seen pecking at trees in search of worms.

Lewis's Woodpecker łiłqʷab "pecking at something" <u>Melaneipes lewis</u> *<u>Asyndesmus lewis</u> Name is descriptive of the activity of this bird. Hairy and downy woodpeckers are also called łiłqʷab. [?? {LD 375}]

<u>Folklore</u>: It is believed that his woodpecker is a doctor who cures trees by removing worms.

Yellow-bellied Sapsucker čəx̌čix̌ <u>Sphyrapicus varius ruber</u> This term is imitation of the call of the sapsucker. My informant was not certain of the habits of this bird. The sapsucker is listed by Ballard as t'tłəqcid.

Flycatchers Tryannidae əast

Western Flycatcher sc̓əp <u>Empidonax difficilis</u> The name describes the color of this bird. Several small yellow birds, including the flycatcher, willow goldfinch, and warblers were all called by the same descriptive term [see below].

Swallows Hirundinidae <əə>

Violet-green Swallow x̌ʷəx̌ʷəl̓q̓ʷiws {LD 361} <u>Tachycineta thalassina</u> The barn swallow and northern cliff swallow are also called the same. Swallows are known to nest in barns. Their food consists of insects.

Jays Corvidae <əə>

Gray Jay sqəq̓ʷiq̓ʷ <u>Perisoreus canadensis</u> The name is imitative of the jay's call. The informant was not certain of the habits of this bird, also known locally as "camp robber."

Stellar's Jay kayʔkayʔ {LD 323} <u>Cyanocitta stelleri</u> The Bluejay is named after the sound of its voice.
<u>Folklore</u>: When the Jay cries qataqata, he is scolding; when he cries skay-aky-kay, he is peaceful.
The flat head of the bluejay is explained in the Snoqualmie version of the Star Husband story (Ballard 1929: 73).

Snoqualmi

Magpies Corvidae <əə>

Black-billed Common Magpie ʔadʔad {LD 291} swədwid <u>Pica pica</u> The magpie was often seen on the back of horse, pecking at a sore. My informant was unaware of the fact that his bird is a notorious nest robber.

Crows Corvidae <əə>

Common Raven qʷəq̓ʷ kaẇqs {LD 291} <u>Corvus corax</u> The raven is known as qʷəq̓ʷ in imitation of its call (described as a croak by Taverner (1926: 258).

<u>Supernatural Beliefs</u>: Shamanistic powers obtained by Doctor Bill Kanim ("uncle" of my informant) included the Raven.

Crow k̓aʔk̓aʔ <u>Corvus brachyrhynchos</u> The term k̓ak̓a is onomatopoetic. The crow, northwestern red-wing, and Brewer's blackbird were all called by the same name; however, the crow was classified as a single species, white the red-wing and blackbird were considered as male and female, respectively [see Warblers].
Crows were known to prey on clams; they were seen along the beach, dropping clams on rocks.

Chickadees Paridae <əə>

Chickadee sc̓əc̓is <u>Parus sp</u> Chickadees appear in flocks. My informant occasionally hunted them for sport. They were taken with bow and arrow. [c̓əlc̓əlkəyus]

<u>Folklore</u>: A bird similar to Oregon Junco, but small er. The head is black with white on the side. He comes in flocks in the spring. He is elder brother to the spring salmon. He calls the salmon, singing, "Come up, come up, sisters." It is then time to spread the nets.
The old people do not like to have children destroy its eggs.

Dippers Cinclidae <əə>

American Dipper əsx̌ʷəc̓q̓ʷ <u>Cinclus mexicanus</u> It is seen along streams diving for salmon eggs.

Wrens Troglodytidae <əə>

Wren sc̓əč̓l The western winter wren (<u>Troglodytes</u>) and Bewick's wren (<u>Thryomanes bewockii</u>) were recognized and classified as a single species. Although this bird was very common in Snoqualmie territory, the informant was not certain of its habits. [təbtəb]

Robins Muscicapidae <əə>

Robin xʷiyisciya k̓ʷəqiq <u>Turdus migratorius</u> Robins were taken with deadfalls and kept as pets. A one foot square deadfall was made of small cedar sticks laid at right angles and built up like a log cabin. One side was elevated and balanced on a stick about six inches in length to which a string was attached. When the string was pulled, the trap, weighted with snow, fell on the bird. Small bird deadfalls were used only by children in winter.

A further description follows with the illustration.

1. Sticks were laid at right angles to each other. Height: two feet.
2. Two binders were placed across the top and tied to bottom sticks with bear grass.
3. A stick 5 inches in length was placed under the trap, raising the trap above the ground and permitting small birds to sit under the trap. A string attached to the supporting stick enabled a child to pull the string, knocking down the supporting stick, bringing the trap down on the birds. Snow was pile on the top for added weight.

Folklore: The appearance of the robin in spring meant that good weather would follow.

Thrushes Turdinae <əə>

Varied Thrush sc̓iyaqʷ Zoothera naevia *Ixoreus naevius naevius The varied thrush was caught by means of a small bird deadfall. It was kept as a pet; the tail feathers were plucked, and a string was tied around the bird's neck. [sxʷət]
Folklore: The appearance of the varied thrush was a sign of cold weather.

Swainson's Thrush sx̌ʷut Catharua ustulatus The name is derived from the notes of the bird's call. The dwarf hermit thrush (Catharus guttatus *Hylocichla) and the Swainson's thrush (*Hylocichla ustulata) were both called sx̌ʷut.
Thrushes were very abundant in summer, particularly during the salmon berry season. The informant had observed that all small birds are regular winter residents; only the thrush disappears in fall and is not seen again until the winter following.

Folklore: The thrush appears during a thunderstorm. If one killed this bird or disturbed its eggs, thunder would follow. In fall, this bird is heard singing "wət-wət" as it returns home to its father Thunderbird. My informant doubted that the thrush actually "goes to its father"; he suggested that this bird probably flies south for the winter. According to Ballard (ms),

> When this bird sings "whut-whut-whut," he is calling his own name. He comes with thunder in the spring time. It take him about two months to come down. He is called "Thunder's child." When he sings a certain song, the salmon berries become plentiful. When he utters a succession of short notes, we say he is calling for rain. He taunts Sparrow, saying "Thin legs, thin legs," and sparrow whips him.

Warblers Parulidae <əə>

Warbler sc̓əp "yellow" Dendroica petechia The term describes the color of the warbler. The following birds were classified as a single species: Orange-crowned warbler (Virmivora celata lutescans), yellow warbler (Dendroica petechia), and Macgillivray's warbler (Oporornis tolmiei).

The western flycatcher (Empidonax difficilis) and willow goldfinch (American goldfinch Carduelis tristis *Spinus tristis) were also called by the same name.

Warblers were very abundant in the area formerly occupied by the Snoqualmie.

Western Meadowlark xʷəlexʷəli Sturnella neglecta
Folklore: The meadowlark speaks the Snoqualmie language. It calls lətʷčad teləebos "Where are you going?" If you answer this bird, you will have bad luck. A meadowlark once spoke to a woman, and she died.

According to Jack Stillman (to Ballard), the meadowlark has two names: a myth name q̓ʷətsxʷa and a common name xwaləxwalə. Jerry, my informant, however, denied this.

Red-winged Blackbird k̓ak̓a Agelaius phoenicus The name is onomatopoetic. k̓ak̓a is imitative of the crow's call; however, this term was also given for the red-wing and Brewer's black bird. The red-wing was the male and Brewer's black bird the female. Although my informant classified the red-wing and black bird as a single species, the crow was definitely recognized as a separate species, distinct from either the red-wing or the black bird.

Red-wings were hunted for sport with bow and arrow.

Western Tanager yetʷad Piranga ludoviciana The informant did not recognize this bird. Ballard records the tanager as yetʷad.

Folklore: He sings, "Yellow salmonberry, my little wife." The old people do not like to kill him.

Rufous-sided Towhee Pipilo erythrophthalmus Its name sxʷeeqʷ is the mimetic term derived from the notes of the towhee's call.

Folklore: The distinctive red-orange color of the towhee's eyes are explained in the myth, How Coyote Stole Towhee's Eyes.

A certain red fungus or moss is called x̣weyoqʷalus "eyes of towhee."

Dark-eyed Oregon Junco scacis Junco phaeonotus *Junco oreganus In winter juncos appear in flocks. They were caught by mean of a small bird deadfall and were kept as pets. [səlus {LD 291}]

Rusty Song Sparrow specxʷ Zonotrichia melodia *Melospiza melodia This sparrow was recognized as commonly occurring in Snoqualmie territory. In winter sparrows were taken with the type of deadfall used for many small birds.

Folklore: After the sparrow was caught, the children sang, calling for warm weather. Then the bird was released.

Snoqualmi

Snoqualmie Charlie (*siatxtə*d), uncle of Jack Stillman, told the following story about specx^w (Ballard 1929: 49-50).

The Man Who Would Not Wash His Face

specx^w was married to one of five sisters; he had four brothers-in-laws. He came from the country in the direction of the rain-wind. Every day he would gather firewood from a burned cedar tree, hollow and charred. His brothers-in-laws did not give him any help, so he had the work to do alone.

Always his face was blackened by the charred wood, and always he left it unwashed. Once when specx^w was out working, the brothers-in-laws said to his wife, "What is wrong? Why does your husband not wash his face? He is getting so dirty from not washing that his face is quite black."

His wife reproached her husband when he came home. In the morning, specx^w said to his wife, "I shall go and wash my face today as your brothers wish."

Down to the river he went to where some boulders lay along the water's edge back from the stream. He said to rain-wind, "Great Uncle, I am about to wash my face now. He began to wash. The clouds began to gather. There came a fine misty rain, and the river began to rise. specx^w kept washing."

His wife told her brothers, "Your brothers-in-law is washing his face now." This she said to reproach them. The river kept rising and flooded all the valley. All was flooded between the hills.

Then specx^w flew to the home of his Great Uncle, Southwest wind. All the people were drowned.

Bird Conclusions

Loon, duck, grouse, and coot were extensively used for food. According to Jerry, ducks were considered more important than all other birds, ranking third in economic significance only to deer and salmon. Several species, including the mallard, green-winged teal, and white-winged scoter gathered in flocks near Lake Sammamish, where they could easily be taken in large numbers (by the hundreds) using horizontal nets and snares. Among the waterfowl available, but not eaten, was wood duck, regarded as inedible because it ate snakes, frogs, and fish.

Snoqualmie used the sharp claws of hawks and eagles for fish hooks. Decorative feathers were obtained from ducks, swans, hawks, eagles, and ruffed grouse.

Children's pets included the robin, varied thrush, junco, and sparrow. Hummingbird eggs were saved for hunting and gambling charms. Jerry, however, had never actually found any eggs except those of grouse, pheasant, and quail.

Jerry emphasized that birds other than those taken for food were never killed or used for target practice, for it was believed that in the mythological era all birds existed in the form of people, and were organized into tribes like the Indians of today. Jerry, however, said that he had occasionally hunted chickadees for sport.

Economically significant birds which appeared as powers included the loon, red-breasted merganser, bald eagle, osprey, and ruffed grouse. Powers could also be obtained from the raven and kingfisher. Traits such as the ability to dive or fish were definitely associated with similar capacities observed among birds. Thus a person who received the merganser for a power would become a skilled diver; of it one obtained a power from the osprey, he would be a good fisher. Strong powers, considered most effective in curing, might be obtained from loon, eagle, or raven. Three birds provided carved images at the top of the poles carried by Indian doctors on their way to the land of the dead during the Redeeming or Spirit Canoe Rite. These were martin (peql), grey swan (sdowauq), and grebe (adač).

Considerable attention was given to several species regarded as birds of ill omen. Snoqualmie bird lore includes references to the bittern, pygmy owl, short-eared owl, and meadowlark, which were associated with bad luck and death. Although these birds brought bad luck, they were never killed, for it was believed that their distinctive calls may be understood by the Snoqualmie. Jerry Kanim was certain that the meadowlark speaks the Snoqualmie and Yakama language; this proves that in the past all birds were formerly human beings. Jerry explained the creation of birds in the following story:

> Birds were formerly orphans, the children who had been taken away by sx^{w}ayuq$^{w'}$ [Ogress]. Moon (słok^{w}alb) changed these children into birds and they flew in different directions. Then he called them back again, and gathered them together again, turning them loose. He repeated this four times. The fourth time, he turned them loose; they all lit on the same tree, which suited Moon.
>
> Then he called them back for the fifth time, and they stayed together, and lit five times, each time on a different tree. On the fifth tree, they flew away, and Moon said, "After this Northern Phalalrope (cicildc), you will always come out before it rains, and give people warning of approaching storms".
>
> The people changed at once into every living bird and animal.

Jerry's knowledge in bird habits might indicate an unusual interest in bird watching for its own sake, perhaps because on the intrinsic fascination of birds. He identified and named about 70 species. Arthur Ballard's checklist includes approximately 82 birds. It is probable that the Snoqualmie formerly recognized at least 82 species, including those which have been recorded by Ballard and were not recognized by Jerry. The following birds have not been included in the annotated list, as there was no additional information available regarding their habits or use in Snoqualmie culture.

Naive terminology has been recorded by Ballard.

1	brown pelican	sts'awał (Puyallup)
2	trumpeter swan	sxowauq' (Lake Washington)
3	white-footed goose	sdjitcilelabc
4	snow goose	təkaxad
5	spruce grouse	kaxadu
6	white tailed ptarmigan	q'ax^{w}ap
7	downey woodpecker	tcextex
8	purple martin	pe•qł
9	common bushtit	tłeq'tcils
10	bluebird	xoq^{w}eq^{w}ex^w
11	white-crowned sparrow	xalq'ed

Snoqualmi

    12 common tern   qpəs

It would appear that many birds formerly recognized have disappeared from the territory occupied by the Snoqualmie. A comparison of Ballard's checklist with those species identified y Jerry would indicate that traditional bird lore is particularly vulnerable. The significant vocabulary loss within several decades reflects not only the unstable habitats and changing bird fauns in the Northwest, but also rapid culture change.

The following birds have been listed as not satisfactorily recognized:

black brant	California condor	American widgeon
common snipe	shoveller	long-billed dowitcher
canvasback	owls	oldsqwawk
greater scaup	lesser scaup	yellow-bellied sapsucker
western tanager	Brewer's blackbird	red-winged blackbird

The following birds were recognized as introduced:

California quail	mountain quail	ring-necked pheasant
Lophortyx cal.	Oreortyx pictus	Phasianus colchicus

Snoqualmi bird lore also includes at least 14 mimetic names derived from bird calls:

common mallard	xatxat
American widgeon	wasilka
Common goldeneye	wəx wəx wəx
oldsqwawk	sa•gi
osprey	tsex^w
sandpiper	wiłwił
pileated woodpecker	qataqata
yellow-bellied sapsucker	tcəxtcex
gray jay	sq^{w}əq^{w}iq^w
Stellar's jay	skaykay
American raven	q^{w}aq^w
western crow	kaka
thrush	sx^{w}ət'
Oregon towhee	sx^{w}e•q^w

    There is no specific name for 'bird'. The term st'łit'ła•lq^{w}ab refers to any bird or mammal, or it may also designate 'game'.
    All ducks, the pigeon guillemot, and the coot are known collectively as sq^{w}alec . This term refers only to the swimming birds. The name xe'bxeb, 'grabs with the claws', is descriptive of the predatory habits of eagles and large hawks. xe'bxeb is combined with an infix to form the name xexebxeb to designate small hawks.
    All large owls are called t'klos, while small owls are known as t^{i}tklos. There is no specific term for small birds.

The names for shoveller, lesser scaup, and western harlequin duck are derived from the appearance of these birds. Names may also reflect the unique predatory or flight habits of certain birds including Cooper's hawk, osprey, northern phalarope, and Lewis woodpecker. The mimetic term xatxat is combined with a diminutive infix to form the name for the green-winged teal (xaxətxat ~ 'small mallard').

Small yellow birds, including the western flycatcher, willow goldfinch, and warblers were all called by the same descriptive name (sts'əp) referring to the yellow color of these birds.

The male bird is designated stopc [stubš]; the female is known as sładay. An immature bird or mammal is called bədbəda stłitła•lq^{w}ab.

Several birds were classified as distinct species, although only one name was given. The western mourning dove, coot, and band-tailed pigeon were all called by the same term (habo'). Jerry classifies the dove as a single species, distinct from either the coot or the pigeon. The coot and pigeon were considered as one species by Jerry.

There may be crossed of species lines in sex identification for certain birds. The term qaqa referred to crow, northwestern red-wing, and Brewer's blackbird. However, the crow is classified as a single species, while the red-wing and blackbird were considered as male and female, respectively. The adult and juvenile herring gull were classified as two separate birds.

It is probable that the Snoqualmie concept of species is based largely upon general field characteristics such as behavior, size, flight, color, or plumage. It appears, however, that a few basic relationships are recognized, e.g. swimming birds (sq^{w}alɛc) are distinct from either hawks or owls.

It was not known how various organs functioned; however, it was observed that young birds develop from eggs. The term uwa'yel, meaning 'hatched', refers to hatcing of birds and fish eggs, and is distinct from ubda•b, which means 'born alive'. Jerry had seen only chicks hatching from eggs.

Jerry's observations concerning bird migration might perhaps reflect a critical attitude toward traditional Snoqualmie bird lore:

There is a place in the North were ducks nest. When they are through, they come here fore food. All little birds stay here in winter except thrush (sx^{w}ut Hylocichla sp.). They go way up because they are Thunder's children. I believe they go away where it is warm. The old people say they go to their father. I don't' believe it; I think they go to a warmer climate".

It is probably that the Snoqualmie recognized that birds are distributed according to ecological niches:

Certain birds are seen in each locality. Each one has a certain thing to go after.

Snoqualmi

Mammals

Skins and mounted specimens in the Burke Museum were used in identification of the mammals. Species have been listed according to Larrison's Washington Mammals (1970).

Both informants were interested in the habits of wild creatures, and obviously enjoyed sharing the rich tradition of Coast Salish animal lore. Jerry's observations of animal behavior are listed in the beginning paragraph of each section, immediately following the native term for the animal. Ed Davis recalled all of the Snoqualmie animal names provided by Jerry Kanim.

Trowbridge Shrew <əə> Sorex trowbridgii The shrew was recognized as a burrowing animal. It was observed in the lowlands. Although the informant could not recall the specific name, he was certain that this animal is distinct from the mole.

Shrew Mole <əə> Neurotrichus gibbi gibbi The shrew mole was recognized by the informant, although he could not remember the name.

Townsend's Mole ṗilk̇či Scapanus townsendi townsendi Moles are seldom seen. They live underground, an may be observed bringing dirt to the surface. The snout and front feet are used to dig the soil. [ṗəłq̇ʷəčiʷ ṗəlqači?ʷ puɫyə? {LD 331}] Moles were not killed or used in any way.

Folklore: If one finds a dead mole, it means that misfortune will occur, Jerry did not actually believe that a dead mole is a warning.

Little Brown Bat pəpəčdya qəbqəbəyus {LD 288} Myotis lucifugus Bats were classified as birds. They were known to be nocturnal in habit. Bats were clubbed by children.

Folklore: Children were told that they should fast for three days after killing a bat. Chief Kanim could not recall the significance of this belief.

Pika sčit Ochotona princeps The name is onomatopoetic. This animal is seen high in the mountains, where it builds hay piles among the rocks. It feeds on leaves and the outer bark of small bushes. The pika was never hunted.

Snowshoe Hare k̇ʷəčdi? {LD 344} Snowshoe Hares were formerly abundant, but now they are scarce. Hares are active throughout the year. Food includes grass, sprouts, and leaves. This animal makes a nest of dry leaves under logs, gathering the leaves in summer for this purpose. In winter these animals were often hunted for sport, and the young were taken as pets. After tracking them into the nest, they could be easily taken by hand.

Pets: Children caught rabbits for pets. They swung them by the ears singing təlaya, xʷəq xʷəq təlaya. This means we will have good weather.

Mythology: Rabbit was a gambler. His brother was Grizzly Bear. They played slahal, Rabbit sang "saxˍ saxˍ təlaya." According to Jerry,

Snoqualmi

When the North wind comes, it will be clear. Rabbit always won.

Townsend Chipmunk sqʷəčɬ Eu<u>tamias townsendi</u> The chipmunk nests in hollow logs and trees. It feeds on berries. [x̌ix̌ipič̓ʷ sk̓ʷəƛ̓čʷ sqətx̌λ̌əx̌, sk̓ʷətɬ {LD 298}]

<u>Food</u>: This animal was hunted with bow and arrow. It was taken only in summer, during the berry season. The whole chipmunk was roasted over the fire.

<u>Charms</u>: According to Ballard's Snoqualmie informant, Lucy Bill,

> The one who casts a love charm may go away. If he does not return within five days, she will kill herself. Only a few knew of this mixture. One mixture consists of the heart and nose of a chipmunk, and the heart of a very good bird of the prairie, with a little grass thrown in. This is called pləx.

Chief Kanim had also heard of such a charm, although he had never paid much attention to "those things."

<u>Mythology</u>: The chipmunk's stripes are explained in the following story, told by Jerry:

> Chipmunk lived with his grandmother xəxəlkayakayd. One day he was picking berries, and he said, "I will eat the ripe berries and save the green berries for grandmother."
> Then he saw swayuqʷ, one of the five ogre sisters who ate children. She tried to coax him to come down to the ground. As he was running under a log, she scraped him.
> That is why he has stripes.

Mountain Beaver šaẁkʷɬ <u>Aplodontia rufa rufa</u> This animal lives in underground burrows. It feeds on berries, bark, and leaves which are carried to the nest. Mountain beavers were very abundant near blackberry patches.

<u>Food</u>: The mountain beaver wa taken in summer after it had grown fat on a diet of berries and leaves. The meat was considered best at this time of the year. The informant could not recall the methods used in hunting this animal.

The whole beaver was roasted flat on a stick. It was eaten only in summer, and was not considered an important item in the diet.

<u>Materials</u>: Jerry could not recall how the fur was used.

Hoary Marmot sq̓ʷiqʷəd {LD 329} <u>Marmota caligata</u> The marmot or Whistling Jack is found high in the mountains, near rock slides. The call resembles a whistle. This animal was never hunted. [swaxʷəbš]

Folklore: There is a power that brings wealth. It is called yabadad. The whistling marmot brings that power [Betsy Losier to Ballard].

Douglas's Squirrel sqədʷuʔ {LD 358} <u>Tamiasciurus douglasi</u> This squirrel is both arboreal and terrestrial in habit. It was not used in any way. [sqʷiʔəqʷ]

Northern Flying Squirrel skədʷu skədʷu <u>Glaucomys sabrinus</u> The Flying squirrel is strictly arboreal; it may be observed gliding from one tree to another. The tail acts as a rudder, so that the animal can change direction when it is flying. When the tail is raised, the squirrel goes down; when the tail is lowered, the animal glides upward.[18]
Jerry believed that the flying squirrel is active day and night. It was not used in any way.

Mythology: The creation of the flying squirrel is explained in the Snoqualmie version of Wolves and the Flying Squirrel (Haeberlin 1924: 427-428).

> Long ago, flying squirrel was a bad animal. Wolf killed him, and cut off his nose, and threw it into the cedar. Wolf made the flying squirrel out of this nose. For this reason, the flying squirrel does not kill the Indians today.

Beaver stəqaxʷ {LD 289} The beaver builds several beaver houses in the water, just above the dam. Canals are dug, extending from the house or lodge to shore. The food of the beaver consists of roots and bark.
This animal was hunted year around. The water in the beaver dam was drained during the night, and the following morning the animals were first driven out of the lodge by a man who stood on top, shoving a long pole into the lodge. Stakes were set with one end raised, so that the animals were forced to run toward the top of the canal, where they could be easily speared. Stakes were also set in a vertical position, so that when they were disturbed, the beaver could be shot by a gun placed under water.
The beaver house was not completely destroyed; a few animals were left "for seed."

Food: The meat is considered very choice. It was usually baked and steamed in a pit. A sausage made of blood and fat was cooked together with the meat. Fat and blood were wrapped around a small stick, and placed in the animal's intestine. The stick was removed when the sausage was cooked. The sausage was three inches long.

Chief Kanim emphasized that only important, "respected" people. or older persons ate this sausage [made of beaver blood and fat]. The blood was regarded as medicine, since the Beaver ate roots and bark. The meat was rarely boiled or roasted.

Materials: Beaver fur was used for clothing; however my principal informant could not recall how it was used.

Pets: Jerry mentioned that beavers are easily tamed and make good pets.

---

[18] The gliding of the flying squirrel is always downward (Larrison 1970: 77).

My cousin Charlie Kanim had two pet beavers. They went away when they got older. Beavers were often kept as pets.

Mythology: The large flat tail of the beaver is explained in th story of Beaver and his brother Muskrat. Chief Kanim gave the following version:

> Beaver and Muskrat were brothers. Beaver said, "Let's trade tails. My tail is too little." Beaver pulled his tail out and put it on muskrat. muskrat dived with the little tail and liked it. Beaver put on muskrat's big tail.
> Beaver said, "What do you think, brother ?" "Fine," said muskrat, "that tail was too big for me anyhow."

Mouse kʷiƛad {LD 332} Rat k̓ədayuʔ k̓ədayuʔ {LD 344}

Folklore: Mice and rats are regarded as thieves. The children were told never to accept powers from mice or rats, because these animals steal, and are considered most undesirable (Haeberlin and Gunther 1930: 37-41).[19]

> The people told the children, "Don't listen to a bad spirit. Don't accept Rat or Mouse who steal, because they are bad powers."[20]

Muskrat sqʷədix̌ {LD 332} <u>Ondatra zibethicus</u> The muskrat is found in marshes where it feeds on roots and grasses. This animal build houses of rushes about four feet in height. It also builds underground nests in the banks. [q̓əɬq̓əɬ]

Food: The meat was roasted on a stick over the fire. This animal was rarely used for food.

Materials: Muskrat fur was considered the best. It was used for caps, shirts, and vests. My principal informant said that caps were worn by both men and women. Four pelts were used to make a cap, which was lined with the belly fur.

Mythology: The long narrow tail of the muskrat is explained in Jerry's version of beaver and muskrat.

Pacific Jumping Mouse skekəwats <u>Zapus trinotatus trinotatus</u>

> My informant believed that this species was not a true mouse, but rather a completely different type of animal. He noted that the word skekəwats resembles skegʷats the native term for deer.[21]

---

[19] Snoqualmie men wore caps of wolf, otter, beaver, and bears, with the fur on the outside.
[20] Both Jerry and Ed agreed on this statement.
[21] Thom Hess (1979) has traced dialect changes in a word to wave-like patterns precipitated by the tabooing of an original word that was close in sound to the name of a person who had died.

Coyote sbiaw sbiyaw {LD 302} <u>Canis latrans</u> The coyote was seen in wooded areas. This animal will attack deer and dig out mountain beaver, coyote feed on anything including rotten food.[22]

This animal was not killed or used in any way. Jerry said that the fur was not used because it smells.

<u>Mythology</u>: Arthur Ballard (1927: 75) has recorded the following story:

How Coyote Stole Towhee's Eyes

Somebody stole the eyes of coyote. He replaced them with the tips of a red fungus (gwuskwiokkalop). He picked two of these for eyes. He went on. He met Towhee (sxaweuq). He asked Towhee to look up. "Can you see that?" "No." "Oh, your eyes are weak, you had better wear mine." "Very well."

Coyote exchanged eyes, putting the eyes of Towhee on himself, and his own on Towhee. Now towhee cannot see plainly.

According to Jack Stillman,

Coyote exercised the power of transforming to some degree, but he was beaten, and Dokʷibəɬ became the most powerful, and coyote became a mere animal, as we see him today.

Gray Wolf stq̓ayuʔ {LD 274} Wolves were formerly abundant in Snoqualmie territory. Now they are seldom seen. Wolves were known to attack deer, though it is mostly shy and nocturnal (Larrison 1970: 144). This animal was never hunted.

<u>Supernatural Beliefs</u>: One who obtained the Wolf for a power would be a skillful hunter or fighter. Haeberlin and Gunther (1930: 74) write

This spirit brought success in hunting and fighting, and also was good for handling dead bodies. Little Sam had this spirit and could hunt deer.

<u>Mythology</u>: In the story The Wolves and the Flying squirrel (Haeberlin 1924: 427-428), five Wolf brothers who were the first Snoqualmie met flying squirrel. Four of the brothers were killed by flying squirrel, the youngest Wolf cut off the nose of flying squirrel and made the harmless flying squirrel as we see him today.

Domestic Dog sqʷəbayuʔʷ sqʷubayʔ {LD 306} <u>canis sp</u> Dogs are the only domestic animal found among the people of the Northwest Coast (Amoss 1975).

Vancouver (1801, II: 130-131) writes about the dogs near Port Orchard,

---

[22] Coyote is both a carnivore and a carrion feeder, existing mostly on animal flesh (Larrison 1970: 142).

They were all shorn as close to the skin as sheep are in England; and so compact were their fleeces that large portions could be lifted up by a corner without causing any separation. They were composed of a mixture of a coarse kind of wool, with very fine long hair, capable of being spun into yarn.

There were several varieties of dogs on the Pacific coast. Suckley (1859: 112) describes Indian dogs,

The dogs of the Indians of the Pacific coast differ among themselves. Some common kinds are believed to be a cross of the coyote. Throughout Oregon the native dog is largely intermingled with imported dogs; but the Clallam on Puget Sound have a white dog with very soft hair, which is sheared like the wool of sheep, and of which they make blankets.

All the Clallam dogs I saw were pure white, but they have the sharp nose, pointed ear, and hang-dog thievish appearance of other Indian dogs.

Materials: The Snohomish and the Klallam raised dogs for their wool. When these dogs were sheared the forelegs were tied together and the wool was cut with a stone knife. The wool was often dyed pink with hemlock or alder bark. The Snoqualmie, Skykomish, and Nisqually did not have these dogs (Haeberlin and Gunterh 1930: 30).

Stuckley (1859: 112) had a blanket made of dog's wool mixed with duck feathers.

Supernatural Beliefs: Ed Davis mentioned that a dog might be a sklaletut:

If a dog talks to you, it will be a sklaletut. You could contact a spirit with a dog too, and when that dog speaks to you, then you'll answer, and that dog will say, "I'll be with you, and I'll see that you're going to get along." And then when he grows up to be past middle age man or past 50 or 60, then he'll sing that song, what he learned from that dog.

Black Bear sčətxʷəd {LD 288} Ursus americanus altifrontalis Jerry observed that the brown bear isqʷitil = brown is a color phase of the black bear xebač = black. Bears are still abundant and may be seen in swamps early in the spring feeding on skunk cabbage. Huckleberries, salmonberries, elderberries, and fish are also eaten. This animal was often seen at night, eating salmon. During the winter, the bear sleeps either at the base of a tree, or in a hollow tree ċwals bear's winter home. [spaʔc]

Bears were hunted the year around. Sleeping bears were smoked out of hollow trees and shot. In winter, they were also trapped near streams, where they went for water. A stick was shoved into the tree to distract the bear. On the other side of the tree, a fire was built. Holes were dug around the tree so that the smoke drove the bear out. Then he was shot. Jerry had never seen a bear trap.

A trap was made, but I never saw one. Meat and fish were put in the trap. When he grabs the meat, the whole trap, loaded with rocks and sticks fell down on him. I never saw one although I heard of this trap.

Ballard (ms) records the bear trap as stɬaladgad. The bear deadfall, used near a creek, is listed as siyalap.

Food: The meat was steamed (skəls steaming) and baked above ground. Jerry thought that bear meat was very rich. Large rocks were placed over an alder fire. Then the charcoal was removed, and cedar limbs and meat were set on hot rocks. Water was sprinkled over the meat, which was then covered by mats and leaves. Meat was steamed until the rocks cooled.

Materials: According to Jerry skins were used for rugs and blankets. The Snoqualmie, Snohomish, Skykomish, and Nisqually had bear skin and seal skin capes without sleeves.

Folklore: Warren Snyder (1968b: 78-79) has recorded the following story, told by Jerry Kanim.

The Origin of the Seasons

Bear has a younger brother, Rabbit. One day Bear said, "All right now, we'll gamble. Then, if you beat me, it will be the way that you want it. If I beat you, it will be the way that I want it with respect to the way day and night will be. Now then, we'll gamble. And if you're going to beat me, sing your spirit power song." The Bear said, "If I beat you, it will be the way I want it."

Then they gambled. The Bear sat at the board and the rabbit sang his power song from the north. He sang it and said, "Clear, clear the sky. Dry, dry, the sky." He called the freezing weather and cold. That is the song of the Rabbit. Rabbit wanted it to get cold.

Then Bear sings for cloudy weather. bear says, "Get warm, get warm." He calls for clouds.

Then they were gambling. The Bear was beaten by Rabbit. When the Rabbit would be outguessed (made to fall) by Bear, the Bear would jump at the Rabbit until the Bear was being beaten by the Rabbit. Rabbit won.

It froze and became cold. It would crackle until it froze. The sky would clear. Bear said, "You beat me. Now it will be the way you want it."

Then for winning, Rabbit got the freezing weather. So now it freezes and gets cold.

Jerry said that this bear speaks in the Snoqualmie language.

The Bear talks our language. When he is badly hurt, he cries "A-da-da!" This cry is the same as the cry of pain in our language.[23]

Grizzly Bear sčatqɬəb stəbtabəl {LD 288} <u>Ursus arctos horribilis</u> Jerry said that in the early days grizzly bears from eastern Washington were occasionally seen near Mount Si. Jerry had never seen a grizzly. This animal was not hunted. Suckley (1859: 120) writes about the grizzly bear,

---

[23] "A bear in pain will bawl and sob like a human" (Van Wormer 1966: 99).

I have never received any intimation of its existence in the western part of Washington territory; but in the Rocky mountain portion it is rather common.

Supernatural Beliefs: Grizzly bear, black bear, cougar, wildcat, and coon were all sklaletut and xʷdab spirits, effective both in war and in curing. Jack Stillman said that there was an old Indian doctor at Fall City who had Grizzly Bear and Rainbow powers. "He was like a woman." Jerry Kanim recalled that this man, known as haywič was a "killing doctor." He lived alone. Ed Davis remembers haywič who was Lucy Johnnie's uncle. Lucy Johnnie told Ed that haywič has a woman's sklaletut, and therefore could not marry, because his wife would not live.[24]

Mythology: Haeberlin (1924: 377-8) has recorded the story of Dokʷibeł and the Animals in which grizzly bear was originally a person and lived with his brothers and cousins, Black Bear, Wildcat, Cougar, and Raccoon. They all lived together in one house. Because Grizzly Bear was very powerful and killed many Indians, Fox cut off Grizzly Bear's nose and killed him, while he was asleep. Fox changed the nose into Grizzly Bear, and told the Bear that he would not be so powerful.

Skykomish attitudes toward the Grizzly Bear are described by Haeberlin and Gunther (1930: 73).

> The Grizzly Bears were Skykomish before the world was changed. Therefore, the grizzly bears would never kill a Skykomish, even if the man has no grizzly bear spirit. When a Skykomish met a grizzly bear, he sang the grizzly bear spirit songs, and the bear would not attack him, but would sing and dance and then go away. When a Skykomish woman met a grizzly bear, she drummed with a stick on the bottom of a coiled basket and sang. A Skykomish would never kill a grizzly bear.

When Little Sam was young, his grandfather wanted him to get the grizzly bear spirit. He could have done this because he was partly Skykomish. He went to the trail where the grizzly bears pass but none came so Little Sam did not get the spirit (Haeberlin and Gunther 1930: 377-8).

Raccoon bəlups x̌ax̌alus {LD 244} Procyon lotor This animal lives in trees and hollow logs. It is active the year around. Coons were formerly very abundant until 1925, when they were killed by Cougar Peterson's dogs. Raccoons were never used for food.

Materials: Jerry recalled that the skin was used for caps and quivers. Quivers were made with the fur on the outside and fastened with a buckskin strap. According to Haeberlin and Gunther (1930: 38), among the Nisqually, little boys wore caps of coonskin. The Snohomish men also wore coon skin caps. Some of the Snohomish caps had the ears on them (Haeberlin and Gunther 1930: 38).

---

[24] Original note # 28 "Lucy Johnnie was mother-in-law of Mr Davis. haywič lived in a cabin near McCann's Shingle Mill at the mouth of Raging River. He was reported to be 130 years of age at the time of his death in 1970 (The Valley Record, Centennial Edition June 1972: 1, 11).

Supernatural Beliefs: Coon was a brave animal. One who had bəlups for a power would become a skillful fighter, according to Jerry.

Marten piq̓s {LD 329} Martes caurina The marten was seen at high elevation. It was never killed or used in any way [but it "is a valuable fur-bearing mammal," Larrison 1968: 153.] [səltups]

Fisher sčačəb Martes pennanti   Fishers lived in wooded areas near marshes and rivers. Although formerly very common, they are now scarce. This animal was not used [though natives who hunted in the Cascades and Blue Mountains made quivers of fisher skins, Suckley 1859: 114].

Supernatural beliefs: Doctor Bill Kanim (łəlčkədb) received sčačəb for a power. In the sbitidaq or Soul Recovery [Redeeming] Ceremony łəlčkədb was the leader.

Long-tailed Weasel łəčəb {LD 373} Mustela frenata Jerry recognized several color phases; white, brown, and yellow. He had also observed white weasels throughout the year. [łiłq̓əb {LD 373}]
   The weasel preys on deer, biting the neck.[25] My principal informant could not remember how weasels were caught.
Materials: Jerry stated that the fur was used as trimming on caps.

   The men among the Nisqually parted their hair in the middle, and either braided it or let it hang loose. Sometimes they wore a band of mink or weasel around the head (Haeberlin and Gunther 1930: 38).

Mink c̓əbəl̓qid {LD 331} Lutreola lutreola The mink lives in swamps and dry areas. It preys on mountain beaver, fish, and frogs. This animal is never used. [bəščəbʷ piq̓s]

Mythology: Mink plays an important role in Coast Salish myths and Folklore. Haeberlin (1924: 382-383) has recorded the following story,

Dokʷibəł Transforms Mink

Mink caught a dog salmon and roasted it. When Dokʷibəł found this out, he put Mink to sleep. He ate the salmon and smeared the fat on Mink's hands and mouth. As Dokʷibəł went away, Mink woke up and saw him. He reprimanded Dokʷibəł.
   The latter turned back and converted Mink into different forms. The first time, at Mink's own request, he changed him into a doll. Mink wanted to be a doll because the girls would play with him. As soon as Dokʷibəł turned away, Mink attained his real form again and scolded Dokʷibəł.

---

[25] "Weasels themselves are ferocious little creatures utterly without fear, whose jaws lock when they bite into a rabbit or chicken. They quietly seize the blood vein of the neck of a fowl and kill their victim before it can warn others in the flock" (Packard 1961: 53).

Snoqualmi

The latter then changed Mink into a flat rock. Mink wanted to have this form because the girls would sit down on him. As soon as Dokʷibəɬ turned away, he changed back to his real form and scolded Dokʷibəɬ.

The latter then changed Mink into a tree. Mink liked this because the girls would sit astride on him when they went bathing. Again Mink assumed his real form and scolded Dokʷibəɬ.

Then he was changed into a sandy beach. This also pleased Mink for the girls would slide down on him. Once more, as soon as Dokʷibəɬ started to go, Mink attained his real form.

Now Dokʷibəɬ lost his patience, so he turned around, split Mink right in two, tore off his nose, and threw it into a snag and called it "Mink!"

This is the end of Mink.

Ed Davis tells this amusing sx̌ʷiyab.

Mink and Weasel

The Mink come along on the river and he found a fish and he start cookin' that fish in a fire. Then he turned this fish he's cooking over so the other side could get cooked. And all that time, the weasel was watchin' him.

And he lay down. This Mink lay down and he fell asleep, and he went to sleep, and while he was sleeping, why this Weasel come along, and he started eatin' his fish. Then when he got done eatin' everything, he took his hand where he was handlin' this fish he was eatin'.

He walks up to the Mink while he was asleep, and he starts rubbin' it on his lips and rubbin' it on his teeth. And the Weasel went off and left him then.

And he finally woke up, rub his eyes and looked around, and no more fish. He knew he didn't eat that fish, but while he was thinkin' that, he started in lickin' his lips, and he tastes the fish in his lips. He says, "I'm sure I didn't eat that fish. It must have happened."

But anyway, the Weasel he went off and left him, after he pulled that joke on him.

Well they're human beings at that time, and they turned into animals after that, Mink and Weasel.

I just picked that up. Come to my mind. my mother-in-law (Lucy Johnnie) used to talk about it, tellin' about it. And we would sit up an evening, after supper, and she'd start tellin' stories. They call that sx̌ʷiyab in the native tongue.

That's when those people turn into animals when the Dokʷibəɬ came along.

Striped Skunk sq̓əbya {LD 354} <u>Mephitis mephitis</u> The skunk is found in hollow trees or logs. It is gregarious; often as many as twenty animals may be observed in a single den. Skunks are active the year around. Jerry noted that skunks are sill abundant in Snoqualmie territory. This animal was never hunted.

River Otter sq̓aƛ {LD 336} <u>Lutra canadiensis pacifica</u> Otters are seen near streams where they feed on fish. During the spawning season, this animal swims with the salmon pretending to spawn while it preys on the fish. The otter's den is in a bank near the water. The otter is a playful animal. It was seen playing on logs or sliding on its belly down otter slides. Jerry recognized light and dark color phases. He could not remember how the otter was trapped.

Food: The otter was not used for food. It was emphasized that the people of the Suiattle River eat otter, but the Snoqualmie do not.

Materials: My principal informant stated that the pelt was worn around the waist, and fastened by tying the two ends together. According to Haeberlin and Gunther (1930: 37-39), the skin was also used for caps and sleeve trimming. A wealthy man often braided otter skin in his hair for ceremonial occasions.

Supernatural Beliefs: One who received the otter for a power would become a skillful diver, fisherman, or hunter. The otter could also appear as a doctor's power. Jerry said that his uncle, Old Man Sam, had otter power.

Mythology: The following story was told by Jerry (cf. Snyder 1968b: 80-83):

> A Snohomish man had received the spirit of swoqʷad. He came here, and married a Snoqualmie girl. He had Loon tattooed on his forearm.
> This Snoqualmie man received otter for power. Otter told him, "Boy, look at me; I can cross from lake to lake under the ground. You can do the same. I also have runways from any lake underground and above."
> The two men went hunting. They stopped by Lake Langois ('bit = fish stew). There Snoqualmie said, " There is a hole in this lake. The hole goes deep." The Snohomish didn't believe the Snoqualmie; he said that "I must see this hole before I believe you."
> The Snoqualmie man said, "I'll go first; you come after. My power is Otter," said the Snoqualmie. The Snohomish man said, "My power is Loon."
> The Snoqualmie went down into the lake; he waited for the Snohomish. The Snohomish went down the hole. He came out near Everett. His head was gone. The old people saw the body. They recognized their son. This shows that the otter is a more powerful animal than Loon.

Cougar swəwa <u>Felis concolor</u> The cougar or mountain lion preys on deer. This animal was never hunted. Jerry had never heard of a power from cougar.
Jerry told the following story,

> My brother-in-law Joe once saw a cougar fighting two deer. He caught one by the throat, the other by the tail. The cougar crushed the rubs of one deer with his tail, and killed the other by biting at the throat.

Bobcat pəčab {LD 293} <u>Lynx rufus</u> The principal informant noted that the bobcat is both terrestrial and arboreal in habitat. It feeds on poultry. The bobcat was not killed or used in any way.

Elk kʷagʷičəd {LD 308} <u>Cervus elaphus roosevelti</u> The animal was formerly abundant near Silver lake, according to Chief Kanim.[26] Willy Martin said that,

> They used to hunt elk years ago on the Sultan River clean down to Marysville.

> Neither Jerry nor Ed had seen elk. Suckley (1859, XII: 133-134) writes,

> The elk extends throughout the mountainous timbered districts of Washington and Oregon territories and all the way down the Coast to San Francisco. Elk are found in the Rocky, Cascade, and Coast ranges of mountains. They run in large droves following well-beaten trails, and at that season are an easy prey to the hunter.

Black-tailed Deer sqigʷəc {LD 304} <u>Odocoileus hemionus columbianus</u> Deer were formerly very common in Snoqualmie territory. They fed on grass and leaves. Their enemy was the cougar. Deer were hunted at any time of the year. However, it was emphasized that the meat was considered best in summer and undesirable in winter. The doe was never killed.

Poison arrows and snares were used in hunting deer. A spring pole snare was set on open trails. The loop was made of bear grass, and was tied to the upper end of a small growing tree (hazel or vine maple). Deer were seldom caught by this method, since the meat is not good if the animal fights for any length of time.

The Snoqualmie used dogs for hunting deer. Chief Kanim explained,

> My "uncle" Charlie Kanim caught deer with dogs. Deer were driven into the stream where they could be shot from a canoe.

Food: Deer was the principal item of food. The meat was barbecued and dried. Haeberlin and Gunther (1930: 23) state that deer meat was wrapped with grease in a strip of cedar bark and placed over hot stones. Jerry said that the liver and heart were opened and roasted on a stick [as a snack].

Materials: Deer skin was tanned on both sides and used for shirts, trousers, leggings, moccasins, and belts. A cluster of dew claws was tied to buckskin, and used as a rattle. Jerry emphasized that only persons who had certain powers could use this type of rattle.

The spinal cord was removed and dried. It was split into long strips, and used for fishing line, thread, and string (tidš). Deer horns were boiled and used for spear points. The deer stomach was dried and used as a sack. Salmon eggs were placed in this sack, and tied with bear grass. Haeberlin and Gunther (1930: 39) write that deer tallow was rubbed in the hair to make it smooth.

---

[26] A Silver Lake in Snohomish county is at T 29 N R 11 E.

Snoqualmi

<u>Trade</u>: According to Ballard, buckskins were traded with the Yakima for bear grass. Skins were traded for horses at Yakima. The rate was ten deerskins for one big horse (Haeberlin and Gunther 1930: 39).

<u>Mythology</u>: Chief Kanim told the following story, which explains the creation of this animal.

Dokʷibəɬ and Deer

When Dokʷibəɬ was travelling. sqigʷəč heard that Dokʷibəɬ was changing things. He was sharpening a bone so he could change the transformer himself.

"sqigʷəč You are singing a fine song. Sing again. What are you making?, Dokʷibəɬ said. Transformer said, "Let me see what you are making." Deer showed it to him. Changer stuck the bone in sqigʷəč's hand. Then transformer said, "The people will come and you will be food for the Indians."

He clapped his hands. sqigʷəč became a deer. You can find that bone in the wrist of a deer.

<u>Folklore</u>: Deer were often kept as pets. A woman must not break the deer bones to take out the marrow till the hunt is over, or the hunter will break his leg. Jerry also explained that

When my uncle would hunt he would sleep by himself, keep away from his wife, and bathe, so the animals would not pick up the scent.

Chief Kanim had never heard of a power received from the deer.

Cascade Mountain Goat sx̌ʷiƛ̕əyʔ {LD 316} <u>Oreamnos americanus</u> goats were seen near rocky slopes, high in the mountains. Jerry noted that this animal does not permit close approach by man. They were hunted with bow and arrow at any time of the year. A few able-bodied women went along.
Samuel Hancock (1927: 124) writes:

I learned from them that mountain goat is very difficult to kill, being very wild and only found on the side of precipices and rocky mountains, where it is almost impossible for a human to climb, yet the Indians engage in their pursuit with great interest, and from appearances pretty successfully, for this party of five had been out three days, and had procured twelve of fine order, saying they had seen a great many but they were hia squos ["very wary" in Wawa jargon], afraid of men; they availed themselves of out campfire to cook some of the meat which I found deliciously flavored and very tender.

<u>Food</u>: The meat was considered superior to deer. It was barbecued before packing it home. Sticks were placed over a framework of upright poles. The meat was laid on the top. A fire was kept going underneath all night until meat was partly cooked. The meat was flattened by trampling. The moisture was squeezed out.

Snoqualmi

<u>Materials</u>: According to Haeberlin and Gunther (1930: 38), the Skykomish wore caps made of a mountain goat head with the animal's horns and ears intact. Chief Kanim said that higher class persons had blankets made of mountain goat wool. The Coast Salish used a roller loom to weave these blankets (1930: 30-31).

> Goat horn was considered best for spear points, according to my principal informant. Charcoal and pitch were mashed on the string wrapped around the spear point, to keep the string from wearing.

<u>Supernatural Beliefs</u>: Chief Pat Kanim was a great leader because he had a "good" power, according to his nephew Chief Jerry Kanim.

> My "uncle" Pat Kanim received mountain goat for a spirit. He became a brave man. When he was a boy, he went to a mountain and heard the Marmot sq̓ʷiq̓ʷiəd, who spoke to him, "I am not the one you are looking for. You are searching for someone higher up." He sang a song, telling him to go to the mountain goat.
> The mountain goat said, "Look at me, boy. I am watching the people. I am higher than all the others. You will be like me. You will be a high man." That is why Pat Kanim became Chief.

<u>Mythology</u>: The creation of this animal is explained in "Transformer" told by Chief Kanim in 1955 (Snyder 1968b: 30-31):

> Transformer went on, high into rocky mountains. He came upon some people high up in the rocks. He asked them: "How do you like these rocky mountains where you are?"
> The people said: "We like the place where we are." Transformer said, "What would you like to have me make you?" The people said, "Make us what you wish."
> Transformer said: "I'm changing everything. I'll make you mountain goats. You will be here on the high rocky mountains. You'll be meat for the people who are coming soon. Your skin will be used for their clothes. Your fur will make good blankets for the future people."

SUMMARY

In evaluating this material, one must first consider that the data have been obtained primarily from two informants who had not actually participated in functioning native culture.

In consideration of the fact that recent biotic changes have also made it almost impossible to observe wild creatures in their normal habitats, it would seem that my informants were unusually efficient game watchers, well aware of the great diversity of an life. Jerry Kanim was not only a competent naturalist, but could also portray with extraordinary skillthose memories of the old way of life.

It is probable that typical Coast Salish life style – seasonal migration from clam digging sites on the saltwater to the foothills of the Cascade mountains, must have greatly extended one's knowledge of the unique wildlife of the north west. Moreover, the belief that animal actions are significant in the search for spirits (sklaletut or xʷdab) might create a heightened awareness and sensitivity toward the total environment.

Man's place in nature is reflected in mythology and folk tales. Dokʷibəł, the Transformer, changed the Mythological era into the world of today, creating sticks, rocks, people, birds, salmon, and all other game.

It was believed that Dokʷibəł came and "settled everything," transforming the people of the past into all the contemporary forms of animal and human life. Since the Bear and Meadowlark speak the Snoqualmie language, the people can therefore understand the calls of these two creatures. Both informants, Jerry and Ed, emphasized that this was proof that animals and birds were formerly people.

One received strength and power from the deep involvement with wild creatures. Human emotional needs, particularly prestige and success in hunting, fishing, or curing, were closely interwoven with animal actions, and were explained within the guardian spirit concept.

Supernatural experiences usually involved meeting an animal or bird who appeared in half-human form, hopefully conferring powers needed for an appropriate self-concept. Thus both informants recalled that children were told never to accept Rat or Mouse as sklaletut because these animals steal.

However, Loon, Fisher, or Cutthroat Trout were "good spirits." A person who received a good spirit might become a leader or a doctor. For example, it was mentioned that Chief Patkanim became a great leader of his people because he had received mountain goat for a spirit. The mountain goat lived high in the mountains, and could look down on all the other animals.

In the search for a spirit or power, human or animal frontiers change. Meeting an animal in a dream-like state was a profoundly creative experience; perhaps it was this highly significant alteration of a young child's perceptual state which revealed important insights and understandings concerning the elusive animal world.

Supernatural concepts not only provided a basis for a highly individualized interpretation of animal behavior, but also transfigured animal and human boundaries. Is there a possibility that these two planes overlap? It would appear that the duality of the two worlds -- animal and human -- is not always clearly defined. Perhaps it is the common emotional language which often reveals the unity of creatures.

For example, by projecting such human attributes as curiosity or insight into wild animals, the Snoqualmie could understand the call notes of the meadowlark who asks, "Where are you going?"

It is probable that the Snoqualmie had also developed concepts of animal behavior that may not necessarily be integrated with the supernatural world. Thus Jerry Kanim recognized that certain birds have specific predatory habits, as well as ecological niches and life styles. The observation that changes in pelage and coloration among mammals are correlated with seasonal variations in climate is perhaps based upon a foundation of practical skills needed in hunting.

The critical attitude regarding time-honored explanations of bird migrations probably reflects the inevitable breakdown of native conceptual systems.

The available data suggest that among the Snoqualmie, man's close relationship with nature may be explained in terms of typical Coast Salish attitudes toward wildlife.

(1) The belief that people and animals are friends. "The animal 'agrees' to help a youngster," according to Ed Davis.

(2) The concept that man is separate in the world of living creatures.

Chief Kanim speaks:

Dokʷibəɬ stuck the bone in [deer's] hand. Then he said, "The people will come, and you will be the food for the Indians." He clapped his hands. sqigʷəc became a deer.

Bibliography

Amoss, Pamela 1975 "Ancient Man's Best Friend." Pacific Search 10 (2): 16-17.

Ballard, Arthur C 1927 Some Tales of the Southern Puget Sound Salish. University of Washington Publications in Anthropology 2 (3): 57-81.

　　　　1929 Mythology of Southern Puget Sound. University of Washington Publications in Anthropology 3 (1): 31-150.

　　　　1957 The Salmon Weir on Green River in Western Washington Davidson Journal of Anthropology 3 (1): 37-53.

Bates, Dawn, Thom Hess, and Vi Hilbert 1994 Lushootseed Dictionary. Seattle: University of Washington Press.

Carrighar, Sally 1965 Wild Heritage. New York: Ballantine Books.

Castetter, Edward 1944 "The Domain of Ethnobiology." The American Naturalist 78: 158-170.

Dembeck, Herman 1965 Animals and Man. Garden City, New York: Natural History Press.

Gunther, Erna 1928 A Further Analysis of the First Salmon Ceremony. University of Washington Publications in Anthropology 2 (5): 129-173.

　　　　1973 Ethnobotany of Western Washington. Seattle: University of Washington Press.

Haeberlin, Herman 1924 Mythology of Puget Sound. Journal of American Folklore 37 (143-144): 371-438.

Haeberlin, Herman, and Erna Gunther 1930 The Indians of Puget Sound. Seattle: University of Washington Press.

Hancock, Samuel 1927 The Narrative of Samuel Hancock 1845-1860. London: Harrop and Co Ltd.

Hess, Thom 1966 Snohomish Chameleon Morphology. International Journal of American Linguistics 32:350-56.

　　　　1971 Prefix Constituent With /xʷ/. Studies in Northwest Indian Languages. James Hoard and Thom Hess, eds. Sacramento Anthropological Society, Paper 11: 43-69.

　　　　1973 Agent in a Coast Salish Language. International Journal of American Linguistics 39: 89-94.

　　　　1976 Dictionary of Puget Salish. Seattle: University of Washington Press.

　　　　1977 Lushootseed Dialects. Anthropological Linguistics 19 (9): 403-419.

　　　　1979 Central Coast Salish Words for Deer: Their Wavelike Distribution. International Journal of American Linguistics 45: 5-16.

　　　　1995 Lushootseed Reader with Introductory Grammar (Four Stories from Edward Sam). University of Montana, Occasional Papers in Lingusitics, 11.

Henderson, J, and JP Harrington 1914 Ethnozoology of the Tewa Indians. Bureau of American Ethnology Bulletin 56.

Krutch, Joseph W, and Paul S Eriksson, eds. 1962 <u>A Treasury of Bird Lore</u>. New York: Doubleday.

Larrison, Earl J, and Klaus Sonnenberg 1968 <u>Washington Birds</u>. Seattle: Seattle Audubon Society.

Larrison, Earl J 1970 <u>Washington Mammals</u>. Seattle: Seattle Audubon Society.

Layon, WE, and W N Tavolga, eds. 1960 <u>Animals Sounds and Communication</u>. Washington, DC: Institute of Biological Sciences.

Levi-Strauss, Claude 1973 <u>The Savage Mind</u>. University of Chicago Press.

Matthiessen, Peter 1962 Our Vanishing Condor, in Krutch and Eriksson: 106-109.

Meigs, Robert C and Clarence Pautzke 1941 Additional Notes on the Life History of the Puget Sound Steelhead (Salmo gairdnerii). Washington State Department of Game, Biological Bulletin 5. Seattle, Washington.

Mery, Fernand 1968 <u>The Life, History, and Magic of the Cat</u>. New York: Madison Square Press, Gross and Dunlap.

{Miller, Jay 2005 Regaining Dr Herman Haeberlin. Seattle: Lushootseed Press. }

Muir, John 1918 <u>Steep Trails</u>: The Writings of John Muir. Boston: Houghton Mifflin, Sierra Edition 8: 256-260.

Packard, Vance 1961 <u>The Human Side of Animals</u>. New York Dial Press.

Pickwell, Gayle 1947 <u>Amphibians and Reptiles of the Pacific States.</u> Stanford University Press.

Rice, Tom 1972 <u>Marine Shells of the Pacific Northwest</u>. Tacoma, Washington: Ellis Robinson Publishing Co.

Schrenkeisen, Ray 1938 <u>Field Book of Fresh Water Fishes of North America</u>. New York: Putnam.

Smith, Marian W, ed. 1949 Indians of the Urban Northwest. New York: <u>Columbia University Contributions to Anthropology</u> 36.

Snyder, Warren A 1968a Southern Puget Sound Salish: Phonology and Morphology. Sacramento, Ca: <u>Sacramento Anthropological Society</u> 8.

1968b Southern Puget Sound Salish: Texts, Place Names, and Dictionary. Sacramento, Ca: <u>Sacramento Anthropological Society</u> 8.

Speck, Frank, and John Witthoft 1947 Some Notable Life Histories in Zoological Folklore. <u>Journal of American Folklore</u> 60: 345-49.

Stebbins, Robert C 1968 <u>A Field Guide to Western Reptiles and Amphibians</u>. Boston: Houghton Mifflin.

Taverner, PA 1926 Birds of Western Canada. Ottawa: Canada Department of Mines, Victoria Memorial Museum, <u>Museum Bulletin</u> 41, Biological Series 10.

Vancouver, George 1801 <u>A Voyage of Discovery to the North Pacific Ocean and Round the World</u>. London.

Van Wormer, Joe 1966 <u>The World of the Black Bear</u>. New York: Lippincott.

Witthoft, John 1946 Birdlore of the Eastern Cherokee. <u>Journal of the Washington Academy of Sciences</u> 36 (11): 372-384.

Yokum, Charles, and Vinson Brown 1971 <u>Wildlife and Plants of the Cascades</u>. American Wildlife Region Series 8. Hearldsburg, Ca: Naturegraph Publishers.

Documents, Letters, Newspapers

Ballard, Arthur C ms. Ethnographic Notes.

Coombs, Howard n.d Letter to Mrs Marge Qualle. Printed by permission of Mary Ferrell, director, Snoqualmie Valley Historical Society, North Bend, Washington,

Cooper, James, George Gibbs, and George Suckley 1859 Reports of Explorations and Surveys, 1853-55. 32nd Congress, 2nd Session, Executive Document 78, vols 10, 12.

Marine Fishes of the North Pacific. Washington DC: US Government Printing Office #0320-00051.

George Suckley 1859 Reports of Explorations and Surveys 1853-55. 32nd Congress, 2nd Session, Executive Document 78, volume XII.

Tilton, James n.d Court of Claims of the US F 274: 402.

Valley Record. 1972 Centennial Edition. June. Snoqualmie Valley.

Index

A

Aberdeen, 16, 52, 96, 102, 165
Adams, 101f, 172, 194, 206, 214, 225f, 231
Adamson, Thelma, 3, 96f, 98, 141, 164f, 170
Allens, 1, 160f
Andrade, Manuel, 14f, 20
Angeline, 201
ayaxos, 142

B

Ballard Seattle, 3f, 55
Ballard, Arthur, 2, 172, 236f, 251f, 264f, 272f, 280f, 288
Bangor, 210
Bay Center, 96f, 103f, 112f
beads, 28, 55, 58f, 62, 107f, 119f, 131, 140f, 150f, 160, 198, 249f
Beavers, 75, 84f, 100f, 135f, 153f, 239, 279f, 285, see mountain beavers
bells, 70f, 122, 147
Bennetts, 70f, 72f, 84f
Bens, 101f
Bertelson, Ernest, 172
Black, Carl, 69
bladders, 33f, 40, 111, 185, 251
blankets, 37f, 50f, 60f, 99, 103f, 112f, 140, 180f, 196f, 217f, 280f, 290f
blimp, 16
Bluejay, 98, 110, 114, 138, 140f, 151f, 211, 222, 250f, 269
Boas, Franz, 2f, 96f, 164
Bogachiel River, 17, 45, 50, 83f
brains, 107, 112
Bruseth, Nels, 1
Burke Museum, 16, 172, 231, 248, 258, 276

C

Calawah, 17, 50f, 64, 83f
canoes, 1, 22, 30f, 36, 40f, 50f, 60f, 123f, 150f, 180, 230f
Cape Flattery, 33f
Cape Rock, 64
Caplanaho, Molly, 60
Captain Mason, 34f, 60
Carnation, WA, 236
Carpenter, Cecilia Svinth, 1
caskets, 70f, 118, 131
cattails, 103f, 170f, 180f, 195, 203f, 243, 260f
Cattle Point, 16
Centralia, 96f, 133f, 149
Chehalis dialects, 99
Chemawa, 138
chickamin money, 125
Chico, 171f, 203
Chief Kitsap, 187f, 210, 231f
Chief Masin, 126
Chief Tsinitiya, 118, 127
Chief Yawnish, 100f, 113f, 138, 142, 147, 150
Chile, 127
Choke, Robbie, 99f, 130
Claquato, 92, 96, 100
Cloquallam, 133
Clubs, social, 17f
Club, tool, 33, 39, 44
coffin, 70f, 118, 130, 140f, 203
Coles, 38, 41, 48, 57f, 67, 72
Columbia University, 2f, 95
Cosmopolis, 19, 96, 112
Costima, Lewy, 128
Coupeville, 41
Cultees, 96, 99
Curly, 178, 191, 204, 209, 212, 217, 227

D

Dangers, 98, 122, 143, 150, 158
Daugherty, RD "Doc", 13f, 16f, 236 #1,
Davis, Ed, 236f, 240f, 250 #6, 290f
Davis, Marion, 99f, 129f, 136f, 141, 158
deaf, 121
death, 48f, 60, 67, 105, 126f, 129f, 135f, 144f 153f, 172f, 187f, 195f, 213f, 251, 273
deformed jaw, 205
dentalia shells, 49, 55, 116, 165f, 198, 248
Destruction Island, 33, 83f
Devil's Hole, 210

diapers, 107, 115, 194, 198f
dice, 134
dicta, 113, 123f, 129, 135f, 145, 164
Dog Eaters, 212
Dokʷibəł, 244, 249, 283f, 288f, 290
Dr Lester, 20, 52, 67
Dr Obi, 67, 72
Dragon, 64
drills, 22
Duvall, 243

E

Eells, Myron, 1
eels, 96, 100, 112, 128, 132, 155f
effigies, 56, 145, 166
Eley, Mary, see Iley
Elk, 18, 29f, 30f, 41f, 44f, 50f, 60f, 84f, 100, 110, 123, 131, 141f, 153f, 173, 183, 218, 223, 287
Elmendorf, William, 1, 163, 231
Enatai, 167
Erland Point, 171, 183
eye of the earth, 110
eyes, 22, 28f, 48, 54, 64f, 101, 112, 122, 133, 135, 140f, 153f, 174f, 203f, 219, 221, 271, 280f

F

fire, 2, 8, 24, 28, 40f, 50f, 60f, 100f, 110f, 120f, 130f, 140f, 150f, 160f, 170f, 80f, 190f, 210f, 220f, 230f, 240f, 250f, 260f, 270f, 280f
firedrill, 28, 106, 183f, 226
Fisher, Lila, 70
Forest Grove, Oregon, 138
Fort Rupert, 191
Frachtenberg, Leo, 20

G

Gambling, 105, 110f, 130f, 151, 160, 202, 270, 280
Gate City, 92, 97, 102, 126, 132, 155
George, Hal, 15
Georges, 21, 22, 51, 53, 61, 89, 90, 91, 99, 124, 143, 167, 169, 171, 172, 168, 171
Gibbs, George, 1, 19, 248 #4

Goodman Creek, 17, 46, 79
Grand Mound, 92, 95f, 101, 106f, 109, 110f, 129
Green River, 216
Grey, Mrs S, 22, 66
Grey, Stanley, 14, 16, 18, 45f, 50f, 60f, 70, 81f
Gunther, Erna, 3, 83, 94, 132, 169, 238

H

Harrington, JP, 2f, 169, 171
heart, 38, 44, 69, 113f, 122, 127, 132, 140f, 158f, 184, 217, 221f, 250f, 260f, 280f, 287
Heck, Silas, 99f, 101, 109, 118, 121, 134f, 138
Hecks, 99f, 110f, 122f, 130f, 140f, 150f
Herring rake, 184
Hess, Thom, 237f, 248 #4, 279 #21
Heydens, 105, 117f, 148
Hilbert, Vi, 1, 173, 231
Hobucket, 31, 54, 60f, 86
Hood Canal, 18, 90f, 100, 134f, 162f, 170f, 210, 230f
hoop, 25, 39, 108, 131f, 157, 176
Hoquiam, 1, 96, 112, 138, 141
Houses, 13, 20, 24, 46, 55, 64, 85f, 105f, 110f, 117, 126, 137, 145, 160f, 185, 201, 243
Howeattles, 19, 54f, 70, 84, 86
Hudson, Billy, 14, 66f
Hudson, Pansy, 44, 68

I

Iley, Mary, 101f, 120f, 124f, 130f, 140f, 150f, 160f
Illahee, 104

J

Jacobs, Mel, 1, 3, 14, 97f, 128, 163, 172
James Island, 37f, 54, 83
Jones, Bernice, 62, 65f

Index

K

Kanim, Jerry, 236f, 243, 253f, 260f, 270f, 280f, 290
kettles, 45, 62, 109f, 128, 141
Kettle, John, 191
Kinkade, MD, 97f, 133
Kirk, Ruth, 13f
Kitsap Peninsula, 95, 170f, 238
Kwati, 18

L

La Push, 2, 3, 8, 14f, 20f, 35f, 45f, 50f, 60f, 70f, 80f
Leschi, 142, 209, 230f
lice, 155, 194
Little Earths, 143, 146, 166f
Losier, Betsy, 236, 245, 277
Lushootseed, 95, 98, 100f, 118, 146, 165f, 170f, 231f

M

Martin, Willy, 237, 287
masks, 31, 49, 59f, 67f, 122
massage, 47, 120
Meany, Edmond, 1f, 8
Meeker, Jerry, 104
Miller Bay, 172f, 180
Mima Mounds, 96, 99
Misp[h], 18
Morgenroth, Chris, 28, 82
Montesano, 96, 101f, 143
mountain beavers, 106, 112, 242, 277f, 284
Mora, 52f, 83
Moseses, 182, 230f
Mossy Rock, 102f, 128
Mount Si, 240f
Mt Rainier, 96, 103, 109
Mt Olympus, 17
Mud Bay, 72, 95, 99, 103, 112f, 133, 152, 227f, 238

N

Nappie, Julia, 210
Neah Bay, 19f, 31, 44, 55, 59, 63f, 69, 71, 191, 196
nipples, 47
Nisqually Delta, 114
Noah, 158, 172
Nordquist, Del, 237
North Bend, 240f, 293

O

Ogress, 122, 155, 225, 273
Old Man House, 10, 170, 220
Oldman House, 187

P

Paine, Thomas ~ whaler, 34f, 67
Patkanim, 236, 290
Penn, Morton, 49, 59, 63, 69
Pete, Maggie, 100f
pets, 110, 125, 272, 278
Pettitt, George, 3, 14, 20, 49
Place names, 15, 82, 98f, 172f, 231
Plateau prophets, 193
Point Brown, 96
Point Glover, 182
Point No Point, 18, 183, 208, 229f, 234
Port Discovery Bay, 176
Portland, 1f, 100
potlatches, 14, 98, 105, 117f, 124f, 144, 147, 148f, 150, 167, 189f, 200, 206, 210, 216f, 220, 229
Poulsbo, 171f, 183, 210, 218, 226
Powell, JV, 3, 13f, 17, 20f
predictions, 138, 141f
privileges, 18
Putnam, John, 237
Putsenay ~ sturgeoner, 112

Q

Queen Susan, 102, 118, 139f, 142

R

raffia, 110
Rainbow, 110, 211, 284
Rainbow Falls, 96f, 99, 155
Ray, Verne, 3, 14, 16, 21, 96
Reagan, Albert, 14, 20,
reduplications, 93

re-weds, 121, 125
Rochester, 92, 95f, 98, 111, 127, 131
Ruby Beach, 38, 78

S

saddles, 129, 152
salves, 129
Sampson, Martin, 1
Saniwa, 229
Scatter Creek, 92, 95, 98, 101, 106, 120f, 132f, 147
Seattles, 18, 170f, 186f, 201, 210f, 230f
Secena, Mrs Dan, 95, 100, 107, 164, 165
Secenas, 99, 100f, 126f, 132, 140f, 156, 165
Shaker Church, 1, 20, 53, 70f, 141, 147, 244
sharks, 122, 138, 142f, 251
shinny, 135
Silverdale, 171, 214
Skykomish, 204, 230f, 238f, 241, 251, 282f, 291, 292, 293, 294, 300
slaves, 18, 55, 105, 112, 116f, 125f, 133f, 140f, 150f, 160f, 189f, 202f, 214, 230f
Smith, Alanson Wesley, 20
Smith, John, 127, 148
snakes, 64, 129, 132f, 140f, 155f, 208f, 257, 261, 268
Snyder, Warren, 95, 170f, 189, 239, 283
Sol Duc Hot Springs, 52
Sol Duc River, 42, 52, 83f
songs, 18, 31, 51f, 60f, 66f, 103, 113, 120f, 134f, 140f, 164f, 206, 211f, 282f, 289f
Spanish, 19, 127, 152
Spencer, Yakama chief, 100
Spier, Leslie, 2f
Spilyai ~ Coyote, 150
Squax, 244
Star Husband, 219f, 242, 260f
Starr, Phillip, 237, 249
Steilacoom, 228
Stillman, Jack, 237, 255, 258, 272, 281f
Svihla, Dr Arthur, 238
Swan, James, 1, 20

T

Tacoma, 228,
Tahmanawas, 49f, 69, 98, 124, 137, 140f, 155, 164, 196
Taholah, 58, 67, 82, 95f, 107, 113, 126, 149, 155
Taitnapams, 98, 100f, 113f, 132, 160f
Talibot, 228, 233
Tarakanov, Timofei, 19
tattoos, 129
Teams, 133f
Tillamook, 119
Toke Point, 96
Tokeland, 104
Tolt, 251f, 262f
Toms, 19, 36, 103, 209
Toutle River, 102f
trance, 137f, 145f
Tsailto, 60, 68
Tumwater, 100f
Twilight books, 3, 20
twins, 47f, 120, 142

U

U&A, 171
urine, 36, 47f, 158, 199

V

Vancouver Island, 95, 107, 191, 225, 231f
vine maple, 22f, 40f, 78f, 108, 156, 288
vomiting, 31, 135f, 205

W

Wahelchu, Chief Jacob, 172f, 186f, 193
Waterman, TT, 2f, 172f
weirs, 25f, 115f, 177f, 181, 264
Westport, 96f, 133, 149, 165f
whaling, 3, 23, 34f, 49, 56f, 64f, 85, 154
Whidbey Island, 229
Wickersham, Judge James, 1
Willamette Falls, 100
Willapa, 20, 95f, 100f, 165
Williams, Taft, 64
willow bark, 108f, 206
Wilsons, 42, 169f

Index

Witchpec, 72
wooden disks, 204
woolly dogs, 105, 180

X

Xwane ~ Changer, 142f, 151f, 155f

Y

Yakama, 99, 100f, 113f, 129, 132, 140f, 163f, 174f, 211, 230, 273
Youcktons, 99f, 103f, 107f, 127
Young Doctor, 62

Typo Gnomes are ever present, corrections & improvements welcome

Harriet Estelle Turner
Monday 5 April 1920
Sunday 13 June 2015
Purdy & Walters at Floral Hills
Lynnwood, WA

Sold @ Amazon.com